AF575552

TRADIVOX

VOLUME XIV

TRADIVOX

CATHOLIC CATECHISM INDEX

VOLUME XIV

Joseph Deharbe

Edited by
Aaron Seng

SOPHIA INSTITUTE PRESS
MANCHESTER, NEW HAMPSHIRE

South Bend, Indiana
www.Tradivox.com

This book is an original derivative work comprised of newly typeset and reformatted editions of the following Catholic catechisms, once issued with ecclesiastical approval and now found in the public domain:

Deharbe, Joseph. *Small Catechism*. English ed., translated from the German ed. New York: Benziger Brothers, 1882.

———. *A Complete Catechism of the Catholic Religion*. 6th Amer. ed. Translated by John Fander. Edited by James J. Fox and Thomas McMillan. New York: Schwartz, Kirwin, & Fauss, 1912.

Scripture references follow the Douay-Rheims Bible, per the imprint of John Murphy Company (Baltimore, 1899).

Cover and interior design by Perceptions Design Studio.

Sophia Institute Press
Box 5284, Manchester, NH 03108
1-800-888-9344

www.SophiaInstitute.com

ISBN 978-1-64413-376-7
LCCN 2022951862

Dedicated with love and deepest respect
to all the English Martyrs and Confessors.
Orate pro nobis.

CONTENTS

ACKNOWLEDGMENTS

THE publication of this series is due primarily to the generosity of countless volunteers and donors from several countries. Special thanks are owed to Mr. and Mrs. Phil Seng, Mr. and Mrs. Michael Over, Mr. and Mrs. Jim McElwee, Mr. and Mrs. John Brouillette, Mr. and Mrs. Thomas Scheibelhut, Mr. and Mrs. Kyle Barriger, as well the visionary priests and faithful of St. Stanislaus Bishop and Martyr parish in South Bend, Indiana, and St. Patrick's Oratory in Green Bay, Wisconsin. May God richly reward their commitment to handing on the Catholic faith.

FOREWORD

The Catholic faith remains always the same throughout the centuries and millennia until the coming of our Lord at the end of the time, likewise "Jesus Christ is the same yesterday, today and forever" (Heb 13:8). The Catholic faith is "the faith, which was once delivered unto the saints" (Jude 1:3). The Magisterium of the Church teaches us solemnly the same truth in the following words of the First Vatican Council: "The doctrine of the faith which God has revealed, is put forward not as some philosophical discovery capable of being perfected by human intelligence, but as a divine deposit committed to the spouse of Christ to be faithfully protected and infallibly promulgated. Hence, too, that meaning of the sacred dogmas is ever to be maintained, which has once been declared by holy mother Church, and there must never be any abandonment of this sense under the pretext or in the name of a more profound understanding. May understanding, knowledge and wisdom increase as ages and centuries roll along, and greatly and vigorously flourish, in each and all, in the individual and the whole Church: but this only in its own proper kind, that is to say, in the same doctrine, the same sense, and the same understanding (cf. Vincentius Lerinensis, *Commonitorium*, 28)."[1]

An authentically Catholic catechism has the function of learning and teaching the unchanging Catholic faith throughout all generations. The Roman Pontiffs indeed, taught: "There is nothing more effective than catechetical instruction to spread the glory of God and to secure the salvation of souls."[2] Saint Pius X said, that "the great loss of souls is due to ignorance

[1] Vatican I, Dogmatic Constitution *Dei Filius de fide catholica*, Ch. 4

[2] Pope Benedict XIV, Apostolic Constitution *Etsi minime*, n. 13

of divine things."[3] Therefore, the traditional catechisms have enduring value in our own day and age, which is marked by an enormous doctrinal confusion, which reigns in the life of the Church in the past six decades, and which reaches its peak in our days.

I welcome and bless the great project of the "Tradivox" in cataloguing and preserving the hundreds of long-lost Catholic catechisms issued with episcopal approval over the last millennium. This project will convincingly show the essentially unchanging nature of the apostolic doctrine across time and space, and so I invite the faithful of the entire world to support this historic effort, as we seek to restore the perennial catechism of the Church. The project of a catechism restoration on behalf of "Tradivox" will surely be of great benefit not only to many confused and disoriented Catholic faithful, but also to all people who are sincerely seeking the ultimate and authentic truth about God and man, which one can find only in the Catholic and apostolic faith, and which is the only religion and faith willed by God and to which God calls all men.

+Athanasius Schneider, O.R.C.,
Titular Bishop of Celerina
Auxiliary Bishop of the Archdiocese of Saint Mary in Astana

[3] Cf. Pope St. Pius X, Encyclical *Acerbo nimis,* n. 27

SERIES EDITOR'S
PREFACE

SOME are surprised to find that when a given Catholic is asked to "look something up in the catechism," he may well respond: "Which one?" The history of the Catholic Church across the last millennium is in fact filled with the publication of numerous catechisms, issued in every major language on earth; and for centuries, these concise "guidebooks" to Catholic doctrine have served countless men and women seeking a clear and concise presentation of that faith forever entrusted by Jesus Christ to his one, holy, Catholic, and apostolic Church.

Taken together, the many catechisms issued with episcopal approval can offer a kind of "window" on to the universal ordinary magisterium—a glimpse of those truths which have been held and taught in the Church *everywhere, always, and by all.* For, as St. Paul reminds us, the tenets of this Faith do not change from age to age: "Jesus Christ yesterday and today and the same for ever. Be not led away with various and strange doctrines" (Heb 13:8-9).

The catechisms included in our *Tradivox Catholic Catechism Index* are selected for their orthodoxy and historical significance, in the interest of demonstrating to contemporary readers the remarkable continuity of Catholic doctrine across time and space. Long regarded as reliable summaries of Church teaching on matters of faith and morals, we are proud to reproduce these works of centuries past, composed and endorsed by countless priests, bishops, and popes devoted to "giving voice to tradition."

In This Volume

This volume contains two catechisms by a priest widely considered to be the most renowned German catechist of the nineteenth century: Fr. Joseph Deharbe, S. J.

Fired with a love of teaching and missionary labors, the young Deharbe entered the Society of Jesus at age seventeen, going on to teach at the Jesuit College of Switzerland, and later to serve as a missionary and catechist in Cöthen. Being stationed there in 1840, he immediately saw the need for a new German catechism designed to serve both children and adults, sufficient to answer various modernist errors that were emerging in the Rhineland countries—above all, in the revisionist "world histories" that were beginning to insinuate themselves. Believing himself unfit to compose such a work, he did not begin writing until commanded to do so by his superior, Fr. Devis, after 1843.

Drawing upon the best texts available in both German and French, Deharbe completed his first catechism, *Katholischer Katechismus oder Lehrbegriff*, in 1847, just as a heated persecution of the Jesuits broke out in Switzerland. Barely escaping with his life, his catechism was published anonymously at Ratisbon in the following year, and immediately hailed as a "solution" to the bewildering proliferation of catechetical manuals available in German at the time: for, Deharbe's work combined the catechetical tradition with a new textual division and charming style, with a large introductory outline of salvation history that served to place readers in the ongoing "story of the Church." His book was introduced into the German diocese of Linsburg that year, in Trier and Hildesheim the next, and was soon an international success. Bishops in Bavaria, Switzerland, Austria-Hungary, and the United States all welcomed it with acclaim over the next few years, and the author was compelled to prepare several variants of the original—editions of which would be translated into Magyar, Bohemian, Italian, French, English, Swedish, Marathi, Polish, Lithuanian, Slovenian, Danish, Spanish, and Portuguese over the next two decades. By the early twentieth century, "Deharbe's Catechism" was still in wide use throughout most German dioceses, Denmark, Sweden, Austria, Brazil, Chile, East India, and the United States—being widely known as "Fander's Catechism" in the latter, after the name of its English translator.

Of the many iterations of Deharbe's work, the present volume reproduces two of the later and more polished English editions of his *Small Catechism* for children, and his *Complete Catechism of the Catholic Religion* suitable for older children, young adults, and converts. Our only notable change to the *Small Catechism* has been to replace the original "X" designating questions that "beginners are not expected to learn" with an asterisk throughout, and to omit the explanation of this system from the body text. The *Complete Catechism* is especially valuable in its sixth American edition of 1924, which expanded the historical section and added a number of observations and notations derived from both the First Vatican Council and the experience of teachers over several decades using the text. Our only change to this content has been to more clearly mark the use of examples and scriptural catenas within each answer, and to move the "review questions" to section endings for the sake of greater readability.

Although occasionally critiqued for its precise language and theological terminology, Deharbe's catechisms effectively served to foster the faith of children and adults across an astounding span of time, especially for German Catholics. Published before the invention of aeroplanes and in-home electricity, they would be read during the German state revolutions, through the days of Bismarck's *Kulturkampf*, and into the trenches of the Great War on both sides of the battle line. We trust that the work of such a master catechist—admirable for its theological accuracy, brevity, clarity, and sensible arrangement—will once again prove beneficial in the work of handing on the Catholic doctrine. As quoted in the Preface of his *Complete Catechism*, St. Augustine insists that this work is largely dependent on the very love and zeal that once animated Fr. Joseph Deharbe:

> If you do not love God and your brethren, how will you laboriously spell out the first words of faith to the ignorant? Where will you discover the secret of repeating again and again the same truth in a variety of ways? Whence will you draw the courage and industry necessary to cultivate this soil abounding only in briars and thistles? ... You must repeat and repeat the same things. Let the love which animates you give them an appearance of novelty.

Editorial Note

Our *Catholic Catechism Index* series generally retains only the doctrinal content of those catechisms it seeks to reproduce, as well as that front matter most essential to establishing the credibility of each work as an authentic expression of the Church's common doctrine, e.g., any episcopal endorsement, *nihil obstat*, or *imprimatur*. However, it should be noted that especially prior to the eighteenth century, a number of catechisms were so immediately and universally received as reliably orthodox texts (often simply by the reputation of the author or publisher), that they received no such "official" approval; or if they did, it was often years later and in subsequent editions. We therefore include both the original printing date in our Table of Contents, and further edition information in the Preface above.

Our primary goal has been to bring these historical texts back into publication in readable English copy. Due to the wide range of time periods, cultures, and unique author styles represented in this series, we have made a number of editorial adjustments to allow for a less fatiguing read, more rapid cross-reference throughout the series, and greater research potential for the future. While not affecting the original content, these adjustments have included adopting a cleaner typesetting and simpler standard for capitalization and annotation, as well as remedying certain anachronisms in spelling or grammar.

Woodcut depicting an early method used in the production of Catholic catechisms, circa 1568.

At the same time, in deepest respect for the venerable age and subject matter of these works, we have been at pains to adhere as closely as possible to the original text: retaining archaisms such as "doth" and "hallowed," and avoiding any alterations that might affect the doctrinal content or authorial voice. We have painstakingly restored original artwork wherever possible, and where the rare explanatory note has been deemed necessary, it is not made in the text itself, but only in a marginal note. In some cases, our editorial refusal to "modernize" the content of these classical works may require a higher degree of attention from today's reader, who we trust will be richly rewarded by the effort.

We pray that our work continues to yield highly readable, faithful reproductions of these time-honored monuments to Catholic religious instruction: catechisms once penned, promulgated, and praised by bishops across the globe. May these texts that once served to guide and shape the faith and lives of millions now do so again; and may the scholars and saints once involved in their first publication now intercede for all who take them up anew. *Tolle lege!*

Sincerely in Christ,
Aaron Seng

TRADIVOX

VOLUME XIV

DEHARBE'S

SMALL CATECHISM.

TRANSLATED BY

A FATHER OF THE SOCIETY OF JESUS

Of the Province of Missouri,

FROM THE GERMAN EDITION PREPARED

FOR THE UNITED STATES

WITH THE

Approval and Co-operation of the Author.

NEW YORK, CINCINNATI AND CHICAGO:

BENZIGER BROTHERS,

Printers to the Holy Apostolic See.

DEHARBE'S

SMALL CATECHISM.

TRANSLATED BY

A FATHER OF THE SOCIETY OF JESUS

Of the Province of Missouri,

FROM THE GERMAN EDITION PREPARED

FOR THE UNITED STATES

WITH THE

Approval and Co-operation of the Author.

NEW YORK, CINCINNATI AND CHICAGO:

BENZIGER BROTHERS,

Printers to the Holy Apostolic See.

Imprimatur:
+ JOHN CARD. MCCLOSKEY,
Archbp. of New York

NEW YORK, May 20, 1882.

Christian Doctrine

SECTION I
Faith

1. **For what end did God create us?**
God created us, that we might know him, love him, and serve him upon earth, and be happy with him forever in heaven.

2. **What must we do to know, love, and serve God?**
We must take as true all that God has revealed, and keep his commandments.

3. **Why must we take as true all that God has revealed?**
Because God is the eternal and infallible truth.

4. **Who teaches us what God has revealed?**
The Catholic Church teaches us what God has revealed.

* 5. **What must a Christian believe?**
A Christian must believe all that God has revealed and the Catholic Church teaches.

6. **Is faith necessary for salvation?**
Yes; faith is necessary for salvation, for "without faith it is impossible to please God,"[1] and "he that believeth not shall be condemned."[2]

7. **Will any faith save us?**
No; only the true faith which the Catholic Church teaches will save us.

[1] Heb 11:6
[2] Mk 16:16

* 8. **Why has the Catholic Church alone the true faith?**
Because the Catholic Church alone received its faith from Christ, and has always kept it incorrupt.

* 9. **Is it enough to believe only what is contained in holy scripture?**
No; for holy scripture does not contain all that Christ has taught.

* 10. **Where do we find the teachings of Christ not contained in the scripture?**
In tradition; that is, in the revealed truths of the Church handed down to us in other writings than the scripture, and also by word of mouth.

11. **What must be the qualities of our faith?**
Our faith must be so firm and constant that nothing can make us fall away from it.

12. **By what sign does the Catholic Christian profess his faith?**
Chiefly by the sign of the cross.

The Apostles' Creed in General

13. **Where do we find the principal truths that we must know and believe?**
We find them in the twelve articles of the Apostles' Creed.

14. **Say the Apostles' Creed.**
I believe in God, etc.[3]

[3] See "Prayers" section below, p. 71–72.

The First Article of the Creed

"I believe in God the Father Almighty, Creator of heaven and earth."

GOD

15. **Who is God?**
God is the Maker and Lord of heaven and earth and the author of all good.

16. **Are there more gods than one?**
No; there is but one God.

17. **Can we see God?**
No; we cannot see God, for he is a pure Spirit and has no body.

18. **Had God a beginning?**
No; God always was and always will be; that is, he is eternal.

19. **Where is God?**
God is everywhere: in heaven, on earth, and in all places.

20. **Does God know and see all things?**
Yes; God knows and sees all things, even our most secret thoughts.
Think, in whatsoever place thou art,
God sees into thy very heart.

21. **Can God do all things?**
Yes; God can do all things, whatsoever he pleases, without the use of anything.

22. **How, then, do we express that God can do all things?**
We say God is Almighty, that is, all-powerful.

THE THREE DIVINE PERSONS

23. **How many Persons are there in God?**
In God there are three Persons: the Father, the Son, and the Holy Ghost.

24. **Is each of the three divine Persons God?**
Yes; the Father is God, the Son is God, and the Holy Ghost is God.

25. **Since all three divine Persons are God, are there not more gods than one?**
No; the three divine Persons are but one God.

26. **Is any one of the three divine Persons older or more powerful than the others?**
No; all the three divine Persons are from eternity; all three are equally powerful, good, and perfect.

27. **What do we call the mystery of one God in three divine Persons?**
We call it the mystery of the most Holy Trinity.

Our Father, God, all praise to thee,
Both now and for eternity:
The same unto thy only Son.
And Holy Spirit, three in one.

THE CREATION AND GOVERNMENT OF THE WORLD

28. **Why is God called "Creator of heaven and earth"?**
Because God made heaven and earth and everything that is in them.

29. **How did God make the world?**
God made the world out of nothing, by the mere power of his will.

There is one true and only God,
Our Maker and our Lord;
And he created everything
By his almighty Word.

30. **What does God continually do for the world?**
God preserves and governs the world.

* 31. **What do you mean by saying, "God preserves the world"?**
God keeps the world in existence as long as he pleases.

* 32. **What do you mean by saying, "God governs the world"?**
God takes care of all things, orders and directs all things, as he pleases.

The heavens, the earth, and the sea
Their Maker's commandments fulfill;
And are become teachers to me
To yield with delight to his will.

* 33. **What do we call the care God takes to preserve and govern the world?**
The care God takes to preserve and govern the world we call divine providence.

34. **Does God provide also for us?**
Yes; God provides for us: from him we receive life and health, food and drink, shelter and clothing, and everything good for body and soul.

All around and all above
Hath this record: "God is love."

35. **Why does God bestow so much good on us?**
God bestows so much good on us because he is our Father—the kindest of fathers.

36. **Since God is so kind a Father, what should we do?**
We should love him above everything as good and devoted children.

God! may thy holy will be blest
For this one gift above the rest,
That having made all things for me,
Thou, Lord, hast made myself for thee.

THE ANGELS

37. **Has God created only this visible world?**
God has also created countless spirits, called angels.

38. **In what state were the angels when God had created them?**
They were all good and happy.

39. **Did all the angels remain good and happy?**
No; many rebelled against God and were cast into hell.

40. **What are the fallen angels called?**
The fallen angels are called devils or evil spirits.

41. **Why are the devils called evil spirits?**
Because they hate God, and seek to draw us into sin.

42. **What do the good angels do for us?**
The good angels love us, pray for as, and protect us from harm in soul and body.

43. **What is the guardian angel?**
The guardian angel is that angel whom God has set over us for our special protection.

44. **What is your duty toward your guardian angel?**
I must venerate my holy guardian angel; I must pray to him, thank him, and follow his promptings.

O God, how ought my grateful heart
To praise thy bounteous hand!
Thou send'st thy angel from above,
To be my guide and friend.

CREATION AND FALL OF MAN

45. **Which is the most perfect creature of God on earth?**
Man is the most perfect creature of God on earth.

46. **How did God make the first man?**
God made the first man by forming a body out of the earth and breathing into it an immortal soul.

47. **Of what does man consist?**
Man consists of body and soul.

* 48. **What is the soul?**
The soul is an immortal spirit, made to the image and likeness of God, without which we can neither think nor live.

By sin do ne'er thy soul degrade;
To God's own image it is made.

49. **Who were the first man and woman?**
Adam and Eve were the first man and woman.

50. **Were Adam and Eve good in the beginning?**
Yes; Adam and Eve were perfectly good; they were holy and just.

51. **Were Adam and Eve happy?**
Yes; Adam and Eve were very happy in the earthly paradise, and were never to die.

52. **Did Adam and Eve remain happy?**
No; they disobeyed God by eating of the forbidden fruit; and God punished them for their disobedience.

53. **How did God punish Adam and Eve for their disobedience?**
God banished them from paradise, and made them subject to the many miseries of this life and to death.

54. **Did the sin of Adam and Eve injure them only?**
No; sin with its punishments passed on all mankind; so that we all come into the world infected with sin.

55. **What do we call the sin in which all are born?**
The sin in which all are born is called "original sin."

56. **What would have become of man if God had not shown him mercy?**
He would have been lost forever.

* 57. **How did God show mercy to man?**
God promised him a Savior, who should save him from sin, and regain heaven for him.

* 58. **To whom did God first promise a Savior?**
To our first parents, immediately after their fall.

59. **When did the promised Savior come?**
The Savior came about four thousand years after the creation of the world.

The Second Article of the Creed

"And in Jesus Christ, his only Son our Lord."

60. **Whom did God send as Savior?**
God sent Jesus Christ, his only Son, to save us from sin and hell.

61. **What does the name *Jesus* signify?**

The name *Jesus* signifies "Savior" or Redeemer.

Name adored on bended knee,
Name of grace and majesty!

62. **What does the word *Christ* signify?**

The word *Christ* signifies "the Anointed."

* 63. **Why is Jesus Christ called "the only Son of God"?**

Because Jesus Christ is, by nature and from all eternity, the true and only Son of God.

* 64. **Are we not also children of God?**

Yes; we are children of God, but not by nature and from all eternity; we are only adopted children, through grace.

65. **Why is Jesus Christ called "our Lord"?**

Jesus Christ is called "our Lord": first, because he is our God; and second, because he is our Redeemer who has bought us with his blood.

Heart and voice with one accord
Praise, adore, and bless the Lord!

The Third Article of the Creed

"Who was conceived of the Holy Ghost, born of the Virgin Mary."

66. **What does the third article of the Creed teach us?**

The third article of the Creed teaches us that the Son of God, through the power of the Holy Ghost, became man.

67. **How did the Son of God become man?**
He took to himself a body and a soul like ours.

68. **What do we call this mystery of Christ's taking a body and soul like ours?**
We call this mystery the incarnation of the Son of God.

69. **What do we believe concerning Jesus Christ?**
We believe that Jesus Christ is true God and true man.

70. **Was Jesus Christ always both God and man?**
Jesus Christ was always God from eternity; but he was not always man.

71. **How long is it since Jesus Christ became man?**
Over eighteen hundred years.

72. **Where was Jesus, our Savior, born?**
Our Savior was born at Bethlehem, in a stable.

73. **Who first came to adore the infant Jesus?**
Devout shepherds from the neighborhood first came, and then the Magi, or the three holy kings from the East.

74. **How was the birth of Christ made known to the shepherds and to the Magi?**
The birth of Christ was made known to the shepherds by an angel, and to the Magi by means of a wonderful star.

75. **Who is the Mother of Jesus?**
The Blessed Virgin Mary is the Mother of Jesus.

76. **What is the Blessed Virgin Mary, therefore, called?**
The Blessed Virgin is called the "Mother of God."

77. **Had Jesus Christ a father?**
As man, Jesus Christ had no father.

78. **Who was St. Joseph?**
St. Joseph was only the foster-father of Jesus.

THE LIFE OF JESUS

79. **What took place when Jesus was forty days old?**
When Jesus was forty days old, he was presented in the Temple at Jerusalem.

80. **Did the Child Jesus remain always in Judea?**
No; Joseph and Mary fled with the Child Jesus into Egypt, because King Herod sought to take his life.

81. **Where did Jesus dwell after his return from Egypt?**
Until the thirtieth year of his age, Jesus dwelt at Nazareth with his parents and "was subject to them."[4]

82. **Why did Jesus wish to be subject?**
Jesus, the Son of God, wished to be subject, to teach children to obey their parents.

83. **What did Jesus do at the age of twelve years?**
At the age of twelve years, Jesus went with his parents to Jerusalem, and there remained three days in the Temple.

84. **What did Jesus do at the age of thirty years?**
At the age of thirty years, Jesus began to preach in public and to work miracles.

* 85. **What did Jesus teach?**
Jesus taught what we are to believe and to do in order to be saved.

[4] Lk 2:51

* 86. **Mention some of his miracles.**

Jesus changed water into wine; with five loaves, he fed over five thousand people; by a word, he calmed the winds and the waves; he cured all sorts of diseases, and raised even the dead to life.

* 87. **Why did Jesus work miracles?**

Jesus worked miracles to show that he was the Son of God.

Jesus, though my Lord and God,
Chose humble poverty.
Oh! let me love the paths he trod,
And strive like him to be.

The Fourth Article of the Creed

"Suffered under Pontius Pilate, was crucified, dead, and buried."

88. **What did Jesus Christ do to redeem us?**

Jesus Christ suffered and died on the cross to redeem us.

* 89. **Did Jesus Christ suffer as God or as man?**

Jesus Christ suffered as man; that is, according to his human nature.

90. **What did Jesus Christ suffer for us?**

He suffered much during his whole life. At last, after a terrible agony in the Garden of Olives, he was seized, mocked, scourged, crowned with thorns, and finally nailed to the cross.

91. **Who condemned Jesus to death?**

Pontius Pilate, the Roman governor of Judaea, condemned Jesus to death.

92. **Where was Jesus crucified?**
Jesus was crucified on Mount Calvary, near Jerusalem.

93. **On what day did Jesus die?**
Jesus died on Good Friday, about the third hour after noon.

Come, fall before his cross
Who shed for us his blood,
Who died the victim of pure love
To make us sons of God.

94. **How did Jesus die?**
Jesus said, "Father, into thy hands I commend my spirit,"[5] and bowing his head he gave up the Ghost.

* 95. **How did Jesus suffer such torments and death?**
Jesus, so innocent, suffered everything willingly and patiently, out of compassion and love for us.

96. **For whom has Jesus died?**
Jesus has died for me and for all mankind.

97. **What happened after the death of Jesus?**
The body of Jesus was taken down from the cross and laid in a tomb.

Thou didst go forth, O blessed Lord,
To suffer death for me,
And I too wish for thee to live,
I wish to die for thee!

[5] Lk 23:46

The Fifth Article of the Creed

"He descended into hell; the third day he rose again from the dead."

98. **Where did the soul of Jesus go after separating from the body?**
The soul of Jesus went down into limbo, which was the place where the souls of the just who had died before Christ were detained.

* 99. **Why were the souls of the just who had died before Christ detained in limbo?**
Because heaven was closed by the sin of Adam, and was first to be opened again by Christ.

100. **How long did the soul of Jesus remain in limbo and his body in the tomb?**
Until the third day, Sunday; when Jesus united his soul to his body and rose gloriously from the tomb.

101. **Did Jesus go to heaven immediately after his resurrection?**
No; after his resurrection, Jesus still remained forty days on earth, and often appeared to his disciples.

The Sixth Article of the Creed

"He ascended into heaven; sitteth at the right
hand of God the Father Almighty."

102. **What did Jesus do forty days after his resurrection?**
Forty days after his resurrection, Jesus, with soul and body, went up into heaven.

103. **From what place did Jesus go up into heaven?**
From Mount Olivet, in the presence of his disciples.

* 104. **Did Jesus ascend alone into heaven?**
No; he took with him into heaven the souls of the just whom he had freed from limbo.

105. **What is meant by the words "sitteth at the right hand of God"?**
They mean that Christ, even as man, partakes of the power and glory of his Father in heaven.

106. **Can we also go to join Jesus in heaven?**
Yes; if we believe in him, keep his commandments, and follow his example.

May I live to know and fear him,
Trust and love him all my days,
Then to dwell forever near him,
See his face and sing his praise!

The Seventh Article of the Creed

"From thence he shall come to judge the living and the dead."

107. **Will Christ come again from heaven to earth?**
Yes; at the end of the world, Christ will come again on earth in a visible manner.

108. **How will he come?**
Christ will come with great power and majesty.

109. **Why will Christ come again?**
Christ will come to judge all men, both the good and the wicked.

110. **What do we call the judgment at the end of the world?**
"The general judgment," "the last judgment," or "the judgment of the world," because then all men shall be judged.

111. **Where shall men go after the last judgment?**
The wicked shall go to hell, the good to heaven.

112. **Is there any other than the general judgment?**
Yes; there is also the particular judgment, which immediately follows death.

113. **Where does the soul go after the particular judgment?**
After the particular judgment, the soul goes to heaven, to hell, or to purgatory.

* 114. **What souls go at once to heaven after death?**
The souls of the just, such namely as are perfectly pure, go at once to heaven.

* 115. **What souls go to hell?**
The souls of the wicked, who die in mortal sin, go to hell.

* 116. **What souls go to purgatory?**
The souls of the just, who are not perfectly pure, or who have still to atone for past sins, go to purgatory.

117. **Will there be a purgatory after the general judgment?**
No; after the general judgment, there will be only heaven and hell.

The Eighth Article of the Creed

"I believe in the Holy Ghost."

118. **Who is the Holy Ghost?**
The Holy Ghost is the third Person of the Blessed Trinity, true God with the Father and the Son.

119. **Why is the Holy Ghost represented in the form of a dove?**
Because, at the baptism of Jesus, the Holy Ghost appeared over him in the form of a dove.

120. **How did the Holy Ghost appear on Whitsunday?**
On Whitsunday, the Holy Ghost came down on the apostles in the form of fiery tongues.

* 121. **What does the Holy Ghost perpetually do in the Catholic Church?**
The Holy Ghost teaches, sanctifies, and directs the Church in an invisible manner, to the end of the world.

*** 122. What effects does the Holy Ghost produce in the soul?**

The Holy Ghost enlightens, strengthens, consoles, purifies, and sanctifies the soul by his grace.

123. What particular benefit have you received from each Person of the Holy Trinity?

God the Father has created me; God the Son has redeemed me; God the Holy Ghost has sanctified me.

The Ninth Article of the Creed

"The holy Catholic Church, the communion of saints."

THE CHURCH IN GENERAL

124. Has Christ established a Church?

Yes; Christ has established a Church which is to continue to the end of the world.

*** 125. What is the Church?**

The Church is the congregation of all the faithful on earth, professing the true faith, governed by their lawful bishops, and united under one visible head.

126. Is not Christ the head of the Church?

Christ is indeed the head of the Church, but the invisible head.

127. Did Christ give his Church a visible head?

Yes; Christ made St. Peter the visible head of the Church.

128. Who has been the visible head of the Church since the death of St. Peter?

Our holy father the pope, the lawful successor of St. Peter in the episcopal See of Rome.

129. **Are there other pastors or rulers of the Church?**
Yes; the bishops of the Catholic Church, who govern their respective dioceses.

130. **Who are the assistants of the bishops?**
The priests, subject to them, are the assistants of the bishops.

THE MARKS OF THE CHURCH

131. **Has Christ established more than one Church?**
Christ has established but one Church.

132. **By what marks may the true Church of Christ be known?**
The true Church of Christ may be known by these four marks:
1. She is one.
2. She is holy.
3. She is catholic.
4. She is apostolic.

133. **Which Church has all these four marks?**
The Roman Catholic Church alone has these four marks.

* 134. **Why is the Catholic Church also called Roman Catholic?**
Because the pope at Rome is her head.

* 135. **How is the Roman Catholic Church one?**
The Roman Catholic Church is one because she has at all times and in all places:
1. The same faith.
2. The same sacrifice and the same sacraments.
3. The same common head.

* 136. **How is the Roman Catholic Church holy?**

The Roman Catholic Church is holy:

1. Because she has a holy founder and a holy doctrine.
2. Because she faithfully preserves and dispenses all the means of holiness.
3. Because she always has saints, whose holiness God confirms by miracles.

* 137. **What does the word *catholic* mean?**

Catholic means "universal."

* 138. **How is the Roman Catholic Church catholic or universal?**

The Roman Catholic Church is catholic or universal:

1. Because she has always existed from the time of Christ.
2. Because she is spread over the entire world.
3. Because she always teaches the whole doctrine of Christ.

* 139. **How is the Roman Catholic Church apostolic?**

The Roman Catholic Church is apostolic:

1. Because her origin and her doctrine are derived from the apostles.
2. Because her rulers, the pope and the bishops, are the lawful successors of the apostles.

140. **Can the Catholic Church err in what she teaches?**

No; the Catholic Church cannot err in what she teaches; she is the "pillar and ground of truth."[6]

* 141. **Why cannot the Catholic Church err?**

The Catholic Church cannot err because the Holy Ghost guides her.

THE COMMUNION OF SAINTS

142. **Are only the faithful on earth united as one Church?**

No; all those that have died in the grace of God are spiritually united to the faithful on earth.

[6] 1 Tm 3:15

143. **What is this spiritual union called?**
The communion of saints.

144. **Who are members of the communion of saints?**
1. All the members of the Catholic Church on earth.
2. All the souls in purgatory.
3. All the saints in heaven.

* 145. **In what manner are these members of the Church united?**
They are all members of one body, whose head is Christ; and they help each other.

146. **How do the saints in heaven help us?**
The saints in heaven help us by their merits, and by their intercession with God in our behalf.

* 147. **Can we help the souls in purgatory?**
Yes; we can help the souls in purgatory by our prayers, good works, and especially by the Holy Sacrifice of the Mass.

The Tenth Article of the Creed

"The forgiveness of sins."

148. **What does the tenth article of the Creed teach?**
The tenth article of the Creed teaches that in the Catholic Church we can obtain the forgiveness of sins, and the remission of the punishment due to them.

149. **How are sins forgiven in the Catholic Church?**
Sins are forgiven through the merits of Jesus Christ applied to the repentant sinner, chiefly in the sacraments of baptism and penance.

150. **Can all sins be forgiven in the Catholic Church?**
Yes; all sins without exception can be forgiven in the Catholic Church.

The Eleventh Article of the Creed

"The resurrection of the body."

151. **What happens to man at his death?**
The soul separated from the body appears before the judgment seat of God, while the body returns into dust.

152. **How long shall the body remain separated from the soul?**
The body shall remain separated from the soul till the day of the last judgment, when God will reunite it to the soul and raise it to life.

153. **What do we call the raising of the body to life?**
The resurrection of the body.

* 154. **Shall all bodies be alike when raised to life?**
No; the bodies of the wicked shall be hideous and wretched, while the bodies of the good shall be glorious and happy.

The Twelfth Article of the Creed

"And life everlasting. Amen."

155. **What does the twelfth article of the Creed teach?**
The twelfth article of the Creed teaches that the just shall live forever in heaven.

156. **What is heaven?**

Heaven is the place of perfect and everlasting happiness.

157. **Shall not the damned also live forever?**

Yes; the damned shall live forever, in hell, where they shall be miserable for all eternity.

158. **What is hell?**

Hell is the place of everlasting, unspeakable misery and torment.

159. **Which are the four last things?**

The four last things are:

1. Death.
2. Judgment.
3. Hell.
4. Heaven.

Whilst I dwell, O my God, in this valley of tears,
For refuge and comfort I fly unto thee.
And when death's awful hour with its terrors appears,
O merciful Jesus! have mercy on me.

SECTION II

The Commandments

160. **Is it sufficient to believe all that God has revealed?**
No; we must also love and serve God by keeping his commandments.

161. **Which are the chief commandments that include all the others?**
The commandment of the love of God and the commandment of the love of our neighbor.

THE LOVE OF GOD

162. **How is the commandment of the love of God expressed?**
"Thou shalt love the Lord thy God with thy whole heart, and with thy whole soul, and with thy whole mind, and with thy whole strength."

163. **What does the commandment of the love of God require of us?**
It requires of us to love God above all things.

* 164. **When do we love God above all things?**
We love God above all things when we love him more than all else, and would rather lose all else than be separated from him by sin.

165. **Why must we love God?**
We must love God because he is the sovereign and most perfect good, and all good comes from him.

* 166. **How do we show that we love God?**
We show that we love God by doing what is pleasing to him and shunning what is displeasing to him.

Oh, may I love thee, dearest Lord,
Almighty as thou art!
For thou hast stooped to ask of me
The love of my poor heart.

THE LOVE OF OUR NEIGHBOR

167. **How is the commandment of the love of our neighbor expressed?**
"Thou shalt love thy neighbor as thyself."

168. **Who is our neighbor whom we should love?**
Everyone, friend or enemy.

* 169. **Must we love even our enemies?**
Yes; we must love even our enemies, and pray for them.

170. **Why must we love all, even our enemies?**
We must love all:

1. Because our Lord commanded us to love them.
2. Because all men are children of one Father in heaven.

* 171. **When do we love our neighbor as ourselves?**
We love our neighbor as ourselves when we observe the command of Christ: "All things, therefore, whatsoever you would that men should do to you, do you also to them."[7]

[7] Mt 7:12

The Ten Commandments of God

172. **Where shall we find our duty to God and our neighbor more fully explained?**

In the ten commandments of God.

173. **From whom have we the ten commandments of God?**

From God himself, who gave them to Moses on Mount Sinai, amidst thunder and lightning.

174. **Say the ten commandments.**

I am the Lord thy God, who brought thee out of the land of Egypt, and out of the house of bondage.

1. Thou shalt not have strange gods before me; thou shalt not make to thyself any graven thing, nor the likeness of anything that is in the heavens above, or in the earth beneath, or in the waters under the earth. Thou shalt not adore them nor serve them.
2. Thou shalt not take the name of the Lord thy God in vain.
3. Remember that thou keep holy the sabbath day.
4. Honor thy father and thy mother that it may be well with thee, and thou mayest live long on the earth.

5. Thou shalt not kill.
6. Thou shalt not commit adultery.
7. Thou shalt not steal.
8. Thou shalt not bear false witness against thy neighbor.
9. Thou shalt not covet thy neighbor's wife.
10. Thou shalt not covet thy neighbor's goods.[8]

The First Commandment of God

"I am the Lord thy God. Thou shalt not have strange gods before me; thou shalt not make to thyself any graven thing, nor the likeness of anything that is in the heavens above, or in the earth beneath, or in the waters under the earth. Thou shalt not adore them nor serve them."

175. **What does God command by this first commandment?**
By this first commandment, God commands us to pay him due honor and adoration.

176. **How many kinds of honor do we owe God?**
We owe God two kinds of honor, namely: interior and exterior honor.

[8] Cf. Ex 20:2-17

177. **How do we honor God interiorly?**
We honor God interiorly by believing in him, hoping in him, loving him above all things, and adoring him alone.

178. **How soon are children obliged to make acts of faith, hope, and charity?**
As soon as they have come to the use of reason.

* 179. **What should we hope for from God?**
We should hope, above all, for the forgiveness of our sins, for the grace of God and for life everlasting.

* 180. **How do we sin against the interior honor we owe God?**
When we neglect to pray, or pray badly; when we doubt in matters of faith, or listen to people talking against it; when we do not trust in God or murmur against his dispensations.

181. **How do we honor God exteriorly?**
We honor God exteriorly by attending divine service, by bending the knee or bowing the head, and otherwise showing our respect.

182. **How do we sin against the exterior worship of God?**
We sin against the exterior worship of God by neglecting to attend divine service, or by being irreverent when present.

THE VENERATION AND INVOCATION OF THE SAINTS

183. **Is it right to honor the saints and to pray to them?**
Yes; it is right and good for the soul to honor the saints and to pray to them.

184. **Why do we honor the saints?**
We honor the saints on account of their great virtue and sanctity, and on account of their glory in heaven.

* 185. **What is the difference between the honor we pay God and the honor we pay the saints?**
We honor and adore God alone as our sovereign Lord; we honor the saints only as his faithful servants and friends.

186. **Why do we pray to the saints?**
We pray to the saints that they may obtain favors for us from God.

* 187. **In what does our praying to God differ from our praying to the saints?**
We pray to God that he may help us by his almighty power; we pray to the saints that they may help us by interceding with God for us.

188. **Whom should we honor and pray to above all the other saints?**
Mary, the ever Blessed Virgin and Mother of God.

189. **Should we honor the images of Jesus Christ and of the saints?**
Yes; for if children honor the portraits of their parents, we certainly ought to honor the images of our Lord and of his saints.

The Second Commandment of God

"Thou shalt not take the name of the Lord thy God in vain."

190. **What does God forbid by this second commandment?**
By this second commandment, God forbids all profanation of his holy name.

191. **How do we profane the holy name of God?**
We profane the holy name of God:

1. By uttering it irreverently.
2. By blaspheming.

3. By sinful swearing and by cursing.
4. By breaking our lawful oaths or vows.

* 192. **What is uttering God's holy name irreverently?**

It is uttering the holy name of God, of the saints, of the holy sacraments, in jest, in anger, or in a careless manner.

193. **What is swearing?**

Swearing is calling God to witness that we speak the truth or that we will keep our promise.

* 194. **When do we sin by swearing?**

We sin by swearing:

1. When we swear falsely or in doubt.
2. When we swear without necessity.
3. When we swear to do what is evil.

195. **What is cursing?**

Cursing is wishing evil either to one's self or to another, thus dishonoring the name of God.

The Third Commandment of God

"Remember that thou keep holy the sabbath day."

196. **What does God command by this third commandment?**
By this third commandment, God commands us to keep holy the Sunday, the Lord's day.

197. **How should we keep Sunday holy?**
We should above all hear Mass, and, if possible, also attend other services of the Church, especially the sermon and Christian doctrine.

198. **What is strictly forbidden on Sunday?**
All unnecessary servile work is strictly forbidden on Sunday.

* 199. **Is Sunday profaned only by unnecessary servile work?**
No; Sunday is also profaned by revelry, intemperance, extravagant games, wild sports, and amusements.

Remember that thou sanctify
Sunday and holy day;
Work not without necessity,
Hear Holy Mass and pray.

The Fourth Commandment of God

"Honor thy father and thy mother, that it may be well with thee, and thou mayest live long on the earth."

200. **What does God command by this fourth commandment?**
By this fourth commandment, God commands that children show reverence, love, and obedience to their parents, and inferiors to their superiors.

* 201. **Why must children revere, love, and obey their parents?**
Because, next to God, parents are their greatest benefactors, and hold his place in their regard.

202. **When do children sin against the reverence, love, and obedience they owe their parents and superiors?**

1. When they treat their parents or superiors harshly or insolently, and cause them trouble or grief.
2. When they do not obey them at all or with reluctance, or disregard their admonitions.
3. When they wish or do them evil, speak ill of them, or go so far as to raise their hand against them.

203. **What awaits those children who grievously fail in their duty toward their parents?**
The curse of God in this world, and eternal punishment in the world to come.

204. **What awaits those children who faithfully discharge their duty toward their parents?**
God's blessing and protection in this world, and eternal happiness in the world to come.

* 205. **What other superiors, besides our parents, must we revere, love, and obey?**
Our guardians, teachers, employers, and all our spiritual and temporal superiors.

The Fifth Commandment of God

"Thou shalt not kill."

206. **What does God forbid by this fifth commandment?**
By this fifth commandment, God forbids us to kill our neighbor unjustly, or to injure our neighbor or ourselves in body or soul.

207. **When do we injure our neighbor's body?**
We injure our neighbor's body when we strike or wound him or injure his health.

* 208. **How do we injure our own body?**
We injure our own body when we take our own lives, or when, without necessity, we expose our lives to danger or impair our health.

209. **Is quarreling forbidden by the fifth commandment?**
Yes; quarreling, abusive words, anger, hatred, and envy are forbidden by the fifth commandment.

210. **When do we injure our neighbor's soul?**
We injure our neighbor's soul when we scandalize him; that is, when we tempt him to sin.

* 211. **What must we do when we have injured our neighbor in body or soul?**
We must not only repent and confess our sin, but we must also, as far as we can, repair the injury we have done.

Thou shalt not kill nor vengeance take;
All thoughts of anger flee.
Forgive and love for Jesus' sake
All that have injured thee.

The Sixth Commandment of God

"Thou shalt not commit adultery."

212. **What does God forbid by this sixth commandment?**
By this sixth commandment, God forbids all sins of impurity, such as immodest looks, words, jests, and whatever else leads to impurity.

213. **Why must we most carefully guard against impurity?**
Because no sin is more shameful in the eyes of God and of men.

* 214. **What should we do to preserve our purity?**
We should shun all unchaste curiosity, bad company, and indecent books and plays; pray fervently and remember that God sees everything.

The Seventh Commandment of God

"Thou shalt not steal."

215. **What does God forbid by this seventh commandment?**
By this seventh commandment, God forbids us to injure our neighbor in his property, by stealing or cheating or in any other unjust way.

216. **Is it a sin for children secretly to take things from their parents?**
Yes; it is a sin for children to take things from their parents.

217. **How do we injure our neighbor in his property?**
We injure our neighbor in his property by damaging his houses, fields, goods, or anything belonging to him.

* 218. **What must we do when we have goods stolen or found?**
We must restore the goods stolen or found to the owner and, as far as we can, repair the injury done.

Thou shalt not steal, nor keep, nor waste,
Nor cheat in any way;
Ill-gotten goods restore in haste
And lawful debts repay.

The Eighth Commandment of God

"Thou shalt not bear false witness against thy neighbor."

219. **What does God forbid by this eighth commandment?**
By this eighth commandment, God forbids us to tell a falsehood against anybody, especially in a court of justice.

220. **Are lies forbidden by the eighth commandment?**
Yes; all lies, hypocrisy, detraction, and slander are forbidden by the eighth commandment.

221. **What is meant by a lie?**
A lie is the deliberate and intentional denial of the truth.

222. **Are we ever allowed to tell a lie?**
No; we are never allowed to tell a lie, not even in jest or for the sake of preserving ourselves or others from harm.

* 223. **Who are guilty of detraction?**
Those are guilty of detraction who make known their neighbor's faults without necessity.

* 224. **Who are guilty of calumny or slander?**
Those are guilty of calumny or slander who accuse their neighbor of faults of which he is not guilty.

* 225. **Who are guilty of false suspicion?**
Those are guilty of false suspicion who, without sufficient reason, imagine evil of their neighbor.

The Ninth and Tenth Commandments of God

"Thou shalt not covet thy neighbor's wife."
"Thou shalt not covet thy neighbor's goods."

226. **What does God forbid by the ninth commandment?**
By the ninth commandment, God forbids all impure thoughts and desires.

227. **What does God forbid by the tenth commandment?**
By the tenth commandment, God forbids all unjust desire of what belongs to others.

* 228. **Are bad thoughts and desires always sinful?**
Bad thoughts and desires are sinful whenever we willfully keep them in our mind and take pleasure in them.

The Commandments of the Church

229. **Are we bound to keep any other commandments besides the commandments of God?**
Yes; we are bound to keep the commandments of the Church.

230. **Which are the commandments of the Church?**

The commandments of the Church are these six:

1. To rest from servile work, and to hear Mass on all Sundays and holy days of obligation.
2. To fast and to abstain on the days appointed by the Church (that is, to fast in Lent, on the Ember days, on the Fridays in Advent, and on the eves of certain festivals; to abstain from flesh meat on Fridays and other appointed days of abstinence).
3. To confess our sins at least once a year.
4. To receive worthily the Blessed Eucharist at Easter or within the time appointed.
5. To contribute to the support of our pastors.
6. Not to marry within the forbidden degree of kindred, nor to solemnize marriage within the forbidden times.

The First Commandment of the Church

"To rest from servile work, and to hear Mass on
all Sundays and holy days of obligation."

231. **What does the Church command by this first commandment?**

By this first commandment, the Church commands us to keep holy the Sundays and holy days instituted by her in honor of our Lord and of his saints.

* 232. **For what purpose has the Church instituted holy days?**
The Church has instituted holy days to honor our Lord and his saints.

233. **How are we to keep holy the Sundays and holy days of obligation?**
By assisting at the Holy Sacrifice of the Mass with attention and devotion.

234. **Who are bound to hear Mass on Sundays and holy days of obligation?**
All who have attained the use of reason.

* 235. **When do we sin against the commandment of hearing Mass?**
We sin against the commandment of hearing Mass:
1. When through our own fault we lose Mass or a part of it.
2. When during Mass we willfully give way to distractions; when we laugh, talk, or otherwise misbehave.

The Second Commandment of the Church

"To fast and to abstain on the days appointed by the Church."

236. **What does the Church command by this second commandment?**
By this second commandment, the Church commands us to fast and to abstain from flesh meat on certain days appointed by her.

* 237. **Who is obliged to fast in the manner prescribed?**
Every Christian who is fully twenty-one years of age and is not excused by any just cause.

238. **On what days are we commanded to abstain from flesh meat?**
On all fast days of obligation and on all Fridays of the year.

239. **Who are bound to abstain from flesh meat on the appointed days?**
All Christians who have attained the use of reason (commonly at the age of seven).

The Third Commandment of the Church

"To confess our sins at least once a year."

240. **What does the Church command by this third commandment?**
By this third commandment, the Church commands us to confess our sins sincerely, at least once a year, to a lawfully approved priest.

The Fourth Commandment of the Church

"To receive worthily the Blessed Eucharist at
Easter or within the time appointed."

241. **What does the Church command by this fourth commandment?**
By this fourth commandment, the Church commands us to receive Holy Communion at Easter or thereabouts.

Note.—At what age children ought to go to confession and Communion must be left to the decision of their pastors.

The Fifth Commandment of the Church

"To contribute to the support of our pastors."

242. **What does the Church command by this fifth commandment?**
By this fifth commandment, the Church commands us to contribute willingly to the support of our pastors, churches, and religious institutions.[9]

The Violation of the Commandments or Sin

243. **What is sin?**
Sin is any willful transgression against the law of God or of the Church.

* 244. **In how many ways can we sin?**
We can sin:
1. By bad thoughts and desires.
2. By bad words and actions.
3. By the omission of the good we are bound to do.

[9] On the sixth commandment of the Church, see "Matrimony."

245. **Are all sins equal?**

No; there are grievous sins, called mortal, and there are lesser sins, called venial.

* 246. **When do we commit mortal sin?**

We commit mortal sin when we knowingly and willfully transgress the law of God in a serious matter.

* 247. **When do we commit venial sin?**

We commit venial sin when we transgress the law of God in a small matter.

248. **Should we dread only grievous or mortal sins?**

No; we should dread and carefully avoid every sin, whether mortal or venial.

249. **Why should we so much dread every sin?**

We should dread sin more than any other evil on earth, because it is the greatest evil.

250. **Why is sin the greatest evil?**

Because sin offends God and draws upon us his punishment.

251. **What punishment does sin draw upon us?**

Mortal sin draws upon us everlasting punishment in hell; venial sin draws upon us temporal punishment in this world or in purgatory.

* 252. **Are there particular classes of sin?**

Yes; chiefly the seven capital or deadly sins, namely:

1. Pride.
2. Covetousness.
3. Lust.
4. Anger.
5. Gluttony.
6. Envy.
7. Sloth.

Jesus, may we ever live
From sin and sorrow free;
Then let us ever die to sin,
And ever live to thee!

Virtue and Christian Perfection

253. **Should we be content with avoiding sin?**
No; we should also diligently endeavor to practice virtue and to attain perfection.

254. **In what does Christian virtue consist?**
Christian virtue consists in the steady will and constant effort to do what is pleasing to God.

255. **Which are the theological virtues?**
The theological virtues are faith, hope, and charity.[10]

256. **How may we briefly make acts of faith, hope, and charity?**
Thus:
O my God, I believe in thee, the eternal truth.
O my God, I hope in thee, the infinite mercy.
O my God, I love thee, the sovereign, most amiable good.

257. **When are we obliged to make acts of faith, hope, and charity?**
Often in life, and especially in danger of death.

* 258. **What means must every Christian use for attaining perfection?**
1. He must love prayer and Christian instruction.

[10] Acts of faith, hope, and charity, see p. 73.

2. He must perform his actions in the state of grace and in a manner pleasing to God.
3. He must imitate Jesus and often think of the presence of God.

SECTION III
The Means of Grace

GRACE IN GENERAL

259. **Can we by our own strength keep the commandments and be saved?**
No; without the grace of God, we cannot keep the commandments and be saved.

260. **How many kinds of grace are there?**
There are two kinds of grace: actual grace and sanctifying grace.

* 261. **How does God assist us by actual grace?**
By actual grace, God gives us light and strength to avoid evil and do good.

* 262. **How does God assist us by sanctifying grace?**
By sanctifying grace, God makes our soul just and holy in his sight.

263. **When do we receive sanctifying grace?**
We receive sanctifying grace in baptism.

264. **How is sanctifying grace lost?**
Sanctifying grace is lost by mortal sin.

265. **How is sanctifying grace recovered?**
Sanctifying grace is recovered by the sacrament of penance.

* 266. **What fruits do we produce in the state of grace?**
In the state of grace, we produce good works which merit an eternal reward.

267. **Is every Christian bound to do good works?**
Yes; for "every tree that doth not yield good fruit shall be cut down and cast into the fire."[11]

268. **What does God especially consider in our good works?**
In our good works, God especially considers our good intention.

269. **What is a good intention?**
A good intention is the purpose to serve and honor God in whatsoever we do.

270. **How may we briefly make a good intention?**
We may say: "My Lord and my God, all for thy honor and glory!"

271. **When should we make a good intention?**
We should make a good intention often during the day, especially in the morning.

272. **What special means must we use to obtain grace?**
The holy sacraments and prayer.

The Sacraments in General

273. **Who instituted the sacraments?**
Jesus Christ, our Lord, instituted the sacraments.

274. **For what end did Jesus Christ institute the sacraments?**
Jesus Christ instituted the sacraments to give grace and interior sanctification to our souls.

[11] Mt 3:10; Cf. Mt 7:19

275. **How many things are necessary to constitute a sacrament?**

These three:

1. An outward sign.
2. An inward grace.
3. The institution of Christ.

276. **How many sacraments did Christ institute?**

Christ instituted seven sacraments, namely:

1. Baptism.
2. Confirmation.
3. Holy Eucharist.
4. Penance.
5. Extreme unction.
6. Holy orders.
7. Matrimony.

Baptism

277. **Which is the first and most necessary sacrament?**

Baptism is the first and most necessary sacrament.

278. **What is baptism?**

Baptism is a sacrament in which, by water and the word of God, we are cleansed from all sin, sanctified in Christ, and born again to eternal life.

* 279. **How is baptism given?**

Baptism is given by pouring water on the head of the person to be baptized, and saying at the same time: "I baptize thee in the name of the Father, and of the Son, and of the Holy Ghost."

280. **From what sins are we cleansed in baptism?**
In baptism, we are cleansed from original sin and from all sins committed before baptism.

281. **How are we sanctified in baptism?**
In baptism, we receive sanctifying grace, and are made children of God, members of the Church of Christ, and heirs of heaven.

* 282. **Who can and should baptize?**
Priests should baptize; in case of necessity, any person can baptize.

* 283. **What do we promise in baptism?**
In baptism, we promise to renounce Satan and all sin, and to be true children of the Catholic Church.

Confirmation

284. **What is confirmation?**
Confirmation is a sacrament in which, after baptism, we are strengthened by the Holy Ghost steadfastly to profess our faith.

285. **Who has the power to give confirmation?**
Bishops have the power to give confirmation.

286. **How does the bishop give confirmation?**
By the imposition of his hands, by anointing with holy chrism, and by prayer.

287. **Who can be confirmed?**
Everyone who is baptized can be confirmed.

* 288. **Is confirmation necessary for salvation?**
Confirmation is not absolutely necessary for salvation; yet it would be a sin willfully to neglect receiving it.

The Holy Eucharist

THE REAL PRESENCE OF CHRIST IN THE BLESSED SACRAMENT

289. **What is the Holy Eucharist?**
The Holy Eucharist is the true body and true blood of Christ under the appearances of bread and wine.

* 290. **When did Christ institute the Holy Eucharist?**
Christ instituted the Holy Eucharist at the last supper, the evening before his bitter passion and death.

* 291. **How did Christ institute the Holy Eucharist?**
Christ changed bread and wine into his sacred body and blood, and gave it to his apostles.

* 292. **Did Christ give others the power to change bread and wine into his sacred body and blood?**
Yes; he gave the apostles and their successors, the bishops and priests of the Catholic Church, the power to change bread and wine into his sacred body and blood.

* 293. **When do the bishops and priests exercise the power of changing bread and wine into the body and blood of Christ?**
At the consecration in the Mass.

* 294. **Is there no longer bread and wine on the altar after the consecration in the Mass?**
No; after the consecration in the Mass, there is on the altar the true body and true blood of Christ under the appearances of bread and wine.

295. **What should we do when in Church before the Blessed Sacrament?**
We should consider that Jesus Christ is there present; adore him with the deepest humility and respect.

Great sacrament of love divine!
All, all we are or have be thine.
Sweet sacrament, we thee adore;
Oh, make us love thee more and more!

THE HOLY SACRIFICE OF THE MASS

296. **Who instituted the Holy Sacrifice of the Mass?**
Jesus Christ instituted the Holy Sacrifice of the Mass.

297. **Why did Jesus Christ institute the Holy Sacrifice of the Mass?**
Jesus Christ instituted the Holy Sacrifice of the Mass that it should be the perpetual sacrifice of the new law.

298. **What takes place in the Sacrifice of the Mass?**
In the Sacrifice of the Mass, Jesus Christ, under the appearances of bread and wine, offers himself to his heavenly Father by the hands of the priest.

299. **When did Jesus Christ first offer himself to his heavenly Father?**
Jesus Christ first offered himself to his heavenly Father when dying on the cross on Calvary.

300. **Is the Sacrifice of the Mass the same as the sacrifice of the cross?**
Yes; the Sacrifice of the Mass is essentially the same as the sacrifice of the cross.

301. **Is there no difference between the Sacrifice of the Mass and the sacrifice of the cross?**
Yes; there is a difference between the Sacrifice of the Mass and the sacrifice of the cross in the manner of offering.

302. **In what manner did Christ offer himself on the cross?**
On the cross, Christ offered himself in a bloody manner, dying a most painful death.

303. **In what manner does Christ offer himself in the Mass?**
In the Mass, Christ offers himself in an unbloody manner, without suffering or dying.

304. **Which are the principal parts of the Mass?**
The principal parts of the Mass are:
1. The offertory.
2. The consecration.
3. The communion.

* 305. **What is the fruit of the Mass?**
The fruit of the Mass is to procure for God the greatest honor, and for us the greatest blessings.

306. **How should we assist at Mass?**
We should assist at Mass with great devotion and reverence, bearing in mind that Christ himself is present.

HOLY COMMUNION

307. **What do we receive in Holy Communion?**
In Holy Communion, we receive the true body and blood of Christ for the nourishment of our souls.

* 308. **Must we also drink the chalice in order to receive Holy Communion?**
No; for under the appearance of bread Christ is present whole and entire, his body and his blood.

* 309. **What effect does Holy Communion produce in our souls?**
Holy Communion unites us in the most intimate manner with Jesus Christ, and imparts many graces when we receive it worthily.

* 310. **Who receives Holy Communion unworthily?**
He receives Holy Communion unworthily who receives it in mortal sin.

* 311. **What, then, must we do before Holy Communion, in case we have committed a mortal sin?**
We must make a good confession before receiving Holy Communion, to put ourselves in the state of grace.

* 312. **After making a good confession, what other preparation must we make for Holy Communion?**
We must pray with fervor and devotion, and remain fasting from midnight.

Penance

313. **What is the sacrament of penance?**

The sacrament of penance is a sacrament in which the sins we have committed after baptism are forgiven.

314. **How are sins forgiven in the sacrament of penance?**

Sins are forgiven in the sacrament of penance by virtue of the priest's words of absolution, joined with contrition, confession, and satisfaction on the part of the penitent.

* 315. **Who gave the power of forgiving sin?**

Jesus Christ gave the power of forgiving sin to the apostles and their successors, when he said to them: "Receive ye the Holy Ghost; whose sins you shall forgive, they are forgiven them, and whose sins you shall retain, they are retained."[12]

* 316. **Can all sins be forgiven in the sacrament of penance?**

Yes; all the sins we have committed after baptism can be forgiven in the sacrament of penance.

* 317. **Why must we confess our sins in order to have them forgiven?**

We must confess our sins because Christ ordained it so, when he instituted the sacrament of penance.

318. **How many things are required on our part to receive the sacrament of penance worthily?**

To receive the sacrament of penance worthily, these five things are required on our part:

1. Prayer to the Holy Ghost.

[12] Jn 20:22-23

2. Examination of conscience.
3. Contrition with a firm purpose of amendment.
4. Confession.
5. Satisfaction.

PRAYER TO THE HOLY GHOST AND EXAMINATION OF CONSCIENCE

319. **What is the first thing we must do when we prepare for confession?**
The first thing we must do when we prepare for confession is to pray to the Holy Ghost.

* 320. **What should we ask of the Holy Ghost?**
We should ask of the Holy Ghost the grace to know all our sins, to be heartily sorry for them, to confess them properly, and to amend our lives.[13]

321. **What is meant by "examination of conscience"?**
Examination of conscience means: to think seriously on our sins that we may truly know them.

322. **In what manner should we examine our conscience?**
We should recall the commandments of God and of the Church, so as to know in what way and how often we have offended God in thought or desire, in word, deed, or omission.

323. **How may children easily remember their sins?**
By reflecting how they have behaved: in church; in school; at home toward parents, brothers, and sisters; on the street or abroad; alone and in company with others.

[13] See "Prayer to the Holy Ghost," p. 81.

* 324. **Must we examine ourselves on the number of our sins?**
Yes; at least when they are mortal sins.

CONTRITION AND FIRM PURPOSE OF AMENDMENT

325. **What is the most important and necessary part of our preparation for confession?**
The most important and necessary part of our preparation for confession is contrition with a firm purpose of amendment.

326. **What is contrition?**
Contrition is a hearty sorrow for our sins and a detestation of them.

* 327. **What qualities must true contrition have?**
True contrition must be:
1. Interior.
2. Universal.
3. Supernatural.

* 328. **When is contrition interior?**
Contrition is interior when we grieve for our sins not merely in words, but detest them in our heart as the greatest evil, and sincerely wish we had not committed them.

* 329. **When is contrition universal?**
Contrition is universal when we are sorry for all our sins, at least all our mortal sins.

* 330. **If we grieve for our sins on account of temporal loss, disgrace, or punishment, is our sorrow good?**
No; such a sorrow is only a natural contrition.

* 331. **When is contrition supernatural?**

Contrition is supernatural when we are sorry for our sins because we have offended God, or deserved hell, or for other motives which faith teaches us.

* 332. **What must we do to excite supernatural sorrow?**

We must consider:

1. That our sins have made us deserving of God's punishments.
2. That our sins have offended God, our greatest benefactor, the best of fathers, and the supreme good.

333. **What must contrition necessarily include?**

Contrition must necessarily include a firm purpose of amendment.

334. **What is a firm purpose of amendment?**

A firm purpose of amendment is a sincere resolution to amend our life and to sin no more.

* 335. **When is our purpose of amendment true and sincere?**

When it comes from the heart.

* 336. **When must we make an act of contrition with a firm purpose of amendment?**

We must make an act of contrition with a firm purpose of amendment before our confession, at least before the priest gives us absolution.

337. **How do you make an act of contrition with a firm purpose of amendment?**

O my God! I am most heartily sorry, etc.[14]

[14] See p. 73.

CONFESSION

338. **What is confession?**

Confession is the humble recital of our sins to a priest, to obtain his absolution.

339. **What are the necessary qualities of confession?**

Confession must be:

1. Entire.
2. Sincere.
3. Clear.

340. **When is confession entire?**

Confession is entire when we confess at least all the mortal sins we can remember, together with their number and necessary circumstances.

* 341. **What must we do if we cannot recollect the number of our sins?**

We must declare the number of our sins as well as we are able, and say, for instance: "I have committed this sin about...times a day, a week, or a month."

342. **Are we bound to confess also venial sins?**

We are not bound to confess venial sins; but it is good to do so.

343. **When is confession sincere?**

Confession is sincere when we accuse ourselves just as we truly believe ourselves guilty before God.

* 344. **What should the penitent consider if ashamed to make a sincere confession?**

He should consider that when he willfully conceals a mortal sin, he obtains no pardon for any of his sins, but commits another mortal sin—a sacrilege—and makes himself miserable for time and eternity.

* 345. **What must we do if we have left out something in confession which we were bound to confess?**

1. If we have left it out without our fault, it is only required to mention it in the next confession.
2. If we have left it out through our fault, our confession was a bad one, and we must tell in how many confessions we left it out, and repeat them all.

346. **When is confession clear?**

Confession is clear when we so express ourselves that the confessor may clearly see the state of our conscience.

347. **How do you begin your confession?**

Having knelt down, I make the sign of the cross and say: "Bless me, Father, for I have sinned. I confess to Almighty God, and to you, Father, in his stead, that since my last confession, which was...I have committed the following sins." (Here I confess my sins.)

348. **How do you conclude your confession?**

I conclude by saying: "For these and all my other sins, which I cannot at present call to mind, and also for the sins of my past life, especially for...I am heartily sorry. I most humbly ask pardon of God, and penance and absolution of you, my ghostly Father."

349. **What must you do then?**

I must listen with attention to the advice which my confessor may think proper to give me, and to the penance he enjoins; and, whilst he gives me absolution, I must excite my heart to true sorrow.

Note.—Do not leave the confessional until the priest has given you notice by saying, for instance: "Go in peace," or "Praise be to Jesus Christ."

SATISFACTION

350. **What must you do after confession?**

I must make satisfaction; that is, I must do the penance given me by my confessor and amend my life.

* 351. **Why does the confessor give a penance?**

The confessor gives a penance:

1. That we may satisfy for the temporal punishment due to our sins.
2. That we may amend our life.

352. **When God forgives the sin, does he not also remit the punishment due to that sin?**

When God forgives sin, he always remits the eternal punishment, but not always the temporal punishment due to sin.

353. **What is the temporal punishment due to our sins?**

The temporal punishment due to our sins is that which we have to suffer either here on earth or in purgatory.

Extreme Unction

354. **What is extreme unction?**

Extreme unction is a sacrament that gives grace to die well.

355. **How is extreme unction administered?**

The priest anoints the sick with holy oil and prays over them.

356. **What benefit do the sick obtain from extreme unction?**
The sick obtain the grace of God for the good of the soul and often also of the body.

357. **Who can and should receive extreme unction?**
Every Catholic who has come to the use of reason and is in danger of death by sickness.

358. **How are we to receive extreme unction?**
We are to receive extreme unction in the state of grace; wherefore we must first confess our sins, or, if we cannot confess, make an act of perfect contrition.

Holy Orders

359. **What is the sacrament of holy orders?**
The sacrament of holy orders is a sacrament which confers on those who receive it the powers of the priesthood, together with a special grace to discharge its sacred duties.

360. **What are the principal powers of the priesthood?**
The principal powers of the priesthood are:

1. The power to offer the Holy Sacrifice of the Mass.
2. The power to forgive sins.

Matrimony

361. **What is matrimony?**

Matrimony is a sacrament by which two single persons, a man and a woman, are joined together in marriage, and receive grace from God to fulfill faithfully until death the duties of their state, especially to bring up their children in the fear of God.

Prayer

362. **What is prayer?**

Prayer is the raising up of our minds and hearts to God.

363. **Why do we pray?**

We pray to praise God, to thank him, or to beg his grace.

364. **How must we pray that our prayer may be pleasing to God?**

We must pray with devotion and with confidence.

365. **When do we pray with devotion?**

We pray with devotion when we pray from the heart, and avoid all distracting thoughts as much as possible.

366. **What must we do to pray with devotion?**
We must be mindful of God's presence and consider that we are addressing the Almighty.

367. **May we hope that God will hear our devout prayer?**
Yes; we may and should hope that God will hear our devout prayer, if what we ask is good for us.

368. **Why should we hope that God will hear our prayer?**
Because God has promised to hear our prayer through Jesus, his divine Son.

369. **Is prayer necessary?**
Yes; prayer is necessary that we may obtain God's grace and blessing in this life, and eternal salvation in the next.

370. **When ought we to pray?**
We ought to pray often, especially in the morning and at night, before and after meals, when the *Angelus* bell rings, and when we are in church.

THE LORD'S PRAYER

371. **Which is the most excellent of all prayers?**
The Our Father or Lord's Prayer is the most excellent of all prayers.

372. **Why is the Our Father called the "Lord's Prayer"?**
The Our Father is called the "Lord's Prayer" because Christ our Lord made it and commanded us to say it.

373. **Say the Our Father.**
Our Father, etc.[15]

374. **What does the Lord's Prayer contain?**
The Lord's Prayer contains a short preface and seven petitions.

375. **What do you call the preface of the Lord's Prayer?**
These words: "Our Father, who art in heaven."

376. **Of what does the word *Father* remind us?**
The word *Father* reminds us that God is our Father, and that we ought to pray to him with childlike reverence, love, and confidence.

377. **Why do we say, "Our Father," and not, "My Father"?**
We say, "Our Father," because God is the Father of all men; therefore we all should pray for one another.

378. **Why do we add: "Who art in heaven"?**
To call to our minds that when we pray we are to detach our hearts from earth and raise them to heaven.

379. **What do we ask for in the first petition: "Hallowed be thy name"?**
In the first petition, we ask that God may be better known, loved, and revered by us and by all men, and that his holy name may never be profaned or blasphemed.

380. **What do we ask for in the second petition: "Thy kingdom come"?**
In the second petition, we ask that after this life God may admit us all into the kingdom of heaven.

[15] See p. 71.

381. **What do we ask for in the third petition: "Thy will be done on earth as it is in heaven"?**
In the third petition, we ask that we and all men may do the will of God on earth as faithfully as the angels and saints do it in heaven.

382. **What do we ask for in the fourth petition: "Give us this day our daily bread"?**
In the fourth petition, we ask that God would give us all that is daily necessary for soul and body.

383. **What do we ask for in the fifth petition: "Forgive us our trespasses as we forgive them who trespass against us"?**
In the fifth petition, we beg that God would so forgive us all our sins as we forgive them who have offended us.

384. **What do we ask for in the sixth petition: "Lead us not into temptation"?**
In the sixth petition, we beg that God would remove from us all temptations and dangers of sin, or, at least, give us grace to resist them.

385. **What do we ask for in the seventh petition: "But deliver us from evil"?**
In the seventh petition, we beg that God would preserve us from all evil of soul and body, especially from sin and eternal perdition.

386. **What is the meaning of the word *Amen*?**
The meaning of the word *Amen* is: "So be it"—"may all we ask be granted."

THE ANGELICAL SALUTATION

387. **What prayer do Catholics usually say after the Our Father?**
The prayer said in honor of the Mother of God, and called the "Angelical Salutation" or Hail Mary.

388. **How many parts has the Hail Mary?**
The Hail Mary has three parts: two of praise and one of petition.

389. **Of what is the prayer or praise in the Hail Mary composed?**
The prayer of praise is composed:

1. Of the words of the archangel Gabriel: "Hail (Mary) full of grace, the Lord is with thee, blessed art thou among women."[16]
2. Of the words of St. Elizabeth: "And blessed is the fruit of thy womb, (Jesus)."[17]

390. **Why do we call Mary "full of grace"?**
We call Mary "full of grace" because she received more graces from God than all other creatures.

391. **Why do we say, "The Lord is with thee"?**
We say, "The Lord is with thee," because the ever Blessed Virgin Mary was most closely united with God on earth, and is now, as Queen of all saints, near to the throne of God in heaven.

392. **Why do we say, "Blessed art thou among women"?**
We say, "Blessed art thou among women," to praise Mary, because she was chosen from amongst all women to be the Mother of God.

393. **Why do we add these words: "Blessed is the fruit of thy womb, Jesus"?**
We add the words, "Blessed is the fruit of thy womb, Jesus," because we honor and praise the Blessed Virgin chiefly for the sake of Jesus, her divine Son.

394. **Of what words is the prayer of petition in the Hail Mary composed?**
The prayer of petition is composed of the words added by the Church: "Holy Mary, Mother of God, pray for us sinners, now and at the hour of our death. Amen."

395. **Why is the church bell rung morning, noon, and night?**
To invite us to say the *Angelus*. "The angel of the Lord," etc.[18]

[16] Lk 1:28
[17] Lk 1:42
[18] See p. 74.

* 396. **Why do we pray more to the Blessed Virgin than to the other saints?**
We pray more to the Blessed Virgin than to the other saints, because she is the Mother of God, and excels all other saints in grace, holiness, and power with God.

Mother of Mercy, hail, O gentle Queen!
Our life, our sweetness and our hope, all hail!
Children of Eve
To thee we cry from our sad banishment;
To thee we send our sighs,
Weeping and mourning in this tearful vale.
Come, then, our advocate;
Oh! turn on us those pitying eyes of thine:
And our long exile past—
Show us at last
Jesus, of thy pure womb the fruit divine.
O Virgin Mary, Mother blest!
O sweetest, gentlest, holiest!

Prayers

The Holy Sign of the Cross

✠ In the name of the Father, and of the Son, and of the Holy Ghost. Amen.

The Lord's Prayer (7 Petitions)

Our Father who art in heaven,

1. Hallowed be thy name.
2. Thy kingdom come.
3. Thy will be done on earth as it is in heaven.
4. Give us this day our daily bread.
5. And forgive us our trespasses, as we forgive them who trespass against us.
6. And lead us not into temptation.
7. But deliver us from evil. Amen.

The Angelical Salutation (3 Parts)

1. Hail Mary, full of grace, the Lord is with thee, blessed art thou among women.
2. And blessed is the fruit of thy womb, Jesus.
3. Holy Mary, Mother of God, pray for us sinners, now and at the hour of our death. Amen.

The Apostles' Creed (12 Articles)

1. I believe in God the Father Almighty, Creator of heaven and earth.
2. And in Jesus Christ, his only Son, our Lord.
3. Who was conceived of the Holy Ghost, born of the Virgin Mary.
4. Suffered under Pontius Pilate, was crucified, dead, and buried.
5. He descended into hell; the third day he rose again from the dead.

6. He ascended into heaven, sitteth at the right hand of God the Father Almighty.
7. From thence he shall come to judge the living and the dead.
8. I believe in the Holy Ghost.
9. The holy Catholic Church, the communion of saints.
10. The forgiveness of sins.
11. The resurrection of the body.
12. And life everlasting. Amen.

The Gloria Patri

Glory be to the Father, and to the Son, and to the Holy Ghost! As it was in the beginning, is now, and ever shall be, world without end. Amen.

The Confiteor

I confess to Almighty God, to the Blessed Mary ever Virgin, to blessed Michael the archangel, to blessed John the Baptist, to the holy apostles Peter and Paul, and to all the saints, that I have sinned exceedingly in thought, word, and deed, through my fault, through my fault, through my most grievous fault. Therefore I beseech the Blessed Mary ever Virgin, blessed Michael the archangel, blessed John the Baptist, the holy apostles Peter and Paul, and all the saints, to pray to the Lord our God for me.

May the Almighty God have mercy on me, forgive me my sins, and bring me to everlasting life. Amen.

May the Almighty and merciful Lord grant me pardon, absolution, and remission of all my sins! Amen.

THE THREE THEOLOGICAL VIRTUES

An Act of Faith

O my God! I firmly believe all the sacred truths which the Catholic Church believes and teaches, because thou hast revealed them, who canst neither deceive nor be deceived.

An Act of Hope

O my God! relying upon thy infinite goodness and promises, I hope to obtain pardon for my sins, the assistance of thy grace, and life everlasting, through the merits of Jesus Christ, my Lord and Redeemer.

An Act of Love

O my God! I love thee above all things with my whole heart and soul, purely because thou art infinitely perfect, and deserving of all love; I love also my neighbor as myself, for the love of thee; I forgive all who have injured me, and ask pardon of all whom I have injured.

An Act of Contrition

O my God! I am most heartily sorry for all my sins, and I detest them above all things from the bottom of my heart, because they displease thee, O my God! who art most deserving of all my love; and I firmly purpose, by thy holy grace, never more to offend thee, and to do all that I can to atone for my sins and to amend my life.

The Salve Regina

Hail holy Queen, Mother of mercy, our life, our sweetness, and our hope, to thee do we cry, poor banished sons of Eve; to thee do we send up our sighs, mourning and weeping in this valley of tears. Turn, then, most gracious Advocate, thine eyes of mercy toward us, and, after this our exile, show unto us the blessed fruit of thy womb, Jesus. O clement, O loving, O sweet Virgin Mary!

The Memorare

Remember, O most gracious Virgin Mary, that never was it known that anyone who fled to thy protection, implored thy help, and sought thy intercession was left unaided. Inspired with this confidence, I fly unto thee, O Virgin of virgins, my Mother! To thee I come, before thee I stand, sinful and sorrowful.

O Mother of the Word incarnate, despise not my petitions, but in thy mercy hear and answer me. Amen.

The Angelus

To be said morning, noon, and night.

℣. The angel of the Lord declared unto Mary.

℟. And she conceived of the Holy Ghost. Hail Mary! etc.

℣. Behold the handmaid of the Lord.

℟. May it be done unto me according to thy word. Hail Mary! etc.

℣. And the Word was made flesh.

℟. And dwelt among us. Hail Mary! etc.

℣. Pray for us, O holy Mother of God.

℟. That we may be made worthy of the promises of Christ.

Let us pray.

Pour forth, we beseech thee, O Lord, thy grace into our hearts, that we, to whom the incarnation of Christ thy Son was made known by the message of an angel, may, by his passion and cross, be brought to the glory of the resurrection, through the same Christ, our Lord. Amen.

Prayer to the Guardian Angel

Angel of God, my guardian dear,
To whom his love commits me here,
Ever this day be at my side,
To light and guard, to rule and guide. Amen.

For the Faithful Departed

O God, the Creator and Redeemer of all the faithful, grant to the souls of thy servants departed the remission of all their sins, that through the devout prayers of thy Church on earth they may obtain that remission of pain which they have ever desired: who livest and reignest, etc. Amen.

℣. Eternal rest give to them, O Lord!

℟. And let perpetual light shine upon them.

℣. May they rest in peace.

℟. Amen.

Prayer to the Holy Ghost

Come, O Holy Ghost, fill the hearts of thy faithful and kindle in them the fire of thy love.

℣. Send forth thy Spirit and they shall be created.

℟. And thou wilt renew the face of the earth.

Let us pray.

O God! who by the light of the Holy Ghost didst instruct the hearts of the faithful, give us by this same Holy Spirit, a love and relish of what is right and just, and a constant enjoyment of his comforts, through Jesus Christ our Lord. Amen.

MORNING PRAYERS

As soon as you awake make the sign of the cross and say:

Glory be to God the Father, who has created me. Glory be to God the Son, who has redeemed me. Glory be to God the Holy Ghost, who has sanctified me.

Blessed be the Holy and undivided Trinity, now and forevermore. Amen.

When dressed, kneel and say: ✠ In the name of the Father, etc.

O great God, the sovereign Lord of heaven and earth! I prostrate myself before thee. With all the angels and saints, I adore thee. I acknowledge thee to be my Creator and sovereign Lord, my first beginning and my last end. I render to thee the homage of my being and life. I submit myself to thy holy will, and I devote myself to thy divine service this day and forever.

An act of faith, of hope, of love.[19]

To the Blessed Virgin

O Mary, my Queen and my Mother, I offer myself entirely to thee, and in order to prove myself devoted to thee, I consecrate to thee this day my sight, my hearing, my speech, my heart, my whole being.

Since, therefore, I am thine, O good Mother, preserve and defend me as thy property and possession.

To the Angel Guardian and Patron Saint

O blessed spirit, whom God in his mercy has appointed to watch over me, intercede for me this day, that I may not stray from the path of virtue. Thou also, O happy saint whose name I bear, pray for me, that I may serve God faithfully in this life, as thou hast done, and glorify him eternally with thee in heaven. Amen.

[19] See p. 73.

May the divine assistance always remain with us, and may the souls of the faithful departed, through the mercy of God, rest in peace. Amen.

May the peace and blessing of Almighty God, the Father, Son, and Holy Ghost, descend upon us and remain with us forever. Amen.

Before Any Work

Before you begin your work say:

O my God! I offer thee this work; give it thy blessing.

DURING THE DAY

Raise your mind to God from time to time, especially when you hear the clock strike, saying:

Grant, O my God! that all the actions of this hour, and those of every moment of my life, may be to thy honor and glory.

As soon as you perceive you have fallen into any sin, ask pardon for it, saying:

O my God! I am heartily sorry for having offended thee. I make a firm resolution, with the help of thy grace, never more to fall into this sin, to confess it, to do penance for it, and to avoid the occasions of it.

Before meals say:

✠ In the name of the Father, etc., Our Father, etc., Hail Mary, etc.

Bless us, O Lord! and these, thy gifts, which we are about to receive from thy bounty, through Christ our Lord. Amen.

After meals say:

✠ In the name of the Father, etc., Our Father, etc., Hail Mary, etc.

We give thee thanks, O Almighty God, for all thy benefits, who livest and reignest, world without end. Amen.

EVENING PRAYERS

At night, before going to bed, kneel down and say the following prayers:

✠ In the name of the Father, and of the Son, and of the Holy Ghost. Amen.

Blessed be the Holy and undivided Trinity, now and forevermore. Amen.

Come, O Holy Ghost! fill the hearts of thy faithful, and kindle in them the fire of thy divine love.

Place yourself in the presence of God.

Great God! Lord of heaven and earth! I prostrate myself before thee. With all the angels and saints I adore thee. I acknowledge thee to be my Creator and sovereign Lord, my first beginning and my last end. I render to thee the homage of my being and life. I submit myself to thy holy will, and I devote myself to thy divine service now and forever.

Here repeat the acts of faith, hope, and love.[20] *Then return thanks to God for the favors bestowed on you.*

How shall I be able to thank thee, O Lord! for all thy favors? Thou hast thought of me from all eternity; thou hast brought me forth from nothing; thou hast given thy life to redeem me, and thou continuest daily to load me with thy favors. Alas! my God, what return can I make thee for all thy benefits, and particularly for the favors of this day? Join me, ye blessed spirits, and all ye elect, in praising the God of mercies, who is so good to so unworthy a creature.

Ask for light to discover the sins you have committed this day.

O Holy Ghost! Eternal source of light, show me, I beseech thee, the sins I have committed this day in thought, word, and action, and grant me a perfect sorrow for them.

Examine your conscience.—Reflect where you have been this day, in what company, etc. Call to mind the duties of your state and your different offenses.

[20] See p. 73.

Against God. Omission or negligence in religious duties; irreverence in church; willful distractions at prayer; oaths; murmurings; want of confidence and resignation.

Against your neighbor. Rash judgments; hatred; jealousy; contempt; desire of revenge; quarreling; passion; imprecations; injuries; detraction; raillery; damaging in goods or reputation; bad example; scandal; want of obedience, respect, charity, or fidelity.

Against yourself. Vanity; human respect; lies; thoughts, desires, discourses, or actions contrary to purity; intemperance; impatience or rage; sloth.

Say the confiteor.[21] *Act of contrition.*[22]

Pour down thy blessing, O Lord! on thy holy Church, on our holy father the pope, on this diocese, on our Rt. Rev. Bishop (or Most Rev. Archbishop) and all pastors of souls; on this country, on our superiors temporal and spiritual, on our congregation; on this family, on our parents, relations, benefactors, friends, and enemies. Help the poor, the sick, and those that are in their agony; convert all heretics and enlighten the infidels.

O my holy angel! be thou my protector. And thou my holy patron, Saint N., and all the saints of God, pray to the Lord our God for me. Glory be to the Father, etc.

On going to bed say:

✠ In the name of our Lord Jesus Christ crucified, I lay myself down to rest; may he bless, govern, and preserve me, and bring me to everlasting life. Amen.

[21] See p. 72.

[22] See p. 73.

THE ROSARY OF THE BLESSED VIRGIN

✠ In the name of the Father, and of the Son, and of the Holy Ghost. Amen.

I believe in God the Father, etc., Our Father, etc., Hail Mary, *three times*. Glory be to the Father, etc.

The First Part: The Five Joyful Mysteries

First mystery.—The incarnation. Our Father, ten Hail Marys, Glory be to the Father.
Second mystery.—The visitation of the Blessed Virgin to her cousin St. Elizabeth. Our Father, etc.
Third mystery.—The birth of our Lord Jesus Christ in Bethlehem. Our Father, etc.
Fourth mystery.—The presentation of our Blessed Lord in the Temple. Our Father, etc.
Fifth mystery.—The finding of the Child Jesus in the Temple. Our Father, etc.

The Second Part: The Five Sorrowful Mysteries

First mystery.—The prayer and bloody sweat of our Blessed Savior in the garden. Our Father, etc.
Second mystery.—The scourging of our Blessed Lord at the pillar. Our Father, etc.
Third mystery.—The crowning of our Blessed Savior with thorns. Our Father, etc.
Fourth mystery.—Our Savior carrying his cross. Our Father, etc.
Fifth mystery.—The crucifixion. Our Father, etc.

The Third Part: The Five Glorious Mysteries

First mystery.—The resurrection of Christ from the dead. Our Father, etc.
Second mystery.—The ascension of Christ into heaven. Our Father, etc.

Third mystery.—The coming of the Holy Ghost upon the apostles and disciples. Our Father, etc.
Fourth mystery.—The assumption of the Blessed Virgin Mary into heaven. Our Father, etc.
Fifth mystery.—The coronation of the Blessed Virgin Mary in heaven. Our Father, etc.

Prayers before and after Confession

Prayer to the Holy Ghost

O God, my merciful Father! I come to thee with the sincere will to make a good confession of my sins, that in thy mercy and love thou mayest receive me again as thy beloved child. But as I am unable to do anything without thy divine help, I earnestly beseech thee to have pity on me, and to send the Holy Ghost with his assisting grace into my poor heart.

Come, O Holy Ghost! enlighten my mind, that I may clearly know my sins; and move my heart, that I may sincerely repent of them, confess them, and amend my life.

Our Father, Hail Mary, etc.

Examination of Conscience

Seriously reflect when and how you made your last confession, and whether you did the penance then given you by your confessor. Recall the commandments of God and of the Church, and the seven deadly sins, so as to know in what way and how often you have offended God in thought or desire, in word, deed, or omission.

First commandment of God.—Have I willfully doubted in matters of faith, or taken pleasure in hearing our holy religion ridiculed? Have I sinned by presumption?—Have I neglected to say my morning and evening prayers, or said them without devotion?—Have I been ashamed to make the sign of the cross, to take holy water, to kneel while praying?

Second commandment of God.—Have I uttered the holy names of God, Jesus, Mary, etc., irreverently?—Have I cursed? sworn falsely or in trivial matters?—Have I murmured against God? spoken with contempt of holy things and ceremonies?

Third commandment of God.—Have I neglected Mass on Sundays or holy days? Have I been late for Mass through my own fault? Have I been willfully distracted during Mass? spoken, laughed, gazed around, thus distracting others?

Fourth commandment of God.—Have I been rude and insolent, or disobedient; and obstinate to my parents, teachers, or other superiors?—Have I offended, grieved, or angered them?—Have I despised their advice, wished them evil, insulted them and even lifted up my hand against them?

Fifth commandment of God.—Have I, with the intention of provoking them, given nicknames to others, even to my sisters and brothers?—Have I quarreled with them, struck or injured them?—Have I been rude and insolent toward servants? Have I been unkind to the poor?—Have I been stubborn, quarrelsome, and malicious?—Have I provoked others to anger?—Have I, without necessity, exposed my life?—Have I been cruel to animals? Have I induced others to do evil, or was it my desire to do so?—Have I helped others to do wrong, or when they had done wrong, did I praise and justify them?—Have I given bad example to others by word or deed? Have I caused others to quarrel?

Sixth and ninth commandments of God.—Have I looked at immodest things, or thought, spoken, or read of them; and have I liked to hear of them?—Have I entertained immodest and impure desires?—Have I acted immodestly before children or grown persons while I was dressing or undressing?

Seventh and tenth commandments of God.—Have I stolen money, or anything else, or had I the will to steal?—Have I received from others things that were stolen?—Have I kept things that were stolen?—Have I neglected to return things I had found?—Have I injured the property of others?—Have I made presents without the knowledge and consent of my parents?

Eighth commandment of God.—Have I told lies? Have I told lies that injured anyone?—Is it not a habitual sin in me to tell lies?—Have I falsely accused my neighbor, or injured his good name?—Was this done out of hatred or envy? Have I spoken of what I should have concealed? or have I been silent in regard to faults of which I should have informed my parents and teachers?

Commandments of the Church.—Have I eaten flesh meat on forbidden days?—Have I done so out of contempt or indifference for the commandments of the Church?

The seven deadly sins.—Have I been proud of my acquirements, my clothes, of the position and wealth of my parents?—Have I thought myself better than others, and have I, for that reason, despised them, mocked them, and laughed at them?—Have I studied and prayed only to be praised or rewarded?—Have I been avaricious, and have I kept everything for myself, without dividing it with my sisters and brothers, or the poor?—Have I been envious, and therefore angry and sad, if others were praised or were successful, and, on the contrary, have I been glad when they were punished or suffered loss?—Have I been intemperate in eating and drinking: either eating or drinking too much, or eating with greediness, and drinking what was injurious to my health?—Have I been lazy in learning my lessons? Have I spent my time in idleness, that is, in playing and running about? Have I, without sufficient reason, neglected school, or when at school, shown a want of diligence and attention? and have I prevented others from learning their lessons by my talk and malicious conduct?

Considerations to Excite Contrition

1. Consider, my child, that by sin you have deserved to be punished by Almighty God in this world and in the next. Remember what the lost angels and men suffer in hell, and what the poor souls in purgatory

suffer. Alas! what would have become of you if God had punished you in like manner? Make up your mind what you will do; determine in future to be a good and obedient child of your heavenly Father, so that one day you may be with him in heaven.

2. Represent to yourself Christ upon the cross. See how his hands and feet are fastened with nails; how he is crowned with thorns, covered with wounds and blood, and how he suffers and dies for you! Behold, my child! your sins have caused all this; for on account of your sins our Blessed Lord had to suffer so much, and to die upon the cross. And are you therefore not sorry that you have committed them?
3. Remember also the many and great favors which God has bestowed upon you; how he has given you life, health, daily food and clothing, good parents, and a holy guardian angel; how thankful you should be to him that you are not a pagan or a Jew, but a child of the holy Catholic Church! O, how wicked, how ungrateful a child would you not be, if you should continue to offend such an infinitely kind Father, who is at the same time our sovereign and best good; and how wicked it would be for you not to love him! After having reflected upon all this, make, with a penitent heart, an act of contrition.[23] If you have time, say the following:

Prayer.—O my dearest Lord and Savior Jesus Christ! behold at thy feet thy poor, sinful child. Alas! I am ashamed before thee! Thou hast shown me so much kindness, didst come even from heaven into this world, to suffer so many pains and torments, and finally to give thy life for me; and I have been so ungrateful, and have committed so many sins! If thou hadst punished me, as thou, O just Lord, didst punish the wicked angels after the first sin, alas! how unhappy would I be now, and for all eternity! But thou hast always been, and art yet, full of love and mercy toward me, thy ungrateful child. O, my Jesus, I am most heartily sorry for having offended thee so often and so grievously! I beseech thee most humbly, my Lord and my Savior, to forgive me, and to receive me again into thy favor. I hate and detest all my sins, and promise thee, O my God, to sin no more. I will

[23] See p. 73.

in future love thee above all things, and avoid all occasions and dangers of sin, so that I may not have the misfortune to fall again.

O holy Virgin Mary, Mother of God, pray for me now, that I may make a good confession and obtain pardon of my sins. Assist me, my dear holy guardian angel, that from henceforth I may never sin again, but lead a good and pious life.

Prayer after Confession

O my Lord and Father! how great is thy goodness to me! On account of the merits of Jesus Christ, thou hast given me, through the words spoken by the priest, thy representative, the absolution of all my sins; I can now hope to be again thy dear child. I thank and praise thee, Father of mercy, for this great and unmerited grace! I shall never forget it, and I shall be most careful not to fall back into the old sins. Bless, O heavenly Father, this my resolution, and give me strength to be faithful to it unto death. I ask this grace, through the blood of Jesus Christ, shed for me upon the cross, and through the merits of Mary, his Blessed Mother, and of all the saints. Amen.

Renewal of the Baptismal Vows, to Strengthen the Resolutions Made in the Sacrament of Penance

O my God, through thy merciful love, I, a weak child, was cleansed from sin in holy baptism, renewed according to thy image, sanctified through thy grace, and received into thy holy Church!

I cheerfully confess my belief in thee, O Father! in thy Son, and in the Holy Ghost, and, according to this holy faith, without which there is no salvation, I will live and die in the one holy Catholic Church.

I again renounce all sin. I renounce Satan, with all his pomps and vanities; and I promise thee, O my Lord, to keep all thy holy commandments faithfully, to love thee above all things, and my neighbor as myself.

I beseech thee to awaken and renew in me the grace which thou didst give me in holy baptism, through Jesus Christ our Lord. Amen.

Manner of Serving at Mass

Let the server kneel at the left side of the priest, and answer as follows:

PRIEST. In nomine Patris, et Filii, et Spiritus Sancti. Amen. Introibo ad altare Dei.

SERVER. Ad Deum qui laetificat juventutem meam.

P. Judica me, Deus; et discerne causam meam de gente non sancta: ab homine iniquo et doloso erue me.

S. Quia tu es, Deus, fortitudo mea, quare me repulisti? et quare tristis incedo, dum affligit me inimicus?

P. Emitte lucem tuam et veritatem tuam: ipsa me deduxerunt et adduxerunt in montem sanctum tuum, et in tabernacula tua.

S. Et introibo ad altare Dei: ad Deum qui laetificat juventutem meam.

P. Confitebor tibi in cithara, Deus, Deus meus: quare tristis es, anima mea, et quare conturbas me?

S. Spera in Deo, quoniam adhuc confitebor illi, salutare vultus mei, et Deus meus.

P. Gloria Patri, et Filio, et Spiritui Sancto.

S. Sicut erat in principio, et nunc, et semper, et in saecula saeculorum. Amen.

P. Introibo ad altare Dei.

S. Ad Deum qui laetificat juventutem meam.

P. Adjutorium nostrum in nomine Domini.

S. Qui fecit coelum et terram.

P. Confiteor Deo, etc.

Bow your head when the priest begins the confiteor, *and continue bent till the* Dominus vobiscum.

S. Misereatur tui omnipotens Deus, et dimissis peccatis tuis, perducat te ad vitam aeternam.

P. Amen.

S. Confiteor Deo omnipotenti, Beatae Mariae semper Virgini, beato Michaeli archangelo, beato Joanni Baptistae, sanctis apostolis Petro et

Paulo, omnibus sanctis et tibi, Pater *[here turn your head toward the priest, and then go on]*, quia peccavi nimis cogitatione, verbo, et opere *[striking your breast thrice, say]*, mea culpa, mea culpa, mea maxima culpa: ideo precor Beatam Mariam semper Virginem, beatum Michaelem archangelum, beatum Joannem Baptistam, sanctos apostolos Petrum et Paulum, omnes sanctos, et te, Pater *[here turn again toward the priest]*, orare pro me ad Dominum Deum nostrum.

P. Misereatur vestri, etc.

S. Amen.

P. Indulgentiam, etc.

S. Amen.

P. Deus tu conversus vivificabis nos.

S. Et plebs tua laetabitur in te.

P. Ostende nobis, Domine, misericordiam tuam.

S. Et salutare tuum da nobis.

P. Domine, exaudi orationem meam.

S. Et clamor meus ad te veniat.

P. Dominus vobiscum.

S. Et cum spiritu tuo.

After the introit.

P. Kyrie eleison.

S. Kyrie eleison.

P. Kyrie eleison.

S. Christe eleison.

P. Christe eleison.

S. Christe eleison.

P. Kyrie eleison.

S. Kyrie eleison.

P. Kyrie eleison.

P. Dominus vobiscum; *or*, Flectamus genua.

S. Et cum spiritu tuo; *or*, Levate.

P. Per omnia saecula saeculorum.

S. Amen.

At the end of the epistle say, Deo gratias, *and after the gradual and alleluia, or tract, remove the book to the gospel side of the altar, and return to the epistle side—make a genuflection or a low reverence as you pass the middle of the altar, then stand up whilst the gospel is read.*

At the gospel.

P. Dominus vobiscum.

S. Et cum spiritu tuo.

P. Initium, *or* Sequentia, sancti Evangelii, etc.

Here make the sign of the cross—1st, upon your forehead, 2nd, upon your mouth, 3rd, upon your breast, and say, Gloria tibi, Domine.

At the end of the gospel, say,

S. Laus tibi, Christe.

P. Dominus vobiscum.

S. Et cum spiritu tuo.

At the offertory.

Going to the middle of the altar, kneel and make a reverence; then proceed to prepare the wine and water; present them to the priest, making a reverence; afterward, pour water on his fingers, present him with a towel, and return to your place at the epistle side of the altar.

P. Orate fratres, etc.

S. Suscipiat Dominus sacrificium de manibus tuis ad laudem et gloriam nominis sui, ad utilitatem quoque nostram, totiusque Ecclesiae suae sanctae.

At the preface.

P. Per omnia saecula saeculorum.

S. Amen.

P. Dominus vobiscum.

S. Et cum spiritu tuo.

P. Sursum corda.

S. Habemus ad Dominum.

P. Gratias agamus Domino Deo nostro.

S. Dignum et justum est.

When the priest says, Sanctus, sanctus, sanctus, etc., *ring the bell each time he pronounces it. When he spreads his hands over the chalice, ring the bell; then proceed to the center of the altar, where, kneeling, ring the bell with your right, and hold up the vestment with your left hand, during the elevation; then return to your former place; and as often as you pass by the Blessed Sacrament, make a genuflection.*

P. Per omnia saecula saeculorum.

S. Amen.

P. Et ne nos inducas in tentationem.

S. Sed libera nos a malo.

P. Per omnia saecula saeculorum.

S. Amen.

P. Pax Domini sit semper vobiscum.

S. Et cum spiritu tuo.

At the communion.

Each time the priest says, Domine non sum dignus, *ring the bell. When he has received the chalice, serve him with wine only; on his presenting the chalice again, serve him with wine and water. Remove the book to the epistle side of the altar, and retire to your place on the gospel side.*

P. Dominus vobiscum.

S. Et cum spiritu tuo.

P. Per omnia saecula saeculorum.

S. Amen.

P. Dominus vobiscum.

S. Et cum spiritu tuo.

P. Ite, missa est; *or,* Benedicamus Domino.

S. Deo gratias.

[*Note.*—In Masses for the Dead, the priest says,

P. Requiescat in pace.

S. Amen.]

Remove the book if left open, kneel before the center of the altar and receive the priest's blessing.

P. Pater, et Filius, et Spiritus Sanctus.

S. Amen.

Then rise.

P. Dominus vobiscum.

S. Et cum spiritu tuo.

P. Initium, *or,* Sequentia sancti Evangelii secundum, etc.

S. Gloria tibi, Domine.

At the end of the gospel, say,

S. Deo gratias.

Give the priest his biretta or cap, and go before him to the sacristy.

A COMPLETE CATECHISM
OF
THE CATHOLIC RELIGION

TRANSLATED FROM THE GERMAN OF
THE REV. JOSEPH DEHARBE, S.J.
BY THE
REV. JOHN FANDER

PRECEDED BY

A Short History of Revealed Religion, from the Creation to the Present Time

WITH QUESTIONS FOR EXAMINATION

SIXTH AMERICAN EDITION

CONFORMED TO THE
CODEX JURIS CANONICI

EDITED BY
THE REV. JAMES J. FOX, D.D.
AND
THE REV. THOMAS McMILLAN, C.S.P.

✠

NEW YORK
SCHWARTZ, KIRWIN & FAUSS
42 BARCLAY STREET

A COMPLETE CATECHISM

OF

THE CATHOLIC RELIGION

TRANSLATED FROM THE GERMAN OF
THE REV. JOSEPH DEHARBE, S.J.

BY THE

REV. JOHN FANDER

PRECEDED BY

A Short History of Revealed Religion, from the Creation to the Present Time

WITH QUESTIONS FOR EXAMINATION

SIXTH AMERICAN EDITION

CONFORMED TO THE
CODEX JURIS CANONICI

EDITED BY

THE REV. JAMES J. FOX, D.D.

AND

THE REV. THOMAS McMILLAN, C.S.P.

✠

NEW YORK
SCHWARTZ, KIRWIN & FAUSS
42 BARCLAY STREET

Nihil Obstat
Very rev. Edmund T. Shanahan, D. D.
Censor deputatus
Catholic University of America
April 16, 1908
Washington, D. C.

Imprimatur
+ John M. Farley
Archbishop of New York
April 21, 1908

PREFACE TO THE SIXTH AMERICAN EDITION

The catechism of Father Joseph Deharbe, S. J., first translated into English about half a century ago, has become so well known throughout this country that there is no need now to draw attention to its merits. It follows the triple catechetical method, using each in its appropriate place. The historical outline prefixed to the catechism proper furnishes, in sufficient detail, the historic proof of revelation and the divine institution of the Church. The first part of the catechism treats of faith and what is to be believed; the second, of the Christian rule of life, i.e., the commandments of God and of the Church; the third, of the essential means of salvation, grace, and of the channels instituted by our Lord Jesus Christ for its communication. The dogmatic and moral teaching is accompanied by ample citation of proof from scripture and tradition. Finally, the logical relation and sequence of subjects is insisted upon; so that the whole forms a well-articulated, comprehensive statement of our holy religion. It presents that religion truly, as a doctrine and rule of life embracing the whole man; given by God, through his Son, Jesus Christ, who has made it visible to men and fruitful unto salvation in an enduring society of which he is the head, the way, the truth, and the life.

The present edition is based on the fifth American edition. No essential changes have been introduced; but many minor modifications, suggested by experienced teachers who have used the work for many years, have been made. In a few places, the order has been rearranged; simpler and more idiomatic terms and phrases have been substituted for others that were less familiar, or foreign in construction, or too technical. Some questions and answers have been recast for the sake of clearness; and some new ones have been inserted. In many cases where this has been done, as, for example, in the section on the creation of man, the new forms have been taken from the *Catechism of Pius X*.[1] The historical sketch has been brought down to the present day; and, that it might not, in consequence, demand an unduly large share of space, some of the preceding paragraphs

[1] Editor's note: The *Catechism of Pius X*, or *Compendium of Christian Doctrine*, may be found in Volume VIII of this series.

have been condensed. The changes which have been instituted in Church discipline since the publication of the previous edition have been incorporated. In the exposition of duties, more account has been taken to make it meet the conditions of life in this country.

Some more changes in the text, looking toward further simplification, were suggested by persons interested in the work. It must be remembered, however, that, especially on dogmatic subjects, accuracy cannot always be safeguarded without a close adhesion to the language of theology. As Bossuet has wisely said, terms not understood at first may come to be understood later on by the help of reflection; and it is better that the less advanced and less capable should find things which they cannot quite understand, than that the more advanced and intelligent should be deprived of anything useful to them. Besides, this work is not intended for the younger children, but for pupils in the more advanced classes, of elementary schools, for high schools, colleges, academies, Sunday schools, and for private instruction.

THE TEACHING OF THE CATECHISM

From the earliest days of the Church, the instruction of the ignorant, whether adults or children, in the rudiments of the faith has ever been regarded as one of the foremost duties of the pastoral office. This kind of instruction, called "catechetical," differs from the more general forms of religious teaching. The Council of Trent carefully marked this difference, and prescribed catechetical instruction as a distinct duty for all who have the care of souls. In his encyclical on the subject, His Holiness, Pius X, describes the nature of such instruction. He first cites with approbation the words of his predecessor, Benedict XIV: "Two chief obligations have been imposed by the Council of Trent on those who have the care of souls; first, that they address the people on divine things on feast days; and, second, that they instruct the young and the ignorant in the rudiments of the law of God and of the faith." Then Pius X says: "It may be that there are some who, to save themselves trouble, are willing to believe that the explanation of the gospel may serve also for catechetical instruction. This is an error which should be apparent to all. For the sermon on the gospel is addressed to those who may be supposed to be already instructed in the rudiments of the faith. It is, so to say, the bread that is broken for adults. Catechetical instruction, on the other hand, is that milk which the apostle St. Peter wished to be desired with simplicity by the faithful as newly-born children."

Three methods are open to the catechist: the historical, the logical, and the liturgical. Divine revelation is a fact that falls within the domain of history. To relate the events connected with this revelation, their sequence, relations, and results, in order to impart a knowledge of Christian doctrine, is to follow the historical method. In his treatise for catechists, a work which left a lasting impress on the Church's catechetical system, St. Augustine strongly recommends this method. He advises the catechist to give a brief account of religious history from the beginning, in order to explain creation and original sin; to show how the old testament foretells the coming of the Redeemer, and the establishment of the Church; then to relate the events of our Lord's life, the beginnings of the Church, and her subsequent history; and thereby to convey to the pupils a knowledge of Christian belief and precepts.

On the simple enunciation of a truth of faith, the mind may ascend from the ideas expressed to principles on which these ideas depend; or it may develop the consequences contained in the truth. This is the logical plan, based on the natural tendency of the mind to correlate and systematize its knowledge. It is followed by the great catechism published by the authority of the Council of Trent, for the purpose of resisting protestantism, which did not dispute the fact of revelation. The influence of this catechism has caused the logical method to predominate for the last three centuries. The historical method, however, was maintained and perpetuated by Bossuet, who, following the counsels of St. Augustine, composed for his diocese an abridgment of sacred history to be used in conjunction with the catechism in vogue.

The truths of faith and the facts of religious history, associated with revelation and its propagation, are perpetuated in a striking, sensible manner by institutions, laws, customs, ceremonies, symbols, prayers, and other observances. The Church, with her entire constitution, organization, discipline, and worship, is a perpetual living monument embodying and, throughout the ages, witnessing to the doctrine of the faith. To teach this doctrine by interpreting the meaning of the Church's life and action is the liturgical method. These three methods do not exclude one another. Each one of them, in turn, possesses its own special advantages for some divisions of the catechism; and the whole ground is best covered when they are combined. If we examine the homilies of the fathers, we shall find that they make use of the three plans.

Along with Benedict XIV, the present supreme pontiff calls the office of catechist the most useful of institutions for the glory of God. He observes that the teaching of the catechism is a work more important than that of the sacred orator who eloquently defends religion; or than that of the priest who laboriously compiles learned books to illustrate the truths of faith. The proper fulfillment of this office, he warns us, is not an easy task: "It is much easier to find a preacher capable of delivering an eloquent and elaborate discourse than a catechist able to impart instruction in a manner entirely worthy of praise. It must, therefore, be carefully borne in mind that whatever facility of ideas and language a man may have inherited from nature, he will never be able to teach the catechism to the young and the adult without preparing himself thoughtfully for the task."

The first indispensable condition for fruitful work is, according to St. Augustine, that the catechist bring to his task a spirit of love: "If you do not love God and your brethren how will you laboriously spell out the first words of faith to the ignorant? Where will you discover the secret of repeating again and again the same truth in a variety of ways? Whence will you draw the courage and industry necessary to cultivate this soil abounding only in briars and thistles?...You must repeat and repeat the same things. Let the love which animates you give them an appearance of novelty."

Catechetical instruction, Piux X observes, is the basis of all other kinds of religious instruction. Ignorance of the catechism he declares to be the chief cause of that rapid increase of infidelity and immorality which he witnesses, not only among the poorer classes, "but in the highest walks of life and among those who, inflated with knowledge, rely upon a vain erudition and think themselves at liberty to turn religion into ridicule and to blaspheme that which they know not." His words confirm the solemn warning which a late learned prelate addressed to his clergy: The most effectual of all preaching, and that without which all other preaching is nearly useless, is the teaching of the catechism to the young. The priest who would neglect every other instruction and teach the catechism to the children of his parish would have done a great deal. The priest who would discharge every other duty and neglect this one would have done nothing. The one will be preparing for his successor a generation of, at least, believing Christians; the other, a generation of baptized pagans.

A Short History of Revealed Religion

Introduction

The word *revelation* signifies an unveiling or manifestation of something hidden by a veil. As the Council of the Vatican teaches, God, the beginning and end of all things, may be certainly known by the natural light of human reason, by means of created things. But it pleased his wisdom and bounty to reveal himself and the eternal decrees of his will to mankind by another and supernatural way, by speaking, in times past, through his prophets, and last of all by his Son, our Lord Jesus Christ.

We owe it to this divine teaching that, among things divine, such truths as of themselves are not beyond human reason can, even in the present condition of mankind, be known by everyone with ease, with certainty, and with no admixture of error.

Besides, God has revealed truths which regard the supernatural end to which he has destined man.

This divine revelation is "contained in the written books and unwritten traditions which, received by the apostles themselves, from the dictation of the Holy Spirit, transmitted as it were, from hand to hand, have come down even to us."[2]

The books containing this revelation are called the Bible. The Bible consists of two parts, the old and the new testament. The old testament contains the revelations made in the beginning to man and those which God made subsequently through the patriarchs and the prophets of Israel

[2] First Vatican Council, *Dogmatic Constitution on the Catholic Faith*, Ch. 2, n. 5

before the coming of Christ. The new testament, written by the apostles and evangelists, records the life of our Lord Jesus Christ, the foundation of his Church, and the early events of her history.

Frequently, the true sense of the scriptures is obscure. Sometimes the words are to be taken in their exact literal meaning; at other times they are figurative. "The sacred writers," as Pope Leo XIII has said, "put down what God, speaking to men, signified in the way that men could understand and were accustomed to."[3]

The Church alone, guided by the Holy Ghost, can infallibly declare what is the true sense of the sacred text. In comparatively few cases has the Church declared whether the words are to be taken literally or in a figurative sense. She has never, for instance, taught that the six days of creation mean days of twenty-four hours each; nor has she determined the age of the world, or the date at which man was created. On the other hand, she has always clearly insisted on the great truths taught in the history of the creation, related in the Bible, which are the unity, the eternity, the goodness, and the omnipotence of God; his creation of all things out of nothing; the spirituality and the immortality of the human soul; the fall of man; the wickedness of sin; the transmission of the effects of original sin from our first parents to all their descendants; the character of marriage as a union for life between one man and one woman; and the necessity of a divine Savior for all the human race. Whenever the Church is silent regarding the meaning of a text or passage of the Bible, no private person, however learned he may be, has the right to pronounce with authority upon what is the meaning of God's words in that particular case.

The Council of the Vatican declares "that in matters of faith and morals, appertaining to the building up of Christian doctrine, that is to be held as the true sense of holy scripture which our holy mother Church hath held and holds, to whom it belongs to judge of the true sense and interpretation of the holy scripture: and, therefore, that it is permitted to no one to interpret the sacred scripture contrary to this sense or likewise contrary to the unanimous consent of the fathers."[4]

[3] Leo XIII, *Providentissimus Deus*, n. 18

[4] First Vatican Council, *Dogmatic Constitution on the Catholic Faith*, Ch. 2, n. 8

Between the holy scripture as interpreted by the Church on the one side and science on the other, there never can be any real contradiction; for God, who is the author both of faith and reason, cannot contradict himself. And as Leo XIII says, "There can never, indeed, be any real discrepancy between the theologian and the physical scientist as long as each confines himself within his own lines, and both are careful, as St. Augustine warns us 'not to make rash assertions, or to assert what is not known as known.'"[5]

History of Revealed Religion before Christ

FROM ADAM TO MOSES

In the beginning, God created heaven and earth. He said: "Let them be made," and they were made. In six days, God made the whole world—the sun, moon, and stars; the plants, trees, and animals; and, last of all, he made man to his own image and likeness. The first man was called Adam, and the first woman Eve. They were just and holy, and the favorites of God. They lived happy in a delicious garden called paradise, and they and their descendants were never to die.

God commanded Adam and Eve not to eat of the fruit of the tree that stood in the midst of the garden, lest they should die. But the serpent said to them: "If you eat thereof, you shall be as gods." Adam and Eve believed the serpent, and broke the command of God. For this sin of disobedience, punishment immediately came upon them and all their descendants. They were driven from the garden of paradise, were doomed to death and many hardships, and were to be banished from God forever. Nevertheless, God had compassion on them, and promised them a Savior, who should reconcile them again to him, and make them partakers of eternal happiness in heaven, provided they did penance.[6]

[5] Leo XIII, *Providentissimus Deus*, n. 18

[6] Cf. Gn 3:15

Cain and Abel, sons of our first parents, offered sacrifice to Almighty God. God was pleased with that of the virtuous Abel, but not with that of the wicked Cain. Cain, being exceedingly angry at the preference given to his brother, killed him; and in punishment for this crime, he was cursed by God, and became a vagabond upon earth.

The descendants of Cain were wicked, like their father, and gradually seduced even the good; insomuch that, in process of time, all men turned away from God and sank deeper and deeper into sin and vice. God then resolved to destroy the degenerate race of Adam by a universal deluge. The rain fell upon the earth for forty days and forty nights, and the waters rose fifteen cubits, or twenty-seven and a half feet, above the highest mountains. All living creatures on the face of the earth perished in the flood, except the pious Noe, with his family, and the animals that were with him in the ark, which he had built by the command of God. In thanksgiving for this escape, Noe erected an altar and offered a burnt sacrifice to the Lord, who, in return, blessed him and his sons, and promised him that "there should no more be waters of a flood to destroy all flesh."[7]

The descendants of Noe became so numerous that they soon began to spread abroad into all lands. However, before separating, they determined to build a tower, the top of which should reach to heaven. But God confounded their language, so that they were unable to understand one another and were obliged to desist from building it; and the tower was called the "Tower of Babel," or "Confusion." Noe's descendants also gave themselves up to their wicked inclinations, and degenerated so far that, instead of adoring the true God, they worshipped the sun and moon, men and animals, and even idols of gold and silver, and of stone and wood. This shameful idolatry brought with it all kinds of sins and vices, which again prevailed in a frightful manner among mankind.

God, however, provided that the true faith and the hope in a future Redeemer should not entirely vanish from the earth. For this purpose, he chose Abraham (1920 B.C.), made a particular covenant with him, and promised him that the Messiah should be born of his posterity, saying: "In

[7] Gn 9:15

thee shall all the kindreds of the earth be blessed."[8] Therefore, God also distinguished Abraham and his descendants—who were called "Hebrews," and afterward, "Israelites," or "Jews"—from all other nations, and, during the course of time, often revealed himself to them in a wonderful manner.

In order to try the faith of Abraham, God commanded him to offer his only son Isaac in sacrifice upon Mount Moria. Abraham set out without hesitation. He himself placed the wood for the burnt offering upon his son, and ascended the mountain with him. When they had reached the summit, Isaac willingly laid himself on the wood to be offered up in sacrifice; but God saved the pious Isaac through an angel, blessed Abraham for his obedience, and renewed his former promises to him.

Isaac was here a figure of the future Savior of the world, who, in obedience to his Father, took the wood of the cross upon his shoulders, and carried it to Mount Calvary, to sacrifice himself upon it for our redemption.

The patriarch Jacob was the son of Isaac, and lived with his family in the land of Chanaan, the country into which God had called Abraham. He had twelve sons, who became the fathers of the twelve tribes of Israel. One of them, Joseph, was chosen by God to be, through what happened to him in his life, a figure of Jesus Christ. Having been sold by his brothers, he was carried into Egypt, where he was falsely accused and cast into prison. After recovering his liberty, the king made him chief ruler over all Egypt; and as, by his wisdom and prudence, he saved the country during seven years from a dreadful famine, he was called "savior of the world."[9] Jacob also, at his invitation, went down with all his family into Egypt and settled there. Before his death, he pronounced this remarkable prophecy regarding the Redeemer: "The scepter (supreme power) shall not be taken away from (the tribe of) Juda (his son)...till he come that is to be sent; and he shall be the expectation of nations."[10] And, in fact, when Christ, who was sent by God, was born, Herod, an Idumean, sat on the throne of the kings of Juda, and the kingdom was evidently approaching its end.

[8] Gn 12:3
[9] Gn 41:45
[10] Gn 49:10

FROM MOSES TO CHRIST

After Joseph's death, the Israelites grew into a great people, insomuch that the Egyptians, fearing they might become too powerful, reduced them to the hardest slavery. At length, the Lord appeared to Moses in a flame of fire out of the midst of a bush, and commissioned him to lead the children of Israel back to Chanaan. Pharao, king of Egypt, would not let them go; and therefore Almighty God sent dreadful plagues over all his dominions. At last, an angel in one night slew all the firstborn of the Egyptians. But the destroying angel did not harm the Israelites, because they had sprinkled the doors of their houses with the blood of the paschal lamb, which, according to God's command, they ate that very night.

By this was foreshown how, one day, mankind should be delivered from eternal death by the blood of Jesus Christ, the true divine paschal Lamb, which we eat in the Holy Eucharist.

Then Pharao permitted the Israelites to depart; but he soon regretted it. In all haste he collected his troops, and pursued the unarmed Israelites to the shores of the Red Sea. Here, struck with alarm and dread of being drowned or slaughtered, they implored the assistance of God; and Moses, by the command of God, stretched forth his rod over the Red Sea; and, behold, the waters were divided before them, and stood like a wall on their right hand and on their left, and they passed through on dry ground. Pharao rushed furiously after them into the midst of the sea; whereupon Moses once more stretched forth his rod over the waters, and they suddenly returned to their former place, and buried Pharao with his whole army in the deep.

The children of Israel had now to travel through a vast wilderness, and came, fifty days after their departure from Egypt, to Mount Sinai, where God, amidst thunder and lightning, gave them the ten commandments, written on two tables of stone. He also renewed with them the covenant he had made with their fathers, and regulated their religious and civil duties by most salutary laws. But the people soon forgot the commandments and blessings of God, and continually complained and murmured; nay, they debased themselves to such a degree that they made a golden calf, and adored it as their god.

In punishment of these and many other grievous sins, the Israelites had to remain forty years in the desert, until another and better generation had grown up. Nevertheless, God continually bestowed favors upon them. He rained bread, called "manna," from heaven for them, and gave them water from a rock; and at last, after Moses' death, he conducted them into Chanaan, or Palestine, the promised land, which they conquered with his powerful assistance, and divided into twelve parts, giving one of them to each of the twelve tribes.

All this was a figure of the future salvation of mankind.[11] The deliverance from the bondage of Egypt signifies our liberation from the slavery of Satan by Jesus Christ. The journey through the wilderness signifies our pilgrimage in this world, where God gives us his laws, nourishes us with the true bread of heaven, and strengthens us with the life-giving fountains of grace. The land of promise refers us to heaven, which we can conquer and take possession of only after combating the world, the flesh, and the devil.

In this beautiful country, the Israelites lived happy, and were blessed by God, until, contrary to his express command, they united themselves by marriage to the Gentiles, or pagans, and thereby fell again into vice and idolatry. As often as they turned away from God, he abandoned them to their enemies; but when they returned to him, he raised among them pious heroes called "judges," such as Gedeon, Jephte, and Samson, who rescued them from their foes.

For more than four hundred years the people of Israel were ruled by the high priests and judges, who were invested with supreme authority over them; but at length they desired to be governed, like the neighboring nations, by a king. In compliance with their wish, God appointed Saul to be their king, and the prophet Samuel anointed him about 1095 B.C. He was, however, afterward rejected by God for his disobedience, and was succeeded by David. David was strong and mighty: when only a youth, he had slain the giant Goliath; and having been made king, he extended his kingdom by splendid victories. He served God with an upright heart, and composed in his honor those beautiful sacred songs called "psalms,"

[11] Cf. 1 Cor 10:6

in which, by divine inspiration, he prophesied many things concerning the Redeemer of the world, who was to be born of his family, and whose kingdom should have no end. For this reason, Christ is also called the Son of David.

Solomon, his son and successor, was a wise and great king. He built a magnificent Temple to the Lord in Jerusalem about the year 1000 B.C. The sanctuary, or holy of holies, was overlaid with plates of the purest gold; and in it was kept the ark of the covenant, which contained the two tables of laws written by God himself. The high priest was the only person who was allowed, once a year, to enter the sanctuary. The people of Israel had no other temple, nor was anyone permitted to offer up sacrifice in any other place than the Temple of Jerusalem. Solomon, however, did not persevere in wisdom and goodness. He married pagan wives, and, toward the end of his life, had the misfortune of being seduced by them from the service of God into the impious practices of idolatry.

After Solomon's death, his kingdom was divided. The tribes of Juda and Benjamin remained faithful to King Roboam, his son, and formed the kingdom of Juda, the chief city of which was Jerusalem. The other ten tribes chose Jeroboam for their king, and made Samaria the capital of their kingdom, which from that time was called the kingdom of Israel. At the same time, they abandoned the religion of their fathers, built a temple for themselves at Samaria, and introduced many kinds of the most abominable idolatry. God, therefore, delivered them into the hands of the pagan king, Salmanasar, who destroyed the kingdom of Israel forever, and led the people to Ninive, into the Assyrian Captivity, about seven hundred years before Christ. The kingdom of Juda was also repeatedly chastised by God for its many transgressions. Nabuchodonosor (Nebuchadnezzar) II took Jerusalem, pillaged the Temple, and sent the sacred vessels and a large number of Jews to Babylon; and in 588, he entirely demolished the Temple and the city, carried Sedecias, the last king of Juda, with the rest of the inhabitants, into the same Babylonian Captivity. But the kingdom of Juda was not destroyed forever, like the kingdom of Israel that had forsaken the religion of its fathers.

These severe judgments of God did not by any means overtake Juda suddenly and unexpectedly. Men, enlightened by God, who were called prophets, had announced them long before, confirming their words by great miracles, in order to rouse the people to repentance. These same prophets also promised pardon to those who should repent, and prophesied of the Redeemer who was to come. In their books, written many centuries before Christ, we read all the circumstances of his life and sufferings: his birth of a Virgin at Bethlehem, his office of teaching, his miracles, his passion, his death, his resurrection, the sending of the Holy Ghost, the destruction of Jerusalem, the conversion of the Gentiles, and the splendor of the Christian Church; nay, Daniel foretold the very year in which the Savior was to appear. The most remarkable amongst the prophets are Elias, Eliseus, Isaias, Jeremias, Ezechiel, and Daniel.

During the time of the captivity, illustrious examples of rare virtues were given by Tobias at Ninive; and at Babylon, by the chaste Susanna, by the three young men in the fiery furnace, and by Daniel in the lions' den. The Babylonian Captivity had already lasted seventy years, when Cyrus, king of Persia, took Babylon, and, by divine inspiration, gave permission to the Jews to return to their own country (536 B.C.) and to rebuild the Temple at Jerusalem. In a short time, the second Temple was finished; and when the old men began to complain that its magnificence was far inferior to that of the first, the prophet Aggeus foretold to them that the glory of this latter house should be greater than that of the former, because the "Desired of All Nations," the Messias, would enter it.[12]

Esdras and Nehemias now reestablished the divine service in conformity to the law, and collected the sacred scriptures, which thenceforth were diligently read and interpreted. All the people shed tears and repented most sincerely. They never more returned to the sin of idolatry, which had brought upon their fathers the grievous sufferings of their captivity. When, some time later, Antiochus, king of Syria, tried to compel them to adore idols, they resisted most courageously under the command of the high priest Mathathias and his sons; nay, many of them, animated by the glorious example of the aged Eleazar, of the seven brothers, commonly called the Machabees, and of their heroic mother, preferred to suffer the most atrocious of deaths, rather than disobey the law of God.

[12] Cf. Agg 2:8-10

At length, the time fixed by God for the fulfillment of his promise arrived; and the signs that were to precede the coming of the Redeemer of mankind were accomplished. The Jews longed for it with the greatest anxiety, and even among the Gentiles there was a current opinion that a great ruler was to rise in Judea. The corruption in which the world was sunk was unbounded. The Jews, indeed, still acknowledged the one true God; but impious sects, such as the Pharisees and Sadducees, had sprung up amongst them, and a great corruption of morals had gained ground. Most of them honored God only with their lips, but their conduct was according to the sinful desires of their heart. All other nations, even the most enlightened among them, the Greeks and Romans, were devoted to the most shameful idolatry. Innumerable were the gods and goddesses to whom they built temples and altars, and offered sacrifices, even of human beings; and whom they believed they particularly honored when they extolled their infamous vices and imitated them without shame or fear. Such were the heathens, as St. Paul testifies: "Filled with all iniquity, malice, fornication, avarice, wickedness, full of envy, murder, contention, deceit, malignity, whisperers, detractors, hateful to God, contumelious, proud, haughty, inventors of evil things, disobedient to parents, foolish, dissolute, without affection, without fidelity, without mercy."[13] Who was then able to help and save mankind? God alone; and he did help and did save them. As he had promised to our first parents in paradise, and foretold by the prophets, he now showed mercy to mankind, when in their utmost degeneracy, and sent them a Redeemer and Savior; for "God so loved the world as to give his only begotten Son, that whosoever believeth in him may not perish, but may have life everlasting."[14]

[13] Rom 1:29-31
[14] Jn 3:16

History of Christ

The world was at peace; Augustus was emperor of Rome, and Herod, the Idumean, king of Judea, when the promise of God and the predictions of the prophets were accomplished. Jesus Christ, the Son of God and Redeemer of the world, was born, in a stable at Bethlehem, of Mary, a Virgin, descended from the royal family of David. His birth was announced by angels to the shepherds at Bethlehem, and by a star to the wise men in the East. The cruel Herod made every effort to discover the divine infant, that he might put him to death; but by the Lord's command, Joseph, the foster-father of Jesus, fled with him and his mother to Egypt, and did not return till after the death of Herod. Jesus then led a retired life at Nazareth in Galilee, was subject to his parents, and "advanced in wisdom, and age, and grace with God and men."[15] When he was twelve years old, he went with his parents to Jerusalem to celebrate the Pasch, or Passover, and remained there three days in the Temple, astonishing even the scribes, or doctors of the law, by his wise questions and answers. At the age of thirty, he went to the river Jordan to be baptized by John the Baptist. When he came out of the water, the Holy Ghost descended upon him in the shape of a dove, and a voice came from heaven, saying: "This is my beloved Son, in whom I am well pleased."[16]

Jesus then retired into the desert, and after having fasted and prayed there forty days and forty nights, he began to preach the gospel—that is, the good tidings of the kingdom of God on earth. He traveled about the towns and villages, and proved his divine mission and the truth of his doctrine by his holy life, by miracles and prophecies. Those who heard him were filled with wonder and amazement. Multitudes of people followed him, praised and extolled him as the true Messias, and said: "Never did man speak like this man."[17] Jesus selected from his followers twelve men whom he called his "apostles"

[15] Lk 2:52
[16] Mt 3:17
[17] Jn 7:46

or messengers. They were to be witnesses of his doctrine and works, that, after his ascension into heaven, they might preach what they had seen and heard of him to all nations. These are the names of the twelve apostles: Simon, who is called Peter, and Andrew, his brother; James (the elder), the son of Zebedee, and John, his brother; Philip and Bartholomew; Thomas and Matthew; James (the Less), the son of Alpheus, and Thaddeus, his brother, sometimes called Jude; Simon, the Chanaanite, and Judas Iscariot, which afterward betrayed him. Moreover, he chose seventy-two disciples, "and he sent them two and two before his face into every city and place, whither he himself was to come."[18] The twelve apostles, the seventy-two disciples, and the others who adhered to Jesus, formed the beginning of that society of all the faithful which we call the Church of Christ. He appointed Peter to be the visible head of his Church on earth, called him the Rock upon which he said he would build his Church, against which the gates of hell should never prevail, and promised him the keys of the kingdom of heaven.[19]

Jesus bestowed favors upon the Jews such as no one had ever witnessed before: he made the blind to see and the lame to walk; he restored the sick to health, and raised the dead to life; in a word, he relieved every kind of suffering and misery. Nevertheless, he had many enemies, especially among the scribes and Pharisees, who hated him because he reprimanded them for their sins and vices, and also because he would not establish a temporal kingdom and elevate them to high dignities. They watched all his words and actions; but they could not convict him of any sin. In the third year of his public teaching, and shortly before the Pasch or Easter, Jesus raised Lazarus to life after he had lain four days in the grave. The people, hearing of this miracle, greatly rejoiced; and when Jesus went to Jerusalem, they came forth in crowds to meet him, with branches of palms and olives in their hands, spread their garments in the way, and cried, saying: "Hosanna to the Son of David: Blessed is he that cometh in the name of the Lord. Hosanna in the highest."[20] This triumphant entry of Jesus exasperated his enemies still more, and from that day they sought to put him to death.

[18] Lk 10:1
[19] Cf. Mt 16:18-19
[20] Mt 21:9

Jesus knew that the time of his bitter passion was at hand. Resigned to the will of his heavenly Father, he prepared to pass out of this world. Whilst, in conformity with the Jewish law, he was eating the paschal lamb with his apostles, he took bread into his holy and venerable hands, lifted up his eyes toward heaven, to God his Almighty Father, gave thanks, blessed and broke it, and gave it to his disciples, saying: "Take ye, and eat; this is my body which shall be delivered for you." After that, he took the chalice with wine in it, again gave thanks, blessed and gave it to his disciples, saying: "Drink ye all of this; this is my blood of the new testament, which shall be shed for you and for many unto the remission of sins. As often as you do this, do it for the commemoration of me." Thus Jesus instituted the Holy Eucharist, wherein, under the appearance of bread and wine, he gives himself truly to us for the nourishment of our souls. After the last supper, Jesus continued speaking for some time to his apostles in the most affectionate manner, and promised to send them, for their Comforter, the Holy Ghost, the Spirit of truth, who should teach them all things, and abide with them forever. After this, he went into the Garden of Gethsemane, on the Mount of Olives, to pray.

There all his coming sufferings were most sensibly displayed before his soul. A violent agony came over him, and his sweat became as drops of blood trickling down upon the ground. "My Father," said he, "if it be possible, let this chalice pass from me. Nevertheless, not as I will, but as thou wilt."[21] In the meanwhile, Judas, who was about to betray him, approached with a band of armed men; and Jesus suffered himself to be taken, bound, and led before the chief council, where he was mocked, spat upon, and buffeted. The chief priests then delivered him up as guilty of death to Pontius Pilate, the Roman governor of Judea, who, on his part, sent him to King Herod; but neither of them could find any evil in him. Nevertheless, he was scourged and crowned with thorns; and at last, in compliance with the clamorous and threatening demands of the chief priests and the Jewish rabble, who preferred the murderer Barabbas before him, Pilate delivered him unto them to be crucified.

[21] Mt 26:39

Jesus, like one of the greatest criminals, was loaded with a heavy cross, and conducted to Mount Calvary, a place of execution, where he was crucified between two thieves. As the prophets had foretold, so it was now accomplished: his hands and feet were pierced with nails; the soldiers divided his garments among them, and upon his vesture they cast lots. When tormented with burning thirst, they gave him vinegar and gall to drink. Even the chief priests and ancients scoffed at him; but Jesus suffered all these cruelties with the most wonderful patience and meekness. Nay, he even prayed for his enemies, saying: "Father, forgive them, for they know not what they do." For three hours Jesus was hanging upon the cross suffering the most dreadful pains. The sun was darkened, and all nature mourned. At last, with a loud voice, he exclaimed: "It is consummated; Father, into thy hands I commend my spirit"; and bowing his head, he gave up the Ghost. The moment he expired, the earth quaked, the rocks split asunder, the veil of the Temple was rent in two from the top to the bottom, the graves were opened, and many bodies of the saints that had slept arose and appeared in Jerusalem. The centurion or captain and the soldiers, who stood near the cross, were struck with awe, and said: "Indeed this was the Son of God." Thus Jesus became "the propitiation for our sins; and not for ours only, but also for those of the whole world."[22]

It was on Good Friday, about three o'clock in the afternoon, that Jesus expired. In order to assure themselves that he was dead, one of the soldiers with a spear opened his side, and immediately there came out blood and water. His body was taken down from the cross, and laid in a new sepulchre hewn out in a rock. The Jews sealed it and set a guard before it. But early on the third day, before sunrise, there was a great earthquake, and Christ crucified arose glorious from the sepulchre. During forty days afterward, he often appeared to his disciples, instructed them concerning the kingdom of God—that is, the Church—gave them power to forgive sins, and installed Peter head of the Church, with these words: "Feed my lambs; feed my sheep."[23] When he appeared for the last time in the midst of

[22] 1 Jn 2:2
[23] Jn 21:15, 17

the eleven, he commanded them to go into the whole world, to preach the gospel to all nations, and to baptize them "in the name of the Father, and of the Son, and of the Holy Ghost." For that purpose, he gave them the same power which he had received from his heavenly Father, and promised to be with them all days, even to the consummation of the world. Finally, on the fortieth day after his resurrection, he led his disciples to the Mount of Olives, where he lifted up his hands over them, and, whilst he blessed them, ascended in their sight up to heaven.

History of the Church of Christ

FROM THE ASCENSION OF CHRIST TO THE CONVERSION OF CONSTANTINE

After the ascension of our Lord, his disciples returned to Jerusalem, where they persevered in prayer, expecting the coming of the Holy Ghost, whom he had promised to send them. In the meantime, the apostles chose Matthias, one of the disciples, in the place of Judas. On the tenth day, the feast of Pentecost, there came suddenly a sound from heaven, as of a mighty wind, and it filled the whole house where they were assembled. Over the head of each one there appeared the form of a fiery tongue; and all of them, being filled with the Holy Ghost, began to speak in divers languages and to praise the Lord their God. Peter, the head of the apostles, stood up and declared to the innumerable multitude of the Jews who had come together that the same Jesus whom they had crucified, and whom God had raised from the dead, was their Lord and Redeemer, and he called upon them to believe in him. His discourse was so powerful that no less than three thousand came at once and asked to be baptized. Soon after, Peter and John went to the Temple to pray. A lame man was lying there at the gate, and asked an alms of them. Peter said to him: "Silver and gold

I have none; but what I have I give thee: in the name of Jesus Christ of Nazareth, arise and walk"; and forthwith the lame man sprang to his feet and walked joyfully with them into the Temple, thanking and praising God. All the people were filled with amazement at this miracle, and five thousand more of them asked to be baptized.

The apostles preached the resurrection of Jesus Christ with great power, and did many signs and wonders. By this their authority increased so much that the people brought the sick into the streets, in order that, when Peter passed by, his shadow, at least, might fall upon them, and deliver them from their infirmities. The chief priests and their adherents, seeing all this, were greatly exasperated. They caused the apostles to be apprehended and scourged, and forbade them to preach in the name of Jesus; they stirred up the people against them, insomuch that St. Stephen was stoned to death; and they perpetrated many other acts of violence. But no earthly power was able to prevent the spreading of the doctrine of Jesus. The apostles did not cease to preach the crucified Savior, both in the Temple and from house to house; and the number of those who presented themselves to be baptized increased exceedingly every day. Even Saul, afterward called Paul, the most furious enemy and persecutor of the Christians, became, through the grace of God, an apostle of Jesus Christ and the most zealous propagator of the gospel.

The new converts in Jerusalem and its neighborhood formed the first Christian community, called the "Church." Their conduct was unblemished and irreproachable; they served God with gladness and in simplicity of heart. They all lived in the greatest harmony, and had but one heart and one soul. None of them suffered want; for the rich willingly sold, for the relief of the poor, what they could spare, such as houses and lands, and laid the proceeds at the feet of the apostles, that they might divide them among the needy. The apostles were the rulers of the Church, as Christ had ordained; they taught, baptized, and administered the other sacraments; they managed all ecclesiastical affairs, and governed the community.

Although many of the Jews embraced the doctrine of Christ, yet the greater part of them remained obstinate and hardened. God, therefore, permitted the punishment they had been threatened with to be inflicted upon them; about the seventieth year after the birth of Christ, Jerusalem was destroyed, and the Temple burnt by the Romans. An immense number of Jews lost their lives, and the rest were banished from their country and dispersed all over the world, that they might be everywhere and at all times living witnesses of the divine judgment. The stubbornness of the Jews, and still more an express command of God, had early determined the apostles to go and preach to the pagans or heathens. Poor and persecuted though they were, they announced to the nations of the earth the good tidings of salvation, under thousands of hardships and perils, even of death. Therefore God visibly blessed their efforts; and thirty years had scarcely elapsed after the descent of the Holy Ghost, when there were already Christian communities in all parts of the world. Over these Churches the apostles placed bishops, to whom they communicated their powers by special forms of prayer and the imposition of hands, and whom they appointed their substitutes and successors. All these communities were most closely united together, and formed, under their common head, St. Peter, the one, Universal—that is, Catholic—Church. St. Peter was first bishop of Antioch, and afterward bishop of Rome, where he suffered martyrdom under Nero, 67 A.D.; and then the supreme authority over the whole Church devolved on his successors, the bishops of Rome, or the popes.

The pagans were greatly alarmed at the rapid spreading of the Christian religion, which openly condemned their vicious lives and their monstrous idolatry, and they resolved to exterminate it. The Christians had either to abjure their faith or to die under the most cruel torments. They were scourged and lacerated, and were cast before wild beasts; their sides were torn with iron hooks or burnt with torches. They were thrown into caldrons of boiling oil, mutilated, sawn in pieces, and crucified. They were covered with pitch and set fire to, that they might serve to light the nocturnal games of the pagans. Everywhere the Christians suffered tortures beyond all description. Many countries were drenched with their blood, and hundreds of thousands of every age, sex, and condition died under the most dreadful torments. Rome especially, the capital of paganism, and the seat of all the abominations of idolatry, overflowed, as it were, with the blood of the Christians. The number of those who suffered martyrdom in that city surpasses all belief; and their bones, which are still to be seen in the subterraneous caverns or catacombs, where they were entombed by their fellow Christians, are witnesses of it to this day.

These terrible persecutions lasted, with few interruptions, for three hundred years. Had Christianity been the work of man, it would certainly have been extirpated by the blind fury of its enemies; but being the work of Jesus, the Son of God, it took deeper and deeper root, and spread more and more over the world. The signs and wonders which the confessors of Christ did, but, above all, the imperturbable serenity of mind and cheerfulness of heart with which they suffered the most cruel torments and the most painful deaths, convinced the pagans that only the God of the Christians could be the true God. It even often happened that, whilst the Christians were suffering these most horrible tortures, many of the pagan spectators were heard to cry out: "We also are Christians; kill us together with them!" and thus the blood of the martyrs was the fruitful seed from which new Christians continually sprang up.

By permitting all this, God had sufficiently shown to the world that the establishment of the Church was his work, and that all the powers of the earth could not prevail against her. He now bestowed peace on her by calling Constantine the Great to be the protector of Christianity. This emperor, while still a pagan, was at war with Maxentius. Seeing that his enemy's army was far greater than his, Constantine prayed fervently to the true God for assistance; and behold, a bright cross appeared in the sky to him and to his whole army, with the following inscription upon it: "In this sign thou shalt conquer." In imitation of this cross, Constantine ordered a banner to be made, and had it carried before his army in battle. He then bravely attacked the superior forces of Maxentius, and overcame them; and from that time (312 A.D.) Constantine became the defender and protector of Christianity.

FROM THE CONVERSION OF CONSTANTINE TO THE RISE OF PROTESTANTISM IN THE SIXTEENTH CENTURY

The cross, that had hitherto been the sign of the greatest ignominy, now became a sign of honor and victory. It glittered on the imperial crown of Constantine, and was displayed in Rome—till then the principal seat of paganism—on the pinnacle of the temple of Jupiter, the Capitol; and it thus announced the triumph of the crucified God-man to the whole world. Constantine granted the free practice of their religion to the Christians, built splendid churches for them, and showed marks of great honor and distinction to priests, and especially to the popes. His example prompted thousands of the pagans to embrace the divine doctrine; and the idols were soon abandoned and their temples deserted. In a short time, paganism was completely overthrown throughout the Roman Empire, and the Christian religion was permanently established.

The Catholic Church had now to gain victories of another kind—namely, over her internal enemies, the heretics. Several heretical and schismatical doctrines had already been broached at different times and in different places; they had, however, soon disappeared. But now, by God's permission, some new heretics arose, and gained many followers by cunning and fraud. They impudently left the Church, and formed separate and vast communions or sects, which were mostly named after their founders; as the Arians, Nestorians, Eutychians, Pelagians, etc. These heretics often succeeded in gaining the favor of princes and emperors, under whose protection they most cruelly oppressed and persecuted the faithful. In the same way as the apostles had formerly assembled in order to settle, by the inspiration of the Holy Ghost and under the presidency of St. Peter, such differences as had arisen in matters of religion,[24] so now also their successors, the bishops of the Catholic Church, assembled under the presidency of the pope, or of his legates, consulted about the heretical doctrines, and then condemned them. Such an assembly of bishops is called a general

[24] Cf. Acts 15

council; and the decisions of such a council in matters of faith, when confirmed by the pope, are infallible, because they proceed from the Church, which the Holy Ghost invisibly governs and preserves from all error. One of the most famous councils is that of Nice, in Bithynia, which was held in 325. Three hundred and eighteen bishops were assembled there; and amongst them were many holy men who, during the persecutions, had suffered for Christ's sake, and had lost their hands or eyes. They unanimously condemned the impious doctrine of Arius, who obstinately maintained that Jesus Christ was not God from all eternity, and they cut him off from the communion of the faithful. Although this sect, called Arians, was at that time very powerful, the Church, by her solemn decision, had set the seal of reprobation on it, and consequently it was gradually to vanish from the face of the earth. The same sentence of condemnation was passed on all the other heresies that sprang up in subsequent ages; and, however hard the conflicts were in which the Church had to engage, she has always come off victorious.

During this period, God illustrated his Church also by many holy and learned men who gloriously defended the true doctrine. They are called "doctors of the Church," or "fathers of the Church." Such were St. Athanasius, patriarch of Alexandria, who had to endure from the Arians a long and severe persecution for the true faith (d. 373); St. Basil the Great, archbishop of Caesarea (d. 379); St. Gregory Nazianzen (d. 389), and St. John, surnamed "Chrysostom," that is, "Golden Mouth" (d. 407), both patriarchs of Constantinople; St. Cyril, archbishop of Jerusalem (d. 386), and St. Cyril, patriarch of Alexandria (d. 444); St. Ambrose, archbishop of Milan (d. 397); St. Jerome, celebrated for his Latin translation of the holy scriptures, called the "Vulgate" (d. 420); St. Augustine, bishop of Hippo in Africa, one of the brightest luminaries of the Church (d. 430); and the holy popes St. Leo the Great (d. 461) and St. Gregory the Great (d. 604).

Whilst the holy fathers of the Church especially distinguished themselves as defenders of the true faith, the "hermits," or "solitaries," and monks, shone as models of the most austere penance. The hermits were pious Christians who fled from the seductive pleasures of the world, to prepare themselves in solitude, by prayer and self-denial, for a happy death.

A cavern in a rock, or a hut made of branches, was their abode; the bare ground, or a few leaves their bed; roots and herbs were their food, and water was their drink. They renounced all the comforts of life, that they might entirely die to the world, and live only for God. The first hermit was St. Paul, who died about 340. St. Anthony, to satisfy the importunities of others, built the first monastery, and is called the "Patriarch of Monks" (d. 356). Thus the solitary life gave rise to the monastic life, which was so opportunely and successfully propagated in the West by the great St. Benedict, noted for the wonders he had done. For, not to speak of his miracles, we may safely say that Europe is especially indebted to the religious order he established for the cultivation of its soil and the conversion of its inhabitants. He died in 543. St. Augustine, the apostle of England, was a Benedictine monk, and introduced this order into England in 596.

In the fifth and sixth centuries, the Church was exposed to new dangers, when rapacious pagan nations left their own wild homes, and overran the Christian countries in countless swarms, laying waste all before them with fire and sword. This is called the "migration of nations." Some of them were named Huns, Alans, Heruli, Goths, Suevi, Lombards, Burgundians, Vandals, Franks, Angles, Saxons; but the most merciless and savage of all these barbarian tribes were the Huns, under their king, Attila, who called himself the "Scourge of God." The most celebrated towns were utterly destroyed, and whole countries laid waste and almost depopulated. The Roman Empire, more than one thousand years old, and once so powerful, could no longer resist these savage tribes, and was at last completely overthrown. Odoacer, king of the Heruli, took Rome, and was proclaimed king of Italy in 476. It is impossible to describe the extent of misery which these barbarous hordes inflicted on all Europe, until finally God subdued and civilized them by means of that very Church which they had threatened with destruction.

Holy men were sent by the popes to announce the good tidings of salvation to them. These took the cross and the gospel in their hands; and although they were exposed to the greatest dangers, they preached, with no less courage and confidence in God, the doctrine of the Savior of the world. St. Patrick was sent by Pope Celestine, in 432 A.D., to Ireland, and labored there for many years, converting the entire country to Christianity, and establishing many episcopal sees, churches, and monasteries. This is the only instance in the history of the Church of the conversion of an entire people without a single martyrdom. St. Patrick has been deservedly styled the "apostle of Ireland," and Ireland was called the Island of Saints.

In the fifth, sixth, seventh, and eighth centuries, Germany was also converted and civilized. St. Severinus is called the "apostle of Austria," because he converted that country to the Christian faith. He died in 482. St. Columban and St. Gall, both natives of Ireland, preached near the Lake of Constance and elsewhere in Switzerland; St. Kilian, a holy Irish monk, and St. Willibald, an English West-Saxon, in Franconia; St. Rupert and St. Corbinian, both French missionaries, in Bavaria and the surrounding countries; St. Ludger, a native of Friesland, in Westphalia; St. Anscharius, a French Benedictine monk, in Scandinavia and Lower Germany (d. 865). But the most indefatigable and successful preacher of the gospel in Germany was St. Winfrid or Boniface, who is therefore justly called the "apostle of the Germans." He was born at Crediton, in Devonshire, about the year 680, and was a Benedictine monk at Exeter. On account of his great merits, he was created archbishop of Mentz in 732, by Pope Gregory III; and whilst he was engaged in preaching the gospel to the infidel inhabitants of the northern parts of Friesland, he was martyred, in 755.

As soon as the missionaries had got a footing in a country, they made it their first business to erect one or several monasteries. These sanctuaries of religion then sent forth holy men to spread the seeds of Christianity over the country, established schools for the education of young priests, and taught the barbarians to leave off their savage manners, and to follow peaceful and useful occupations. Thus the wild Germans were taught agriculture, the duties of domestic life, trades, and mechanical arts. By the industry and labor of the monks, deserts were changed into rich fields, and dark forests into pleasant abodes; in all respects, they were the greatest benefactors of mankind. The emperor Charlemagne, who had especially the propagation and prosperity of the Christian Church at heart, founded more than twenty-four monasteries, and erected several episcopal sees, which he most liberally endowed with lands and estates. His example was followed by the pious king Stephen, to whom Hungary is indebted for her conversion to Christianity.

Whilst the Christian faith was propagated in the West with gratifying success, most fatal and deplorable disturbances arose in the East. The Greek emperors at Constantinople, instead of humbly submitting themselves to the Church, wanted to rule her, and obtrude upon her their opinions as articles of faith. The people were heedless, the clergy frequently forgot their duties, and pride and dissension supplied at last what was still wanting to bring about that lamentable schism by which the greater portion of the Greek or Eastern Church seceded from the pope, the common head of the Church of Christ (1054 A.D.).

But God did not delay to inflict upon them the punishment they had so well deserved. As in former times he had chastised the Israelites for the neglect of his laws, so he now punished the degenerate Christians also. In the beginning of the seventh century (622 A.D.), there had appeared in Arabia an arrogant impostor called Mahomet, who pretended to be a messenger of God, and patched up a new religion out of pagan, Jewish, and Christian observances and doctrines. At the head of a band of robbers, he first plundered caravans, soon after took cities and countries, and, sword in hand, forced the inhabitants to embrace his religion. His successors, who were called caliphs, continued, by the force of arms, to subdue one country after another in Asia and Africa, and to spread the doctrine of their false prophet, and, at the same time, barbarism, profligacy, and the most oppressive slavery. Christianity, it is true, was not entirely rooted out in those countries; but being separated from the true Church, it fell into a state of torpidity and debasement, under which it is still languishing at the present time.

In the year 637, Jerusalem, the capital of the Holy Land or Palestine, had fallen under the power of the Mahometans or Saracens (i.e., Arabians; so called from *sara*, "a desert"), and had groaned under their yoke 442 years, when, in 1079, it was conquered, together with the fairest portions of Western Asia, by the Seljukian Turks, a Tartar tribe, who came in 1048 from the Caspian Sea, and had in the eighth century embraced Mahometanism. The latter were the most relentless foes of Christianity. The enormities which they committed in the Holy Land, and the cruel treatment which they inflicted upon the Christian pilgrims who resorted thither from the West, gave rise, about the close of the eleventh century, to the Crusades.

Peter of Amiens, a pious hermit, who had made a pilgrimage to Jerusalem, reported to Pope Urban II how the holy places, where our Savior had lived and suffered, were profaned by the infidels, and to what outrages the Christians were there exposed. The pope was so sensibly affected that he resolved to put an end to the insolence and insatiable rapacity of the Mahometans. He summoned the Christian princes and knights to a council at Clermont in Auvergne (1095 A.D.), called upon them to engage in a military expedition against the infidels, and excited their enthusiasm to such a pitch that the whole assembly spontaneously exclaimed: "God wills it! God wills it!" This cry reechoed through the whole West, and shortly after there stood ready a tremendous host of men armed at all points. They wore, as a badge of their engagement, a red cross on their right shoulder, whence originated the name of *Crusaders* and *Crusade*. Full of joy and courage, they marched to Palestine.

After having endured inexpressible hardships, and fought many a hot battle, they at last took Jerusalem; and the brave hero, Godfrey of Bouillon, Duke of Lorraine, was proclaimed king, 1099 A.D. Being presented with a golden crown, he refused to wear it, saying that he would never consent to wear a crown of gold where the Redeemer of the world had worn a crown of thorns; and he never gave himself any other title but that of Duke Godfrey. The new kingdom, however, lasted only eighty-eight years. Owing to the treachery of the Greeks, and to the want of discipline and harmony among the Crusaders, it was unable to resist the superior forces of the Turks, although it repeatedly obtained auxiliaries from the West; and thus Jerusalem was taken by Saladin, sultan of Egypt, in 1187.

About the year 1300, fresh hordes of Turks, called the Ottomans, poured down from Tartary, subdued the Seljukians, and extended their conquests over Western Asia, Rumelia, Moldavia, Servia, Bulgaria, Greece, and the Morea; until at last, under that monster of brutality and voluptuousness called Mahomet (II) the Great, they rendered themselves masters of Constantinople, the capital of the Greek empire (1453 A.D.), which calamity God no doubt permitted in punishment for the grievous offenses it had committed against him.

The further progress of the Turks, however, was checked by the ardent zeal and heroic valor of the Christian princes Huniades and Scanderbeg, of the Knights Hospitallers of St. John of Jerusalem (who from 1310 were called Knights of Rhodes, and from 1530 Knights of Malta), and of other Christian orders of Chivalry, till they were at last completely overthrown by the united forces of the pope, of Spain, and of Venice, and by the evident help of the glorious Mother of God, in the famous battle of Lepanto (1571 A.D.). The result of this victory was not only a check to the progress of the Ottomans, but also the beginning of the decline of their power; and thus Catholic Europe, and especially Germany, was saved from the imminent danger of being likewise overrun and subjugated by those ferocious infidels.

In the Western countries of Europe, the Crusades everywhere roused the people to a more vigorous exertion of their mental powers, and to a new spiritual life. During the destructive migration of nations, the sciences had found an asylum in the monasteries; but now they spread among the people, and were ardently cherished by them. Celebrated schools and universities were established; and men of wonderful erudition, as St. Anselm (d. 1109), Albertus Magnus (d. 1280), St. Thomas of Aquino (d. 1274), and others, occupied the professorial chairs. Those times, generally called the "Middle Ages," are still more renowned for the luster of Christian virtues, for the firmness of faith, for childlike simplicity, and for an ardent love of God and man.

Even at the present time we behold with surprise and wonder those ancient gigantic cathedrals which were erected by the piety of our ancestors; and we are enraptured at the most tender devotion, expressed in the paintings and statues with which they adorned the buildings consecrated to God. Such great and charming works could only be produced by the religion which filled their hearts and governed all their actions.

This same religion also poured out the greatest blessings over the earth through the holy founders of religious orders, St. Romuald (d. 1027), St. Bruno (d. 1101), St. Norbert (d. 1134), St. Bernard (d. 1153), St. Dominic (d. 1221), St. Francis of Assisi, surnamed the Seraphic (d. 1226), and many other men of God. The numerous monasteries which they built not only produced many great saints and enlightened prelates, but they also cherished piety and religious zeal among the lower classes of the people. They relieved the wants of the poor, sheltered and nursed the sick, and redeemed those who had been made prisoners and slaves; they sent missionaries into all parts of the world, and obtained, by their devout prayers, abundant graces from heaven on countries and nations.

In the meantime, there appeared also an exuberant growth of cockle among the wheat in the field of God.[25] There were pernicious feuds and wars, various acts of injustice and violence, and many scandals. In several places, and particularly in Germany, the custom had been introduced by temporal princes of putting the newly elected bishops and abbots in possession of their benefices by giving them the ring and the crosier, the symbols of pastoral authority, which ceremony was called "investiture," and seemed to imply the conferring of spiritual jurisdiction. Not content with this, the emperor Henry IV used to bestow bishoprics and abbeys upon the most unworthy candidates, and even on such as offered him the largest sums of money. Pope Gregory VII courageously inveighed against those crying abuses; and hence ensued, about 1076, a long and tedious contest, called "The Contest of Investiture," out of which the Church indeed came forth victorious, but not till after many hard trials.

After that there arose heretics who kindled the fire of revolt first against the ecclesiastical, and then against the secular authorities; as in France the Albigenses, in Upper Italy the Waldenses, in England the Wickliffites or Lollards, in Bohemia the Hussites. Peace, it is true, was restored to the Church, and men, mighty in words and deeds, as St. Vincent Ferrer (d. 1419) and St. John Capistratt (d. 1456), went through the countries of Europe, preaching penance to princes and people. Nevertheless, an unholy fire lay hidden under the ashes; feelings of disrespect and hostility to the Church, and a fondness for innovations, had gained ground, and were increased by many other attendant evils. Nothing was wanted for the fatal eruption of this volcano of wickedness and rebellion but an opportunity; and this presented itself in the beginning of the sixteenth century in Germany. Like a contagious disease, this lamentable evil spread abroad; thousands and thousands abandoned the Catholic Church; bloody wars, revolts, and corruption of morals ensued; the most splendid establishments, founded

[25] Cf. Mt 13

by the piety of former ages, were destroyed, and unspeakable misery was prepared both for time and eternity.

FROM THE RISE OF PROTESTANTISM TO THE PRESENT TIME

Martin Luther, an Augustinian monk and a professor in the University of Wittenberg, a man of an irritable and turbulent disposition, began in 1517 by exclaiming against the abuses which are said to have been practiced in the publication of the indulgences granted by Pope Leo X to those who should contribute to the rebuilding of St. Peter's Church in Rome. But soon after, he arbitrarily set himself up as a reformer of the Church, inveighed against the ecclesiastical authorities, especially against the pope, whose supreme power he denounced as usurpation and tyranny, and which he said he would bring to a miserable end. In pursuance of his wrong views, he rejected many articles of faith which the Church had received from Christ and his apostles. He repudiated the Holy Sacrifice of the Mass, fasting, confession, prayers for the dead, and many other pious practices; he declared good works to be useless, and taught that man is justified and saved by faith alone.

Moreover, he threw open the monasteries and convents, and gave leave to the monks and nuns to marry; and he presumed to award to princes and sovereigns the right of confiscating the property of churches and convents, and of assigning it to any use they pleased. Finally, he broke the vow of chastity which he had solemnly made as a monk and as a priest, and committed the double sacrilege of taking a nun for his wife. Luther boasted that he took his doctrine from the Bible only; but being misled by the false rule of private judgment in its interpretation, he soon fell into the most palpable contradictions and errors. Thus he asserted that "man has no free will, and consequently can neither keep the commandments nor avoid evil";[26] "that sin does not condemn man, provided he firmly believe,"[27] etc. Nevertheless,

[26] Luther, *De Servo Arbitrio*

[27] Luther, *Epistle to Melanchthon*, Anno 1521; *De Captivitate Babylonica Ecclesiae*, tom. 2, fol. 284

he soon obtained many followers; for the thoughtless multitude were very much pleased with such easy doctrine, which allowed them to lead a dissolute life, and covetous princes found nothing more conformable to their wishes than the suppression of churches and monasteries. Besides, Luther eagerly embraced any opportunity of increasing his party, and for this purpose he permitted the Landgrave of Hesse to contract a second marriage whilst his first wife was still living.

The way of innovation and revolt being once opened by Luther, several others soon followed him, and they went even further than he did. Zwinglius, in Switzerland, denied the real presence of Jesus Christ in the Holy Eucharist. Calvin, at Geneva, taught that "God has predestined a part of mankind, without any fault of theirs, to eternal damnation, and that therefore he blinds and hardens the heart of sinners."[28] The Anabaptists proclaimed a kingdom of Christ on earth, in which there was to be no private property, no law, no magistrates. Zwinglius, Calvin, and other sectarians totally demolished in the churches what had been spared by Luther. The images of the crucified Redeemer and of the saints, pictures as well as statues, and masterpieces of art, were hewn in pieces; the organs and altars were shattered; nay, even the graves were ransacked, and the bones of the saints trampled upon and burnt to ashes. Although these pretended reformers combated and anathematized one another, nevertheless their several doctrines spread most rapidly. United only in their hatred against the Catholics, they contrived all imaginable measures to gain the superiority over them. By thousands and thousands of pamphlets, they disseminated their erroneous principles, and, at the same time, they most virulently attacked and calumniated the pope and the Catholic clergy. Moreover, in many places, crying acts of violence were committed, and people were forced by all sorts of oppression and persecution to renounce the holy Catholic faith.

The Catholics, on their part, made several attempts to restore peace to the Church, by entering into amicable discussions with their opponents; but the hatred which Luther bore to the pope, the head of the Church,

[28] Calvin, *Institutes of the Christian Religion*

continued implacable. To check the progress of heresy and wickedness, the emperor Charles V assembled in 1529 a second diet at Spires, where a decree was issued that, until the decision of a general council, Lutheranism should be tolerated wherever it had already been established, but should not be spread any further; that no one should be hindered from saying or hearing Mass; and that all invectives against any religion should be prohibited. The Lutherans protested against this decree, and from this circumstance is derived their name of "protestants"; which appellation has since been given also to the other sects into which they have divided.

At length, the holy father convoked a general council at Trent, in the Tyrol, in the year 1545. The doctrine of the innovators was examined and unanimously condemned; at the same time, many excellent decrees concerning ecclesiastical institutions and the reformation of abuses were issued; in a word, the vigorous and decisive action of this council gave fresh beauty and new life to the Catholic Church. The protestants had been repeatedly invited to the council, as they had in the beginning expressly wished for it in order to adjust their differences; but they refused to appear at Trent. Consequently, the unfortunate schism continued, and brought unspeakable misery and endless calamities upon the greater part of Europe. Luther had preached liberty and reviled the emperor, the princes, and bishops; the peasants lost no time in freeing themselves from their masters. They traversed the country in lawless bands, burnt down the castles and monasteries, and committed the most horrible cruelties against the nobility and clergy. More than one hundred thousand persons were slain during this frightful insurrection (1525 A.D.). Other religious wars ensued, and Germany, which once had been so flourishing, became at last the scene of the most frightful desolation and of the most horrible atrocities during the Thirty Years' War (1618-1648).

The other countries which had embraced the new doctrine were likewise devastated by religions and civil wars. In Switzerland, Zwinglius fell in a bloody battle which he fought against his own countrymen. In France, the Calvinists, called Huguenots, with a devastating army, kept the field for many years against the crown and the Church. In their blind fury, they massacred numbers of priests, monks, and nuns; they ravaged villages and towns, and burnt or pulled down many thousands of churches, some of which were magnificent monuments of Christian art. England also suffered severely for her apostasy, begun by King Henry VIII, who abandoned the Catholic Church because the pope would not allow him to repudiate his lawful wife, Catharine, and marry Anne Boleyn. From that time, the country was drenched in human blood; even King Charles I, a successor of the tyrannical Henry, was beheaded by rebels who boasted of professing and practicing the "purest" of all Christian doctrines.

The loss which the Church had suffered from the apostasy in Europe was to be compensated by the conversion of innumerable heathens in other parts of the globe. Missionaries went forth in every direction, and announced the salutary doctrines of the gospel with wonderful success. It is truly astonishing what St. Francis Xavier, the apostle of the Indies, who was so eminently favored by heaven, alone accomplished. Glowing with zeal for the salvation of the pagans, he crossed the vast ocean, and, landing at Goa in the year 1542, he began his mission by walking through the streets with a bell in his hand, and calling the children to come and be instructed. They joyfully attended and listened to the holy man, who spoke to them so affectionately of their dear Redeemer. When they had returned home, they repeated what they had heard, and so induced the adult persons to come likewise and hear the holy preacher.

God rewarded his zeal, and granted him, as he had done to the first apostles, the power of healing the sick, of raising the dead to life, of commanding the storms; in short, the power of working the most stupendous miracles. With untiring energy, he went from country to country, from island to island, through all India and Japan, and converted, in the short period of ten years, many tribes and kingdoms. He himself testifies in one of his letters that in one month he administered holy baptism to ten thousand heathens.

After his death, other missionaries continued the pious work, and introduced the religion of Jesus into China also, that immense, unknown, and till then inaccessible empire. That these heathens had been truly converted was proved in the most convincing manner when the persecution of the Christians broke out in Japan. About 1,100,000[29] died for their faith,

[29] Some authors reckon 1,200,000.

and the greater part of them were most horribly tortured. Even tender children, weak old men, and women of rank hastened with joy to martyrdom, dressed in their holiday attire, as if they were going to a wedding feast. So sincere and strong was their faith that even the survivors and their children have continued to preserve it under most adverse circumstances. Though shut out for over two hundred years from the Christian world, and without a priest, and subjected to tyranny and persecution, they taught the catechism, recited the Catholic prayers they had learned, baptized their children, and strove to live piously. Ultimately the Japanese were forced to repeal their laws for the total exclusion of foreigners. Missionaries have again entered, and have found villages of these faithful Japanese Catholics.

In America also, that newly-discovered world, the light of the gospel spread, and overthrew the most abominable idolatry with all its horrors and vices. No people on earth offered up more human sacrifices than the natives of America. The Mexicans sacrificed about twenty thousand human victims every year, and when they had no captives for this purpose, they did not spare even their own children. It is impossible to describe what the heroic missionaries suffered, and what dangers they incurred among those bloodthirsty men. They had to struggle not only against the cruelties and vices of the natives, but also against the insatiable avarice of the European settlers. Yet their labors were crowned with success, and the Christian faith was firmly and permanently established on this continent.

The mission of Paraguay, in South America, especially flourished. The brutish natives, who lived among the wild beasts in the forests, who thought of nothing but plundering, murdering, and revenge, who delighted only in eating human flesh, in voluptuousness and drunkenness, were transformed by the indefatigable missionary priests into devout Christians. They became models of modesty and charity, of innocence and piety, and by their untiring industry and labor changed their wild country into a delicious paradise.

The holy men who, with such indefatigable zeal, and often even to the shedding of their blood, devoted themselves to the conversion of the pagans, belonged for the most part to religious orders. St. Francis Xavier, and those others who planted the faith in China and Paraguay, were

Jesuits—that is, members of the Society of Jesus. This order was founded in 1540 by St. Ignatius of Loyola, a man filled with the most ardent zeal for the honor of God. These religious exerted themselves especially in propagating the Catholic faith, and defending it against the newfangled doctrines; and consequently they drew upon themselves implacable hatred and grievous persecutions from the enemies of religion.

God raised also other orders, that might, in concert with the secular clergy, heal the wounds which Luther and other heretics had inflicted on the Church. The pious Capuchins, who sprang in 1528 from the Order of St. Francis of Assisi, labored especially for the salvation of souls, and distinguished themselves by their affectionate zeal and austere life. The Oratorians, or Fathers of the Oratory, which was founded in 1574 by St. Philip Neri, devoted themselves to prayer and the instruction of the people, to visiting the hospitals, to attending the poor and the sick, and to literary pursuits. The Fathers of the Pious Schools occupied themselves with the instruction of youth, and other religious, again, with the nursing of the sick. There arose also communities of religious women for the training up of young girls to a pious and godly life; as the orders of the Visitation, of the Ursulines, and of the Good Shepherd, and the Institute of English Ladies.[30]

Above all, this period was exceedingly rich in heroes of faith and virtue. St. Charles Borromeo, cardinal archbishop of Milan (d. 1584), set a bright example of true Christian charity during the plague, by visiting the sick in the most dangerous places, in lazarettos and hospitals, and by giving up all his property, even his bed, for the relief of the sufferers. St. Francis of Sales, prince-bishop of Geneva (d. 1622), converted, by the irresistible power of his meekness and humility, seventy-two thousand Savoyards from the errors of Calvin to the true faith. St. Vincent of Paul (d. 1660) devoted his whole life to the poor and distressed; no misery, of whatever kind or form, escaped the ardor and abundance of his love. He founded orphanages and foundling hospitals; he established a congregation of missionary priests

[30] This institute was established in the Netherlands for English ladies who were persecuted under Queen Elizabeth for their attachment to the Catholic faith, and soon spread over Germany, where it is still flourishing under the above name, though its members have long ceased to be English.

(called Lazarists, from St. Lazarus' College in Paris) for the instruction of ignorant country people; an association for the reforming of convicts, and also the admirable institute of the Sisters of Charity for nursing the sick.

In Germany, especially in Austria and Bavaria, and in Switzerland, the venerable Peter Canisius opposed himself as a mighty barrier against heresy; he combated it by his writings and incessant preaching, and founded schools and pious institutions for preserving and enlivening the true faith established by Christ and his apostles.

The sixteenth and seventeenth centuries were also illustrated by St. John of God, St. John of the Cross, St. Thomas of Villanova, St. Cajetan, St. Peter of Alcantara, St. Camillus of Lellis, St. Joseph Calasanctius, St. Joseph of Cupertino, St. Francis Borgia, St. Pius V, St. Fidelis of Sigmaringen, St. Aloysius Gonzaga, St. Stanislas Kostka, and by many other men eminent for the sanctity of their lives; and among the female sex were especially distinguished St. Teresa, St. Rose of Lima, St. Angela of Brescia, St. Mary Magdalen of Pazzi, St. Jane Frances de Chantal, St. Catherine of Ricci, etc. In the eighteenth century, there shone among others, as one of the brightest ornaments of the Catholic Church, St. Alphonsus Maria Liguori, bishop of St. Agatha, near Naples (d. 1787), who established the Congregation of the Redemptorists for the instruction of the people. All these saints did great deeds and wrought innumerable miracles by their mighty intercession with God; and thus they irrefragably proved that the true spirit of Christianity, the spirit of charity, of humility, and self-denial, had not departed from the Church, as the blind adversaries of our faith unfortunately often assert.

Awful events, which make nature shudder, remain as yet to be related. We would fain pass them over in silence, if they were not most instructive for us. As with all human productions, so it fared with the doctrine of Luther; it became antiquated, it altered, and entirely changed. Sects upon sects arose: Baptists, Presbyterians, Episcopalians, Quakers, Methodists, Moravians, etc. Each one of these sects presumed, after the example of Luther, to reform the faith. At last, impious freethinkers, first in England and afterward in France, carried their presumption to the highest pitch, and contrived the infernal scheme totally to abolish religion, and to exterminate forever the belief in Christ. Under the pretense of enlightening mankind, they deluged the world with writings in which they scoffed at all holy things, grossly calumniated the pope and the clergy, and openly advocated the most shameful licentiousness. Their books, written in most attractive language, and sparkling with witticism and satire, found their way too readily among all classes of people, and, at the same time, the spirit of profligacy and impiety spread with surprising rapidity. At the same time, the masses of the people were suffering from misgovernment, oppressive taxation, and excessive privileges enjoyed by the upper classes. These causes combined with the spread of infidel philosophy and the decay of religious faith brought about the French Revolution at the close of the eighteenth century.

The Church was attacked, ecclesiastical property was confiscated; religious orders were suppressed by violence; monks and nuns were turned out of their peaceable abodes by force, and many religious houses were plundered and pulled down. Soon after, a sanguinary edict was issued against all priests who should continue faithful to the discharge of their duties. Was any one discovered refractory, he was cast into prison, or immediately hanged up to the nearest lamppost. The Christian era was annulled, the celebration of the Sundays and festivals was abolished, the churches were profaned and devastated. Everything that reminded them of Christianity was destroyed.

Finally, the madness of these men arrived at such a pitch, that they proclaimed reason to be the supreme being, and conducted a vile woman as an emblem of the deity, on a triumphal car, into the Cathedral of Paris, where they placed her on the high altar, in the place of the figure of our crucified Redeemer, and sang hymns in her honor. Order, prosperity, and public safety disappeared together with religion; even the throne was overturned and shattered to pieces. France was for two years the scene of such horrible atrocities as are unequalled in the annals of history. Human blood flowed in torrents. Neither age nor sex was safe from the fury of those monsters. The total number of the people slaughtered in this Reign of Terror was, according to some, two million. And all this was done under the pretense of promoting the happiness of mankind. *Enlightenment* was their word when they abolished religion; *liberty* and *equality*, when they murdered their fellow men. At last, in order to stop the complete anarchy that prevailed, the leaders solemnly proclaimed that the nation should once more believe in God and the immortality of the soul.

In the year 1799, Napoleon, in quality of First Consul, seized upon the sovereign power; but he did not venture to govern a people without religion. He therefore restored the Catholic religion in France, and made a solemn concordat with the pope (1801 A.D.). However, the Church did not long enjoy this peace. Napoleon, blinded by fortune, attempted to extort from the supreme head of the Church certain concessions which he could not grant. The French troops invaded Rome, and carried away Pius VII prisoner in 1809. But as God had visibly protected his Church ten years before, when Pope Pius VI had died a captive at Valence in France, so now he did not abandon her to her enemies. Napoleon was vanquished by the Confederate Powers of Europe, and dispossessed of his crown, and the pope reentered triumphant into Rome (1814 A.D.).

With the establishment of peace, after the Napoleonic Wars, in 1815, a more favorable era opened for the Church. In France, she recovered some of her old prosperity. What has been called the Catholic Revival, began, first in Germany, to the great progress of religion, and afterward in England. In 1829, the disabilities under which Irish and British Catholics had so long labored were removed. A few years after, in England, the hierarchy, which had been suppressed at the time of the Reformation, was restored; numerous and notable conversions from protestantism took place; and the number of Catholics and Catholic institutions has since grown very rapidly. The infidel doctrines, however, of the French philosophers and subsequent freethinkers have continued to spread unbelief, so that the Church has to contend everywhere with a spirit of irreligion.

In 1848, Pius IX was obliged to quit Rome through the machinations of Italian revolutionists. During his short exile he received the respectful sympathy of the Catholic world; and, in 1850, amid the rejoicings of the Eternal City, he returned to his See.

In 1869, Pope Pius IX convoked the General Council of the Vatican, which defined the dogma of the pope's infallibility. Before the council could finish its labors, it was obliged to suspend its sittings, because of the war which, in 1870, broke out between France and Germany. The Italian army took possession of Rome, and the pope was unjustly deprived of the temporal power and sovereignty enjoyed by his predecessors for ages, and necessary to the complete independence of the Holy See. Pius IX lived eight years longer, as a prisoner in the Vatican Palace, protesting against the iniquitous spoliation of the Church. The next pope, Leo XIII, passed his long pontificate in the same way. Yet from his prison walls his power reached to the ends of the earth. The enemies of the Church had predicted that the fall of the temporal power would prove the end of the papacy. But never has the moral and spiritual authority of the Holy See been more powerful throughout the world than it is today. The German government, at the instigation of Bismarck, instituted a campaign of legislative persecution against the Church. But the fidelity of German Catholics proved victorious.

In 1903, Leo XIII died and was succeeded by His Holiness, Pius X. His reign was marked in France by the culmination of a violent anti-Christian movement which began during the reign of his predecessor. Laws were enacted to suppress all religious orders, Catholic schools, and religious instruction in the government schools. The concordat established with the Holy See was most unjustly abolished, and the Church was robbed of all her property throughout the country.

Shortly after the outbreak of the World War in 1914, Pius X died and was followed by Benedict XV, whose heroic efforts to promote peace among the nations became fully known only after his death. The present pontiff, His Holiness, Pius XI, elected in the year 1922, is the 266th pope, including St. Peter. He is regarded as a highly gifted ruler, well informed on the problems of the day.

The most wonderful and most consoling fact in recent history has been the Church's unexampled growth in the United States during the past century. From a mere handful a hundred years ago, her children have increased to fourteen million or more. This growth, too, is as sound and vigorous as it is extensive. Among the external indications of its strength enumerated with admiration by Leo XIII (*Longinqua Oceani*, Jan., 1895) are: our unnumbered religious and useful institutions, sacred edifices, schools for elementary instruction, colleges for the higher branches, homes for the poor, hospitals for the sick, convents, and monasteries. Besides, as he observed, there are still surer signs of the faith of the people; for the numbers of the clergy are steadily increasing, pious sodalities and confraternities are held in esteem, schools for religious teaching are in a flourishing condition; the strength of popular piety is further manifested by associations for mutual aid, for the relief of the indigent, and for the promotion of temperance. Truly the judgment of the secular historian was well grounded who said that the Church's gains in the New World have compensated her for what she has lost in the Old.

Concluding Remarks

ON THE HISTORICAL EVIDENCES OF THE TRUTH OF OUR DIVINE RELIGION

We have now, in a small compass, surveyed the history of our holy religion, and considered the blessings it has conferred upon mankind from Adam, our first parent, to our Lord and Savior Jesus Christ, and from him, the divine head and founder of our Church, to his present vicegerent, Pius X. How sublime and beautiful is the religion we profess! Everything connected with it calls out to us: God alone could have given such a religion to mankind. Man has not invented it: God himself has taught it to us, and has commanded us to observe it. He revealed it by holy men in the old testament; and in the new, precisely as the prophecies of the old testament had foretold. His only begotten, eternal Son appeared on earth, and most convincingly confirmed his divine doctrine by numerous miracles, especially by his resurrection from the dead. God has spoken, and no one has a right to be indifferent to his word; to despise or reject it would be to condemn one's self to everlasting hell fire.

The religion to which we belong did not take rise only a few centuries ago; properly speaking, it dates from the creation of man. For its first seeds were laid in paradise when God promised a Redeemer to our first parents after their fall; and the whole of the old law, with its sacrifices and wonderful events, was but a figure of the new law, which contains the fulfillment and accomplishment of the old. The old law believed in the Redeemer to come, and the new believes in him already come. But it is the same belief in the same Redeemer, and therefore it is essentially the same religion.

Although our holy religion is coeval with the beginning of mankind, yet its beginning is not lost in obscure fables of ancient times; on the contrary, its truth is evident and obvious to all. For it exhibits, from the remotest antiquity down to the present time, an uninterrupted series, as it were, of public and universally known facts and events, which perfectly agree with one another, and with all the monuments of past ages, and with the annals of the various nations of the world. They have been so manifoldly and irrefragably attested that he who would not believe them might just as well deny any other historical truth. We count the generations as they succeeded one another from Adam to Christ,[31] and all the supreme pastors or popes from St. Peter to our holy father, Pius X, who is now gloriously governing the Church established by the Son of God. What a wonderful chain of events, and what an unparalleled succession!

Even the Jews, the most obstinate adversaries of our faith, bear witness to its truth. For they carefully keep upon record, in their holy books, the whole history and all the prophecies of the old testament, to which we appeal in order to prove the divine origin of Christianity; insomuch that no one can for a moment suppose that the Christians have perverted or invented such passages in the old testament as refer to our Savior.

Nor can it be denied that it is entirely through the mighty help of God that the Christian religion has spread over the whole earth. The apostles who first preached it were from the lowest class of the people, poor, unknown, even without eloquence or learning. Their doctrine of the cross, which contains the inscrutable mysteries of penance, humility,

[31] Cf. Lk 3; Mt 1

and mortification, was not likely to please the proud and licentious pagans, who found in their abominable mythology (i.e., fabulous history of their gods), not only an excuse, but even a justification for all their vices. The rich and the great looked with disdain upon the poor fishermen; the witty and the learned derided them; and the mighty rulers of the earth, as even pagan writers testify, took all possible pains to destroy them with fire and sword. During three centuries, persecution and martyrdom were the common lot of the Christians. Nevertheless, the doctrine of the poor fishermen, as we have seen, triumphed over all its enemies, and thus proved to be the doctrine of God. It spread so rapidly that, soon after the death of the apostles, St. Justin ventured to affirm before the whole world: "There is no people, neither among the barbarians, nor among the Greeks, nor in any other known nation, among whom prayers and thanksgivings are not offered up to the Father and Creator of the universe in the name of Christ crucified." Who else but the Almighty could have performed such an inexplicable wonder? St. Augustine, the celebrated father of the Church, makes a striking observation upon this: "If the miracles," he says, "wrought by the apostles could be denied, this would be the greatest miracle: that the world believed without miracles."

But the Christian Church is not only founded on miracles; her duration itself is a continual and perpetual miracle. Kingdoms and empires, in spite of their power, perish in the course of time; the kingdom of Christ alone outlasts them all, and is constantly increasing. If it decreases in one part of the world, it spreads so much the more in another. From the time of its foundation, it has been assailed by innumerable enemies from within and from without; their power is terrible, their hatred implacable. The Church of Christ, on her part, has no army to repulse their assaults, no sword to oppose their rude violence. Had not the arm of God protected her, she would long since have been overcome by the force and fraud of her enemies.

The Christian Church appears still more glorious, if we consider the benefits and blessings which she has at all times conferred on mankind. It was she that subdued the brutality of the barbarians, that abolished slavery and human sacrifices, and promoted public and domestic happiness. It was she that founded charitable institutions and innumerable hospitals for the reception of the sick and distressed; it was she that amended the existing laws or made new ones; it was she that taught concord and charity, and diffused learning and true enlightenment. She can truly be called the "tree of life" which God has planted, that all men should peacefully rest under its shade, and refresh themselves with its fruit. Never has a nation abandoned this tree of life without plunging itself into religious confusion and misery. We know very well what has become of the nations in Asia and Africa who were formerly so happy, and what fruit the anti-Christian freethinkers have produced in Europe. If "the tree is to be known by its fruits,"[32] everyone must see that the Christian faith, which diffuses nothing but happiness and blessings, is the most valuable gift of God; that, on the contrary, infidelity, which produces but misery and vexation, can only proceed from the spirit of evil.

Now, this Church which Almighty God has founded on miracles, nay, which is herself a continual miracle; this Church which incessantly pours out the greatest benefits over the universe, can be no other but the Roman Catholic Church. History clearly proves that it is she, and no other, that forms that community of the faithful which Christ has established for the salvation of the world, in which the bishops, as the successors of the apostles, under the supreme authority of the pope, the successor of Saint Peter, exercise their teaching and pastoral offices in an uninterrupted succession. It is impossible that any sect, whatever may be its name, should be the Church founded by Christ; for it is well known that every one of them began to exist long after Christ, and that even then they owed their origin to their defection and separation from the Church of Christ. We see, therefore, that in all these sects the words of Jesus are sooner or later fulfilled: "Every plant which my heavenly Father hath not planted shall be rooted up."[33] Their existence is not lasting; they spring up, make some noise, and disappear again. It is not so with the Catholic Church. Thousands of years pass away; neither does she vanish, nor does she grow old; for to her was made the promise of our Lord: "Upon this rock I will build my Church, and the gates of hell shall not prevail against her."[34]

[32] Lk 6:44; Cf. Mt 7:16
[33] Mt 15:13
[34] Mt 16:18

Review Questions

From Adam to Moses

How did God create heaven and earth? In how many days did he create all things? When did he create man? How did he distinguish man from the other creatures? What were the names of the first man and woman? Were they also liable to sin, as we are? Where did they live? Were they and their children ever to die?

What commandment did God give to Adam and Eve? What did the serpent tell them? What did Adam and Eve do? Were they punished for it? Were they alone punished? What punishment came upon them? Did God then abandon them? What did he promise them?

Who were Cain and Abel? How did they worship God? Was God pleased with their sacrifices? What did Cain do, and what became of him?

Were the descendants of Cain good or wicked? What evil did they do? What did God then resolve to do? How long did it rain? To what height did the flood rise? Did all living creatures perish? What did Noe do when he came out of the ark? What new kindness did God show to Noe and his sons?

Did the descendants of Noe multiply much? What did they attempt to do? How was their undertaking frustrated? What was the tower called? Did the descendants of Noe remain faithful to God? What was the consequence of their idolatry?

Were the true religion and the hope in the Redeemer entirely to vanish? How did God prevent it? How were the descendants of Abraham called? What favor did God bestow on them?

How did God try the faith of Abraham? How did he fulfill the command of God? What did Isaac do? Did God suffer him to be killed? How did God reward Abraham? What mysterious signification does the sacrifice of Isaac contain?

Who was Jacob, and where did he live? How many sons had he, and what did they become afterward? What was Joseph chosen by God to be? What happened to him? Did Jacob remain in Chanaan? What did he prophesy before his death, and about whom? How was it fulfilled?

From Moses to Christ

What happened to the children of Israel in Egypt? Whom did God appoint to deliver them? How did he appear to Moses? Did Moses meet with any opposition? What did God do to the Egyptians? Did the angel hurt also the Israelites? Why did he not hurt them? What did the blood of the paschal lamb signify?

Did Pharao continue keeping the Israelites in bondage? What did he do soon after? What did the Israelites do on their part? How were they delivered? How did God punish Pharao?

Did the Israelites now go on straight to Chanaan? How long were they journeying from Egypt to Mount Sinai? What happened at Mount Sinai? Did God give them the ten commandments only? What return did they make for all these benefits?

How was their ingratitude punished? Did God abandon them altogether? What favors did he still show them? When, and how, did they get possession of Chanaan? Is there not a figure in all this? What does the deliverance from Egypt signify? What does the journey through the desert signify? What does the promised land call to our mind?

How long did the Israelites remain happy in the promised land? What happened to them when they offended God? How did God help them when they repented?

Who were the first rulers of the people of Israel? How long were they governed by them? Who was the first king of Israel? Why was he rejected by God? By whom was he succeeded? What can you tell me of David? Was he also pious? Why are his psalms so very remarkable? Why is Christ also called the Son of David?

Who was Solomon? What famous building did he erect? How was the sanctuary decorated, and what was kept in it? What did the ark of the covenant contain? Who was permitted to enter the sanctuary, and how many times a year? Had the people of Israel any other temples, or altars? Did Solomon remain wise and good? What made him leave the service of God?

What happened after Solomon's death? Which tribes formed the kingdom of Juda? Who was its first king? Which was its capital? How many tribes constituted the kingdom of Israel? Whom did they choose for their king? Which was the capital of the kingdom of Israel? Did it remain faithful to God? How did God punish it? Did the kingdom of Juda also sin against the Lord? Was it also chastised, and how? Was not its punishment less severe than that of the kingdom of Israel, and why?

Did the judgments of God come upon them quite unexpectedly? How did God forewarn the people? Did the prophets only announce God's judgments? What have they foretold of the Messias? Which prophet foretold the time of his coming most precisely? Which are the most remarkable among the prophets?

Who distinguished themselves by their virtues at Ninive and Babylon? How long did the Babylonian Captivity last? How was it brought to an end? What did the Jews most urgently set about after their return? Was the new Temple as magnificent as the one that had been demolished? In what was it superior to the first one?

What is to be observed about Esdras and Nehemias? How did the people then behave? Did they remain faithful to their Lord and God? How did they show their fidelity? Who especially distinguished themselves at that time?

Were all the signs that were to precede the coming of the Messias fulfilled at the time of Christ's birth? Were all the signs of his coming accomplished at that time? What was the prevalent feeling of the Jews and the pagans? What was the state of the world? How did this corruption appear among the Jews? And how amongst the other nations? In what did the abomination of idolatry consist? What character does St. Paul give of the heathens? Was there anyone then who could help mankind? Did he help them, and how? What did Christ himself say on this subject?

History of Christ

Under what emperor and what king was the Redeemer born? Where, and of whom, was he born? Who was first told of his birth, and by whom? What did King Herod try to discover, and why? What did St. Joseph do? Where did Jesus spend his childhood after his return from Egypt? How did he live there? What did he do when he was twelve years old? What did he do when he was thirty? What happened at his baptism?

What did Jesus do after his baptism? What does the word *gospel* mean? How did Jesus prove his divine mission? What impression did he make upon the people? How many apostles did he choose? What does the word *apostle* signify? Why did he choose them? What are their names? How many other disciples did he elect, and for what purpose? Who formed the beginning of the Christian Church? What did Jesus promise to his Church? Whom did he appoint to be her visible head on earth? By what expressions did he intimate this? What did he promise to give him?

What sort of favors did Jesus confer upon the Jews? How did the Jews behave toward him? Why did the scribes and Pharisees especially hate him? Why did they watch all his words and actions? Could they convict him of any sin? What special miracle did Jesus perform in the third year of his teaching? What impression did this make on the people? In what words did they express their feelings? What effect did this reception of Jesus produce on his enemies?

How did Jesus meet his approaching passion? How did he celebrate the last supper with his apostles? What commandment did he give them at the end of it? What sacrament did he institute by this? What did he promise to his apostles after the last supper? Whither did he go afterward?

What did Christ suffer in the Garden of Gethsemane? What memorable prayer did he say there? By whom was he then betrayed? And how was he apprehended? Whither did they lead him then? How was he treated before the chief council? To whom did the chief priests, and to whom did Pilate, deliver him up? What did Pilate and Herod think of him? What else had Christ to suffer?

What did they make Jesus carry? Where, and between whom, was he crucified? How were then the prophecies fulfilled in him? When hanging on the cross, how did he suffer, and for whom did he pray? How long did he hang on the cross? What great miracle happened during that time? How did our Lord expire? What miracles illustrated his death? What benefit did Jesus confer by his death on us and on the whole world?

On what day, and at what hour, did Jesus expire? How did they assure themselves of his death? And what resulted from this? What was done with his sacred body? What did his enemies then do? When, and how, did Christ rise to life? How long did he yet remain on earth? What did he do during that time? What did he command his apostles to do when he appeared the last time among them? What power, and what promise, did he give them? When, where, and how did he ascend into heaven?

From the Ascension of Christ to the Conversion of Constantine

How did the disciples prepare for the coming of the Holy Ghost? Whom did the apostles choose in the place of Judas? When, and how, did the Holy Ghost come? What change did he produce in them? What did Peter, the head of the apostles, do? What was the result of his sermon? How was the lame man at the Temple-gate healed? What effect had this miracle on the Jews?

By what else did the apostles spread the doctrine of Christ? What did the people do in consequence of this? What impression did this make upon the chief priests and their adherents? What did they do to the apostles? Who was the first martyr? Did the apostles, on being persecuted, cease preaching? What can you relate of St. Paul?

Of whom was the first Christian community composed? What was their conduct, and how did they serve God? Was there any dissension amongst them? Did any of them suffer from want? How were the poor relieved? By what authority, and how, did the apostles govern this first community?

Were the Jews all converted? Did those who refused to believe in Christ remain unpunished? What punishment was inflicted on them? Why were they dispersed all over the world? What determined the apostles to go and preach to the pagans? Under what difficulties, and with what success, did they preach to them? How did the apostles organize the new Christian communities? Were these communities separated, and independent of one another? Who was their common head? What do we call all these communities together? What is the meaning of *catholic*? Where was St. Peter bishop, and where did he die? Upon whom did his supremacy over the whole Church devolve?

What impression did the spreading of Christianity make on the pagans? How did they expect to exterminate it? What torments did they inflict upon the Christians? Were there many thus tortured and killed? Where did the persecution of the Christians chiefly rage? Have we any evidence of this nowadays?

How long did these persecutions last? Was the Christian religion extirpated by them? Why not? What convinced the pagans of the divine origin of Christianity? What occurred oftentimes while the Christians were tortured? With what, then, may the blood of the martyrs justly be compared?

Why did God permit these persecutions? Whom did he call to put an end to them? Who was Constantine, and what can you relate concerning his victory? In what year did Constantine gain the battle and become the protector of Christianity?

From the Conversion of Constantine to the Rise of Protestantism in the Sixteenth Century

What had the cross been before this, and what did it become now? Where was it particularly seen, and what did it announce to the world? What did Constantine do for the Christian religion? What effect had his example upon the pagans? What became of paganism, and what was established in its place?

Were the contests of the Church now at an end? Who were her new enemies? Had there not been heresies before? And what was the difference between them and these new ones? Whence did the sects take their names? How did they behave toward the faithful? How did the Church oppose these heresies? What is the name of a general assembly of the bishops of the Catholic Church? When and why are the decisions of a general council infallible? When was the Council of Nice held? How many, and what, bishops were assembled there? What sentence did they pass? What error did Arius maintain? What became of these sectarians after their condemnation? How did it fare with all subsequent heresies? And what became of the Catholic Church?

By whom did God especially illustrate his Church at this time? How are those holy and learned men called? Can you name any of them? Did any other men distinguish themselves in the Church about this time? Who were the hermits? What was their abode? What was their food and drink? Why did they renounce all comforts? Who were the first and most famous hermits? What did the solitary life give rise to afterward? Who built the first monastery? Who particularly advanced the monastic life in Europe? For what is Europe especially indebted to the Benedictine order? When, and by whom, was it introduced into England?

What was the cause of the dangers to which the Church was exposed during the fifth and sixth centuries? What is this called in history? Can you name any of these rapacious tribes? Which of them was the most savage and cruel? Who was their king, and what did he call himself? Did these savage tribes do much harm? What became of the Roman Empire? Who was made king of Italy? In what year? By what means did God subdue the barbarians? How was this done? When was Ireland converted, and by whom? What peculiarity was there in the conversion of the Irish? In what centuries was Germany converted and civilized? Who is the apostle of Austria? Can you name any more of the missionaries to whom Germany owes its conversion? Who is called the apostle of the Germans? Where was he born? To what order did he belong? Of what town was he made archbishop? How, and in what year, did he die? What did the missionaries usually do when they had settled in a country? What did, then, the monasteries do for the spreading and strengthening of the faith? For what else is Germany indebted to the monks? What emperor in those days interested himself particularly for the prosperity of the Christian Church, and what did he do? To whom does Hungary owe her conversion?

What happened in the East, whilst the Christian faith was successfully spread in the West? Who was the chief cause of those disturbances? To what were the people and the clergy inclined? What was the unfortunate result of all this? Did God suffer all this to remain unpunished? Who was Mahomet? What did he pretend to be? Of what did he form his new religion? How did he spread it? What did his successors do? Was the Christian religion totally destroyed under them? What became of it, and what was the reason?

In what year did Jerusalem fall under the power of the Mahometans? What do you understand by *Mahometans*, and what by *Saracens*? When was Jerusalem conquered by the Turks? What do you call those Turks, and whence did they come? What was their religion? Were they friends of the Christians? What was the cause of the Crusades? Who was Peter of Amiens, and what did he report to Urban II? What did the pope do? What did he effect at the Council of Clermont? In what year was the Council of Clermont held? What ensued in the West? What is the origin of the name of *Crusade*? What can you relate of the first Crusade? In what year was Jerusalem taken? What can you relate of Godfrey of Bouillon? How long did the Christian kingdom of Jerusalem last? What caused its fall? When, and by whom, was it conquered? About what year, and by what Turks, were the Seljukians subdued, and how far did they extend their conquests? In what year, and by whom, was Constantinople taken? Who checked the further progress of the Turks? By whom were they at last completely overthrown? In what battle, and in what year? What was the result of this victory?

What influence had the Crusades on Western Europe? Where had the sciences found an asylum during the invasions by the barbarians, and among whom were they now spread? What learned men of those times can you name? What do we call those times, and what are they particularly remarkable for? What monuments give, even at the present time, evidence of the piety of our ancestors? What enabled them to produce such stupendous works? Through whom in particular did the Catholic religion pour out its blessings at that time? What fruits did the numerous monasteries bring forth?

Was there in those times no cockle in the field of God? What kind of cockle was it? What custom had been introduced in some places by the temporal princes? What is symbolized by the ring and crosier? What was this ceremony called, and what did it seem to imply? What did the emperor Henry IV use to do? Who opposed him? What is this contest called, and when did it take place? How did the Church get out of it? What evil came afterward on the West of Europe? Which were the most notorious heretics of that time? Whom did God send to preach penance to them? Was the evil then entirely suppressed? How and when did the slumbering fire break out into a flame? What was the consequence of this?

From the Rise of Protestantism to the Present Time

Who was the author of protestantism? What sort of a man was he? When and how did he begin his conflict with the Church? Did he stop there? How did he behave toward the pope? What innovations did he introduce? What did he do with regard to monasteries, monks, and nuns? What pretended right did he give to princes and sovereigns? Was his conduct edifying? Whence did he pretend to take his doctrine? How did he interpret the Bible? Did he teach the pure word of God? Can you name any of his errors? How was his doctrine received by the people, and how by some princes? What did he do to gain the favor of the Landgrave of Hesse! Did any imitate Luther's example? Where and what did Zwinglius teach? Where and what did Calvin teach? What did the Anabaptists proclaim? What havoc did the Zwinglians and the Calvinists make? Did the different sects agree among themselves? Did their disagreement prevent the spread of their doctrines? In what were they united? What measures did they contrive to propagate their principles? What means did they use in many places to make the Catholics renounce their faith?

What did the Catholics do for the restoration of peace, and what was the result? In what year, and by whom, was the Diet of Spires assembled? What famous decree was issued there? How did the name of *protestants* originate? Are only the Lutherans now called protestants? What measures did the holy father at last take? In what year was the Council of Trent convoked, and what was done by it? What did the Church gain by this council? Did the protestants come to it? What was the effect of Luther's preaching liberty? What took place during the war of the peasantry? Were there any other wars in Germany, and how long did the great religious war last in that country? What was the consequence of this war? Were any other countries involved in war, and which? Where and how did Zwinglius end his life? What are the French protestants called, and what atrocities did they commit? Who introduced protestantism into England, and for what reason? Did England gain anything by the change? What do you know of Charles I?

How was the Church compensated for her loss in Europe? How was this effected? What is the name of the apostle of the Indies? Where did he land, and in what year? How did he begin his mission? What did the children do? How did God reward and assist his zeal? In what countries did he work, and how long? What was the result of his labors? How many heathens did he christen or baptize in one month? Was Christianity also introduced into China? How was the sincerity of the new Christians, especially in Japan, proved? How many were martyred in Japan? Does the hatred against the Christians still continue there? What can you relate of America in general, and of Mexico in particular? Was the work of the missionaries easy there? What particular obstacles did they encounter? Did they succeed the less for all that? How did the savages of Paraguay live? What did they become after their conversion to Christianity?

To what class of men did most of the missionaries belong? Of what order were the apostles of the Indies, and the first planters of Christianity in China and Paraguay? When, and by whom, was this order established? In what did these religious especially exert themselves? How were they requited for their labor by the enemies of religion? Did God raise any other orders at that time, and for what purpose? When and how did the Order of Capuchins originate, and by what were they particularly conspicuous? When and by whom was the Oratory founded, and to what does it devote itself? What was the object of the Fathers of the Pious Schools and of other orders? What communities of religious women arose at that time? What do they devote themselves to? What is the origin of the Institute of English Ladies? In what was this epoch especially rich? Can you tell me anything remarkable of St. Charles Borromeo? What do you know of St. Francis of Sales? What did St. Vincent of Paul in general do for the temporal and eternal welfare of his fellow men? What charitable institutions did he found in particular? Who especially labored in the sixteenth century in Germany and Switzerland for the preservation of the true faith? Were there any other principal saints who shone in the sixteenth and seventeenth centuries, and who were they? By what saints was the female sex distinguished at that time? What saint did particularly illustrate the eighteenth century? What religious order did he found? What did all these saints especially do, and what did they prove by their works and miracles?

What became, in process of time, of the doctrine of Luther? What was the final result of its alterations and changes? What did the sectarianism lead to? What did the freethinkers contrive to do? What principal means did they make use of? Why were their books well received by the people? Whom did the infidels first attack? What became of the ecclesiastical property, the monks and nuns, and the religious houses? What edict was issued against the priests? What did the infidels do to destroy the very name of Christianity? With what particular infamy did they brand themselves in their madness? Why did prosperity and public safety disappear? What became then of France? How many people are said to have been slaughtered during the Reign of Terror? Under what pretense were all these horrible crimes committed? What did the impious wretches finally do in the utmost necessity? By whom, when, and why was the Catholic religion restored in France? Did Napoleon act as a faithful son of the Church? How did he treat Pius VII? Did God ever withdraw his hand from the Church? What became of Napoleon, and what of the pope? In what year did Pius VII return to Rome?

When did a more favorable era open for the Church? When did the Catholic revival occur? What changes took place in Ireland and England? Relate the flight of Pius IX from Rome, and his return. Give an account of the Council of the Vatican. When and by whom was the pope unjustly despoiled of his temporal power? Did this change ruin the Church? What happened during the reign of Leo XIII? When did he die and by whom was he succeeded? What has happened in France since the opening of the reign of Pius X?

What is the most consoling fact in the recent history of the Church? What are the external signs of this growth? Are there other signs indicating the strength of the people's faith? What have we now surveyed? What have we chiefly considered in the history or our religion?

Concluding Remarks

Whence does our religion come? By whom has God revealed it to us? How did Jesus Christ confirm his divine doctrine? Is it indifferent which religion we profess?

How old is our religion? How do you explain and prove its great age?

Is the history of our religion perhaps uncertain, because it dates from the creation of man, and embraces so long a period? Why not?

What evidence do even the Jews give to the truth of our religion? What does this prove?

How do you prove that the Christian religion was spread through the help of God? About what time did St. Justin live? What does he testify of the propagation of Christianity? What observation does St. Augustine make?

How do you prove that the duration or permanent continuance of the Christian Church is a miracle?

What fruits did the Christian faith produce for mankind? What, on the contrary, were the fruits which heresy and infidelity brought forth? What conclusion must we draw from these different fruits?

How do you prove from history that the Church established by God can be no other than the Roman Catholic? What has Christ foretold of all sects? What promise has he given to the Catholic Church?

List of Roman Pontiffs

WITH BIRTHPLACE, DATES OF ACCESSION AND DEATH, AND LENGTH OF PONTIFICATE, AS IN THE BASILICA OF ST. PAUL, ROME

1. St. Peter, native of Bethsaida in Galilee, prince of the apostles, who received from our Lord and Savior Jesus Christ the supreme pontificate, to be transmitted to his successors; and, having resided for a time at Antioch, established his See at Rome, where he suffered martyrdom on the 29th of June, 67.—...–67—25yrs, 2mo.
2. St. Linus, Volterra Mart.—67–78—11 yrs, 3 mos.
3. St. Cletus, Rome, Mart.—78–90—12 yrs, 1 mo.
4. St. Clement I, Rome, Mart.—90–100—10 yrs., 2 mos.
5. St. Anacletus, Greece, Mart.—100–112—12 yrs., 10 mos.
6. St. Evaristus, Syria, Mart.—112–121—9 yrs., 7 mos.
7. St. Alexander I, Rome, Mart.—121–132—10 yrs., 7 mos.
8. St. Sixtus I, Rome, Mart.—132–142—9 yrs., 3 mos.
9. St. Telesphorus, Greece, Mart.—142–154—11 yrs., 3 mos.
10. St. Hyginus, Greece, Mart.—154–158—4 yrs., 3 mos.
11. St. Pius I, Aquileia, Mart.—158–167—8 yrs., 3 mos.
12. St. Anicetus, Syria, Mart.—167–175—8 yrs., 4 mos.
13. St. Soter, Naples, Mart.—175–182—7 yrs., 3 mos.
14. St. Eleutherius, Epirus, Mart.—182–193—11 yrs., 4 mos.
15. St. Victor I, Africa, Mart.—193–203—10 yrs., 2 mos.
16. St. Zephyrinus, Rome, Mart.—203–220—17 yrs., 2 mos.
17. St. Calixtus I, Rome, Mart.—221–227—5 yrs., 2 mos.
18. St. Urban I, Rome, Mart.—227–233—6 yrs., 7 mos.
19. St. Pontian, Rome, Mart.—233–238—5 yrs., 2 mos.
20. St. Anterus, Greece, Mart.—238–239—1 yr., 1 mo.
21. St. Fabian, Rome, Mart.—240–253—13 yrs., 1 mo.
22. St. Cornelius, Rome, Mart.—254–255—1 yr., 10 mos.

23. St. Lucius I, Rome, Mart.—255–257—1 yr., 4 mos.
24. St. Stephen I, Rome, Mart.—257–260—3 yrs., 3 mos.
25. St. Sixtus II, Greece, Mart.—260–261—0 yrs., 11 mos.
26. St. Dionysius, Turin—261–272—11 yrs., 3 mos.
27. St. Felix I, Rome, Mart.—272–275—2 yrs., 5 mos.
28. St. Eutychian, Tuscany, Mart.—275–283—8 yrs., 10 mos.
29. St. Caius, Dalmatia, Mart.—283–296—12 yrs., 4 mos.
30. St. Marcellinus, Rome, Mart.—296–304—7 yrs., 11 mos.
31. St. Marcellus I, Rome, Mart.—304–309—4 yrs., 1 mo.
32. St. Eusebius, Calabria—309–311—2 yrs., 1 mo.
33. St. Melchiades, Africa—311–314—3 yrs., 7 mos.
34. St. Sylvester I, Rome—314–337—23 yrs., 10 mos.
35. St. Marcus, Rome—337–340—2 yrs., 8 mos.
36. St. Julius I, Rome—341–352—11 yrs., 2 mos.
37. St. Liberius, Rome—352–363—10 yrs., 7 mos.
38. St. Felix II, Rome—363–365—1 yr., 3 mos.
39. St. Damasus, Spain—366–384—18 yrs., 2 mos.
40. St. Siricius, Rome—384–398—13 yrs., 1 mo.
41. St. Anastasius I, Rome—399–402—2 yrs., 10 mos.
42. St. Innocent I, Albano—402–417—15 yrs., 2 mos.
43. St. Zozimus, Greece—417–418—1 yr., 9 mos.
44. St. Boniface I, Rome—418–423—4 yrs., 9 mos.
45. St. Celestine I, Rome—423–432—9 yrs., 10 mos.
46. St. Sixtus III, Rome—432–440—8 yrs., 1 mo.
47. St. Leo I (the Great), Tuscany—440–461—21 yrs., 1 mo.
48. St. Hilary, Sardinia—461–468—6 yrs., 3 mos.
49. St. Simplicius, Tivoli—468–483—15 yrs., 0 mos.
50. St. Felix III, Rome—483–492—8 yrs., 11 mos.
51. St. Gelasius I, Africa—492–496—4 yrs., 8 mos.
52. St. Anastasius II, Rome—496–498—1 yr., 11 mos.
53. St. Symmachus, Rome—498–514—15 yrs., 7 mos.
54. St. Hormisdas, Frosinone—514–523—9 yrs., 0 mos.
55. St. John I, Tuscany, Mart.—523–526—2 yrs., 9 mos.
56. St. Felix IV, Benevento—526–530—4 yrs., 2 mos.

57. Boniface II, Rome—530–532—2 yrs., 0 mos.
58. John II, Rome—532–535—2 yrs., 4 mos.
59. St. Agapitus, Rome—535–536—0 yrs., 10 mos.
60. St. Silverius, Frosinone, Mart.—536–538—2 yrs., 0 mos.
61. Vigilius, Rome—538–555—16 yrs., 0 mos.
62. Pelagius I, Rome—555–560—4 yrs., 10 mos.
63. John III, Rome—560–573—12 yrs., 11 mos.
64. Benedict I, Rome—574–578—4 yrs., 1 mo.
65. Pelagius II, Rome—578–590—11 yrs., 2 mos.
66. St. Gregory I (the Great), Rome—590–604—13 yrs., 6 mos.
67. Sabinianus, Volterra—604–606—1 yr., 5 mos.
68. Boniface III, Rome—607–607—0 yrs., 8 mos.
69. St. Boniface IV, Marso—608–615—6 yrs., 8 mos.
70. St. Adeodatus I, Rome—615–619—3 yrs., 0 mos.
71. Boniface V, Naples—619–625—5 yrs., 10 mos.
72. Honorius I, Capua—625–638—12 yrs., 11 mos.
73. Severinus, Rome—640–640—0 yrs., 2 mos.
74. John IV, Dalmatia—640–642—1 yr., 9 mos.
75. Theodorus I, Greece—642–649—6 yrs., 5 mos.
76. St. Martin I, Todi, Mart.—649–655—6 yrs., 2 mos.
77. St. Eugenius I, Rome—655–656—1 yr., 7 mos.
78. St. Vitalian, Segni—657–672—14 yrs., 5 mos.
79. Adeodatus II, Rome—672–676—4 yrs., 2 mos.
80. Domnus I, Rome—676–678—1 yr., 2 mos.
81. St. Agatho, Greece—678–682—3 yrs., 6 mos.
82. St. Leo II, Sicily—682–683—0 yrs., 10 mos.
83. St. Benedict II, Rome—684–685—0 yrs., 10 mos.
84. John V, Antioch—685–686—1 yr., 0 mos.
85. Conon, Thracia—686–687—0 yrs., 11 mos.
86. St. Sergius I, Siculiana—687–701—13 yrs., 8 mos.
87. John VI, Greece—701–705—3 yrs., 2 mos.
88. John VII, Greece—705–707—2 yrs., 7 mos.
89. Sisinnius, Syria—708–708—0 yrs., 0 mos.
90. Constantine, Syria—708–715—7 yrs., 0 mos.

91. St. Gregory II, Rome—715–731—15 yrs., 8 mos.
92. St. Gregory III, Syria—731–741—10 yrs., 8 mos.
93. St. Zacharias, Greece—741–752—10 yrs., 3 mos.
94. Stephen II, Rome—752–752—0 yrs., 0 mos.
95. Stephen III, Rome—752–757—5 yrs., 0 mos.
96. St. Paul I, Rome—757–767—10 yrs., 1 mo.
97. Stephen IV, Syracuse—768–771—3 yrs., 5 mos.
98. Adrian I, Rome—771–795—23 yrs., 10 mos.
99. St. Leo III, Rome—795–816—20 yrs., 5 mos.
100. Stephen V, Rome—816–817—0 yrs., 7 mos.
101. St. Paschal I, Rome—817–824—7 yrs., 0 mos.
102. Eugenius II, Rome—824–827—3 yrs., 6 mos.
103. Valentine, Rome—827–827—0 yrs., 1 mo.
104. Gregory IV, Rome—827–844—16 yrs., 0 mos.
105. Sergius II, Rome—844–847—2 yrs., 11 mos.
106. St. Leo IV, Rome—847–855—8 yrs., 3 mos.
107. Benedict III, Rome—855–858—2 yrs., 6 mos.
108. St. Nicholas I (the Great), Rome—858–867—9 yrs., 6 mos.
109. Adrian II, Rome—867–872—4 yrs., 10 mos.
110. John VIII, Rome—872–882—10 yrs., 0 mos.
111. Marinus I, Gallicia—882–884—1 yr., 5 mos.
112. Adrian III, Rome—884–885—1 yr., 4 mos.
113. Stephen VI, Rome—885–891—6 yrs., 0 mos.
114. Formosus, Ostia—891–896—4 yrs., 6 mos.
115. Boniface VI—896–896—0 yrs., 0 mos.
116. Stephen VII, Rome—897–898—1 yr., 2 mos.
117. Romanus, Gallese—898–898—0 yrs., 3 mos.
118. Theodorus II, Rome—898–898—0 yrs., 0 mos.
119. John IX, Tivoli—898–900—2 yrs., 0 mos.
120. Benedict IV, Rome—900–903—3 yrs., 2 mos.
121. Leo V, Ardea—903–903—0 yrs., 1 mo.
122. Christophorus, Rome—903–904—0 yrs., 6 mos.
123. Sergius III, Rome—904–911—7 yrs., 3 mos.
124. Anastasius III, Rome—911–913—2 yrs., 2 mos.

125. Landus, Sabina—913–914—0 yrs., 6 mos.
126. John X, Ravenna—915–928—14 yrs., 2 mos.
127. Leo VI, Rome—928–929—0 yrs., 8 mos.
128. Stephen VIII, Rome—929–931—2 yrs., 1 mo.
129. John XI, Rome—931–936—4 yrs., 10 mo.
130. Leo VII, Rome—936–939—3 yrs., 6 mos.
131. Stephen IX, Rome—939–942—3 yrs., 4 mos.
132. Marinus II, Rome—943–946—3 yrs., 6 mos.
133. Agapitus II, Rome—946–956—10 yrs., 3 mos.
134. John XII, Rome—956–964—7 yrs., 9 mos.
135. Benedict V, Rome—964–965—1 yr., 1 mo.
136. John XIII, Rome—965–972—6 yrs., 11 mos.
137. Benedict VI, Rome—972–973—1 yr., 3 mos.
138. Domnus II, Rome—973–973—0 yrs., 3 mos.
139. Benedict VII, Rome—975–984—9 yrs., 5 mos.
140. John XIV, Pavia—984–985—0 yrs., 8 mos.
141. Boniface VII, France—985–985—0 yrs., 7 mos.
142. John XV, Rome—985–996—10 yrs., 4 mos.
143. John XVI—996–996—0 yrs., 4 mos.
144. Gregory V, Germany—996–999—2 yrs., 8 mos.
145. John XVII—999–999—0 yrs., 10 mos.
146. Sylvester II, France—999–1003—4 yrs., 1 mo.
147. John XVIII, Rome—1003–1003—0 yrs., 4 mos.
148. John XIX, Rome—1003–1009—5 yrs., 7 mos.
149. Sergius IV, Rome—1009–1012—2 yrs., 8 mos.
150. Benedict VIII, Rome—1012–1024—11 yrs., 11 mos.
151. John XX, Rome—1024–1033—9 yrs., 8 mos.
152. Benedict IX, Rome—1033–1044—11 yrs., 0 mos.
153. Gregory VI, Rome (abdicated in 1046)—1044–...—2 yrs., 8 mos.
154. Clement II, Saxony—1046–1047—0 yrs., 9 mos.
155. Damasus II, Bavaria—1048–1048—0 yrs., 0 mos.
156. St. Leo IX, Germany—1049–1054—5 yrs., 7 mos.
157. Victor II, Svevia—1055–1057—2 yrs., 3 mos.
158. Stephen X, Germany—1057–1058—0 yrs., 7 mos.

159. Benedict X—1058–…—0 yrs., 9 mos.
160. Nicholas II, France—1059–1061—2 yrs., 6 mos.
161. Alexander II, Milan—1061–1073—11 yrs., 6 mos.
162. St. Gregory VII, Soana—1073–1085—12 yrs., 1 mo.
163. Victor III, Benevento—1087–1087—0 yrs., 4 mos.
164. Urban II, Reims—1088–1099—11 yrs., 4 mos.
165. Paschal II, Tuscany—1099–1118—18 yrs., 5 mos.
166. Gelasius II, Gaeta—1118–1119—1 yr., 0 mos.
167. Calixtus II, Burgundy—1119–1124—5 yrs., 10 mos.
168. Honorius II, Bologna—1124–1130—5 yrs., 1 mo.
169. Innocent II, Rome—1130–1143—13 yrs., 8 mos.
170. Celestine II, Citta di Castello—1143–1144—0 yrs., 5 mos.
171. Lucius II, Bologna—1144–1145—0 yrs., 11 mos.
172. Bl. Eugenius III, Montemagno—1145–1153—8 yrs., 4 mos.
173. Anastasius IV, Rome—1153–1154—1 yr., 4 mos.
174. Adrian IV, England—1154–1159—4 yrs., 8 mos.
175. Alexander III, Siena—1159–1181—21 yrs., 11 mos.
176. Lucius III, Lucca—1181–1185—4 yrs., 2 mos.
177. Urban III, Milan—1185–1187—1 yr., 10 mos.
178. Gregory VIII, Benevento—1187–1187—0 yrs., 1 mo.
179. Clement III, Rome—1187–1191—3 yrs., 3 mos.
180. Celestine III, Rome—1191–1198—6 yrs., 9 mos.
181. Innocent III, Anagni—1198–1216—18 yrs., 6 mos.
182. Honorius III, Rome—1216–1227—10 yrs., 8 mos.
183. Gregory IX, Anagni—1227–1241—14 yrs., 5 mos.
184. Celestine IV, Milan—1241–1241—0 yrs., 0 mos.
185. Innocent IV, Genoa—1243–1254—11 yrs., 5 mos.
186. Alexander IV, Anagni—1254–1261—6 yrs., 5 mos.
187. Urban IV, Troyes—1261–1264—3 yrs., 1 mo.
188. Clement IV, France—1265–1269—3 yrs., 9 mos.
189. Bl. Gregory X, Piacenza—1271–1276—4 yrs., 4 mos.
190. Innocent V, Savoy—1276–1276—0 yrs., 5 mos.
191. Adrian V, Genoa—1276–1276—0 yrs., 1 mo.
192. John XXI, Lisbon—1276–1277—0 yrs., 8 mos.

193. Nicholas III, Rome—1277–1280—2 yrs., 8 mos.
194. Martin IV, France—1281–1285—4 yrs., 1 mo.
195. Honorius IV, Rome—1285–1287—2 yrs., 0 mos.
196. Nicholas IV, Ascoli—1288–1292—4 yrs., 1 mo.
197. St. Celestine V, Lavoro (resigned)—1294–...—0 yrs., 5 mos.
198. Boniface VIII, Anagni—1294–1303—8 yrs., 9 mos.
199. Bl. Benedict XI, Treviso—1303–1304—0 yrs., 8 mos.
200. Clement V, France (removed to Avignon)—1305–1314—8 yrs., 10 mos.
201. John XXII, France—1316–1334—18 yrs., 3 mos.
202. Benedict XII, France—1334–1342—7 yrs., 4 mos.
203. Clement VI, France—1342–1352—10 yrs., 6 mos.
204. Innocent VI, France—1352–1362—9 yrs., 8 mos.
205. Bl. Urban V, France—1362–1370—8 yrs., 1 mo.
206. Gregory XI, France (restored See to Rome)—1370–1378—7 yrs., 2 mos.
207. Urban VI, Naples—1378–1389—11 yrs., 6 mos.
208. Boniface IX, Naples—1389–1404—14 yrs., 11 mos.
209. Innocent VII, Sulmona—1404–1406—2 yrs., 0 mos.
210. Gregory XII, Venice (resigned)—1406–...—2 yrs., 6 mos.
211. Alexander V, Bologna—1409–1410—0 yrs., 10 mos.
212. John XXIII, Naples (resigned 1415)—1410–...—5 yrs., 0 mos.
213. Martin V, Rome—1417–1431—13 yrs., 3 mos.
214. Eugenius IV, Venice—1431–1447—15 yrs., 11 mos.
215. Nicholas V, Sarzana—1447–1455—8 yrs., 0 mos.
216. Calixtus III, Spain—1455–1458—3 yrs., 3 mos.
217. Pius II, Siena—1458–1464—5 yrs., 11 mos.
218. Paul II, Venice—1464–1471—6 yrs., 10 mos.
219. Sixtus IV, Savona—1471–1484—13 yrs., 0 mos.
220. Innocent VIII, Genoa—1484–1492—7 yrs., 10 mos.
221. Alexander VI, Spain—1492–1503—11 yrs., 0 mos.
222. Pius III, Siena—1503–1503—0 yrs., 0 mos.
223. Julius II, Savona—1503–1513—9 yrs., 3 mos.
224. Leo X, Florence—1513–1521—8 yrs., 8 mos.
225. Adrian VI, Utrecht—1522–1523—1 yr., 8 mos.
226. Clement VII, Florence—1523–1534—10 yrs., 1 mo.

227. Paul III, Rome—1534–1549—15 yrs., 0 mos.
228. Julius III, Tuscany—1550–1555—5 yrs., 1 mo.
229. Marcellus II, Montepulciano—1555–1555—0 yrs., 0 mos.
230. Paul IV, Naples—1555–1559—4 yrs., 2 mos.
231. Pius IV, Milan—1559–1565—5 yrs., 11 mos.
232. St. Pius V, Bosco—1566–1572—6 yrs., 3 mos.
233. Gregory XIII, Bologna—1572–1585—12 yrs., 10 mos.
234. Sixtus V, Ancona—1585–1590—5 yrs., 4 mos.
235. Urban VII, Rome—1590–1590—0 yrs., 0 mos.
236. Gregory XIV, Cremona—1590–1591—0 yrs., 10 mos.
237. Innocent IX, Bologna—1591–1591—0 yrs., 2 mos.
238. Clement VIII, Florence—1592–1605—13 yrs., 1 mo.
239. Leo XI, Florence—1605–1605—0 yrs., 0 mos.
240. Paul V, Rome—1605–1621—15 yrs., 8 mos.
241. Gregory XV, Bologna—1621–1623—2 yrs., 5 mos.
242. Urban VIII, Florence—1623–1644—20 yrs., 11 mos.
243. Innocent X, Rome—1644–1655—10 yrs., 3 mos.
244. Alexander VII, Siena—1655–1667—12 yrs., 1 mo.
245. Clement IX, Pistoia—1667–1669—2 yrs., 5 mos.
246. Clement X, Rome—1670–1676—6 yrs., 2 mos.
247. Innocent XI, Como—1676–1689—12 yrs., 10 mos.
248. Alexander VIII, Venice—1689–1691—1 yr., 3 mos.
249. Innocent XII, Naples—1691–1700—9 yrs., 2 mos.
250. Clement XI, Urbino—1700–1721—20 yrs., 3 mos.
251. Innocent XIII, Rome—1721–1724—2 yrs., 9 mos.
252. Benedict XIII, Rome—1724–1730—5 yrs., 8 mos.
253. Clement XII, Florence—1730–1740—9 yrs., 6 mos.
254. Benedict XIV, Bologna—1740–1758—17 yrs., 8 mos.
255. Clement XIII, Venice—1758–1769—10 yrs., 6 mos.
256. Clement XIV, S. Angelo in Vado—1769–1774—5 yrs., 4 mos.
257. Pius VI, Cesena—1775–1799—24 yrs., 6 mos.
258. Pius VII, Cesena—1800–1823—23 yrs., 5 mos.
259. Leo XII, Spoleto—1823–1829—5 yrs., 4 mos.
260. Pius VIII, Cingoli—1829–1830—1 yr., 8 mos.

261. Gregory XVI, Belluno—1831–1846—15 yrs., 3 mos.
262. Pius IX, Sinigaglia—1846–1878—31 yrs., 7 mos.
263. Leo XIII, Carpineto—1878–1903—25 yrs., 5 mos.
264. Pius X, Riese—1903–1914—11 yrs., 0 mos.
265. Benedict XV, Genoa—1914–1922—7 yrs., 4 mos.
266. Piux XI, gloriosamente regnate—1922

EXPLANATION OF THE LIST

Owing, chiefly, to the fact that during what is called the great schism of the West, there were sometimes several claimants to the Holy See, only one of whom could be the lawful successor of St. Peter, authorities differ concerning the correct list of the popes. Some reckon that Pius XI is the 261st successor of St. Peter.

The foregoing list is taken from a series of portraits, painted in medallions, on the nave walls of the Basilica of St. Paul, on the Ostian Way, near Rome. This magnificent church was built over the tomb of the great apostle, under the reign of Constantine the Great, by Pope St. Sylvester, about the year 320 A.D. The portrait of that pope, and of Marcus, his successor, and of the thirty-three popes who had preceded them, were all painted apparently by the same hand. The portraits of the succeeding popes were generally added, one by one, by different hands, probably soon after death, and by the care of their successors. This, however, seems to have been omitted in some instances, possibly on account of the troublous times; for we find that the series has been continued by medallions of two or three popes evidently executed by the same artist. The most considerable interruption of such a character was in the fourteenth and fifteenth centuries, when seven medallions seem to have been painted during the reign of Martin V.

This is the largest and most interesting series of historical portraits in existence. Artists are able to read, as it were, and recognize the work and painter as easily and as surely as ordinary mortals read and recognize the varying handwriting of individuals. Even in the case of the earlier popes before St. Sylvester, they see evidences that the artist was in possession of such knowledge as enabled him to give to each face the marked individuality of a portrait. For the subsequent popes down to the present time, there is no difficulty. However imperfect the workmanship, even in the medieval centuries, and although the fading colors may have been retouched by equally unskillful hands, it is always evident that the painter originally presented the features of a real face—not an ideal or fancy sketch.

The Basilica of St. Paul was destroyed by fire in 1823, and this series of portraits unfortunately perished in the flames. But half a century before, all these portraits had been carefully engraved on copperplate and published. From these engravings Pope Pius IX caused the portraits to be reproduced in imperishable mosaics, and they again decorate the nave of the splendid Basilica of St. Paul, which has been rebuilt, and which he consecrated a few years ago. From the copperplates, other copies have been made in copperplate, steel, lithograph, and photograph, of various sizes, and may be easily obtained. Under each medallion in the Church was an inscription giving the name of the pontiff, and the length of his pontificate. Ordinarily, in the case of contemporary popes, this is testimony of the highest character. Where, as in the case of the earlier popes, the inscription could only give the judgment of the painter as to dates long past, it obviously cannot claim the same high value. It might be, and in some cases has been, held to be uncertain, and in others erroneous. Some popes, also, have been inserted in this list. Doubtless in deference to the claims urged at the time by their adherents, and perhaps for the sake of peace. A more critical and impartial spirit has doubted or denied their right to such honor, and classed them as antipopes. In these two points we find the explanation of the difference between this list of popes and those found elsewhere. We give the list as published in the *Gerarchia Cattolica*, Rome, 1875, with a few corrections, which were evidently typographical errors.

JOSEPH DEHARBE

A Complete Catechism of the Catholic Religion

Introduction

On the End of Man

1. **For what end are we in this world?**
We are in this world that we may know God, love him, and serve him, and thereby attain heaven.

2. **What is heaven?**
Heaven is a place of eternal and perfect happiness.

3. **Are not the things of this world intended to make us happy?**
No; the things of this world cannot possibly make us happy.

4. **Why cannot the things of this world make us happy?**
1) Because all earthly things are vain and perishable; and 2) because man is made for God and for everlasting happiness in heaven.

"I heaped together for myself silver and gold, and the wealth of kings and provinces...And whatsoever my eyes desired, I refused them not, and I withheld not my heart from enjoying every pleasure...But I saw in all things vanity and vexation of mind, and that nothing was lasting under the sun."[35] Thus spoke Solomon, the happiest of kings. "What is your life? It is a vapor which appeareth for a little while, and afterward shall vanish

[35] Eccles 2:8, 10-11

away."[36] "For thyself, O God, thou hast made us; therefore our heart will be restless until it rest in thee."[37]

5. **For what end, then, were the things of this world principally given to us?**
That we may use them for the purpose of knowing and serving God.

"All men are vain, in whom there is not the knowledge of God, and who by these good things that are seen could not understand him that is, neither by attending to the works have acknowledged who was the workman."[38] "Whether you eat or drink, or whatsoever else you do, do all to the glory of God."[39]

6. **Why does God require us to know him, love him, and serve him?**
God requires us 1) to know him, because he is the eternal truth; 2) to love him, because he is the most bountiful and most lovable God; and 3) to serve him, because he is the sovereign Lord.

7. **What will become of those who will not know, love, and serve him?**
God will cast them from him forever.

"The unprofitable servant cast ye out into the exterior darkness. There shall be weeping and gnashing of teeth."[40]

8. **What is, then, most necessary in this life?**
In this life the most necessary thing is that we should know, love, and serve God, and thereby obtain eternal happiness.

"Seek ye first the kingdom of God and his justice."[41] "For what doth it profit a man, if he gain the whole world and suffer the loss of his own soul."[42]

[36] Jas 4:15
[37] Augustine, *Confessions*, Bk. 1, Ch. 1, n. 1
[38] Ws 13:1
[39] 1 Cor 10:31
[40] Mt 25:30
[41] Mt 6:33
[42] Mt 16:26

9. **What must we do, if we would know and serve God, and be eternally happy?**
1) We must believe all that God has revealed; 2) we must keep all the commandments which God has ordered to be kept; and 3) we must use the means of grace which God has ordained for our salvation.

Or, in other words: we must have religion; for religion (from *religare*) is the lively union of man with God, which springs from faith, charity, and grace, and is confirmed by the faithful observance of the divine commandments.

10. **Why must we, in order to be saved, believe, keep the commandments, and make use of the means of grace?**
We must, in order to be saved, 1) believe, because it is only by faith that we get a right knowledge of God; 2) we must keep the commandments, because by keeping the commandments we serve God; and 3) we must also use the means of grace, because by them we obtain the help necessary to salvation.

11. **Where do we get a right knowledge of the truths of divine faith, of the commandments, and of the means of grace?**
In the Christian doctrine.

12. **What do you call the book which briefly contains the Christian doctrine in question and answer?**
The catechism.

13. **What, then, does the catechism treat of?**
1) Of faith; 2) of the commandments; and 3) of the means of grace, namely, the sacraments and prayer.

Application. Never neglect going to the instructions on Christian doctrine; and when there, be always attentive, that you may learn to know and love God properly, and thus attain your last end, which is eternal happiness in heaven. "Blessed is the man that findeth wisdom (i.e., the knowledge and love of God)...She is more precious than all riches; and all the things that are desired are not to be compared with her...She is a tree of life to them that lay hold on her; and he that shall retain her is blessed."[43]

[43] Prv 3:13, 15, 18

SECTION I
Faith

Faith in General

Nature and Necessity of Faith

14. **What is faith?**

Faith is a virtue infused by God into our souls, by which we believe, without doubting, all those things which God has revealed, and proposes by his Church to our belief.

To believe means, in general, to hold to be true what another says, and for this reason, because he says it. *To believe God* means, therefore, to hold firmly and without doubting what God has revealed, and because he has revealed it, although we can neither see nor completely understand it; for faith is founded not on our seeing or complete understanding, but on the Word of God. "Faith is…the evidence of things that appear not."[44]

15. **Why do we say that faith is infused by God into our souls?**

Because it is a gift of God, and an effect of his grace, which enlightens our understanding and moves our will to believe, without doubting, all those things which God has revealed.

"For by grace you are saved through faith, and that not of yourselves: for it is the gift of God."[45]

[44] Heb 11:1
[45] Eph 2:8

16. **Why must grace not only enlighten our understanding, but also move our will?**

Because a good will also belongs to faith; for no one can believe but he who is willing to believe.

Therefore, faith is also rewarded by God, and unbelief punished. "He that believeth, and is baptized, shall be saved; but he that believeth not shall be condemned."[46]

17. **Why must we believe all that God has revealed?**

Because God is the eternal and infallible truth.

18. **Is faith necessary to salvation?**

Faith is absolutely necessary to salvation; for "without faith it is impossible to please God."[47]

"He that doth not believe is already judged."[48] "He that believeth not shall be condemned."[49]

19. **Will any faith save us?**

No; only the true faith, which Christ our Lord has taught, will save us.

"He that believeth in the Son hath life everlasting: but he that believeth not the Son shall not see life; but the wrath of God abideth on him."[50]

20. **Why will that faith only which Christ has taught save us?**

Because by this faith alone, and by no other, we are made partakers of Christ, and without Christ there is no salvation.

"For there is no other name under heaven given to men whereby we must be saved."[51]

[46] Mk 16:16
[47] Heb 11:6
[48] Jn 3:18
[49] Mk 16:16
[50] Jn 3:36
[51] Acts 4:12

21. **Is it, then, a sin to say that it does not matter what faith we profess?**
Yes, it is a grievous sin to say so, or even only to think so; for we despise God by it, who has given us the one true faith, and, therefore, has sent his only begotten Son into the world.[52]

If it did not matter what we believe, it would not have been necessary for God to reveal a religion, and our ancestors might all have remained heathens or Jews. But "this is the judgment," says Jesus Christ, "because the light is come into the world, and men love darkness rather than the light"[53]; i.e., because many were obstinate in their unbelief, although they saw the truth, or could have seen it, provided they had been sincere.

22. **But is it not written: "He that feareth God, and worketh justice, is acceptable to him"?**[54]
Yes; but he who fears God does also believe all that he has revealed, as Cornelius did.[55] He, on the contrary, who does not believe all that God has revealed does not fear him either, but rejects his word, and denies his veracity.

Object and Rule of Faith

23. **What means, "all that God has revealed"?**
It means all that God has made known for our salvation by the patriarchs and prophets, and at last by his Son Jesus Christ and the apostles.

"God, who, at sundry times and in divers manners, spoke in times past to the fathers by the prophets, last of all, in these days hath spoken to us by his Son."[56]

[52] See our "Concluding Remarks" of the "Short History of Revealed Religion," p. 151, above.

[53] Jn 3:19

[54] Acts 10:35

[55] Cf. Acts 10

[56] Heb 1:1-2

24. **Was it necessary that God should have revealed to us the truths of salvation, in order that we might know them?**
Yes, because without divine revelation we should have known some of them only with great difficulty, and very imperfectly; and most of them would have remained entirely unknown to us.

"And hardly do we guess aright at things that are upon earth: and with labor do we find the things that are before us. But the things that are in heaven, who shall search out? And who shall know thy thought, except thou give wisdom, and send thy Holy Spirit from above?"[57]

25. **How do we know the truths which God has revealed?**
We know the truths which God has revealed by means of the Catholic Church, which is infallible; that is, by means of the pope, the successor of St. Peter, and by the bishops, the successors of the apostles, who were taught by Christ himself.

26. **Are we certain of the truths which the Church teaches?**
We are most certain of the truths which holy Church teaches, because Jesus Christ has pledged his word that the Church shall never be deceived.

27. **Have not the protestant sects also received their doctrine from Christ himself, and preserved it uncorrupted?**
No; for 1) it is impossible that they should have received it from Christ himself, since they did not begin to exist till long after Christ; and 2) it is equally impossible that they should always have preserved uncorrupted whatever portion of the doctrine of Christ and his apostles may be held among them, because they teach at different times different principles, whereas Christ and the apostles always taught the same.

28. **What, therefore, must the Catholic believe?**
He must believe all that God has revealed and the Catholic Church proposes to his belief, whether it be contained in the holy scripture or not.

[57] Ws 9:16-17

The Church is considered to "propose" a truth to our belief when she recognizes it to be revealed by God, and commands us to believe it.

29. **By what sinful act is faith lost?**
Faith is lost by denying or willfully doubting any single article proposed to us by the Church to be believed.

30. **How is faith regained if it has been lost?**
Faith when lost is regained by repenting of the sin committed and believing anew all that the Church believes and teaches.

31. **If, then, the true faith is essentially necessary to salvation, and the Catholic faith is the only true one, is it not a great grace to be a Catholic Christian?**
To be a Catholic Christian is an invaluable grace, for which we cannot thank God enough, and which we ought most earnestly to turn to our advantage.

Application. Rejoice, and often thank God that you are a child of the Catholic Church; for "there is," as St. Augustine says, "no greater wealth, no greater treasure, than the Catholic faith," provided we live as our faith teaches us. The truth of this is especially felt by Catholics at the hour of death. In matters of faith, never trust your own judgment, but always humbly submit to the decisions of holy Church; for when you believe what the Church teaches, you believe the Word of God.

Mysteries

32. **Can we understand all the truths of faith?**
No; we cannot understand all the truths of faith, because some of them are mysteries.

33. **What are mysteries?**
Mysteries are truths beyond reason, which we cannot completely understand; but we believe them to be.

"The divine mysteries by their own nature so far transcend the created intelligence that, even when delivered by revelation and received by faith, they remain covered with a veil of faith itself, and shrouded in a certain degree of darkness, so long as we are pilgrims in this mortal life, not yet with God: 'for we walk by faith and not by sight.'"[58]

34. **Are mysteries contrary to reason?**
Mysteries are beyond reason, but not contrary to it.

"Although faith is above reason, there can never be any real discrepancy between faith and reason; since the same God who reveals mysteries and infuses faith has bestowed the light of reason on the human mind, and God cannot deny himself, nor can truth contradict truth."[59]

Holy Scripture

35. **Where are the truths revealed of God contained?**
The truths revealed by God are contained in the holy scripture and tradition.

36. **What is the holy scripture?**
The holy scripture is a collection of books which were written by the inspiration of the Holy Ghost, and acknowledged by the Church as the word of God.

"Prophecy came not by the will of man at any time; but the holy men of God spoke, inspired by the Holy Ghost."[60]

37. **How is the holy scripture divided?**
The holy scripture is divided into the books of the old and the new testament, or of the old and the new law.

[58] 2 Cor 5:7; First Vatican Council, *Dogmatic Constitution on the Faith*, Ch. 4, n. 4
[59] First Vatican Council, *Dogmatic Constitution on the Faith*, Ch. 4, n. 5-6
[60] 2 Pt 1:21

38. **What revelations does the old testament contain?**
The old testament contains the divine revelations which were made to man before the coming of Christ.

39. **Of what books does the old testament consist?**
The old testament consists: 1) of twenty-one historical books, which relate the creation of the world, the lives of the patriarchs, and the history of the Jewish nation; 2) of seven moral books, which are collections of psalms, of holy maxims, and of rules of life; and 3) of seventeen prophetical books, which mostly contain prophecies.

The historical books are: the Pentateuch, or five books of Moses (Genesis, Exodus, Leviticus, Numbers, Deuteronomy); the book of Josue; the book of Judges; the book of Ruth; the four books of Kings; the two books of Chronicles or of Paralipomenon; the book of Esdras; the book of Nehemias, which is also called the second of Esdras; the book of Tobias; the book of Judith; the book of Esther; and the two books of the Machabees.

The moral books are: the book of Job; the Psalms; the Proverbs; Ecclesiastes, or the Preacher; the Canticle of Canticles; the book of Wisdom; and Ecclesiasticus, or Jesus, the Son of Sirach.

The prophetical books: Isaias; Jeremias; Baruch; Ezechiel; Daniel; Osee; Joel; Amos; Abdias; Jonas; Micheas; Nahum; Habacuc; Sophonias; Aggeus; Zacharias; and Malachias.

40. **What revelations does the new testament contain?**
The new testament contains the revelations which we have received through Jesus Christ and the apostles.

41. **Of what books does the new testament consist?**
The new testament consists: 1) of the four gospels according to St. Matthew, St. Mark, St. Luke, and St. John, which relate the history of Jesus; 2) of the Acts of the Apostles, by St. Luke; 3) of fourteen epistles of St. Paul, and seven by other apostles, which contain dogmatical and moral instructions; and 4) of the Apocalypse, or the Revelation of St. John, which foretells the combats and victories of the Church.

The epistles of St. Paul are: one to the Romans; two to the Corinthians; one to the Galatians; one to the Ephesians; one to the Philippians; one to the Colossians; two to the Thessalonians; two to Timothy; one to Titus; one to Philemon; and one to the Hebrews.

The other epistles are: one of St. James; two of St. Peter; three of St. John; and one of St. Jude, surnamed Thaddeus.

42. **From whom alone can we know the true sense of holy scripture?**
We can know the true sense of holy scripture from the Church alone; because the Church alone cannot err in interpreting it.

43. **May no one, then, presume to explain the scripture contrary to the interpretation of the Catholic Church?**
No; for this would be as if he understood the scripture better than the Holy Ghost, who inspires the Church with the true meaning of it.

44. **But is the meaning of the holy scripture not clear in itself, and easy to be understood by everyone?**
No; for the holy scripture is a divine and mysterious book, "in which," as St. Peter says, speaking of the epistles of St. Paul, "are certain things hard to be understood, which the unlearned and unstable wrest to their own destruction."[61]

"What else gives rise to so many heresies, save that the scripture, which, good in itself, is ill understood!"[62]

45. **Is it not, then, true that the Bible alone is the only rule of faith? Or, in other words: Is not every private individual to search the Bible, and nothing but the Bible, until he finds out what he has to believe?**
No; for not the Bible alone, but the Bible and tradition, both infallibly interpreted by the Church, are the right rule of faith.

[61] 2 Pt 3:16
[62] Augustine

1. If it were the will of our Savior that we should arrive at the knowledge of the truths of salvation simply by reading and searching the scripture, why is it written: "Faith cometh by hearing, and hearing by the [preaching of the] word of Christ"?[63] And why, then, did not Christ himself write? Why did he not commission his apostles to write? Why did they write only after the lapse of a long space of time, and only upon special occasions? Why did they not all write? Why did he himself "give some apostles, and some prophets, and other some evangelists, and other some pastors and doctors"?[64] Why did he not command that everyone, or at least every Christian, should learn to read? Why did God allow printing to be invented so late? Etc.

2. The Christian religion had been spread, and flourished, before the books of the new testament were written; and even after they had been written, there were many Christian nations, as St. Irenaeus testifies, who did not so much as possess the holy scriptures.

46. **What has the Church decreed with regard to the reading of the Bible in the vulgar tongue?**

1) That we should have the learning and piety requisite for it; and 2) that the translation should be accompanied with explanations, and that both should be approved of by the Church.

By this wise provision the Church by no means intends to withhold the word of God from the faithful, since she desires nothing more than that all should know it and meditate upon it; she merely wishes to guard them against corrupted Bibles, which are often designedly offered to ignorant people, and against erroneous interpretations, sects, and schisms.

[63] Rom 10:17

[64] Eph 4:11; Cf. 1 Cor 12

Tradition

47. **Is it enough to believe only those doctrines which are contained in the holy scripture?**

No; we must also believe tradition—i.e., those revealed truths which the apostles preached, but did not commit to writing.

St. Paul, therefore, exhorts the first Christians by saying: "Therefore, brethren, stand fast: and hold the traditions which you have learned, whether by word or by our epistle."[65]

48. **Have not, then, the apostles written all that Jesus Christ has taught?**

No; the apostles have not even written all that Jesus has done, far less all that he has taught; for Christ did not commission them to write, but to preach his doctrine.[66]

"Many other signs also did Jesus in the sight of his disciples, which are not written in this book."[67]

The Bible, therefore, does not contain the entire revelation of God. The Bible nowhere tells us how many divine books there are, and which they are; if we did not know this for certain from tradition, we should not even have a Bible.—The Bible does not, in doubtful passages, decide upon the true meaning of its words; therefore, all sects have always appealed to the Bible, in order to prove their contradictory doctrines, and each one of them pretended to have hit on its true meaning.—If we would consult the Bible only, without tradition, we ought, for instance, still to keep holy the Saturday with the Jews, instead of Sunday, and to refrain ourselves from things strangled, and from blood;[68] moreover, we ought, with the Anabaptists, to let little children, who are incapable of being instructed, die without baptism, since, according to the mere words of the text, Christ has commanded, first to teach, and then to baptize.[69]

[65] 2 Thes 2:14
[66] Cf. Mk 16:15; Mt 28:19
[67] Jn 20:30
[68] Cf. Acts 15:20
[69] Cf. Mt 28:19

49. **Why is the unwritten doctrine of the apostles called "tradition"?**
It is called "tradition"—that is, "a handing down"—because, since the times of the apostles, it has, without interruption, been handed down in the Catholic Church from generation to generation.

"And the things which thou hast heard of me by many witnesses, the same commend to faithful men, who shall be fit to teach others also."[70]

50. **Where are the teachings of tradition contained?**
The teachings of tradition are contained chiefly in the decrees of the councils, in the writings of the holy fathers, in the acts of the Holy See, and in the words and usages of the sacred liturgy.

51. **What value must be placed on tradition?**
The same value as is placed on the word of God revealed in the holy scripture.

52. **Why must we believe tradition as well as the holy scripture?**
Because tradition is revealed by God just as well as what is contained in holy scripture.

53. **From whom are we to learn the true meaning of tradition?**
From the Church alone, because she alone has received from God the authority and the guidance necessary to interpret infallibly all the doctrine that he has revealed, whether in holy scripture or in tradition.

Qualities of Faith

54. **What must be the qualities of our faith?**
Our faith must be 1) universal; 2) firm; 3) lively; and 4) constant.

[70] 2 Tm 2:2

55. **When is our faith universal?**

Our faith is universal when we believe not only some but all the truths which the Catholic Church proposes to our belief.

56. **Is, then, no one at liberty to admit and believe only some points of the Christian faith?**

No; for 1) Christ says without exception: "Preach the gospel to every creature;...he that believeth not shall be condemned."[71] And again: "Teach them to observe all things whatsoever I have commanded you."[72] And St. John says: "Whosoever revolteth, and continueth not in the doctrine of Christ, hath not God."[73] And 2) he who believes of the doctrine of Christ only what he pleases has no faith at all; for such a one does not believe God, but his own judgment.

57. **When is our faith firm?**

Our faith is firm when we believe without the least doubt.

Examples. Abraham, rewarded for his firm faith: "In the promise of God he staggered not by distrust, but was strengthened in faith;...and therefore it was reputed to him unto justice."[74] Moses and Aaron, punished on account of a doubt.[75]

58. **When is our faith lively?**

Our faith is lively when we live up to it; that is, when we avoid evil, and do good in the manner our faith prescribes.

"As the body without the spirit is dead, so also faith without works is dead."[76]

[71] Mk 16:15-16
[72] Mt 28:20
[73] 2 Jn 1:9
[74] Rom 4:20, 22
[75] Cf. Nm 20:12
[76] Jas 2:26

59. **Will a dead faith also save us?**

No; our faith must prove itself active by charity, or else it is not sufficient for obtaining eternal salvation.

"In Christ Jesus neither circumcision availeth anything, nor uncircumcision; but faith, that worketh by charity."[77] "And if I should have all faith, so that I could remove mountains, and have not charity, I am nothing."[78]

60. **When is our faith constant?**

Our faith is constant when we are ready to lose all, even our life, rather than fall away from it.

"Take heed, brethren, lest perhaps there be in any of you an evil heart of unbelief, to depart from the living God."[79]—*Example* of the holy martyrs.

61. **What leads people to fall away from their faith?**

1) Pride and excessive reasoning on the mysteries of our religion; 2) neglect of prayer and of the other religious duties; 3) worldliness and a wicked life; and 4) reading irreligious books, intercourse with scoffers at religion, and such matrimonial or other connections as endanger the true faith.

"I confess to thee, O Father, Lord of heaven and earth, because thou hast hid these things from the wise and prudent, and hast revealed them to little ones."[80] "The kingdom of God shall be taken from you, and shall be given to a nation yielding the fruits thereof."[81] "Having faith and a good conscience, which some rejecting have made shipwreck concerning the faith."[82] "Beware of false prophets, who come to you in the clothing of sheep, but inwardly they are ravening wolves."[83] "A little leaven corrupteth the whole lump."[84]

[77] Gal 5:6
[78] 1 Cor 13:2
[79] Heb 3:12
[80] Mt 11:25
[81] Mt 21:43
[82] 1 Tm 1:19
[83] Mt 7:15
[84] Gal 5:9

62. **How do we especially show that our faith is firm and constant?**
By never denying it, not even in appearance, but by candidly professing it on every occasion by word and deed.

"Every one that shall confess me before men, I will also confess him before my Father who is in heaven. But he that shall deny me before men, I will also deny him before my Father who is in heaven."[85] "With the heart, we believe unto justice: but, with the mouth, confession is made unto salvation."[86]—*Example* of Eleazar.

63. **Is there also a particular sign by which Catholics profess their faith?**
Yes, the sign of the cross.

64. **Why do we use the sign of the cross in order to profess our faith?**
Because it expresses the two principal mysteries of our religion—namely, the mystery of the most Blessed Trinity, and the mystery of our redemption by Christ on the cross.

65. **Whence comes the custom of making the sign of the cross?**
This custom is very old, and descends from the apostolic times.

66. **When should we make the sign of the cross?**
It is good and wholesome to make it frequently, as the first Christians did; especially when we rise and when we go to bed, before and after prayers, before every important occupation, and in all temptations and dangers.

67. **Why is it wholesome frequently to make the sign of the cross?**
Because, by devoutly making the sign of the cross, we arm ourselves against the snares of the devil, and draw down the blessings of heaven upon us.

[85] Mt 10:32-33
[86] Rom 10:10

68. **Why do we usually make the sign of the cross on our forehead, mouth, and heart, at the reading of the gospel?**
That God, through the merits of Christ crucified, may give us grace to comprehend the gospel with our mind, to profess it with our mouth, and to love it with our heart.

Application. Never be ashamed of the Catholic faith, or of the sign of the cross; let this be your motto: "God forbid that I should glory, save in the cross of our Lord Jesus Christ."[87] Shun most carefully all intercourse with irreligious and wicked persons, and especially beware of such books as might stagger you in the true faith, or lead you astray from the path of virtue.

The Apostles' Creed

69. **Where are the chief things, which we must above all know and believe, briefly contained?**
In the twelve articles of the Apostles' Creed.

70. **Why is it called the "Apostles' Creed"?**
It is called the "Apostles' Creed," because it is an abridgment of the truths of the faith taught by the apostles.

[87] Gal 6:14

THE FIRST ARTICLE

"I believe in God the Father Almighty, Creator of heaven and earth."

On God and His Attributes or Perfections

"I believe in God."

71. **Who is God?**

God is an infinitely perfect Spirit, the Lord of heaven and earth, and the author of all good.

72. **Can we see God?**

No; we cannot see God with corporeal eyes, because he is a Spirit.

73. **How, then, can we come to a knowledge of God?**

God has made himself known to us in two ways; that is, in a natural, and in a supernatural way.

74. **How has God made himself known to man in a natural way?**

1. By the visible world, which he has created and continually governs; for nobody can reasonably think that the world has made itself, or that the regular and perfect order in it originated and subsists by itself. Only "the fool hath said in his heart, 'There is no God.'"[88]

Therefore, St. Paul says of the Gentiles that they are inexcusable, if they do not believe in God: "For the invisible things of him, from the creation of the world, are clearly seen, being understood by the things that are made: his eternal power also, and divinity."[89] "Nevertheless, he left not himself without testimony, doing good from heaven, giving rains and fruitful seasons, filling our hearts with food and gladness."[90]

[88] Ps 13:1
[89] Rom 1:20
[90] Acts 14:16; Cf. Ws 13

2. By the voice of conscience, which admonishes us to dread an invisible avenger of sin, and to hope in a rewarder of virtue.[91]

Conscience has not been made by man. Its action is often so painful that man would prefer, if he could, to be without it. It exists in us by the will of God, who made it an essential part of our human nature, in order that we might be taught by its voice.

75. **How has God made himself known to man in a supernatural manner?**
By the revelation, which he has given us by the prophets, and last of all by his Son.[92]

"No man hath seen God at any time; the only begotten Son who is in the bosom of the Father, he hath declared him."[93]

76. **Why do we say, "I believe in God," and not only, "I believe God"?**
Because we must not only believe that there is a God, and that all that he has said is true; but we must likewise give ourselves up to God with love and confidence.

77. **Why do we call God a Spirit?**
We call God a Spirit because he has understanding and free will, but no body.[94]

78. **And why do we say that "God is infinitely perfect"?**
Because God is not like created beings, good only in some measure, but because he unites in himself all good perfections without measure, or bounds, or number.

79. **Which are the principal attributes or perfections of God?**
These: God is eternal and unchangeable, omnipresent, omniscient or all-knowing, all-wise, all-powerful; he is infinitely holy and just; infinitely good, merciful, and long-suffering; infinitely true and faithful.

[91] Cf. Rom 2:15
[92] See p. 167, q. 23.
[93] Jn 1:18
[94] Cf. Jn 4:24

80. **What means, "God is eternal"?**

"God is eternal" means that he is always without beginning and without end.

"Before the mountains were made, or the earth and the world was formed; from eternity to eternity, thou art God."[95]

81. **What means, "God is unchangeable"?**

"God is unchangeable" means that he remains eternally the same, without any change either in himself or in his decrees.

"With whom [God] there is no change, nor shadow of alteration."[96] "My counsel shall stand, and all my will shall be done."[97]

82. **What ought we to do, since God is eternal and unchangeable?**

We ought to serve and love him forever and ever.

"Thou art the God of my heart, and the God that is my portion for ever."[98]

83. **What means, "God is omnipresent"?**

"God is omnipresent" means that he is everywhere: in heaven, on earth, and in all places.

"Do not I fill heaven and earth? saith the Lord."[99] "God is not far from every one of us; for in him we live, and move, and are."[100] Although God fills all space, nevertheless he is everywhere entire and perfect, and encompassed by no space; for he is immense.

84. **What means, "God is all-knowing"?**

"God is all-knowing" means that he knows all things perfectly and from all eternity; he knows all things past, present, and to come, even our most secret thoughts.

"The eyes of the Lord are far brighter than the sun, beholding round about all the ways of men, and the bottom of the deep, and looking into

[95] Ps 89 2
[96] Jas 1:17
[97] Is 46:10
[98] Ps 72:26
[99] Jer 23:24
[100] Acts 17:27-28

the hearts of men, into the most hidden parts; for all things were known to the Lord God before they were created: so also after they were perfected he beholdeth all things."[101] See the whole Psalm 138.—*Examples*: Predictions of Christ and of the prophets.

85. **What benefit do we derive from the frequent remembrance of God's omnipresence and omniscience?**

1) It keeps us everywhere, even in secret, from evil, and incites us to good; and 2) it gives us courage and consolation in all difficulties and troubles.

"It is better for me to fall into your hands without doing it, than to sin in the sight of the Lord."[102] "That thy alms may be in secret, and thy Father who seeth in secret will repay thee."[103] "Though I should walk in the midst of the shadow of death, I will fear no evils, for thou art with me."[104] "Behold my witness is in heaven, and he that knoweth my conscience is on high."[105]

86. **What means, "God is all-wise"?**

"God is all-wise" means that he knows how to dispose all things in the best manner, in order to attain his end.

"How great are thy works, O Lord! Thou hast made all things in wisdom."[106]—*Examples*: The child Moses saved; Joseph exalted; Aman disgraced.

87. **What means, "God is all-powerful or Almighty"?**

"God is all-powerful" means that he can do anything, and has only to will, and the thing is done.

"Whatsoever the Lord pleased he hath done, in heaven, in earth, in the sea, and in all the deeps."[107] "Because no word shall be impossible with God."[108]—*Examples*: The creation; the wonders in Egypt and in the desert.

[101] Ecclus 23:28-29
[102] Dn 13:23
[103] Mt 6:4
[104] Ps 22:4
[105] Jb 16:20
[106] Ps 103:24
[107] Ps 134:6
[108] Lk 1:37

88. **To what should our belief in God's infinite power and infinite wisdom incite us?**

It should incite us: 1) to place all our confidence in God; and 2) to be always resigned to his dispensations.

1) "Put not your trust...in the children of men, in whom there is no salvation...Blessed is he...whose hope is in the Lord his God."[109]—*Example*: Gedeon. 2) "Commit thy way to the Lord and trust in him and he will do it."[110]—*Example*: Job.

89. **What means, "God is holy"?**

"God is holy" means that he loves and wills only what is good—i.e., what is in accord with his perfections—and that he abhors all that is evil.

"Thou hast loved justice, and bated iniquity."[111]—*Example*: The giving of the law on Mount Sinai.

90. **What means, "God is just"?**

"God is just" means that he rewards and punishes men according to their deserts.

"He will render to every man according to his works:...for there is no respect of person with God."[112]—*Examples*: The world punished by the deluge, and Sodom and Gomorrha destroyed by fire from heaven; but Noe and Lot preserved.

91. **When will perfect retribution be made?**

1) Perfect retribution will not be made until the soul is in the other world; 2) there is, however, even in this life, no true happiness for the wicked, 3) and no true unhappiness for the just.

1) Parable of the cockle and the wheat;[113] of the rich man and Lazarus.[114] 2) "We wearied ourselves in the way of iniquity and destruction, and

[109] Ps 145:2-3, 5
[110] Ps 36:5
[111] Ps 44:8
[112] Rom 2:6, 11
[113] Cf. Mt 13:30
[114] Cf. Lk 16

have walked through hard ways."[115]—*Examples*: Cain, Absalom, Achab, Antiochus. 3) "The souls of the just are in the hand of God."[116]—*Examples*: Joseph, Tobias, Susanna, Daniel, St. Paul.[117]

92. **To what should the remembrance of God's holiness and justness animate us?**
It should animate us: 1) carefully to avoid all evil, and to become more and more holy; and 2) not to pride ourselves in our pretended righteousness.

"Fear ye not them that kill the body, and are not able to kill the soul: but rather fear him that can destroy both soul and body into hell."[118] "I am the Lord your God: be holy, because I am holy."[119] "I am not conscious to myself of anything, yet I am not hereby justified; but he that judgeth me is the Lord."[120]

93. **What means, "God is good"?**
"God is good" means that out of love he will do good to all creatures, and that he really bestows innumerable blessings upon us.

"Thou lovest all things that are, and hatest none of the things which thou hast made."[121] "Thus saith the Lord: Can a woman forget her infant, so as not to have pity on the son of her womb? And if she should forget, yet will not I forget thee."[122]

94. **Which is the greatest proof of God's love and goodness?**
That he delivered his own Son up to death for the salvation of us sinners.

"God is charity. By this hath the charity of God appeared toward us, because God hath sent his only begotten Son into the world, that we may live by him."[123]

[115] Ws 5:7
[116] Ws 3:1
[117] Cf. 2 Cor 7:4
[118] Mt 10:28
[119] Lv 11:44
[120] 1 Cor 4:4
[121] Ws 11:25
[122] Is 49:15
[123] 1 Jn 4:8-9

95. **What means, "God is merciful"?**

"God is merciful" means that he is disposed to avert all evil from his creatures, and therefore willingly pardons all truly penitent sinners.

"The mercy of God is upon all flesh."[124] "As I live, saith the Lord God, I desire not the death of the wicked, but that the wicked turn from his way, and live."[125]—*Examples*: The Ninivites; parable of the prodigal son.[126]

96. **What means, "God is long-suffering"?**

"God is long-suffering" means that he often waits a long time before he punishes the sinner, in order to give him time for repentance.

"Thou overlookest the sins of men for the sake of repentance."[127]—*Examples*: Manasses;[128] Jerusalem;[129] parable of the barren fig tree.[130]

97. **What should we do, since God is so good, so merciful, and so long-suffering?**

We should: 1) be thankful to God, and love him with all our heart; 2) when we have sinned, we should with confidence beg pardon of him; and 3) we should be good and merciful to our neighbors.

1) "Give glory to the Lord, for he is good; for his mercy endureth for ever."[131]—*Examples*: Ingratitude of the Israelites in the desert punished. 2) "I will arise and will go to my father."[132] 3) "Be ye therefore merciful, as your Father also is merciful."[133]—*Example*: Parable of the unmerciful servant.[134]

124 Ecclus 18:12; Cf. Jon 4:11
125 Ez 33:11
126 Cf. Lk 15
127 Ws 11:24
128 Cf. 2 Par 33
129 Cf. Mt 23:37
130 Cf. Lk 13
131 Ps 106:1
132 Lk 15:18
133 Lk 6:36
134 Cf. Mt 18

98. **What means, "God is true"?**

"God is true" means that he can neither err nor lie, and can reveal nothing but truth.

"It is impossible for God to lie."[135]

99. **What means, "God is faithful"?**

"God is faithful" means that he surely keeps his promises, and executes what he threatens.

"And thou shalt know the Lord thy God, he is a strong and faithful God, keeping his covenant and mercy to them that love him,...and repaying forthwith them that hate him, so as to destroy them."[136]

100. **What does the truth and faithfulness of God oblige us to do?**

1) To believe most firmly in the word of God, and steadfastly to trust in his promise; and 2) always to speak the truth, and to keep the promise we have made.

1) "Blessed are they that have not seen, and have believed."[137]—*Examples*: Abraham. 2) Punishment of Ananias and Saphira.[138]

Application. "My son, give me thy heart."[139] Oh! give it to him, the Eternal, the infinitely perfect, rich, good, and faithful God, without delay, forever and ever. God alone has a right to possess it, and he alone has the power to render it happy through all eternity.

On the Three Divine Persons

"I believe in God the Father."

101. **Why do we say, "I believe in God the Father"?**

1) Because God is our invisible Father in heaven; and 2) because in God there is more than one Person, the first of whom is called the Father.

135 Heb 6:18
136 Dt 7:9-10
137 Jn 20:29
138 Cf. Acts 5
139 Prv 23:26

102. **How many Persons are, then, in God?**
There are three Persons in God: the Father, the Son, and the Holy Ghost.

"Going therefore, teach ye all nations; baptizing them in the name of the Father, and of the Son, and of the Holy Ghost."[140] "There are three who give testimony in heaven, the Father, the Word, and the Holy Ghost, and these three are one."[141]

103. **Is each one of the three Persons God?**
Yes, the Father is true God, the Son is true God, and the Holy Ghost is true God.

104. **Why are the three Persons but one God?**
Because all three Persons have one and the same indivisible nature and substance.

105. **Is any one of these Persons older, or more powerful, than the others?**
No; all three Persons are from eternity; all three are equally powerful, good, and perfect; because all three are but one God.

106. **Is there, then, no distinction at all between the Father, the Son, and the Holy Ghost?**
As to the Persons, they are distinct; but as to the substance, they are one.

107. **How are the three divine Persons distinct from one another?**
By this: that the Father is begotten of no one, nor proceeds from anyone; the Son is begotten of the Father; and the Holy Ghost proceeds from the Father and the Son.

[140] Mt 28:19
[141] 1 Jn 5:7

108. **But if the Son is begotten of the Father, and the Holy Ghost proceeds from both, why, then, is none of the divine Persons older than the others?**
Because the Son is begotten from all eternity, and the Holy Ghost also proceeds from all eternity.

109. **Why is the Father called the "first," the Son the "second," and the Holy Ghost the "third" Person?**
They are so called, not to show any superiority, but the order in which the one proceeds from the other from all eternity.

110. **What works are principally attributed to each of the three divine Persons?**
1) To the Father are attributed the works of omnipotence, and particularly the creation; 2) to the Son, the works of wisdom, and particularly the redemption; and 3) to the Holy Ghost, the works of love, and particularly sanctification; although these works are common to all three Persons.

The works of omnipotence and creation are particularly attributed to the Father, because he is the principle to which the two other Persons owe their eternal origin. The works of wisdom to the Son, because the Father begets the Son by the knowledge of himself, wherefore the Son is also called the essential "Image," the eternal "Word" of the Father. The works of love are attributed to the Holy Ghost, because he proceeds from the mutual love of the Father and of the Son.

111. **What do we call the mystery of one God in three Persons?**
We call it the mystery of the most Blessed Trinity.

112. **Can we comprehend this mystery?**
No; it is impossible that our weak and limited intellect, which cannot understand even created things except imperfectly, should understand a mystery which is infinitely above all created things.

"Great art thou in counsel, and incomprehensible in thought."[142] "For we know in part...We see now through a glass in a dark manner."[143] However incomprehensible this mystery may be, yet it does not contradict any of the truths acknowledged by reason; for we do not say that God has one nature and three natures, but that, though he has but one nature, yet there are three Persons in him. The unity refers to the nature, and the trinity to the Persons. (Comparison with the soul, which has memory, will, and understanding.)

113. **Is the doctrine of the most Holy Trinity also important to us?**

Yes, it is most important; for it is the principal and fundamental doctrine of Christianity, insomuch that to reject it would be to deny the Christian faith.

Application. That the grace of this saving faith may not be withdrawn from you, never forget what thanks you owe to the most Blessed Trinity for the inestimable benefits of your creation, redemption, and sanctification, and what you have solemnly promised to the same Trinity in the holy sacrament of baptism.[144]

On the Creation and Government of the World

"Creator of heaven and earth."

114. **Why is God called "Creator of heaven and earth"?**

Because God created—i.e., made out of nothing—the whole world, the heavens and the earth, and all that is in them.

115. **How has God created the whole world?**

By his almighty will.

"Thou hast created all things; and for thy will they were and have been created."[145]

[142] Jer 32:19
[143] 1 Cor 13:9, 12
[144] Feast of the Blessed Trinity
[145] Apoc 4:11

116. **Did God create the world because he needed it?**

No; God is infinitely rich and happy in himself, and needs nothing besides himself.

"Thou art my God, for thou hast no need of my goods."[146]

117. **If God needs nothing besides himself, why did he create other beings?**

He created them because he is infinitely good, and desired to impart his goodness also to other beings.

"We are, because God is good."[147] "God was not impelled to create by any other cause than a desire to communicate to creatures the riches of his bounty."[148]

118. **Did, then, God create the world for his creatures?**

No; God created the world for himself—that is, for his glory—but, nevertheless, for the good of his creatures.

"The Lord hath made all things for himself."[149] "And every one that calleth upon my name, I have created him for my glory, I have formed him, and made him."[150]

119. **What does God still do, that the world which he has created may not return into its original nothing?**

He preserves and governs it.

120. **How does God preserve the world?**

By the same power of his will with which he created the world he causes it also to continue, in the manner he pleases, and as long as he pleases.

"How could anything endure, if thou wouldst not?"[151]

146 Ps 15:2

147 Augustine, *On Christian Doctrine*, Bk. 1, Ch. 32, n. 35

148 *Catechism of the Council of Trent*. Editor's note: See p. 60 of Volume VII of this series.

149 Prv 16:4

150 Is 43:7

151 Ws 11:26

121. **How does God govern the world?**

1) He takes care of all things, 2) orders all things, and, in his wisdom and goodness, directs all things to the end for which he has created the world.

1) "God made the little and the great, and he hath equally care of all."[152] "But the very hairs of your head are all numbered."[153] 2) "She [the wisdom of God] reacheth therefore from end to end mightily, and ordereth all things sweetly."[154]—*Example*: Deliverance of the Jews through Esther.

122. **What do we call this supreme care of God in preserving and governing the world?**

His divine providence.

123. **But if God orders and directs all things in the world, why, then, is there so much evil done? Does he will it?**

No, God wills not the evil; but he permits it: 1) because he has created man free; and 2) because he knows also how to turn evil into good.

Examples: The history of Joseph in Egypt: "You thought evil against me; but God turned it into good."[155] Thus God, the Almighty, turned even the murder of our Savior by the Jews to the salvation of the world, and the impenitence of the same Jews to the conversion of the heathens. And thus he still avails himself every day of the designs of the wicked in order to glorify his Church; "for there is no wisdom, there is no prudence, there is no counsel against the Lord."[156]

124. **And if God takes care of all things, why are we subject to so many sufferings?**

1) That the sinner may acknowledge the chastisement of God and mend his ways, and not perish forever; and 2) that the just man may be more and more purified, and more abound in merits, and thus obtain a greater reward in heaven.

[152] Ws 6:8
[153] Mt 10:30
[154] Ws 8:1
[155] Gn 50:20
[156] Prv 21:30

1) *Examples*: The brothers of Joseph: "We deserve to suffer these things, because we have sinned against our brother."[157] Manasses;[158] Jonas.[159] 2) "Gold and silver are tried in the fire, but acceptable men in the furnace of humiliation."[160] "Blessed are ye when they shall revile you, and persecute you, and speak all that is evil against you, untruly, for my sake. Be glad and rejoice, for your reward is very great in heaven."[161]

125. **But why does God often permit the wicked to prosper, whilst evil befalls the good?**

1) Because he will not only deter the sinner from his evil ways by punishment, but will also win him by benefits; 2) because he reserves to himself to punish the wicked, and to reward the good, especially in eternity; and 3) because he will not even leave the little good which the wicked may do entirely unrewarded, and, therefore, as he cannot reward it in the next world on account of their impenitence, he will reward it here below.

1) "What is there that I ought to do more to my vineyard that I have not done to it? Was it that I looked that it should bring forth grapes, and it hath brought forth wild grapes?"[162] 2) "The Lord patiently expecteth, that when the day of judgment shall come, he may punish them in the fullness of their sins."[163] 3) "Woe to you that are rich; for you have your consolation";[164] that is, your reward here in this world.—*Example*: Achab: "Because Achab hath humbled himself for my sake, I will not bring the evil in his days."[165]

157 Gn 42:21
158 Cf. 2 Par 33
159 Cf. Jon 2
160 Ecclus 2:5
161 Mt 5:11-12
162 Is 5:4, 2
163 2 Mc 6:14
164 Lk 6:24
165 3 Kgs 21:29

126. **How ought we to receive the sufferings that come upon us?**

We ought to receive them as graces of God; for "whom the Lord loveth he chastiseth";[166] and "before he be glorified, it [his heart] is humbled."[167]

"For it is a token of great goodness when sinners are not suffered to go on in their ways for a long time, but are presently punished."[168]

Application. "Cast all your care upon the Lord, for he hath care of you."[169] "Behold the birds of the air, for they neither sow, nor do they reap, nor gather into barns, and your heavenly Father feedeth them. Consider the lilies of the field,"[170] etc. Take willingly everything that is disagreeable to you as coming from the hand of God: "As it hath pleased the Lord, so is it done; blessed be the name of the Lord";[171] and never be so rash as to complain of the dispensations of God. Whatever may come, "to them that love God, all things work together unto good."[172]

On the Angels

127. **Has God created nothing else but the visible world?**

God has also created an invisible world—namely, innumerable spirits called angels.[173]

The angels are divided into nine different orders or choirs—namely, angels, archangels, virtues, powers, principalities, dominations, thrones, cherubim, and seraphim.[174]

128. **In what state were the angels when God had created them?**

They were all good and happy, and endowed with excellent gifts.

[166] Heb 12:6
[167] Prv 18:12
[168] 2 Mc 6:13
[169] 1 Pt 5:7
[170] Mt 6:26-33
[171] Jb 1:21
[172] Rom 8:28
[173] Cf. Dn 7:10
[174] Cf. Col 1:16; Eph 1:21; Ez 10; Is 6:2

129. **Did the angels all remain good and happy?**

No, many rebelled against God; therefore they were cast away from him forever, and hurled into hell.

"God spared not the angels that sinned, but delivered them, drawn down by infernal ropes to the lower hell, unto torments."[175]

130. **How has God rewarded the angels that remained faithful?**

He has rewarded them with eternal happiness, which consists in seeing and possessing him everlastingly.

"Their angels in heaven always see the face of my Father who is in heaven."[176]

131. **How are the good angels affected toward us?**

The good angels love us; therefore, they protect us in soul and body, pray for us, and exhort us to do good.

"He hath given his angels charge over thee, to keep thee in all thy ways."[177]—*Examples*: Agar, Lot, Tobias, Judas Machabeus;[178] Peter in prison; Cornelius the centurion.

132. **How do we call those angels who are particularly given to man for his protection?**

Guardian angels.

133. **What is our duty toward our guardian angels?**

We must venerate them with great devotion, be thankful to them, and readily follow their admonitions.

"Behold I will send my angel, who shall go before thee…Take notice of him, and hear his voice, and do not think him one to be contemned."[179]

[175] 2 Pt 2:4; Cf. Jude 1:6
[176] Mt 18:10
[177] Ps 90:11
[178] Cf. 2 Mc 10:29-30
[179] Ex 23:20-21

134. **How are the fallen or wicked angels affected toward us?**

The wicked angels, through hatred and envy, lay snares for us, in order to injure us in soul and body, and, by enticing us to sin, to plunge us into eternal perdition.

"Your adversary the devil, as a roaring lion, goeth about seeking whom he may devour."[180]—*Examples*: Eve, Job, Sara, the demoniacs, Judas.[181]

135. **Why does God permit the wicked angels to lay snares for us?**

He permits it because he knows how to make their snares serve unto his own honor and to the salvation of men.

"And they talked among themselves, saying: 'What word is this, for with authority and power he [Jesus] commandeth the unclean spirits, and they go out?' And the fame of him was published into every place of the country."[182] "And the people with one accord were attentive to those things which were said by Philip, hearing and seeing the miracles which he did. For many of them had unclean spirits, who, crying with a loud voice, went out."[183]

136. **What must we do on our part, in order that the snares of the wicked angels may serve to our salvation?**

We must fight against them full of faith and confidence, making use at the same time of the arms of prayer, and availing ourselves of the blessings sanctioned by the Church; and we must firmly resist all temptations to evil.

"For our wrestling is not [only] against flesh and blood; but against... the spirits of wickedness in the high places,"[184] i.e., in the air. "In all things taking the shield of faith, wherewith you may be able to extinguish all the fiery darts of the most wicked one."[185] "Resist the devil, and he will fly from you."[186]—*Example*: Tobias and Sara.[187]

180 1 Pt 5:8
181 See also Lk 8:12 and Apoc 12.
182 Lk 4:36-37
183 Acts 8:6-7
184 Eph 6:12
185 Eph 6:16
186 Jas 4:7
187 Cf. Tb 6:16-19; 8:4-10

Application. Beware of being like the evil spirits by sinning, or of being even their accomplice in seducing others to sin. Imitate the good angels; be innocent, docile, pious, devout, and always ready to promote the welfare of your neighbor. Daily venerate your guardian angel, and recommend yourself to him in all dangers of soul and body.[188]

Man and His Fall[189]

137. **How did God make the first man, Adam?**
God formed a body of the slime of the earth, and breathed an immortal soul into it; and the first man was made.[190]

138. **How did God distinguish man at his creation from all other creatures?**
By creating him to his own image.[191]

139. **How was the first man the image of God?**
By this: that he was endowed with natural and supernatural gifts, which made him resemble God.

140. **In what do the natural gifts consist?**
Especially in this: that the human soul is an immortal spirit, endowed with understanding and free will.

141. **In what do the supernatural gifts consist?**
Especially in this: 1) that the first man possessed sanctifying grace, and together with it the sonship of God, and the right of inheriting the kingdom of heaven; 2) that in him the senses never rebelled against reason; and 3) that he was never to be subjected to hardships and sufferings, nor to death.

[188] Feast of the Holy Guardian Angels
[189] See "Short History of Revealed Religion," p. 102, above.
[190] Cf. Gn 2:7
[191] Cf. Gn 1:27

142. **Why are the latter called "supernatural gifts"?**
They are called "supernatural gifts" because they do not belong to our nature, but are extraordinary and free gifts of God.

143. **Did our first parents receive this divine free gift for themselves alone?**
They received it also for all their descendants; and therefore, according to God's dispensation, not only their natural, but also their supernatural gifts were to descend to the whole human race.

144. **On what condition did they receive these supernatural gifts for themselves and their descendants?**
On condition that they should remain faithful and obedient to God.[192]

145. **Did our first parents observe this condition?**
No; they fell into sin.[193]

146. **What was the sin of Adam?**
The sin of Adam was a sin of pride and grave disobedience.

147. **Was this transgression a grievous sin?**
Yes, it was a very grievous sin; for though they were filled with the knowledge of God, yet they believed the serpent (which is the devil[194]) more than God, rebelled against him, and wanted to be like God.[195]

148. **What punishment came upon Adam and Eve?**
1) They forfeited all their supernatural gifts, and at the same time were also weakened in the faculties of their souls; 2) they were expelled from paradise, in which God had placed them; and 3) they became liable to eternal damnation.

[192] Cf. Gn 2:17
[193] Cf. Gn 3:6
[194] Cf. Apoc 20:2
[195] Cf. Gn 3

149. **Did our first parents lose these supernatural gifts for themselves only?**
No; as by their obedience they would have preserved them not only for themselves, but for all their descendants, so by their disobedience they lost them not only for themselves, but also for us all, and have thereby plunged the whole human race into the greatest misery.

150. **In what does the misery consist into which our first parents have plunged the whole human race?**
In this: that sin, with its fatal consequences, has passed from Adam to all mankind, insomuch that we now all come into this world infected with sin.

"By one man sin entered into this world, and by sin death; and so death passed upon all men, in whom all have sinned."[196] "Behold, I was conceived in iniquities; and in sins did my mother conceive me."[197] The Blessed Virgin Mary alone was, by a particular grace and privilege, perfectly preserved, through the merits of Jesus Christ, not only from all actual sin, but also from every stain of original sin. This privilege is called the "immaculate conception," which was defined as a dogma of faith by Pope Pius IX, December 8, 1854. The modern devotion to the miraculous shrine at Lourdes is closely associated with this doctrine. By decree of the First Council of Baltimore in 1846, the Immaculate Conception was chosen as the patronal feast of the United States.

151. **What do we call this sin in which we are all born?**
We call it "original sin," because we have not actually committed it, but have inherited it from our first parents, who were the origin or source of all mankind.

152. **Is original sin, though not actually committed by us, nevertheless truly sin?**
Yes, it is the death of the soul—it is truly and properly sin.[198]

Owing to the sin of Adam, the entire human race lost its original sanctity and righteousness—i.e., sanctifying grace—and all the supernatural

[196] Rom 5:12
[197] Ps 50:7
[198] Cf. Council of Trent, Session 5, "Decree concerning Original Sin"

gifts which were intended for it. "We all...were by nature children of wrath," because "we were dead in sin."[199]

153. **What fatal consequences have, with original sin, passed to all men?**

1) Their disgrace with God, and at the same time their loss of the sonship of God, and of the right of inheriting the kingdom of heaven;[200] 2) ignorance, concupiscence, and proneness to evil; and 3) all sorts of hardships, pains, calamities, and at last death.

1) "Unless a man be born again of water and the Holy Ghost, he cannot enter into the kingdom of God."[201] 2) "I see another law in my members, fighting against the law of my mind."[202] "The imagination and thought of man's heart are prone to evil from his youth."[203] 3) "Great labor is created for all men, and a heavy yoke is upon the children of Adam, from the day of their birth until the day of their burial."[204] "God created man incorruptible;...but by the envy of the devil death came into the world."[205] This doctrine of divine revelation is confirmed by experience, and by the sad history of mankind.[206]

154. **Did the fatal consequences of sin fall upon man only?**

The punishment of God was also inflicted upon the earth, which had been created for man.

"Cursed is the earth in thy work," said God to Adam, "with labor and toil shalt thou eat thereof all the days of thy life. Thorns and thistles shall it bring forth to thee."[207]

199 Eph 2:3, 5
200 See Eph 2:3.
201 Jn 3:5
202 Rom 7:23
203 Gn 8:21
204 Ecclus 40:1
205 Ws 2:23-24
206 Cf. Rom 7:18-24
207 Gn 3:17-18

155. **What would have become of man, if God had not shown him mercy?**
No one could have received grace and been saved.

156. **Why could no one have anymore received grace?**
Because the divine justice demanded a satisfaction adequate to the sin; and no creature, but least of all man, who had fallen so deeply, was able to give such satisfaction.

157. **How did God show mercy to man?**
He promised him a Savior, who, by a full satisfaction, should take sin away from him, and regain for him grace and the right of inheriting the kingdom of heaven.[208]

"Therefore, as by the offense of one [Adam], judgment came unto all men to condemnation; so also by the justice of one [Christ], grace came unto all men to justification of life;...that as sin hath reigned to death, so also grace might reign by justice unto life everlasting."[209]

158. **If without the grace of the Redeemer no one can be saved, how then could those who lived before the coming of Christ go to heaven?**
Those who lived before the coming of the Redeemer of the world could not indeed enter heaven before him; but with the grace which God gave them on account of the Redeemer to come, they could merit the kingdom of heaven, and then enter into it with him.

The whole of the old testament bears witness of the many eminent graces which God gave to the Israelites, and to the just who lived under the patriarchal law.[210]

159. **Did God give grace also to the pagans for the salvation of their souls?**
Yes; he manifested himself also to the pagans, and in many ways exhorted them to repentance and amendment: 1) by the voice of conscience; 2) by natural benefits; 3) by his judgments; 4) by extraordinary men whom he

[208] Cf. Gn 3:15
[209] Rom 5:18, 21
[210] See "Short History of Revealed Religion," p. 103–108, above.

raised among them or sent to them; 5) by the Israelites whom, with their holy books, he dispersed among them; and 6) sometimes also by angels, dreams, wonderful apparitions, or events.

1) "Who [the Gentiles] show the work of the law written in their hearts, their conscience bearing witness to them."[211] 2) "He left not himself without testimony, doing good from heaven, giving rains and fruitful seasons,"[212] etc. 3) *Examples*: Deluge; punishment of Sodom, of Egypt, of Chanaan, and of other places.[213] 4) *Examples*: Job, Balaam, Jonas, Daniel, etc. 5) "He hath therefore scattered you [Israelites] among the Gentiles, who know not him, that you may declare his wonderful works, and make them known that there is no other Almighty God besides him."[214] 6) Cornelius, the centurion, was advised by an angel;[215] Nabuchodonosor, by dreams;[216] Baltassar, by a mysterious hand;[217] Balaam, by an ass.[218]

160. **Did the Redeemer come immediately after the fall of our first parents?**
No; a long period elapsed: and meanwhile mankind learned by experience into what great misery sin had plunged them, and that no one but God could save them.

Application. My child, be a beautiful image of God and hate sin, which has brought all evils into the world. "Sin maketh nations miserable."[219]

[211] Rom 2:15
[212] Acts 14:16
[213] Cf. Ws 12; 16-18
[214] Tb 13:4
[215] Cf. Acts 10:3
[216] Cf. Dn 2:4
[217] Cf. Dn 5
[218] Cf. Nm 22:22, 28-30
[219] Prv 14:34

THE SECOND ARTICLE

"And in Jesus Christ, his only Son, our Lord."

161. **What does this second article of the Creed teach us?**

It teaches us that the Redeemer whom God promised and sent to us is the only Son of God, Jesus Christ, our Lord.

162. **What does the name *Jesus* signify?**

The name *Jesus* signifies "Savior" or "Redeemer."

"Thou shalt call his name Jesus; for he shall save his people from their sins."[220]

163. **What does the word *Christ* signify?**

The word *Christ*—in Hebrew, *Messias*—signifies "Anointed."

164. **Why is Jesus called "the Anointed"?**

Because, in the old law, the prophets, high priests, and kings were anointed with oil, and Jesus is our greatest prophet,[221] priest,[222] and King.[223]

"Jesus of Nazareth; how God anointed him with the Holy Ghost, and with power."[224] The anointing of Jesus is the plenitude of the divinity that dwells in him.

165. **Why is Jesus called "our prophet," "priest," and "King"?**

Jesus is called, and is: 1) our prophet, because he revealed the mysteries of God to us, and taught us all that we are to believe, to hope, and to do in order to be saved; 2) our priest, because he offered himself for us on the cross, and offers himself daily on the altar, and is also our mediator and intercessor forever in heaven; and 3) our King, because he established a

220 Mt 1:21
221 Cf. Acts 3:22
222 Cf. Heb 4:14
223 Cf. Jn 18:37
224 Acts 10:38

spiritual kingdom (the Church) of which he is, and will be through all eternity, the head.

166. **Why is Jesus Christ called the "only Son of God"?**
Because Jesus Christ, as the second Person of the most Blessed Trinity, is the only true and real Son of God—i.e., Son of God from eternity, of one nature and substance with God the Father.

"To which of the angels hath he said at any time: 'Thou art my Son, today [i.e., at present, from eternity] have I begotten thee'?"[225] The Catholic Church has, in the Ecumenical Council of Nice, expressed this fundamental doctrine of the Christian religion, "respecting the one nature and substance of Jesus Christ with God the Father," in the following terms: "I believe in one Lord Jesus Christ, the only begotten Son of God, and born of the Father before all ages; God of God, light of light, true God of true God; begotten, not made; consubstantial with the Father, by whom all things were made."

167. **Are we not, then, also children of God?**
Yes, we are children of God, but not by nature and from all eternity; we are only children adopted by grace.

"As many as received him, he gave them power to be made the sons of God."[226]

168. **Why is Jesus Christ called "our Lord"?**
Jesus Christ is called, and is, our Lord: 1) as God, because, being one with the Father, he is like him, Lord and Creator of heaven and earth; and 2) as man, because in the human nature, he has redeemed us, and therefore bought us with his blood as his property; and because, in the same nature, he will be one day our judge, and our head and King through all eternity.

[225] Heb 1:5
[226] Jn 1:12

"For you are bought with a great price."[227] "It is he who was appointed by God, to be judge of the living and of the dead."[228] "And he [God] hath subjected all things under his feet, and hath made him head over all this Church."[229]

Application. Constantly cherish the most ardent love and devotion to Jesus, "in whose name every knee should bow, of those that are in heaven, on earth, and under the earth."[230] Often invoke, with the greatest veneration and confidence, this holy name, especially in times of temptation. Take a delight in using this beautiful form of salutation: "Praised be Jesus Christ forevermore. Amen."[231]

This mode of saluting one another is quite common in Germany and Switzerland. An indulgence of one hundred days has been granted by Sixtus V in 1587, and by Benedict XIII in 1728, to those who salute each other, the one saying, "Praised be Jesus Christ," and the other answering, "Amen," or "Forevermore. Amen." To those who have generally used this form of salutation during their life, a plenary indulgence is granted at the hour of death. The same indulgences are imparted to those who teach others this holy practice.

Jesus Christ, the Promised Messias

169. **How do we know that Jesus Christ is the Messias or Redeemer promised by God?**

We know it because in him has been fulfilled all that the prophets have foretold of the Redeemer, as may be seen in the life and sufferings of Christ.[232]

170. **What have the prophets foretold of the Messias?**

1) The time of his coming, the circumstances of his birth, of his life, passion, and death; 2) his resurrection and ascension, and the sending down

[227] 1 Cor 6:20
[228] Acts 10:42
[229] Eph 1:22
[230] Phil 2:10
[231] Feast of the Holy Name of Jesus
[232] On the prophets, see "Short History of Revealed Religion," p. 107–108, above.

of the Holy Ghost; 3) the destruction of Jerusalem, which happened after his death; the rejection of the Jews, and the conversion of the Gentiles; and 4) the founding, spreading, and duration of his Church.

171. **How did they indicate the time of his coming?**
The prophet Daniel[233] foretold that not quite seventy weeks of years—i.e., 490 years—should elapse from the time when it was commanded that Jerusalem should be rebuilt, until the death of Christ; 2) Jacob prophesied that, at the time of the coming of the Messias, the scepter should have been taken away from Juda. Others again foretold that then the Temple of Jerusalem should still exist, and the world be in great expectation. And all this was exactly fulfilled in Jesus.[234]

172. **What did they prophesy of his birth?**
That he should be born at Bethlehem of a Virgin, of the tribe of Juda and family of David, and should be adored by kings from distant countries.[235]

173. **What account do they give us of his life?**
They give us an account of his public teaching, of his miraculous cures, of his forbearing charity and meekness, of his entering into Jerusalem upon an ass, etc.[236]

174. **What do they relate of his passion and death?**
They relate almost all, even the least circumstances; for example, that they would sell him for thirty pieces of silver;[237] strike him, pull out his hair, spit in his face;[238] give him gall and vinegar to drink;[239] pierce his hands and feet, and cast lots for his garment;[240] that those who should see him

233 Cf. Dn 9:24; etc.
234 See "Short History of Revealed Religion," p. 104 and 108, above.
235 Cf. Is 7:14; 11:1; 60:6; Mi 5:2; Ps 71:10
236 Cf. Is 61; 35:3; etc.; Zac 9:9
237 Cf. Zac 11:12-13
238 Cf. Is 50:6
239 Cf. Ps 68:22
240 Cf. Ps 21:17, 19

would mock him, and wag their heads, saying: "He hoped in the Lord, let him deliver him."[241]

The prophets did indeed promise a great King, but not a king of this world, as the Jews are still expecting; otherwise, they would not have described him as "a man of sorrows,"[242] nor called him the "reproach of men, and the outcast of the people";[243] but a King of a spiritual and supernatural kingdom of God (the Church), which was indeed to begin and spread on earth, but is to be consummated only in heaven, and to last forever.

175. **What do they say of his resurrection and ascension, and of his sending down the Holy Ghost?**
They say that his sepulchre shall be glorious, and that he shall not see corruption, but shall mount above the heaven of heavens, and pour out his Spirit upon all flesh.[244]

176. **What did the prophets foretell of the destruction of Jerusalem and of the rejecting of the Jews?**
1) After the Messias shall have been slain, a people with their leader shall come, and destroy Jerusalem and the Temple, and the desolation shall continue even to the consummation, and to the end;[245] 2) the Jews, blinded, rejected, dispersed among all nations, shall have no longer a sacrifice nor a temple; however, they shall not be extirpated by God, but the remnant may be saved at the end of the world.[246]

177. **What did they prophesy of the conversion of the Gentiles, and of the foundation, spreading, and duration of the Church?**
All that we see already accomplished, or being accomplished. They prophesied: 1) that the Messias shall be the light of the Gentiles, and that all

[241] Ps 21:8-9
[242] Is 53:3-4
[243] Ps 21:7
[244] Cf. Is 11:10; Ps 15:10; 67:19, 34; Jl 2:28-29
[245] Cf. Dn 9:26-27
[246] Cf. Ps 68:24-26; 108; Is 10:21; 59:20. How this was accomplished, see "Short History of Revealed Religion," p. 115–116, above.

nations of the earth shall be blessed in him;[247] and 2) that he shall establish a new sacrifice and a new priesthood, and found a kingdom of God, that shall reach from sea to sea to the end of the earth, and shall never be destroyed, but stand forever.[248]

178. **Did the prophets prophesy long before the coming of Christ?**
Malachias, the last of the prophets, prophesied 450 years before Christ.

179. **Were their prophecies also known long before Christ?**
Yes; they had already been written many centuries before Christ, and were preserved and read by the Jews as divine writings; they were also translated into other languages, and spread among the pagan nations.

180. **Did not also Christ and the apostles appeal to the testimony of the prophets?**
Yes; Christ and the apostles proved to the Jews from the writings of the prophets that the Messias was come, and that he himself—Jesus of Nazareth—was the Messias.

"Search the scriptures," said Jesus to the Jews, "and the same are they that give testimony of me."[249] He convinced also the unbelieving disciples from the prophets.[250] St. Peter convinced by the prophecies the three thousand and the five thousand who were baptized.[251] St. Paul protested before King Agrippa, saying: "Being aided by the help of God, I stand unto this day, witnessing both to small and great, saying no other thing than those which the prophets and Moses did say should come to pass."[252] The evangelists, in their narrative, always refer to the prophets. It is also said of Apollo: "With much vigor he convinced the Jews openly, showing by the scriptures that Jesus is the Christ"—i.e., the promised Messias.[253]

[247] Cf. Gn 22:18; Ps 71; Is 42:6; etc.
[248] Cf. Mal 1:11; Is 66:21; Jer 3:15; Zac 9:10; Dn 2:44; 7:14; etc.
[249] Jn 5:39
[250] Cf. Lk 24:25-27, 44-47
[251] Cf. Acts 2-3
[252] Acts 26:22
[253] Cf. Acts 18:23

181. **Do we see nothing else fulfilled in Christ but the prophecies?**
We see also in him the fulfillment of all the figures by which the deeds and sufferings of the Messias were indicated many centuries before.

182. **Which are the most remarkable figures of the Messias?**
1) His passion and death were prefigured by Abel, Isaac, Joseph, David, the paschal lamb, the propitiatory sacrifice, and the brazen serpent; 2) his priesthood chiefly by Melchisedech; 3) his office of prophet and mediator by Moses; 4) his resurrection by Jonas in the whale's belly; and 5) his Church and the holy sacraments by the ark, the Red Sea, the manna, and the Temple with its various appurtenances and sacrifices.[254]

Application. How happy you are to know and possess the promised Savior of the world, for whom the holy patriarchs sighed so long and so ardently! May he always find in your heart a dwelling agreeable to him! Endeavor, therefore, at all times, and especially during the holy season of Advent, to prepare it well for him.

Jesus Christ, True God

183. **Whence do we know that Jesus Christ is the Son of God, and true God?**
We know it: 1) from the prophecies; 2) from the testimony of his heavenly Father; 3) from his own testimony; 4) from the teaching of the apostles; and 5) from the doctrine of the Catholic Church.

184. **What do the prophets say?**
They call the promised Redeemer: "God," "God with us,"[255] "the saint of saints,"[256] "the wonderful," "the father of the world to come."[257] Isaias says

[254] Cf. Heb 9
[255] Is 7:14
[256] Dn 9:24
[257] Is 9:6

of him: "God himself will come and will save you";[258] and Jeremias says: "This is the name that they shall call him, 'The Lord, our just one.'"[259]

185. **What is the testimony of his heavenly Father?**

At the baptism of Christ in the Jordan, and at his transfiguration on Mount Thabor, a voice from heaven was heard, saying: "This is my beloved Son, in whom I am well pleased."[260]

186. **What is the testimony of Christ?**

Christ 1) testified that he is the Son of God, and true God, like his Father; 2) he confirmed his testimony by the holiness of his life, as well as by miracles and prophecies; and 3) he sealed it with his death.

"I and the Father are one;...believe that the Father is in me, and I in the Father."[261] "He that seeth me, seeth the Father also."[262] "All things whatsoever the Father hath are mine."[263] "What things he [the Father] doth, these the Son also doth in like manner...For as the Father raiseth up the dead, and giveth life, so the Son also giveth life to whom he will;...that all men may honor the Son, as they honor the Father."[264] "Amen, amen I say to you, before Abraham was made, I am."[265] When Peter said to Jesus: "Thou art Christ, the Son of the living God";[266] and Thomas said to him: "My Lord and my God,"[267] our Savior confirmed the faith and the declaration of both the apostles.

187. **What are miracles?**

Miracles are such extraordinary works as cannot be done by natural powers, and require for their performance the omnipotence of God.

[258] Is 35:4
[259] Jer 23:6
[260] Mt 3:17; 17:5
[261] Jn 10:30, 38
[262] Jn 14:9
[263] Jn 16:15
[264] Jn 5:19, 21, 23
[265] Jn 8:58; etc.
[266] Mt 16:16
[267] Jn 20:28

188. **Which are the principal miracles wrought by Christ?**
He changed water into wine; with five loaves, he filled several thousands; with one word, he calmed the winds and the waves, cured diseases of all sorts, cast out devils, and raised the dead to life. When he died, all nature mourned; three days after his death, he rose again from the grave; and forty days later, he ascended into heaven in the sight of his disciples.

The miracles of Jesus were such that all Judea must have known whether they had been really wrought or not; and thousands, nay, millions of people have given up all they possessed, even their lives, in testimony of their belief in these miracles.

189. **How do these miracles prove the divinity of Christ?**
They prove: 1) that when Christ said that he is the Son of God, he spoke the truth, since God cannot possibly confirm a lie by miracles; and 2) that Christ possessed divine power, since of himself he wrought miracles.

"If you will not believe me [my words], believe my works, that you may know and believe that the Father is in me, and I in the Father."[268] "What things soever the Father doth, these the Son also doth in like manner... For as the Father raiseth up the dead, and giveth life, so the Son also giveth life to whom he will."[269]

190. **How did Jesus confirm the doctrine of his divinity by prophecies?**
By this: that he foretold many things which God alone could know; for instance, his betrayal by Judas, and his denial by Peter; the manner of his death; his resurrection; his ascension, etc.

191. **Which prophecies of Christ do we still see being accomplished?**
These, for instance: 1) that the gospel shall be preached in the whole world;[270] 2) that the gates of hell shall not prevail against the Church;[271]

[268] Jn 10:38
[269] Jn 5:19, 21
[270] Cf. Mt 24:14
[271] Cf. Mt 16:18

and 3) that of the Temple of Jerusalem there shall not be left a stone upon a stone.[272]

With a view to falsify the prediction of our Lord and of the prophets, the apostate emperor Julian resolved, in 353, to rebuild the Temple of Jerusalem. Full of joy, the Jews came in great haste from all countries, set to work, and cleared away the rubbish of the old Temple, insomuch that not one stone was left upon another. But when they were going to commence the building, terrible flames flashed out of the ground, which partly killed the workmen, and partly put them to flight. This occurred at each fresh attempt that was made, until they gave up their undertaking. This miracle is attested by contemporary pagan as well as Christian writers.

192. **How did Jesus seal the doctrine of his divinity with his death?**

When the high priest adjured him in the name of the living God, he solemnly confessed that he was "the Christ, the Son of God," and that they "shall see [him] sitting on the right hand of the power of God, and coming in the clouds of heaven";[273] and, on account of this confession, he suffered death.[274]

As it would be the most grievous sin falsely to pretend to be God, so it is the greatest dishonor to Jesus Christ not to give credit to his declaration that he is God.

193. **What do the apostles teach of Jesus Christ?**

The apostles explicitly teach: 1) that Jesus Christ is true God; 2) that he possesses all the fullness of the Godhead, and the infinite perfections of God; and 3) that all creatures should adore him.

1) "We know that the Son of God is come...This is the true God and life eternal."[275] "Christ...who is over all things, God blessed for ever. Amen."[276]

[272] Cf. Mk 13:2
[273] Mt 26:63-64
[274] Cf. Jn 19:7
[275] 1 Jn 5:20
[276] Rom 9:5

2) "In him [Christ] dwelleth all the fullness of the Godhead corporally"—i.e., substantially.[277] Of Christ, the Son of God, St. John says: "In the beginning was the Word, and the Word was with God, and the Word was God. The same was in the beginning with God. All things were made by him, and without him was made nothing that was made."[278] "In him [Christ] were all things created in heaven and on earth, visible and invisible, whether thrones, or dominations, or principalities, or powers: all things were created by him and in him; and he is before all, and by him all things consist."[279] "By his Son,...[God] made the world, who, being the brightness of his glory and the figure of his substance, upholds all things by the word of his power."[280]

3) "In the name of Jesus every knee should bow, of those that are in heaven, on earth, and under the earth; and every tongue should confess that the Lord Jesus Christ is in the glory of God the Father."[281] "Let all the angels of God adore him."[282]

The apostles also confirmed their doctrine of the divinity of Jesus by innumerable miracles which they wrought in the name of Jesus, and by the most stupendous of all miracles, the conversion of the world.[283]

194. **What does the Catholic Church teach of Jesus Christ?**
The Catholic Church has ever believed and taught that Jesus Christ is true God, and of one substance with God the Father; and in defense of this fundamental Christian doctrine, she composed, at the Council of Nice, a special Creed, and excommunicated those who taught the contrary.[284]

The holy martyrs also professed this belief, and suffered with joy indescribable torments, nay, death itself, for it; and it often pleased God to confirm their possession by undeniable miracles. One of these

[277] Col 2:9
[278] Jn 1:1-3
[279] Col 1:16-17
[280] Heb 1:2-3
[281] Phil 2:10-11
[282] Heb 1:6
[283] See "Short History of Revealed Religion," p. 114ff, above.
[284] See "Short History of Revealed Religion," p. 118–119, above.

is particularly remarkable. It took place in Africa in 484, and is attested by many unobjectionable eyewitnesses. For when Hunneric, king of the Arian Vandals, who most cruelly persecuted those who professed the divinity of Christ, had had the tongues of the orthodox Christians of the city of Tipisa torn out, they spoke without tongues as fluently and distinctly as before, and proclaimed everywhere that Jesus Christ is true God, and of one substance with the Father. About sixty of them fled to Constantinople, where all the town saw them, and heard them speak daily, and that for many years.

Application. Wickedness dims the understanding. Be always pious and virtuous, and you will never have any doubts respecting the truth of your faith. "If any man will do the will of him that sent me, he shall know of the doctrine, whether it be of God."[285]

THE THIRD ARTICLE[286]

"Who was conceived of the Holy Ghost, born of the Virgin Mary."[287]

195. **What does the third article of the Creed principally teach us?**
It teaches us that the Son of God, the second Person of the Blessed Trinity, became man through the operation of the Holy Ghost, was born of the Virgin Mary, and is called our Lord Jesus Christ.

"The Word [the only-begotten of the Father] was made flesh, and dwelt among us."[288]

196. **What do we call this mystery?**
The incarnation of the Son of God.

[285] Jn 7:16-17

[286] See "Short History of Revealed Religion," p. 110–111, above.

[287] The history of the birth, life, and passion of Christ is to be learned from the "Short History of Revealed Religion."

[288] Jn 1:14

197. **What is, then, our belief concerning Jesus Christ, when we believe the mystery of the incarnation?**
We believe that Jesus Christ is both true God and true man, or that he is a God-man: he is God from eternity, and became man in time.

When Christ says, "I and the Father are one,"[289] he speaks of himself as God; and when he says, "the Father is greater than I,"[290] he speaks of himself as man.

198. **What do we mean by saying Jesus Christ is also true man?**
We mean that he had a human body and a human soul; that he could feel and suffer as we can; and that he was like to us in all things except in sin.

199. **How many natures, then, are there in Jesus Christ?**
There are two natures in Jesus Christ: the divine and the human.

200. **Are there also in Jesus Christ two wills distinct from one another?**
Yes, in Jesus Christ there is a divine will and a human will, which, however, is always in perfect subjection to the divine will.

"Father,...not my will, but thine be done."[291]

201. **Are there also two persons in Jesus Christ?**
No, Jesus Christ is only one divine Person; for the two natures are inseparably united in the one Person of the Son of God.

202. **Why is the incarnation of the Son of God attributed to the operation of the Holy Ghost?**
Because it is especially an effect of the divine love and mercy toward man.

"God so loved the world as to give his only begotten Son."[292]

[289] Jn 10:30
[290] Jn 14:28
[291] Lk 22:42
[292] Jn 3:16

203. **From whom did the Son of God take his human nature?**
From Mary, the purest of virgins; therefore, she is also called "Mother of God."[293]

204. **Why is Mary called "the purest of virgins"?**
Because she always remained a Virgin incomparably pure and entirely undefiled, not only before but also at and after the birth of the divine child.

"Behold, a virgin shall conceive and bear a son, and his name shall be called Emmanuel, that is, God with us."[294] In the holy scriptures, near relations are often called "brethren"; as Lot and Abraham. In like manner, the cousins of Jesus are called "his brethren."[295]

205. **Why is Mary called "Mother of God," since Christ took only his human nature from her?**
She is justly so called because Christ, who was born of her according to the flesh, is true God.

"The Holy One which shall be born of thee, shall be called the Son of God."[296] The doctrine of Nestorius, that Mary is not to be called the Mother of God, was condemned as heretical by the General Council of Ephesus in 431.

206. **Do we believe that, therefore, Mary is equal to God?**
No; Mary is a creature and therefore infinitely below God.

207. **Had Jesus Christ also an earthly father?**
As man, Jesus Christ had no father; for Joseph, the virgin-spouse of Mary, was only his foster father.

"Jesus…being [as it was supposed] the son of Joseph."[297]

[293] Feast of the Annunciation of the Blessed Virgin Mary
[294] Is 7:14
[295] Mt 12:46
[296] Lk 1:35
[297] Lk 3:23

208. **Why did the Son of God become man?**
1) That he might be able to suffer and die for us; for, as God, he could neither suffer nor die; and 2) that by the example of his life, as well as by his word, he might teach us virtue and holiness.

209. **What virtues does Jesus teach us by his example?**
All virtues in the highest degree, especially: 1) zeal for the honor of God, and 2) for the salvation of men; 3) meekness, 4) humility, 5) patience, 6) kindness and mercy toward everyone, 7) even our greatest enemies; and 8) obedience to his heavenly Father unto death.

Examples. 1) Chastisement of the profaners of the Temple. 2) Jesus the good shepherd. 3) Reprimand of the apostles who were going to call fire from heaven. 4) Washing of the feet of the apostles. 5) His passion. 6) Jesus, the merciful Samaritan; Jesus at the well of Jacob; in the house of Zacheus, etc. 7) "Friend, whereto art thou come?"[298] "Father, forgive them."[299] 8) "Father,...not my will, but thine be done."[300]

210. **What example does Jesus give in particular to young people?**
He teaches them, by his example, readily to obey, to take delight in prayer and instruction, to love to stay in the house of God, and to advance in wisdom and grace as they do in age.

Example. The Child Jesus in the Temple and at Nazareth.

211. **Why did Jesus Christ make choice of a poor and humble life?**
1) That he might suffer for us from the very beginning of his life; and 2) to teach us that we ought not to love and seek the vain goods of this world.

Application. Give thanks to God with your whole heart for having taken the form of a servant, and become a poor child for the love of you; especially when you hear the *Angelus* bell ring in the morning, at noon, and at night. Resolve also to perform all your actions in the manner you

[298] Mt 26:50
[299] Lk 23:34
[300] Lk 22:42

know Jesus did his. If you do this, you will be sure to please God, whether you be rich or poor.[301]

THE FOURTH ARTICLE[302]

"Suffered under Pontius Pilate, was crucified, dead, and buried."

212. **What does the fourth article of the Creed teach us?**
It teaches us that Jesus Christ suffered for us, died on the cross, and was laid in the grave.

213. **Did Christ really die?**
Yes; his soul was truly separated from his body.

214. **Why did Christ will to be buried?**
In order that his death might be the more undeniable, and his resurrection the more glorious and credible.

215. **Did Christ suffer as God or as man?**
Christ suffered as man—that is, according to his human nature.

216. **Was Christ compelled to suffer death?**
No; Christ suffered death of his own free will: "He was offered, because it was his own will."[303] "I live in the faith of the Son of God, who loved me, and delivered himself for me."[304]

217. **Why was it the will of Christ to suffer and die?**
In order to satisfy the divine justice for our sins, and thereby to redeem and save us.[305]

[301] Feast of the Nativity of Our Lord, or Christmas day

[302] See "Short History of Revealed Religion," p. 112–113, above.

[303] Is 53:7

[304] Gal 2:20; Cf. Jn 10:17-18; 18:4-9

[305] See above, p. 201, q. 155-157.

By his voluntary obedience unto the death of the cross, Christ has given full, nay, superabundant satisfaction to the Divine Majesty for the manifold offenses given to him by our disobedience, and thus he has redeemed us from the eternal punishment which we had deserved. Therefore St. Paul says: "As by the disobedience of one man [Adam], many were made sinners; so also by the obedience of one [Jesus Christ], many shall be made just."[306] And St. Peter: "Who did no sin,...who his own self bore our sins in his body upon the tree, that we, being dead to sins, should live to justice; by whose stripes you were healed."[307] And Isaias: "Surely he hath borne our infirmities, and carried our sorrows...But he was wounded for our iniquities, he was bruised for our sins."[308]

218. **For what sins has Christ given satisfaction?**
"For the sins of the whole world"[309]—namely, for original sin and all the other sins of mankind.

219. **Why could no one but Christ make full reparation for our sins?**
Because the offense given to the infinite majesty of God demanded a satisfaction of infinite value, which Christ alone was able to give.

"No brother can redeem, nor shall man redeem: he shall not give to God his ransom. Nor the price of the redemption of his soul: and shall labor for ever, and shall still live unto the end."[310]

220. **Why is the satisfaction of Christ of infinite value?**
It is of infinite value because a divine Person made it; for the greater the dignity of the person who satisfies, the greater also is the value and merit of the satisfaction.

[306] Rom 5:19
[307] 1 Pt 2:22, 24
[308] Is 53:4-5
[309] 1 Jn 2:2
[310] Ps 48:8-10

221. **Was it necessary for a perfect satisfaction that Christ should suffer such indescribable torments?**

No; for even the least suffering of a God-man would in itself have been satisfactory, because each of his works is of infinite value.

222. **Why, then, would he suffer so much?**

In order that we might better realize the greatness of his love, and of the punishment which sin deserves; and also that we might bear our cross the more patiently.

223. **From what has Christ redeemed us by his sufferings and death?**

He has redeemed us: 1) from sin; and 2) from eternal damnation, which we have deserved by sin.

"He hath loved us, and washed us from our sins in his own blood."[311] "God hath not appointed us unto wrath [damnation], but unto the purchasing of salvation by our Lord Jesus Christ, who died for us."[312]

224. **What more has Christ gained for us through his sufferings and death?**

He has: 1) reconciled us with God; 2) reopened heaven to us; and 3) merited abundant graces for us, in order to enable us to lead a holy life and to obtain eternal happiness.

"When we were enemies, we were reconciled to God by the death of his Son."[313] "Having therefore, brethren, a confidence in the entering into the holies [heaven] by the blood of Christ; a new and living way which he hath dedicated for us through the veil, that is to say, his flesh."[314] "God hath blessed us with all spiritual blessings in heavenly places [things] in Christ,... according to the riches of his grace, which hath superabounded in us."[315]

[311] Apoc 1:5
[312] 1 Thes 5:9-10
[313] Rom 5:10
[314] Heb 10:19-20
[315] Eph 1:3, 7-8; Cf. Rom 5:15-21

225. **Has Christ merited grace and eternal salvation for those only who are really saved?**

No; he has merited it for all men without exception, as he died also for all without exception.[316]

"Christ Jesus, who gave himself a redemption for all."[317]

226. **If Christ has merited eternal salvation for all men, why, then, are not all saved?**

Because not all do, on their part, what is necessary for obtaining salvation; that is, because they do not all believe, keep the commandments, and use the means of grace.

"He [Christ] became to all that obey him the cause of eternal salvation."[318]—*Example* of St. Paul.[319] "He who made you without your concurrence, will not save you without it."[320]

Application. Oh! that you would never forget how much Jesus has loved you, and what he has suffered for you. For out of mercy, and "for his exceeding charity wherewith he loved us, even when we were dead in sins,"[321] he has redeemed us through his most bitter passion and death, and has placed us in the kingdom of his grace. Let this charity of Christ urge you to live unto him who died for you, and rose again.[322] (Devotion to the sufferings of Christ; the Way of the Cross, or Stations; visiting the Holy Sepulchre in Holy Week; abstinence on Fridays, etc.)

316 Cf. 2 Cor 5:14-15
317 1 Tm 2:5-6
318 Heb 5:9
319 Cf. Col 1:24
320 Augustine, *Sermon 169*, n. 13
321 Eph 2:4-5
322 Cf. 2 Cor 4:14-15

THE FIFTH ARTICLE[323]

"He descended into hell, the third day he rose again from the dead."

227. **What means, "He descended into hell"?**

That the soul of Jesus Christ, after his death, descended into limbo—i.e., to the place where the souls of the just who died before Christ were detained, and were waiting for the time of their redemption.

"He was put to death indeed in the flesh, but enlivened in the spirit; in which also coming he preached to those spirits that were in prison"[324]—that is, announced to them their redemption.

228. **Why were the souls of the just detained in limbo?**

Because heaven was closed through sin, and was first to be opened by Christ.[325]

229. **Why did Christ descend into limbo?**

1) To comfort and set free the souls of the just; and 2) to show forth his power and majesty even there in the lower regions.[326]

230. **What means, "the third day he rose again from the dead"?**

That on the third day after his death Christ reunited, by his own power, his soul to his body, as he had foretold, and rose again from the grave. (Easter day.)

"Destroy this temple, and in three days I will raise it up...But he spoke of the temple of his body."[327]

231. **How did Christ rise again?**

He came forth glorious and immortal from the grave, secured as it was by a heavy stone, and guarded by soldiers.

[323] See "Short History of Revealed Religion," p. 113–114, above.
[324] 1 Pt 3:18-19
[325] Cf. Heb 9:6-8
[326] Cf. Phil 2:10
[327] Jn 2:19, 21; Cf. Jn 10:18

232. **Did Christ retain in his glorified body any mark of his sufferings?**
He still retained, in his hands, feet, and side, the marks of his wounds; therefore he said to Thomas: "Put in thy finger hither [into the place of the nails], and see my hands; and bring hither thy hand, and put it into my side."[328]

233. **Why has he still retained these marks?**
1) In testimony of his victory over hell; 2) as a proof that he rose again in the very same body in which he had suffered; and 3) to show them on the day of judgment, for the consolation of the just and for the confusion of the wicked.

234. **Whence do we know that Christ rose from the dead?**
From the testimony of his apostles and his disciples, who often saw him after his resurrection, touched him, ate, spoke, and conversed with him; and who everywhere loudly proclaimed his resurrection, even before the chief council who had condemned him to death, although by this conduct they drew upon themselves nothing but mortal hatred and persecution.

It is true that the soldiers who guarded the grave, being bribed with a large sum of money, spread the report that, while they were asleep, the disciples of Jesus came and stole his body. But 1) if they were asleep, how could they see, then, that his disciples stole the body? 2) Whence did the timid disciples, who expected now nothing more from their deceased master, get on a sudden such undaunted courage? 3) How did it happen that not even one of the sleeping guards awoke at the rolling away of the heavy stone? 4) Why were the guards not punished for the neglect of their duty?[329]

If the evidence of the apostles and the disciples had not been so certain and quite unexceptionable, they would never have convinced the world, in opposition to the most powerful and crafty enemies of Jesus, that he who, like a malefactor, had been publicly executed and buried, had on the third day risen again glorious from the dead. They have nevertheless so firmly convinced the world of this truth that countless Christian converts endured the most painful martyrdom in testimony of their firm belief in it.

[328] Jn 20:27
[329] Cf. Acts 12:19

235. **What effect ought the doctrine of the resurrection of Christ to produce in us?**

It ought 1) to strengthen our belief in his divinity, and our hope of our own future resurrection; and 2) to incite us to rise from the death of sin to a new and holy life.

"God raised him up from the dead, and hath given him glory, that your faith and hope might be in God."[330] "We are buried together with him by baptism into death; that as Christ is risen from the dead by the glory of the Father, so we also may walk in newness of life."[331]

Application. He who is still deeply buried in the grave of sin—i.e., in evil habits or sinful desires—is not risen yet to a new life. All our thoughts, all our exertions, should tend toward heaven. "If you be risen with Christ, seek the things that are above, where Christ is sitting at the right hand of God. Mind the things that are above, not the things that are upon the earth."[332]

THE SIXTH ARTICLE[333]

"He ascended into heaven, sitteth at the right
hand of God the Father Almighty."

236. **What is meant by "He ascended into heaven"?**

That Jesus Christ, by his own power, with soul and body, went up into heaven.[334]

237. **Did Christ ascend alone into heaven?**

No; he took also with him into heaven the souls of the just whom he had liberated from limbo.

"Ascending on high, he led captivity captive."[335]

[330] 1 Pt 1:21
[331] Rom 6:4
[332] Col 3:1-2
[333] See "Short History of Revealed Religion," p. 113–114, above.
[334] Feast of the Ascension of Our Lord
[335] Eph 4:8

238. **For what purpose did Christ ascend into heaven?**
1) To take possession of his glory as conqueror of death and hell;[336] 2) to be our mediator and advocate with his Father;[337] 3) to send the Holy Ghost to his disciples;[338] and 4) to open heaven, and to prepare a place for us also.[339]

239. **What means, "sitteth at the right hand of God"?**
It means that Christ, as man also, is exalted above all created things, and participates in the power and glory of the Divine Majesty.

"He hath raised him up from the dead, and set him on his right hand in the heavenly places, above all principality, and power, and virtue, and dominion, and every name that is named, not only in this world, but also in that which is to come. And he hath subjected all things under his feet, and hath made him head over all the church."[340]

240. **Is Christ, then, not present in all places?**
As God, he is everywhere; but as God-man, he is only in heaven, and in the Holy Eucharist.

Application. Consider frequently, especially in your troubles and temptations, that we "are pilgrims and strangers on the earth,"[341] and that our true country is heaven, whither Christ has gone to prepare a place for you also. "Be therefore not wearied, fainting in your minds," but "look on Jesus,...who endured the cross,...and now sitteth on the right hand of the throne of God."[342]

[336] Cf. Phil 2:8-11
[337] Cf. Heb 9:24
[338] Cf. Jn 16:7
[339] Cf. Jn 14:2
[340] Eph 1:20-22
[341] Heb 11:13
[342] Heb 12:3, 2

THE SEVENTH ARTICLE

"From thence he shall come to judge the living and the dead."

241. **What does the seventh article of the Creed teach us?**

That Jesus Christ at the end of the world shall come again with great power and glory to judge all men, both the good and the wicked.[343]

242. **What do you call this judgment?**

"The general judgment," "the last judgment," or "the judgment of the world."

243. **When will the day of the judgment of the world come?**

"Of that day and hour no one knoweth, no, not the angels of heaven."[344]

Nevertheless, Christ and his apostles have foretold us many things which shall come to pass on the earth before the end of the world,[345] that the faithful may be on their guard, and not be seduced to fall away. "For there will rise up false Christs and false prophets, and they shall show signs and wonders, to seduce (if it were possible) even the elect."[346]

244. **How shall we be judged?**

We shall be judged according to all our thoughts, words, works, and omissions.

"I say unto you, that every idle word that men shall speak, they shall render an account for it in the day of judgment."[347]

245. **How will the last judgment be held?**

1) Christ will come in the clouds of heaven, and gather all nations together before his throne, placing the good on his right hand, and the wicked on

[343] Cf. Acts 1:11
[344] Mt 24:36
[345] Cf. Mt 24; Mk 13; 2 Thes 2
[346] Mk 13:22
[347] Mt 12:36

his left.[348] 2) He will then make manifest the good and the evil that every man has done, even his most secret thoughts, and also the graces which he has given to each one; and finally, he will pronounce judgment upon all.[349]

"And I saw the dead, great and small, standing in the presence of the throne, and the books were opened;...and the dead were judged by those things which were written in the books, according to their works."[350] "For there is nothing covered, that shall not be revealed; nor hidden, that shall not be known."[351] "The Lord will bring to light the hidden things of darkness, and will make manifest the counsels of the hearts."[352]

246. **What will be the sentence, and the end of the last judgment?**
Christ will say to the good: "Come, ye blessed of my Father, possess you the kingdom prepared for you from the foundation of the world."[353] But to the wicked he will say: "Depart from me, ye cursed, into everlasting fire, which was prepared for the devil and his angels."[354] "And these shall go into everlasting punishment: but the just into life everlasting."[355]

247. **Is there not, besides the general, another judgment?**
Yes, there is also the particular judgment, in which every man shall be judged immediately after his death.

Therefore, the holy scripture says: "It is easy before God in the day of death to reward every one according to his ways."[356]

248. **Why will there be a general judgment besides the particular?**
For three principal reasons: 1) that God's wisdom and justice may be acknowledged by all men; 2) that Jesus Christ may be glorified before the

[348] Cf. Mt 24-25
[349] Cf. 2 Cor 5:10
[350] Apoc 20:12
[351] Lk 12:2; Cf. Mk 4:22
[352] 1 Cor 4:5
[353] Mt 25:34
[354] Mt 25:41
[355] Mt 25:46
[356] Ecclus 11:28

whole world; and 3) that the good may receive the honor due to them, and the wicked the dishonor they have deserved.

"And the heavens shall declare his justice; for God is judge."[357] "They shall see the Son of man coming in the clouds of heaven, with much power and majesty."[358] "Then [shall those that have afflicted them] be amazed at the suddenness of their unexpected salvation, saying within themselves, repenting, and groaning for anguish of spirit: 'These are they whom we had some time in derision, and for a parable of reproach. We fools esteemed their life madness, and their end without honor. Behold how they are numbered among the children of God, and their lot is among the saints,'"[359] etc.

249. **Whither does the soul go after the particular judgment?**

Either to heaven, or to hell, or to purgatory.

250. **How do we know that there is a purgatory?**

1) From the holy scripture and 2) from the tradition of the Church. 3) Also in some measure from reason.

1) In the holy scripture—namely, the old testament—it is said: "It is a holy and wholesome thought to pray for the dead, that they may be loosed from sins."[360] In the new testament, Christ speaks of sins which shall be forgiven in the world to come;[361] and of a prison in the other world, from which there shall be no release till the last farthing has been paid.[362] And St. Paul speaks of such as on the day of judgment "shall be saved, yet so as by fire."[363]

2) That tradition teaches it, follows from the constant practice of the Church to pray for the dead, as well as from the unanimous testimony of the holy fathers and of the councils.

357 Ps 49:6
358 Mt 24:30
359 Ws 5:1-5
360 2 Mc 12:46
361 Cf. Mt 12:32
362 Cf. Mt 5:26
363 1 Cor 3:12-15

3) For as no one goes to heaven except those who are perfectly undefiled, and no one to hell but those who die in mortal sin, we cannot but admit a place between heaven and hell where those souls that are not quite clean, but nevertheless died in the state of grace, suffer until they are worthy of entering heaven.

251. **Who go to purgatory?**
1) Such souls as have departed this life, not in mortal, but in venial sin; and 2) such also as have died without any sin, but have still to suffer the punishment deserved for their past sins.

252. **Will there still be a purgatory after the general judgment?**
No. After the general judgment there will be only heaven and hell.

Application. Never imagine that you are in the dark, or that nobody sees the evil you are doing; for nothing escapes the eye of God: "And all things that are done, God will bring into judgment for every error, whether it be good or evil."[364]

THE EIGHTH ARTICLE[365]

"I believe in the Holy Ghost."

253. **By whom is the fruit or grace of the divine redemption communicated to us?**
By the Holy Ghost.

254. **Where is this grace communicated to us?**
It is communicated to us in the Catholic Church, to which Christ has, for that very purpose, promised and sent the Holy Ghost.

[364] Eccles 12:14

[365] See "Short History of Revealed Religion," p. 114–115, above.

255. **Who is the Holy Ghost?**

The Holy Ghost is the third Person of the Blessed Trinity, true God with the Father and the Son.

Thus the holy scripture teaches. 1) It calls the Holy Ghost God, one with the Father and the Son: "Why hath Satan tempted thy heart, that thou shouldst lie to the Holy Ghost?...Thou hast not lied to men, but to God."[366] "The Father, the Word, and the Holy Ghost, and these three are one."[367] It attributes divine perfections to him—omnipotence, omnipresence, omniscience, eternity, etc.[368] It attributes divine works to him—the creation, regeneration, sanctification, the communication of all spiritual gifts, etc.[369]

2) It represents the Holy Ghost as a Person distinct from the Father and from the Son: "I will ask the Father, and he shall give you another Paraclete, that he may abide with you for ever, the Spirit of truth."[370] "The Holy Ghost descended in a bodily shape, as a dove, upon him; and a voice came from heaven: Thou art my beloved Son."[371]

Thus also the Catholic Church teaches, and has always taught. As early as in the General Council of Constantinople (381 A.D.), she unanimously condemned the heresy of Macedonius, who denied the divinity of the Holy Ghost, and she expressly declared "that the Holy Ghost, the Lord and giver of life, is adored and glorified together with the Father and the Son."

256. **From whom does the Holy Ghost proceed?**

The Holy Ghost proceeds from the Father and the Son, as from one source.

"I will send you...the Spirit of truth, who proceedeth from the Father."[372] "He shall receive of mine."[373]

[366] Acts 5:3-4
[367] 1 Jn 5:7
[368] Cf. 1 Cor 12:8-11; Ps 138:7-10; 1 Cor 2:10-11; etc.
[369] Cf. Ps 103:30; Jn 3:5; 1 Cor 6:11; Rom 5:5; Acts 2:4, 17; etc.
[370] Jn 14:16-17
[371] Lk 3:22; and elsewhere
[372] Jn 15:26
[373] Jn 16:15

257. **Why is the third Person of the Blessed Trinity in particular named the "Holy Spirit," since the name of *Spirit* and *Holy* equally belongs to the first and to the second Person?**

The third Person is in particular called the "Holy Spirit," because to him is especially ascribed the work of our sanctification, and he imparts to us the spiritual life of grace.

Hence the third Person is also called the "Sanctifier" and "giver of life."

258. **Why is the work of our sanctification especially ascribed to the Holy Ghost?**

Because he, as the Spirit of love, is the giver of all inward holiness, and the dispenser of all supernatural gifts and graces, whereby we are sanctified.

It is true, the work of our sanctification is common to all the three divine Persons; nevertheless, as a work of love, it has a special relation to the Holy Ghost—the Spirit of love.

259. **But is it not Jesus Christ, our Redeemer, who sanctifies us?**

Jesus Christ sanctifies us, inasmuch as he has merited and prepared for us the grace which makes us pleasing to God; but the Holy Ghost is said especially to sanctify us, inasmuch as he, through the merits of Christ, actually cleanses us from sin, and makes us just and pleasing to God.

"You are washed, you are sanctified, you are justified in the name of our Lord Jesus Christ, and by the Spirit of our God."[374]

260. **How does the Holy Ghost sanctify us?**

He sanctifies us by means of the supernatural grace which he ordinarily infuses into our souls through the sacraments.

261. **What are in particular the gifts of the Holy Ghost?**

These seven: 1) wisdom; 2) understanding; 3) counsel; 4) fortitude; 5) knowledge; 6) godliness or piety; and 7) the fear of the Lord.[375]

[374] 1 Cor 6:11
[375] Cf. Is 11:2-3

262. **When did Christ send down the Holy Ghost upon his Church?**
Christ sent down the Holy Ghost in a visible manner upon her on Whitsunday, when he descended upon the apostles in the form of fiery tongues.

263. **For what purpose was the Holy Ghost sent upon the Church?**
That he might perpetually teach her, sanctify her, and direct her in an invisible manner; and, in general, that he might impart to her those abundant graces which Christ has merited for her.

By virtue of the Holy Ghost, the Church teaches,[376] cleanses from sin, and sanctifies,[377] guides, and rules.[378]

264. **Is the Holy Ghost still sent at the present time?**
He is still sent at the present time in an invisible manner, as often as he enters with his sanctifying grace into our souls in order to dwell there.

"Know you not, that you are the temple of God, and that the Spirit of God dwelleth in you?"[379]

265. **How long does the Holy Ghost remain in the soul?**
As long as the soul is free from all grievous sin.

266. **Does sin, then, drive the Holy Ghost from the soul?**
Yes, mortal sin drives away the Holy Ghost, and profanes the temple of God.

"But if any man violate the temple of God, him shall God destroy; for the temple of God is holy, which you are."[380]

267. **But is not the Holy Ghost everywhere?**
As God, he is everywhere; but as the author and dispenser of grace, he is especially with the Catholic Church, and in the souls of the just.

[376] Cf. Jn 14:26
[377] Cf. Jn 20:22, etc.
[378] Cf. Acts 20:28; 15:28
[379] 1 Cor 3:16
[380] 1 Cor 3:17

Application. Strive most earnestly, by avoiding sin, to preserve the Holy Ghost in your heart, and to correspond faithfully with his inspirations. "Wisdom will not enter into a malicious soul, nor dwell in a body subject to sins; for the Holy Spirit...will flee from the deceitful."[381]

THE NINTH ARTICLE

"The holy Catholic Church; the communion of saints."

On the Church and the Form of Her Government

268. **What did the apostles do after they had received the Holy Ghost on Whitsunday?**
They went forth into the whole world preaching and baptizing, and gathered all those who believed and were baptized into congregations.[382]

269. **What arose from these congregations of believers?**
There arose in many places communities of Christians,[383] whose rulers were the apostles.[384]

The whole book of the Acts of the Apostles, and all their epistles, bear witness that they did not only preach and baptize, but also rule their communities in every way. They made regulations and laws, threatened, judged, and punished; they excluded the unworthy from the community of the faithful,[385] and received them again when they repented.[386]

[381] Ws 1:4-5
[382] See "Short History of Revealed Religion," p. 114 –115, above.
[383] See Acts 2:41, 44; 4:32.
[384] See "Short History of Revealed Religion," p. 115, above.
[385] Cf. 1 Cor 5:5; 1 Tm 1:20
[386] Cf. 2 Cor 2:10; and elsewhere

270. **What further did the apostles do when the communities of Christians increased?**

They chose elders from amongst them, ordained them bishops, and appointed them everywhere as rulers of the new Christian communities, with the commission that they should likewise ordain and appoint others.[387]

"And when they had ordained to them priests [or elders—i.e., bishops and priests] in every church, and had prayed with fasting, they commended them to the Lord, in whom they believed."[388] "For this cause I left thee in Crete, that thou...shouldest ordain priests [elders] in every city, as I also appointed thee."[389]

271. **Were all these several communities united with one another?**

Yes, they were all closely united with one another: they professed the same faith, partook of the same sacraments, and formed all together one great Christian community under one common head, St. Peter.[390]

272. **What did they call this great community of Christians under one common head?**

The Catholic—i.e., the Universal—Church, or in one word, the Church.

273. **What, then, is the Church even at the present time?**

The Church is the same congregation of all the faithful, who, being baptized, profess the same doctrine, partake of the same sacraments, and are governed by their lawful pastors under one visible head, the pope.

274. **Was the Church thus organized by the apostles?**

No; she was thus organized by Jesus Christ, her founder; the apostles were only the instruments by which he accomplished his will.

[387] See "Short History of Revealed Religion," p. 115–116, above.

[388] Acts 14:22

[389] Ti 1:5

[390] See "Short History of Revealed Religion," p. 115–116, above.

275. **How did Jesus Christ thus organize his Church?**

By conferring his own power upon the apostles, and sending them forth everywhere, 1) to preach; 2) to baptize; and 3) to govern those who were baptized, under the supremacy of St. Peter.

Before Christ ascended into heaven, he said to his apostles: "All power is given to me in heaven and in earth. Going therefore, teach ye all nations; baptizing them in the name of the Father, and of the Son, and of the Holy Ghost. Teaching them to observe all things whatsoever I have commanded you: and behold, I am with you all days, even to the consummation of the world."[391] And even previously to that he said to them: "As the Father hath sent me, I also send you...Whose sins you shall forgive, they are forgiven them; and whose sins you shall retain, they are retained."[392] "Amen I say to you, whatsoever you shall bind upon earth, shall be bound also in heaven; and whatsoever you shall loose upon earth, shall be loosed also in heaven."[393] "He that heareth you, heareth me; and he that despiseth you, despiseth me."[394]

276. **What do you call the threefold office which, together with his power, Christ conferred upon the apostles?**

The teaching, the priestly, and the pastoral office.

277. **In what does this threefold office consist?**

The teaching office consists in the full power to preach the divine doctrine, to condemn heresies, and to decide religious controversies.

The priestly office: in the full power to offer the Sacrifice of the Mass, to administer the sacraments, to consecrate, and to bless.

The pastoral office: in the full power to rule the Church, consequently also to make laws and inflict punishments.

[391] Mt 28:18-20
[392] Jn 20:21, 23
[393] Mt 18:18
[394] Lk 10:16; and elsewhere

278. **Why were the apostles to exercise their office only under the supreme authority of St. Peter?**

Because Christ, in order to maintain unity and union, appointed St. Peter to be his representative upon earth, and the visible head of the whole Church.

279. **But is not Christ himself the head of the Church?**

Christ is undoubtedly the head of the Church, but the invisible head.

280. **Why did Christ ordain that the Church should have also a visible head together with the invisible one?**

Because the Church is a visible community or body, and a visible body must also have a visible head.

Thus, no kingdom can exist without a visible government, although all kingdoms in the world are governed by God in an invisible manner.

281. **From what do we learn that Christ has appointed St. Peter to be the supreme head of his Church?**

We learn it from this: 1) that Christ built his Church upon Peter, as upon the true foundation stone; 2) that he gave him in particular the keys of the kingdom of heaven; and 3) that he commissioned him alone to feed his whole flock.

1) "Thou art Peter [a rock], and upon this rock I will build my Church, and the gates of hell shall not prevail against it."[395] Because Peter was to be the foundation stone of the Church, Christ prayed particularly for him, that his "faith might not fail," and commissioned him "to confirm once his brethren."[396] 2) "And I will give to thee the keys of the kingdom of heaven. And whatsoever thou shalt bind upon earth, it shall be bound also in heaven; and whatsoever thou shalt loose on earth, it shall be loosed also in heaven."[397] 3) "Feed my lambs; feed my sheep."[398] Christ, it is true, made his apostles collectively the foundation of his Church,

[395] Mt 16:18
[396] Lk 22:32
[397] Mt 16:19
[398] Jn 21:15, 17

and gave them all collectively the power of binding and loosing, and of governing the Church; but what he promised and gave to the apostles in common, this he first promised and gave to Peter in particular. Thus, Peter received the full and independent, the apostles, on the contrary, only a subordinate, power.

282. **What facts are there to confirm us in our belief that Peter was appointed by Christ to be the supreme head of the Church?**

These: that after Christ's ascension into heaven, Peter 1) really exercised the office of head of the Church; and 2) that he likewise was always acknowledged by the Church as the head of the apostles, and the pastor of the whole flock of Christ.

1) As often as something of importance was to be decided or executed, Peter arose first, and acted as the head of the rest; as, for instance, at the election of Matthias, on the feast of Pentecost, at the contention about receiving the heathens into the Church, at the council of the apostles in Jerusalem, etc.[399] 2) Even the evangelists, when enumerating the apostles, always put St. Peter the first, although he was neither the oldest of them, nor had been called to the apostleship before all the others. St. Matthew expressly says: "The names of the twelve apostles are these: the first, Simon who is called Peter," etc.[400] The fathers at the General Council of Ephesus (431 A.D.) considered it as "a fact questioned by no one, and known in all ages, that St. Peter was the prince and the head of the apostles, the foundation stone of the Catholic Church," etc.

283. **Was the supremacy of a head of the Church to cease after the death of St. Peter?**

No; for, 1) if the Church was to continue as Christ had established it, the rock also on which he had built it, and the supremacy of a head which he himself had ordained to govern it, were to continue; and 2) if a visible head was necessary when the Church was still small, and there were none, or

[399] Cf. Acts 1:2, 11, 15
[400] Mt 10:2

but few heresies, it was much more necessary afterward when the Church was spread, and heresies and schisms were multiplied.

284. **Who has been the visible head of the Church since the death of St. Peter?** The bishop of Rome, commonly called the pope, who is the lawful successor of St. Peter in the episcopal See of Rome, and who, in consequence, has always been acknowledged as the visible head of the Church, and the vicegerent of Christ on earth.[401]

The councils, as well as the fathers of all ages individually have unanimously and most decidedly, by word and deed, acknowledged in the Roman popes the primacy and supremacy of St. Peter. The Ecumenical Council of Florence (1438) referred to "the decrees of the general councils, and the ecclesiastical statutes," when it declared "that the bishop of Rome (the pope) possessed the primacy over the whole universe; that he was the successor of the prince of the apostles, St. Peter, and the true vicegerent of Jesus Christ, the head of the whole Church, the father and teacher of all Christians; and that he, in the person of St. Peter, had received from our Lord Jesus Christ the full power of feeding, guiding, and governing the whole Church." No general council was ever held at which the pope, or his legates, did not preside; and there never was a decision of the Church universally received before it had been confirmed by the pope; and whosoever refused to recognize the pope as the head of the Church was at all times considered by all the faithful as an apostate.

In the course of time, the successor of St. Peter gained also, by divine dispensation, possession of a secular territory of considerable extent, called the "ecclesiastical states," that he might exercise his spiritual power all the more freely, and be dependent, not on any human favor or force, but on God alone.[402]

[401] See "Short History of Revealed Religion," p. 115–116, above.
[402] See "Short History of Revealed Religion," p. 134–135, above.

285. **Was the threefold office, which was common to all the apostles, to continue at all times?**
Yes; according to the appointment of Christ, it was to pass over from the apostles to their successors, and to continue in them, without interruption, to the end of the world.

286. **How do we know this appointment of Christ?**
From the words which he spoke when he conferred the office upon them: "And behold, I am with you all days, even to the consummation of the world";[403] which evidently cannot be understood to have been said to the apostles alone, since they, of course, were not to live to the end of the world.

287. **Who are the successors of the apostles?**
The bishops who are rightly consecrated, and are in communion with the head of the Church, the pope—i.e., the bishops of the Catholic Church.

288. **Why can no one be a successor of the apostles who is not in communion with the head of the Church?**
1) Because he who is separated from the head cannot even be a member of the Church;[404] and 2) because no power has been conferred on the apostles and their successors, except when united with him to whom Christ has delegated the supreme and full power over the whole Church.

289. **Is the pope alone, by divine appointment, to govern the Church?**
The bishops also are, by divine appointment, to govern the Church, but only with, and under, their head, the pope.

"Take heed to yourselves, and to the whole flock, wherein the Holy Ghost hath placed you bishops, to rule the Church of God."[405]

[403] Mt 28:20

[404] Hence the general rule: "Where Peter [i.e., the pope] is, there is the Church" (Ambrose).

[405] Acts 20:28

290. **In what manner do the bishops rule the Church?**

They rule it in this manner: 1) each bishop governs the diocese or bishopric assigned to him by the pope; and 2) they occasionally assemble from the various dioceses of their province, or of their country, or even of the whole Church, in order to make decrees and regulations subject to the approbation and sanction of the bishop of Rome, our holy father the pope.

291. **Through whom do the bishops exercise their office in the particular congregations (parishes) of their dioceses?**

Through the priests, or pastors, sent to them.

292. **When, then, may a priest discharge the duties of the priesthood?**

When he has been expressly sent, or authorized, for that purpose by his lawful bishop.

The priest receives his ordination and mission, not from the faithful, but from God through a lawful bishop. All and everyone who have thus been ordained and sent are "ambassadors for Christ, God as it were exhorting by [them]";[406] and to all of them is said what Jesus Christ said to his disciples when sending them: "He that heareth you, heareth me; and he that despiseth you, despiseth me; and he that despiseth me, despiseth him that sent me."[407]

293. **By what means are unity and good order maintained in the whole Church?**

By this: that all those who are not priests always continue, with ready obedience, subject to the priests, the priests to the bishops, and the bishops to the pope.

Consequently, Christ has not given to all the members of the Church the same right and the same power, but "hath set the members every one of them in the body [of the Church] as it hath pleased him...And he gave some apostles, and some prophets, and other some evangelists, and other some pastors and doctors, for the perfecting of the saints, for the work

[406] 2 Cor 5:20
[407] Lk 10:16

of the ministry...Are all apostles? Are all prophets? Are all doctors?"[408] Therefore, St. Clement, the disciple and successor of St. Peter, compares the Church to an army, in which the privates are subordinate to the captains, the captains to the colonels, and these again to the general.

Application. Always cherish in your heart a profound reverence and a humble submission to the holy father the pope, and to the bishops and priests united with him; for they are set over you in the place of God, and it is their duty to instruct you in the name of God, to make you partake of the divine graces, and to lead you to eternal salvation. Woe to them who despise the clergy and create schisms! "They have gone in the way of Cain,...and have perished in the contradiction of Core...These are wandering stars, to whom the storm of darkness is reserved for ever."[409]

On the Marks of the Church

294. **Has Christ established one Church, or more than one?**
As in the words of St. Paul, there is but "one Lord, one faith, one baptism, one God and Father of all,"[410] so there is but one Church established by Christ.

Christ said: "Upon this rock I will build my Church"—not "Churches."[411] "There shall be one fold and one shepherd."[412] And the apostles call the Church the "body of Christ."[413] Now, Christ has only one body; therefore he has also established only one Church.

295. **Is it easy to recognize this one Church established by Christ?**
Yes; for 1) Christ has established a visible Church with perceptible marks, so that it is easy to find her; 2) otherwise he could not have commanded us, under pain of eternal damnation, to apply to the Church, and to hear her.

[408] 1 Cor 12:18; Eph 4:11-12; 1 Cor 12:29
[409] Jude 1:11, 13
[410] Eph 4:5-6
[411] Mt 16:18
[412] Jn 10:16
[413] 1 Cor 12:27; and elsewhere

"Neither do men light a candle and put it under a bushel, but upon a candlestick, that it may shine to all that are in the house."[414] "If thy brother shall offend against thee,...go and tell the Church; and if he will not hear the Church, let him be to thee as the heathen and publican."[415]

296. **How is the Church of Christ visible?**

The Church of Christ is visible: 1) in her superiors and members; 2) in her doctrine; and 3) in the Sacrifice of the Mass, and in the administration of the sacraments.

If the Church were not visible in this manner, how would it then be possible, according to the direction of Christ and the apostles,[416] to "obey the prelates" (bishops and priests) of the Church, to hear her teachers, to participate in her sacrifice and sacraments, or, in general, in her divine service?

297. **By what marks may the true Church of Christ be known?**

The true Church of Christ may be known by these four marks: 1) she is one; 2) she is holy; 3) she is catholic; and 4) she is apostolic.

As early as 325 A.D. it was pronounced in the Nicene Creed: "I believe in one, holy, catholic, and apostolic Church."

298. **Why must the true Church of Christ be one, holy, catholic, and apostolic?**

She must be: 1) one, because no kingdom can stand "that is divided against itself";[417] 2) holy, because her founder is holy, and her object is to lead all men to holiness; 3) catholic, or universal, because she has been established for all nations and for all times,[418] and is, according to the promise of Christ and of the prophets, to be spread over the whole universe;[419] and

[414] Mt 5:15
[415] Mt 18:15, 17
[416] Cf. Heb 13:17; Mk 16:15-16; and elsewhere
[417] Lk 11:17
[418] Cf. Mt 18:19
[419] See above, p. 207–208, q. 177; and p. 211–212, q. 191.

4) apostolic, because her origin and her doctrine are apostolic,[420] and her rulers must be lawful successors of the apostles.[421]

299. **Which Church has all these four marks?**
It is evident that no Church has these four marks except the Roman Catholic—namely, that Church which acknowledges the pope of Rome as her head.

300. **Why is the Roman Catholic Church evidently one?**
Because she has at all times and in all places: 1) the same faith; 2) the same sacrifice and the same sacraments; and 3) a common head.

301. **Why is the Roman Catholic Church evidently holy?**
1) Because her founder is holy, and she teaches a holy doctrine; 2) because she faithfully preserves and dispenses all the means of sanctification instituted by Christ; and 3) because there were in her at all times saints, whose holiness God has also confirmed by miracles and extraordinary graces.[422]

Abuses and failings of individual members cannot be imputed to the Church herself, because they did not arise from her doctrine or organization, and were never approved of by her. If a Church were no longer to be the true Church on account of abuses and scandals met within her, why, then, did Christ himself compare his Church to a field in which wheat and cockle grow together, and to a net that contains both good and bad fishes?[423] And where, then, was the true Church in the days of the apostles?—for even then there were scandals,[424] and also blameworthy bishops in the Church.[425]

[420] Cf. Eph 2:20

[421] See above, p. 239, q. 285-288.

[422] See "Short History of Revealed Religion," p. 119–120, 124–125, and 130–132, above.

[423] Cf. Mt 13

[424] Cf. 1 Cor 11

[425] Cf. Apoc 2-3

302. **Why is the Roman Church evidently catholic or universal?**

1) Because from the time of Christ she has continually existed with the same teaching, the same priestly, and the same pastoral office as at the present time; 2) because she is spread over the whole universe; and 3) because she is constantly spreading, in accordance with the divine commission: "Go ye into the whole world, and preach the gospel to every creature."[426]

Therefore, the Roman Church was always called "Catholic," even by apostates and infidels, as St. Augustine testifies; and up to this day she is called throughout the world the "Catholic Church."

303. **Why is the Roman Catholic Church evidently apostolic?**

1) Because her origin is unquestionably traced back to the apostles; 2) because her doctrine is grounded on apostolic tradition; and 3) because her rulers, the pope and the bishops, are lawful successors of the apostles.[427]

It is an undisputed fact that Anglicans and others approach the nearer to the Catholic Church the more diligently and sincerely they search in the writings of the holy fathers for the apostolic traditions.

304. **But are not non-Catholic religious societies also one?**

No; they are not, and cannot be, one: 1) because they have no common head; and 2) because every one of their members has a right to interpret and believe the holy scriptures as he likes.

Therefore "they are children tossed to and fro, and carried about with every wind of doctrine."[428]

305. **And why can none of them be called "holy"?**

1) Because their founders were not holy; 2) because they have rejected many articles of faith and means of sanctification, as, for example, the Sacrifice of the Mass and most of the sacraments, and have, on the contrary,

[426] Mk 16:15

[427] See above, p. 239, q. 287.

[428] Eph 4:14

established principles which are directly opposed to sanctity;[429] and 3) because they cannot produce from among themselves one saint, confirmed as such by his miraculous power.

306. **Why can none of them be called "catholic"?**
Because they arose only in later years, and have not ceased to split again into numerous sects, none of which is universally spread or continually spreading in the manner ordained by Christ.[430]

307. **And why can none of them be called "apostolic"?**
1) Because they did not come into existence till long after the time of the apostles, and then by separating themselves from the old apostolic Church; 2) because doctrine ever wavering and ever changing, as theirs is, cannot certainly be apostolic; and 3) because they have no lawful successors of the apostles, and, therefore, neither teachers nor pastors sent by Christ.

308. **If, then, none but the Roman Catholic Church has the marks of the one Church of Christ, what follows from this?**
That the Roman Catholic Church alone is the true Church established by Jesus Christ.

Application. Pray frequently for the peace and exaltation of the Catholic Church, and for the conversion of the heretics and infidels. "Blessed are all they that love thee [the Church], and that rejoice in thy peace."[431]

On the End of the Church, and on Her Qualities Resulting from This End

309. **For what end did Christ establish the Church?**
Christ established the Church that by her he might lead all men to eternal salvation.

[429] See "Short History of Revealed Religion," p. 126–127, above.
[430] See "Short History of Revealed Religion," p. 126–127 and 132–134. above.
[431] Tb 13:18

310. **What has the Church to do in order to lead men to salvation?**
She has: 1) to preach the doctrine of Christ to them; 2) to administer to them the means of grace instituted by Christ; and 3) to guide and govern them in the way to eternal life.

311. **How has Christ enabled the Church to do all this in a proper manner?**
1) He has entrusted the Church with his doctrine, his means of grace, and his powers, by conferring upon her his teaching, his priestly, and his pastoral office; and 2) he has given her the help of the Holy Ghost, in order that she might also always keep the divine doctrine pure, rightly administer the means of grace, and exercise her powers for the salvation of mankind.

312. **By whom is the divine doctrine always preserved pure and uncorrupted in the Church?**
By the infallible teaching body of the Church.

313. **Who composes this infallible teaching body?**
The pope, and the bishops united with him.

They are also called "the teaching Church," or simply "the Church,"[432] in contradistinction to the rest of the faithful, who are called "the hearing Church."

314. **Why is the teaching Church called "infallible"?**
Because, by the assistance of the Holy Ghost, she is secured against erring both in matters of faith and of morals.

315. **Who assures us that the Church cannot err?**
Christ himself, who has promised us: 1) that he will be with her "all days, even to the consummation of the world";[433] 2) that the "Spirit of

[432] Mt 18:17
[433] Mt 28:20

truth" shall "abide with [her] for ever";[434] 3) that "the gates of hell shall not prevail against [her]."[435]

Were it possible that the teaching Church might err, the hearing Church would likewise fall into error, as she is to be instructed and guided by the former; and then the whole Church would, contrary to the promise of Christ, be prevailed against by the spirit of lies, or the powers of hell.

316. **What does St. Paul call the Church on account of her infallibility?**
St. Paul calls the Church "pillar and ground of the truth."[436]

317. **But have there not also been in the Catholic Church some individual teachers who have fallen into error?**
Yes; but this happened only because they taught differently from the whole teaching body; for infallibility is not granted to each one individually, but to the teachers (bishops) collectively, when united with the pope.

If non-Catholics pretend to say that the whole Catholic Church has, in the course of time, departed from the divine doctrine, and fallen into errors: 1) they manifestly contradict the promises of our divine Savior; 2) they condemn all the holy fathers of the Church, who taught exactly the same as the Catholic Church teaches; 3) they set themselves at variance with one another, since they have always disagreed among themselves about what properly is divine doctrine, and what is not; and 4) they must, if the nations had been deceived by the teaching Church, lay the fault on God, who continually accredited the Catholic Church together with her teachers, and confirmed her authority by evidently protecting her at all times, by spreading her over the whole world, by illustrating her by innumerable miracles, and blessing her labors with the most glorious success;[437] whereas, on the other hand, the sectarians never could corroborate their pretended mission by any miracle, but, on the contrary, fell into many

[434] Jn 14:17, 16
[435] Mt 16:18
[436] 1 Tm 3:15
[437] See our "Concluding Remarks" of the "Short History of Revealed Religion," p. 103–104, above.

manifest contradictions and pernicious errors, by which the world was only more and more corrupted.[438]

318. **If, then, differences arise in matters of faith, what are we to do?**

We must adhere to the decisions of the Church.

"And he gave some apostles,...and other some pastors and doctors,... that henceforth we be no more children tossed to and fro, and carried about with every wind of doctrine by the wickedness of men, by cunning craftiness, by which they lie in wait to deceive."[439]

319. **By whom are the decisions of the Church given?**

Either by the supreme head of the Church, the pope, or by a council confirmed by the pope.[440]

320. **Are all Christians bound to submit to the decisions of the pope?**

Yes, as often as he decides as head and teacher of the whole Church in matters of faith and morals, the pope is as infallible as the Church herself.

321. **Is the pope infallible?**

Yes; the General Council of the Vatican, in 1870, defined that the pope is infallible when he teaches the Church *ex cathedra*.

322. **Is not this a new doctrine?**

No; the Church then defined—that is, solemnly declared in precise words—a doctrine which had always been held and acted on.

In doing this, the Church acted just as she had done in the First General Council of Nicea (325 A.D.), when she similarly defined the doctrine of the divinity of Christ, which had been held and acted on before that date; and as she has acted at other times, in regard to other doctrines, whenever she saw that it was necessary to define them.

438 See "Short History of Revealed Religion," p. 125–126 and 132–134, above.
439 Eph 4:11, 14
440 See "Short History of Revealed Religion," p. 118–119, above.

323. **What is the meaning of the infallibility of the pope? Does it mean that he cannot do wrong?**
By no means. The pope is a child of Adam, and, like other men, can have faults and can commit sin. Infallibility refers not to his life and conduct, but to his official teaching of doctrine, and means that in such teaching he cannot fall into error.

324. **Are the words of the pope, therefore, always infallible?**
No; the words of the pope are always to be received with the respect due to his high authority. But they are infallible only when he teaches *ex cathedra* as pope.

325. **When does the pope speak *ex cathedra*?**
The pope speaks *ex cathedra* when, in the exercise of his office as head of the Church, and chief pastor and teacher of all the faithful, he declares what is to be held by the Universal Church as the true doctrine on any matter of faith or morals.

326. **Why cannot the pope teach error when he speaks *ex cathedra*?**
Because God will not allow him to do so. Infallibility does not depend on the virtue or on the learning of the pope, but on the special assistance of the Holy Ghost, given him according to the promise of Christ, who said to St. Peter: "I have prayed for thee, that thy faith fail not. And thou, being once converted, confirm thy brethren."[441]

327. **Is the infallibility of the pope the same as the infallibility of the Church?**
Yes, precisely. The pope is the supreme pastor and teacher, whose voice all the faithful, clergy, and laity, "lambs and sheep," are commanded by Christ to hear and to follow. If he could teach error *ex cathedra*, the Church would then follow him into error, and would thereby fail; and so the promises of Christ would be falsified, which is impossible.

[441] Lk 22:32

328. **How do we know that this doctrine was always held and acted on in the Catholic Church?**

Because from the beginning whoever obstinately refused to accept and believe a doctrine of Catholic faith, when so declared *ex cathedra* by the pope, was always cut off from the communion of the Church, and condemned as a heretic.

"I will give to thee the keys of the kingdom of heaven, and whatsoever thou shalt bind upon earth, it shall be bound also in heaven; and whatsoever thou shalt loose on earth, it shall be loosed also in heaven."[442] "I have prayed for thee, that thy faith fail not, and thou, being once converted, confirm thy brethren."[443] "Feed my lambs; feed my sheep."[444] The authority of the pope to decide doctrinal controversies conclusively, and to define the true faith for the whole Church, was ever acknowledged and acted on. Those who broached heresies in any part of the world, and were condemned by their own local bishops, often appealed to the supreme decision of the bishop of Rome. On the other hand, Catholic bishops and patriarchs, like St. Athanasius, St. John Chrysostom, and others, who were often persecuted and unjustly condemned by synods, appealed to the pope, who reversed and annulled the unjust decrees, and decided in favor of the condemned ones, as holding the true doctrine. Nestorius, Eutyches, and other heresiarchs were condemned by the popes, and the decisions of the Roman pontiffs were received as conclusive, and were honored as "the voice of Peter speaking through his successor," which it would be heresy to depart from. St. Augustine held that a controversy was closed definitively when the pope had decided it. *Roma locuta est!* In defining the infallibility of the Roman pontiff, the Vatican Council did not introduce a new doctrine, but simply defined the ordinary and normal mode in which Christ has willed and provided that his Church shall in fact be kept infallibly in the path of divine truth and saved from the assaults of hell, ever striving to lead her into error.

[442] Mt 16:19
[443] Lk 22:32
[444] Jn 21:15, 17

329. **How does the Church decide when differences arise in matters of faith?**
She decides according to the tenor of holy scripture and tradition.

330. **Does the Church, then, teach nothing new, when, in such differences, she decides what is to be believed?**
No; she only explains the word of God entrusted to her in holy scripture and tradition, and condemns the opposite errors and innovations.

The doctrine of the Catholic Church is no other than the doctrine of Christ and the apostles, which she has been entrusted with, in order that she may faithfully preserve and preach it. The Church, therefore, perpetually adheres to the old doctrine, inherited from the fathers, and cries out with the apostle to all: "Keep that which is committed to thy trust, avoiding the profane novelties of words, and oppositions of knowledge falsely so called."[445] "But evil men and seducers shall grow worse and worse: erring, and driving into error. But continue thou in those things which thou hast learned, and which have been committed to thee."[446] "If any one preach to you a gospel besides that which you have received, let him be anathema."[447] "What has been believed in all places, at all times, and by all people, that is really and truly Catholic."[448]

On Salvation in the True Church of Christ Alone

331. **If the Catholic Church is to lead all men to eternal salvation, and has, for that purpose, received from Christ her doctrine, her means of grace, and her powers,[449] what, for his part, is everyone obliged to do?**

Everyone is obliged, under pain of eternal damnation, to become a member of the Catholic Church, to believe her doctrine, to use her means of grace, and to submit to her authority.

[445] 1 Tm 6:20; Cf. 2 Tm 1:14
[446] 2 Tm 3:13-14
[447] Gal 1:9
[448] Vincent of Lerins, *The Commonitory*, Ch. 2, n. 6
[449] Compare p. 245–246, q. 309-311.

332. **Who teaches us this obligation?**

Jesus Christ himself, in these words: "If he will not hear the Church, let him be to thee as the heathen and publican";[450] and: "He that believeth not [the apostles and their lawful successors[451]] shall be condemned."[452]

Hence the Catholic Church is justly called the only saving Church. To despise her is the same as to despise Christ; namely, his doctrine, his means of grace, and his powers; to separate from her is the same as to separate from Christ, and to forfeit eternal salvation. Therefore, St. Augustine, and the other bishops of Africa, at the Council of Zirta, 412 A.D., pronounced this decision: "Whosoever is separated from the Catholic Church, however commendable in his own opinion his life may be, he shall for this very reason, that he is at the same time separated from the unity of Christ, 'not see life, but the wrath of God abideth on him.'"[453]

333. **Who is a member of the Catholic Church?**

Everyone who is baptized, and has neither voluntarily separated himself, nor has been excluded from her.

334. **Who have voluntarily separated themselves from the Church?**

1) All those who by their own fault are heretics, i.e., who profess a doctrine that has been condemned by the Church; or who are infidels—that is, who no longer have nor profess any Christian faith at all; and 2) all those who by their own fault are schismatics—that is, who have renounced, not the doctrine of the Church, but their obedience to her, or to her supreme head, the pope.

335. **Who are excluded from the Catholic Church?**

Excommunicates—that is, those who, as degenerate members, have been expelled from the communion of the Church.

[450] Mt 18:17

[451] Compare p. 239, q. 285-286.

[452] Mk 16:16

[453] Jn 3:36

336. **Are not those also who are heretics without their own fault separated from the Catholic Church?**

Such as are heretics without their own fault, but sincerely search after the truth, and in the meantime do the will of God to the best of their knowledge, although they are separated from the body, remain, however, united to the soul of the Church, and partake of her graces.

Even those who are heretics without their own fault are deprived, though not of all, at least of many, graces and blessings of our holy religion; as, for instance, the Holy Sacrifice of the Mass, the true Lord's supper, sacramental absolution, the holy sacraments administered to the dying, etc. Therefore, we should fervently pray for heretics, and by sincere charity, and an edifying life, contribute toward their conversion.

337. **Who is a heretic by his own fault?**

A heretic by his own fault is: 1) he who knows the Catholic Church, and is convinced of her truth, but does not join her; and 2) he who could know her, if he would candidly search, but, through indifference and other culpable motives, neglects to do so.

338. **Does it become us to judge whether this one or that is outside the Church by his own fault or not?**

No; for such judgment belongs to God, who alone is "the searcher of hearts and reins,"[454] and "judges the secrets of men."[455]

"Judge not before the time, until the Lord come, who both will bring to light the hidden things of darkness, and will make manifest the counsels of the hearts."[456]

[454] Ps 7:10

[455] Rom 2:16. On this subject, consult *The Sincere Christian Instructed* (Appendix), by the Right Rev. George Hay.

[456] 1 Cor 4:5

339. **To obtain eternal salvation, is it sufficient to be a member of the Catholic Church?**
No; for there are also rotten and dead members,[457] who by their sins bring upon themselves eternal damnation.

340. **What, then, do we profess to believe by these words of the Creed, "I believe in the holy Catholic Church"?**
We profess to believe that Jesus Christ has established a visible Church, endless in her duration, and infallible in her doctrine, which we must believe and obey without reserve, if we would obtain eternal salvation; and that this is no other than the Roman Catholic Church.

Application. It is right for us to call the Catholic Church our mother; for 1) she has regenerated us in a spiritual manner in baptism, and has made us children of God; 2) she feeds us with the word of God, and with the bread of angels; 3) she brings us up in the fear of the Lord; and 4) she kindly prays for us, comforts us, and assists us, as long as we live here below, and even after we have departed this life. Honor and love, therefore, the Church as your mother; listen diligently to her instructions, and humbly submit to all her laws and directions; for "he shall not have God for his Father who will not have the Church for his mother."[458]

The Communion of Saints

341. **Are only the faithful on earth united together as one Church?**
No; with the faithful on earth are also spiritually united the saints in heaven and the souls in purgatory. The faithful on earth who are members of the Catholic Church constitute the Church militant; the souls in purgatory, the Church suffering; and the saints in heaven, the Church triumphant; yet these three Churches are, strictly speaking, but one in different states.

[457] Cf. Apoc 3:1
[458] Cyprian, *On the Unity of the Church*, n. 6

342. **In what does this spiritual union consist?**
This spiritual union consists in this: that all are members of one body, whose head is Christ Jesus, and that therefore the different members participate in one another's spiritual goods.

"As in one body we have many members,...so we, being many, are one body in Christ, and every one members one of another."[459] "He [Christ] is the head of the body, the church."[460]

343. **What is this spiritual union called?**
The communion of saints.

344. **Why are all the members of this communion styled "saints"?**
Because all are called to be saints,[461] and have been sanctified by baptism; and many of them have already arrived at sanctity.

345. **What benefit do we reap from the communion with the saints in heaven?**
We partake of the merits which they acquired while here below, and are assisted by their intercession with God in our behalf.

346. **But does not death dissolve all union between the living and the dead?**
No; no more than it dissolves their union with Christ, their head.

347. **What benefit do the souls in purgatory receive from our communion with them?**
We come to the assistance of these our suffering brethren, in order that their pains may be mitigated and shortened.

348. **By what means can we assist the poor souls in purgatory?**
By prayers, almsdeeds, and other good works, especially by the Holy Sacrifice of the Mass and the application of indulgences.

[459] Rom 12:4-5
[460] Col 1:18
[461] Cf. 1 Thes 4:3

"Judas [Machabeus] sent twelve thousand drachms of silver to Jerusalem for sacrifice to be offered for the sins of the dead...It is, therefore, a holy and wholesome thought to pray for the dead, that they may be loosed from sins."[462] That the Church has at all times prayed for the dead, and that the apostles themselves ordained to remember them at the Holy Sacrifice of the Mass, is testified by the most ancient fathers of the Church.[463]

349. **What profit do we derive from the mutual communion with the faithful on earth?**

We participate in all the Masses, prayers, and good works of the Catholic Church, and, in general, in all her spiritual goods.

"God hath tempered the body together...that the members might be mutually careful one for another Now, you are the body of Christ, and members of member."[464]

350. **Do sinners, as long as they are not cut off from the Church, also share in this communion?**

Sinners as dead members forfeit, indeed, most of the spiritual goods; nevertheless, in virtue of their union with the Church, they still receive various blessings and graces, which help to their conversion.

Application. Every day pray for your fellow Christians who are either combating on earth or suffering in purgatory, and recommend yourself every morning and night to the protection of the saints in heaven. Above all, strive to lead a holy life; for "we are fellow citizens with the saints, and the domestics of God."[465]

[462] 2 Mc 12:43, 46
[463] All Souls' Day
[464] 1 Cor 12:24-25, 27
[465] Eph 2:19

THE TENTH ARTICLE

"The forgiveness of sins."

351. **What does the tenth article of the Creed teach us?**
That in the Catholic Church we can receive, through the merits of Jesus Christ, forgiveness of sins and of the punishment due to them.

"Blessed be the God and Father of our Lord Jesus Christ,...in whom we have redemption through his blood, the remission of sins, according to the riches of his grace."[466]

352. **What sins can be forgiven in the Catholic Church?**
All sins without exception.

353. **What must the sinner do in order to obtain forgiveness of his sins?**
1) He must truly repent; for Christ says, "Unless you shall do penance, you shall all perish";[467] and 2) he must worthily receive the sacraments instituted by Christ for the remission of sins.

354. **Which sacraments were instituted by Christ for the remission of sins?**
The sacraments of baptism and penance.

355. **Who has power to forgive sins in the sacrament of penance?**
The bishops of the Catholic Church and the priests commissioned by them; for it was to them only that Christ said: "Whose sins you shall forgive, they are forgiven them."[468]

Application. Give hearty thanks to God for having promised you forgiveness of your sins, and go willingly and frequently to confession; but first prepare yourself well for it, that it may be said to you also: "Be of good heart, son, thy sins are forgiven thee."[469]

466 Eph 1:3, 7
467 Lk 13:3
468 Jn 20:23
469 Mt 9:2

THE ELEVENTH ARTICLE

"The resurrection of the body."

356. **What happens to man at his death?**

The soul separates from the body, and appears before the judgment seat of God; but the body returns into the earth.[470]

357. **Why must all men die?**

Because all have sinned in Adam.

"By one man sin entered into this world, and by sin death."[471]

358. **Why has God hidden from us the time of our death?**

1) That we may so much the more honor and fear him as the supreme Lord of life and death; 2) that we may keep ourselves every moment prepared for death; and 3) that the dread with which we are seized when we think of death as at hand may be moderated.

"Be you then also ready; for at what hour you think not, the Son of man will come."[472]—*Example*: Parable of the ten virgins.[473]

359. **How are we to keep ourselves prepared for death?**

We should carefully avoid sin, and lead a godly life.

360. **How long will the body remain in the earth?**

The body will remain in the earth till the day of judgment, when God will raise it again to life, and reunite it forever to the soul, from which death had separated it.

"The hour cometh, wherein all that are in the graves shall hear the voice of the Son of God. And they that have done good things shall come

[470] Cf. Eccles 12:7
[471] Rom 5:12
[472] Lk 12:40
[473] Cf. Mt 25

forth unto the resurrection of life; but they that have done evil unto the resurrection of judgment"—i.e., to hear the sentence of condemnation.[474]

361. **What do we call this raising of the bodies to life?**
The resurrection of the flesh or body.

362. **But how can the bodies, when reduced to dust, rise again?**
By the omnipotence of God, our bodies, reduced to dust, can as easily be raised again to life as they were once made out of nothing.

Parable of the grain of wheat.[475]

363. **Why shall our bodies rise again?**
1) That, as the body was a partner with the soul in the performance of good or evil works, so it may also be a partaker of the reward or punishment;[476] and 2) that the victory of Christ over death may be perfect.

"When this mortal hath put on immortality, then shall come to pass the saying that is written: 'Death is swallowed up in victory.' O death, where is thy victory?"[477]

364. **Shall all men rise from the dead?**
Yes, all men, the good as well as the wicked.[478]

365. **Will the bodies, when raised to life, be all alike?**
No; the bodies of the bad shall be hideous and miserable, but those of the good shall be glorious, and like to the glorified body of Christ.

"We shall all indeed rise again, but, we shall not all be changed"—i.e., glorified.[479] "[Our Lord Jesus Christ] will reform the body of our lowness,

[474] Jn 5:28-29
[475] Cf. 1 Cor 15:35; etc.
[476] Cf. 2 Cor 5:10
[477] 1 Cor 15:54-55
[478] Cf. Jn 5:28-29
[479] 1 Cor 15:51

that it may be made like to the body of his glory."[480] Hence the honor we pay to the bodies of the deceased—funerals, blessed burying-grounds.

According to 1 Corinthians 15:42-44, we distinguish four qualities of the glorified bodies: 1) "It [the body] is sown [i.e., buried] in corruption, it shall rise in incorruption," incorruptible and impassible—i.e., incapable of corruption, and of any suffering. 2) "It is sown in dishonor, it shall rise in glory," bright—i.e., shining with glory, without spot or blemish. 3) "It is sown in weakness, it shall rise in power," agile—i.e., capable of transporting itself with the soul in an instant from one place to another. 4) "It is sown a natural body, it shall rise a spiritual body," subtile—i.e., spiritualized, or capable of penetrating any corporeal substance, like our Savior's body after his resurrection.

366. **Is cremation, or the burning of the bodies of the dead, lawful?**
No; cremation is forbidden by the Church under severe penalties.

367. **What impression should our belief in the resurrection of the body make upon us?**
It should incite us: 1) to honor our body, and never to abuse it by sinning; 2) patiently to suffer all bodily pains, and even death; and 3) to console ourselves at the death of our friends.

1) "Glorify and bear God in your body."[481] 2) *Examples*: Job: "In the last day I shall rise out of the earth, and I shall be clothed again with my skin, and in my flesh I shall see my God...This my hope is laid up in my bosom";[482] the Machabean brothers. 3) "We will not have you ignorant, brethren, concerning them that are asleep, that you may not be sorrowful, even as others who have no hope,"[483] etc.

Application. Never abuse your eyes, tongue, ears, hands, nor your other senses or members by doing evil, but "yield them to serve justice, unto

[480] Phil 3:21
[481] 1 Cor 6:20
[482] Jb 19:25-27
[483] 1 Thes 4:12-17

sanctification";[484] that you may one day rise to everlasting glory, and not to everlasting damnation.

THE TWELFTH ARTICLE

"And life everlasting. Amen."

368. **What does the twelfth article of the Creed teach us?**

1) That after this life there is another, which will last forever; and 2) that the just shall enjoy eternal happiness in it.

"The just shall go into life everlasting"—that is, into eternal glory.[485]

369. **In what does the eternal happiness of the just consist?**

1) They see God as he is, and are united with him in the most intense love; and 2) with this sight and love of God is combined the possession of all good things, eternal joy and glory in the company of all the angels and saints.

"We see now through a glass in a dark manner; but then face to face."[486] "God shall wipe away all tears from their eyes; and death shall be no more, nor mourning, nor crying, nor sorrow."[487] "They shall be inebriated with the plenty of thy house [O God!], and thou shalt make them drink of the torrent of thy pleasure."[488] "They shall receive a kingdom of glory, and a crown of beauty at the hand of the Lord."[489]

370. **Can we conceive this eternal happiness?**

No; the happiness in heaven is so great that it exceeds all that can be said or imagined.

[484] Rom 6:19
[485] Mt 25:46
[486] 1 Cor 13:12; Cf. 1 Jn 3:2
[487] Apoc 21:4
[488] Ps 35:9
[489] Ws 5:17

For "eye hath not seen, nor ear heard, neither hath it entered into the heart of man, what things God hath prepared for them that love him."[490]

371. **Shall all be equally happy?**

No; for "every one shall receive his own reward according to his own labor"—i.e., according to his deserts.[491]

"He who soweth sparingly, shall also reap sparingly; and he who soweth in blessings, shall also reap blessings."[492]

372. **What will be the life of the wicked through all eternity?**

A life without any grace or joy, a life full of pains in hell.

Such a life is called in the holy scripture the "second (eternal) death." "The fearful, and unbelieving, and the abominable, and murderers, and whoremongers, and sorcerers, and idolaters, and all liars, they shall have their portion in the pool burning with fire and brimstone, which is the second death."[493]

373. **What is hell in the words of Christ?**

"A place of torments";[494] "an everlasting punishment";[495] an "unquenchable fire";[496] "the exterior darkness, where there shall be weeping and gnashing of teeth."[497]

374. **Who shall be condemned to the torments of hell?**

Everyone who dies an enemy of God—that is, who dies in mortal sin.

"He that committeth sin is of the devil";[498] therefore, he also deserves to be punished like the devil.[499]

490 1 Cor 2:9
491 1 Cor 3:8
492 2 Cor 9:6; Cf. 1 Cor 15:41-42
493 Apoc 21:8
494 Lk 16:28
495 Mt 25:46
496 Mk 9:44
497 Mt 8:12
498 1 Jn 3:8
499 Cf. Mt 25:41

375. **What sort of pains shall the souls of the damned suffer?**

1) Internal torture and despair at the thought of all the evil they have done, and of the many graces they have abused;[500] 2) unspeakable sadness and misery, because they have, by their own fault, forfeited eternal happiness in heaven;[501] 3) perpetual horror of the dismal company of the devils and of all the damned;[502] and 4) the most intolerable torments and pangs, without any hope of relief or end; for "their fire shall not be extinguished, and their worm shall not die."[503]

"And the rich man also died, and he was buried in hell. And lifting up his eyes when he was in torments, he saw Abraham afar off, and Lazarus in his bosom; and he cried, and said: 'Father Abraham, have mercy on me, and send Lazarus, that he may dip the tip of his finger in water, to cool my tongue; for I am tormented in this flame,'"[504] etc.

376. **Whence do we know that the pains of the damned are eternal?**

1) From the clear testimony of Christ and the apostles; and 2) from the express doctrine of the infallible Church, which has solemnly condemned the erroneous opinion of those heretics who taught that the pains of the devils and of the damned would in time have an end.

"Depart from me, ye cursed, into everlasting fire:...and they shall go into everlasting punishment."[505] "It is better for thee to enter lame into life everlasting, than, having two feet, to be cast into the hell of unquenchable fire, where their worm dieth not, and the fire is not extinguished."[506] "And the smoke of their torments shall ascend up for ever and ever."[507]

[500] Cf. Ws 5:1-15; Mt 8:12
[501] Cf. Lk 13:25-28
[502] Cf. Mt 25:41
[503] Mk 9:45; Cf. Apoc 20:9-10
[504] Lk 16:22-24
[505] Mt 25:41, 46
[506] Mk 9:44-45
[507] Apoc 14:11; and elsewhere

377. **Why are the pains of the condemned souls eternal?**

1) Because the offense against the infinite majesty of God demands of his justice a punishment without end; 2) because all who die in sin remain eternally obdurate in sin; 3) because God, in virtue of his holiness, hates evil no less than he loves what is good, and therefore punishes vice eternally, as he eternally rewards virtue; and 4) because only the everlasting pains of hell are a sufficient means to deter man, even in secret, from evil.

"Sin remains as a propensity to sin, though it can no more be committed in deed."[508] "God showed also mercy to us when he created hell, whereby he will prevent us from being wicked."[509]

378. **Will the pains of all the damned be equal?**

No; for each one shall have to suffer in proportion to his sins, and to the ill use he has made of the graces bestowed upon him.

"As much as she (the city of Babylon) hath glorified herself, and lived in delicacies, so much torment and sorrow give ye to her."[510] "Unto whomsoever much is given, of him much shall be required."[511]

379. **Will all those who are condemned to eternal hell fire be condemned by their own fault?**

Yes; for all men may be eternally happy, provided they will avail themselves of the abundant graces which God gives them.

"[God] will have all men to be saved, for there is...one mediator of God and men, the man Christ Jesus, who gave himself a redemption for all."[512] "Before man is life and death;...that which he shall choose shall be given him."[513]

[508] Innocent III
[509] Chrysostom
[510] Apoc 18:7
[511] Lk 12:48
[512] 1 Tm 2:4-6
[513] Ecclus 15:18

380. **What do you understand by the "four last things" of man?**
I understand by the "four last things": death, judgment, hell, and heaven.

381. **Of what use is the frequent remembrance of the four last things to us?**
It is, as the Holy Ghost testifies, an effectual means to avoid sin, and consequently to escape eternal damnation.

"In all thy works remember thy last end, and thou shalt never sin."[514]

382. **With what word do we conclude the Apostles' Creed?**
With the word *Amen*, which means, "So it is," or, "So be it."

383. **Why do we conclude the Apostles' Creed with this word?**
In order to declare that we firmly believe all that is contained in the twelve articles of the Creed, and that we are determined to live according to this belief, and to die in it.

Application. Often consider, especially at the hour of temptation, this serious truth: "Once lost, lost forever"; or this one: "Momentary joy brings on eternal pain, but short pain eternal joy"; and these words of Jesus Christ: "The kingdom of heaven suffereth violence, and the violent bear it away."[515]

[514] Ecclus 7:40
[515] Mt 11:12

SECTION II

On the Commandments

The Commandments in General and the Chief Commandment of Charity

384. **To obtain eternal salvation is it sufficient that we believe all that God has revealed?**

No; we must also keep his commandments: "If thou wilt enter into life, keep the commandments."[516]

"Not every one that saith to me, 'Lord, Lord,' shall enter into the kingdom of heaven; but he that doth the will of my Father who is in heaven, he shall enter into the kingdom of heaven."[517]

385. **But are we able to keep the commandments of God?**

Yes, with the assistance of God's grace, which he refuses to no one who asks for it.

"His commandments are not heavy."[518] "My yoke is sweet, and my burden light."[519]

386. **How do we know that we are able to keep the commandments?**

We know it: 1) because God inflicts eternal punishment upon those who break them; and 2) because there have been at all times saints who faithfully observed them.

[516] Mt 19:17
[517] Mt 7:21
[518] 1 Jn 5:3
[519] Mt 11:30

1) "And that servant who knew the will of his lord,...and did not according to his will, shall be beaten with many stripes."[520] 2) It is written of Zachary and Elizabeth: "And they were both just before God, walking in all the commandments and justifications of the Lord without blame."[521]

387. **Is there one chief commandment that includes all the others?**
Yes; the commandment of charity—i.e., the commandment of the love of God and of our neighbor.

388. **How is this commandment of charity expressed?**
It is expressed in these terms: "Thou shalt love the Lord thy God with thy whole heart, and with thy whole soul, and with thy whole mind, and with thy whole strength. This is the greatest and the first commandment. And the second is like to this: Thou shalt love thy neighbor as thyself."[522]

On the Love of God

389. **What is the love of God?**
It is a virtue infused by God into our soul, by which we give ourselves up with all our heart to him, the sovereign good, in order to please him by fulfilling his will, and to be united with him.

390. **What qualities must our love of God have?**
It must be: 1) supernatural; 2) sovereign; and 3) active.

391. **When is our love "supernatural"?**
Our love is supernatural when, with the help of God's grace, we love him as we know him, not only by our reason, but by our faith.

"Now the end of the commandment is charity, from a pure heart, and a good conscience, and an unfeigned faith. From which things some, going

[520] Lk 12:47
[521] Lk 1:6
[522] Mk 12:30-31; Mt 22:37-40

astray, are turned aside unto vain babbling."[523] "My just man liveth by faith; but if he withdraw himself, he shall not please my soul."[524] By faith we know God, not only as the Creator of the world, and the giver of all natural goods, which we can likewise perceive by our reason; but also as the author and giver of the supernatural graces and benefits; as the most merciful Father, who has most graciously adopted us, and has given his own Son, in order to save us, to sanctify us, and make us one day eternally happy in the kingdom of his glory.

392. **When is our love of God "sovereign"?**

Our love of God is sovereign when we love him more than all other things, so that we are willing to lose all rather than separate ourselves from him by sin.

"I am sure that neither death, nor life,...nor things present, nor things to come,...nor any other creature, shall be able to separate us from the love of God."[525] This degree of love, by which we are ready to lose all, rather than commit a grievous sin, is absolutely necessary to salvation; but this is not the highest degree. For a higher degree is this: when we are not only determined not to commit any grievous sin, but not even the least sin; and there is a higher degree still, when we are resolved always to do what is most perfect, or most pleasing to God.

393. **When is our love "active"?**

Our love is active when we do what is acceptable to God; that is, when we keep his commandments.

"He that hath my commandments, and keepeth them, he it is that loveth me."[526] "This is the charity of God, that we keep his commandments."[527]

[523] 1 Tm 1:5-6
[524] Heb 10:38
[525] Rom 8:38-39
[526] Jn 14:21
[527] 1 Jn 5:3

394. **Why must we love God?**

We must love God: 1) because he is the sovereign and most perfect good; 2) because he has loved us first, and has bestowed innumerable blessings upon us in soul and body; and 3) because he commands us to love him, and promises us eternal salvation as a reward for it.

395. **When is our love of God "perfect"?**

Our love is perfect when we love God on account of his infinite goodness; that is, when we love him above all things, because he is both infinitely good in himself, and infinitely good to us.

"Let us therefore love God, because God first hath loved us."[528] Of this perfect love it is said: "He that abideth in charity, abideth in God, and God in him";[529] and, "Every one that loveth is born of God."[530]—*Example*: Mary Magdalen: "Many sins are forgiven her, because she hath loved much."[531]

396. **When is our love "imperfect"?**

Our love is imperfect when we love God chiefly because we expect good things from him.

Example. The prodigal son: "How many hired servants in my father's house abound with bread, and I here perish with hunger! I will arise, and will go to my father."[532]

397. **By what means is the love of God increased and perfected in us?**

1) By frequently and worthily receiving the holy sacraments; 2) by meditating on the goodness and mercy of God, especially on the bitter passion and death of Jesus Christ; 3) by self-denial, and patience in afflictions; and 4) by performing good works.

[528] 1 Jn 4:19
[529] 1 Jn 4:16
[530] 1 Jn 4:7
[531] Lk 7:47
[532] Lk 15:17-18

398. **How is the love of God lessened and banished?**
By mortal sin, the love of God is banished from our hearts; and by venial sin, its fervor is lessened.

Application. Exercise yourself assiduously in the love of God by these means: often think of him, and often pray to him; delight in hearing and speaking of him, do and suffer everything for his sake, and fear nothing so much as to offend him.

On the Love of Our Neighbor

399. **Whom must we particularly love after God?**
Our neighbor—i.e., all men without exception.

400. **Is it not enough if we love God?**
No; for, "If any man say, I love God, and hateth his brother, he is a liar."[533]

401. **Why must we love our neighbor?**
1) Because Christ our Lord commands us to love him, and by the fulfillment of this commandment, he will know his true disciples; 2) because he himself in his life and death taught us so by his example; and 3) because everyone is a child and an image of God, was redeemed with the blood of Christ, and is called to eternal salvation.

"By this shall all men know that you are my disciples, if you have love one for another."[534] "Be ye, therefore, followers of God, as most dear children; and walk in love, as Christ also hath loved us, and hath delivered himself for us."[535] "Have we not all one Father? Hath not one God created us? Why then doth every one of us despise his brother?"[536]

402. **What qualities must the love of our neighbor have?**
It must be: 1) sincere; 2) disinterested; 3) general.

533 1 Jn 4:20
534 Jn 13:35
535 Eph 5:1-2
536 Mal 2:10

403. **When is our love "sincere"?**

Our love is sincere when we love our neighbor, not in appearance, but as ourselves.

"My little children, let us not love in word, nor in tongue, but in deed, and in truth."[537]

404. **When do we love our neighbor as ourselves?**

We love our neighbor as ourselves when we observe the command of Christ: "All things whatsoever you would that men should do to you, do you also to them."[538]

"See thou never do to another what thou wouldst hate to have done to thee by another."[539]

405. **When is our love "disinterested"?**

Our love is disinterested when we do good to our neighbor for God's sake, and not that we may be praised or rewarded by men.

"When thou makest a feast, call the poor, the maimed, the lame, and the blind: and thou shalt be blessed, because they have not wherewith to make thee recompense; for recompense shall be made thee at the resurrection of the just."[540]

406. **When is our love "general"?**

Our love is general when we exclude no one from it, whether he be our friend or our enemy.

"For if you love them that love you, what reward shall you have? Do not even the publicans this? And if you salute your brethren only, what do you more? Do not also the heathens this?"[541]—*Example*: The good Samaritan.[542]

[537] 1 Jn 3:18
[538] Mt 7:12
[539] Tb 4:16
[540] Lk 14:13-14
[541] Mt 5:46-47
[542] Cf. Lk 10

407. **Is it not enough if we do not revenge ourselves on our enemies?**

No; God commands us to love our enemies—i.e., to wish them well, and to be ready to assist them in their necessities, as much as lies in our power.

"Love your enemies, do good to them that hate you, and pray for them that persecute and calumniate you; that you may be the children of your Father who is in heaven, who maketh his sun to rise upon the good and the bad, and raineth upon the just and the unjust."[543]—*Example*: St. Stephen.

408. **Why must we love our enemies?**

1) Because the Lord our God commands us to love them; 2) because Christ Jesus, our divine model, has given us the example of loving our enemies; and 3) because we also wish to be forgiven by God.

1) "But I say to you, 'Love your enemies; do good to them that hate you,'"[544] etc. 2) Jesus addressed even his betrayer in the kindest manner, saying: "Friend, whereto art thou come?"[545] And he prayed on the cross for his murderers: "Father, forgive them, for they know not what they do."[546] 3) "Forgive us our trespasses, as we,"[547] etc.—*Example*: Parable of the unmerciful servant.[548]

409. **What has he to expect who will not forgive him by whom he has been offended?**

Judgment without mercy.

"Judgment without mercy to him that hath not done mercy."[549] "But if you will not forgive, neither will your Father that is in heaven forgive you your sins."[550]

[543] Mt 5:44-45
[544] Mt 5:44ff
[545] Mt 26:50
[546] Lk 23:34
[547] Mt 6:12ff
[548] Cf. Mt 18:23-35
[549] Jas 2:13
[550] Mk 11:26

410. **What must we do when we have offended someone?**

We must go and be reconciled to him.[551]

411. **What must we do when someone has offended us?**

We must willingly offer to make peace with him, forgive him from our heart, and suffer injustice rather than return evil for evil.

"To no man render evil for evil...If it be possible, as much as is in you, have peace with all men. Revenge not yourselves, my dearly beloved,...for it is written: 'Revenge is mine; I will repay,' saith the Lord."[552]—*Examples*: Jacob and Esau; David and Saul.

412. **What sort of people does holy scripture particularly recommend to our love?**

The poor, widows and orphans, and in general all those who are in corporal or spiritual need.

413. **How are we to assist them?**

By the corporal and spiritual works of mercy.

"Blessed are the merciful, for they shall obtain mercy."[553]

414. **Which are the corporal works of mercy?**

The corporal works of mercy are these seven: 1) to feed the hungry; 2) to give drink to the thirsty; 3) to clothe the naked; 4) to harbor the harborless; 5) to visit the imprisoned; 6) to visit the sick; 7) to bury the dead.

415. **Is it also a duty to perform corporal works of mercy?**

Yes, it is such an indispensable duty that Christ condemns the unmerciful to everlasting fire.

"Depart from me, you cursed, into everlasting fire...For I was hungry, and you gave me not to eat; I was thirsty, and you gave me not to drink; I was a stranger, and you took me not in; naked, and you covered me not;

551 Cf. Mt 5:23-24

552 Rom 12:17-19; Cf. Mt 5:39-41

553 Mt 5:7

sick and in prison, and you did not visit me...Amen I say unto you, as long as you did it not to one of these least, neither did you do it to me. And these shall go into everlasting punishment."[554] With regard to the dead, the holy scripture says: "My son, shed tears over the dead,...and neglect not his burial."[555]

416. **What good things are promised to those who give alms?**

1) Temporal blessings, and 2) especially spiritual graces, in order to obtain forgiveness of their sins and life everlasting.

1) "He that giveth to the poor shall not want; he that despiseth his entreaty shall suffer indigence."[556]—*Example*: Tobias. 2) "Alms delivereth from death, and the same is that which purgeth away sins, and maketh to find mercy and life everlasting."[557]—*Examples*: Zacheus the publican; Cornelius the centurion.

417. **Which are the spiritual works of mercy?**

The spiritual works of mercy are these seven: 1) to admonish sinners; 2) to instruct the ignorant; 3) to counsel the doubtful; 4) to comfort the sorrowful; 5) to bear wrongs patiently; 6) to forgive injuries; 7) to pray for the living and the dead.

418. **Are we also bound to perform spiritual works of mercy?**

Yes, provided we have sufficient knowledge and an opportunity to perform them; for the spiritual good of our neighbor should affect us far more than his corporal welfare.

"My brethren, if any one of you err from the truth, and one convert him, he must know that he who causeth a sinner to be converted from the error of his way, shall save his soul from death, and shall cover a multitude of sins."[558]

554 Mt 25:41-43, 45-46
555 Ecclus 38:16
556 Prv 28:27
557 Tb 12:9
558 Jas 5:19-20

419. **When are we in general bound to admonish or rebuke our neighbor in a brotherly manner?**
When it is necessary in order to prevent him from committing sin, and when our admonition will evidently be of service.

"If thy brother shall offend against thee, go and rebuke him between thee and him alone,"[559] etc.

420. **How is fraternal rebuke to be given?**
With all possible prudence, love, and meekness.

"Brethren, if a man be overtaken in any fault,...instruct such one in the spirit of meekness."[560]

Application. Be peaceable and kind to everyone, especially to your brothers and sisters, and to your relations. Bear with the faults and frailties of your neighbor; never render evil for evil; but pray for him who may have offended you.

Membership in approved Catholic charitable and other fraternal associations is an excellent means to promote and practice brotherly love.

On Christian Self-Love

421. **May a Christian love himself also?**
Yes, he may and ought to love himself; for Christ says: "Thou shalt love thy neighbor as thyself."[561]

422. **In what does Christian self-love consist?**
Christian self-love consists in being, above all things, solicitous for the salvation of one's soul.

423. **Why must we be solicitous, above all things, for the salvation of our soul?**
1) Because the soul has been created to the likeness of God, has been ransomed with the precious blood of Jesus Christ, and sanctified by the grace

[559] Mt 18:15ff
[560] Gal 6:1
[561] Mt 22:39; Mk 12:31

of the Holy Ghost; and 2) because on the salvation of the soul depends our eternal welfare.[562]

424. **What are we to do in order to secure the salvation of our soul?**
1) We must carefully avoid sin, and every occasion of sin; 2) if nevertheless we have sinned, we must not delay to do sincere penance; and 3) we must earnestly endeavor to practice virtue, and to do good works.

"They that commit sin and iniquity are enemies to their own soul."[563] "Delay not to be converted to the Lord, and defer it not from day to day; for his wrath shall come on a sudden, and in the time of vengeance he will destroy thee."[564] "Wherefore, brethren, labor the more, that by good works you may make sure your calling and election."[565]

425. **May we also love our body and temporal goods in a Christian manner?**
Yes, we may, and are also bound to love, in a Christian and supernatural manner, our body and temporal goods, as health, property, and good reputation.

426. **When do we love our body in a Christian manner?**
When we love it: 1) because it is the dwelling place of our soul, and her instrument for the service of God; and 2) because it also was sanctified in baptism, and is destined for eternal glory.

He who loves his body in this manner will constantly subdue its unlawful desires, and thus, according to the admonition of St. Paul, "present [it] a living sacrifice, holy, pleasing unto God."[566]

[562] Cf. Mt 16:26
[563] Tb 12:10
[564] Ecclus 5:8-9
[565] 2 Pt 1:10
[566] Rom 12:1

427. When do we love the goods of this world in a Christian manner?

When we love them: 1) as far as all created things have their origin in God and are his gifts; and 2) as far as they serve us, to promote the honor of God, to assist the needy, and to fulfill the duties of our state of life.

He who loves the goods of this world in this manner will not turn his heart away from God in order to seek his happiness in them, but will make such a use of them that on their account he will not forfeit those of heaven.

428. What is opposite to this Christian love of one's self?

Inordinate self-love.

429. When is self-love "inordinate"?

1) When man prefers his own honor and will to the honor and will of God; 2) when he is more solicitous for his body and for temporal things than for his soul and eternal salvation; and 3) when he seeks his own welfare to the unlawful injury of his neighbor.

This vicious self-love is the source of all sins. "Men shall be lovers of themselves, covetous, haughty, proud, blasphemers, disobedient to parents, ungrateful, wicked, without affection, without peace, slanderers, incontinent, unmerciful, without kindness, traitors, stubborn, puffed up, and lovers of pleasures more than of God."[567]

430. Is every self-love that is not supernatural, vicious and inordinate?

No; there is also a merely natural self-love, by which we may indeed love ourselves, and all that belongs to us, in a lawful manner, but not meritorious to salvation.

"Thus also those who are evil know how to give [through natural love] good gifts to their children."[568]

Application. Oppose in good time that pernicious self-love by which a person, in all that he thinks, speaks, and does, has not in view the honor

[567] 2 Tm 3:2-4
[568] Cf. Lk 11:13

of God or the welfare of his neighbor, but only his own self, and his pretended advantages over others.

On the Ten Commandments of God[569]

431. **Where is our duty of loving God and our neighbor more fully contained?**
In the ten commandments, which God gave to Moses written on two tables of stone.

432. **What are the ten commandments?**

1. I am the Lord thy God. Thou shalt not have strange gods before me; thou shalt not make to thyself any graven thing to adore it.
2. Thou shalt not take the name of the Lord thy God in vain.
3. Remember that thou keep holy the sabbath day.
4. Honor thy father and thy mother, that it may be well with thee, and thou mayest live long on the earth.
5. Thou shalt not kill.
6. Thou shalt not commit adultery.
7. Thou shalt not steal.
8. Thou shalt not bear false witness against thy neighbor.
9. Thou shalt not covet thy neighbor's wife.
10. Thou shalt not covet thy neighbor's house, nor his field, nor his servant, nor his handmaid, nor his ox, nor his ass, nor anything that is his.

[569] See "Short History of Revealed Religion," p. 105, above.

433. **Why are we Christians also bound to keep these commandments of the old law?**
1) Because Christ is not come "to destroy the law, but to fulfill it"[570]—i.e., to confirm it, and to teach us how to observe it perfectly; and 2) because the ten commandments contain that law which already binds all men, since it is grounded in human nature, and has been written by God in all human hearts.[571]

434. **If the law is written in all hearts, why did God give it to man also by revelation?**
That we may the more surely know the law of God, and be the more strongly impelled to fulfill it; for our capacity to know and to will what is good has been very much weakened by sin.

435. **What in particular ought to induce us faithfully to keep the divine commandments?**
1) The reverence, love, and gratitude which we owe to God; 2) the fear of eternal punishment, and the hope of eternal reward.

THE FIRST COMMANDMENT OF GOD

The Honor and Worship of God

"I am the Lord thy God. Thou shalt not have strange gods before me; thou shalt not make to thyself any graven thing to adore it."

436. **What are we commanded by the first commandment?**
By the first commandment, we are commanded to pay to Almighty God due honor and adoration.

437. **How many kinds of honor do we owe to God?**
We owe to God two kinds of honor—namely, interior and exterior honor.

[570] Mt 5:17
[571] Cf. Rom 2:15

438. **How do we honor God "interiorly"?**

We honor God interiorly: 1) by faith, hope, and charity; 2) by reverence and adoration; 3) by thanksgiving for all his blessings; 4) by zeal for his honor; and 5) by obedience and resignation to his holy will.

439. **How do we sin against faith?**

1) By infidelity, heresy, and skepticism; 2) by impious and profane language, or by willfully listening to it; likewise, by reading or spreading irreligious books and writings; and 3) by indifference in matters of faith, or by actually denying it.

Many popular novels and other books which are commonly found in public libraries are dangerous to faith and morals. All, especially young persons, ought to seek competent advice regarding the selection of books to read.

440. **When do people become guilty of indifference in matters of faith?**

1) When they do not care for any religion, or when they consider all religions as equally good; 2) when they stand in need of being instructed, and neglect to attend the catechism or Christian doctrine; and 3) when parents or guardians allow their children to be brought up in an erroneous belief.

441. **How do we sin against hope?**

1) By despair or by distrust of God; and 2) by presumption or by false confidence.

442. **When do we sin by despair or by distrust?**

1) When we either do not hope at all for that which we ought to hope for from God, or 2) when we do not hope for it with confidence in him.

Examples: 1) Cain and Judas; 2) Moses and the Israelites in the desert.

443. **What are we to hope for from God?**

We are, above all, to hope for life everlasting, and for whatever is necessary and conducive to it—that is, the forgiveness of our sins and the grace of God.

444. **On what grounds are we to hope for these things?**
Because God, who is infinitely powerful, merciful, and faithful, has promised them to us, and Jesus Christ has merited them for us.

445. **What, then, is Christian hope?**
Christian hope is a virtue infused into our souls, by which we most confidently expect all the things which God has promised us through the merits of Jesus Christ.

446. **May every sinner hope for pardon?**
Yes, every sinner, even the greatest, may and ought to hope for pardon, provided he will be converted with all his heart, and do penance.

"If the wicked do penance for all his sins which he has committed, and keep all my commandments,...living he shall live, and shall not die."[572]—*Examples*: The Ninivites, Mary Magdalen, the thief on the cross, and others. Parable of the lost sheep and of the prodigal son.[573]

447. **How far may we also expect temporal goods from God?**
As far as they help us, or at least do not hinder us, to obtain eternal salvation.

448. **When do we sin by presumption and false confidence?**
1) When, relying on the mercy of God, we continue to sin without fear, or delay our repentance to the end of our life; 2) when we rashly expose ourselves to a danger from which we confidently expect God will extricate us.

449. **Is Christian hope also consistent with fear?**
1) Confidence in God does not exclude diffidence in ourselves; therefore, 2) we should neither be excessively timid about our salvation, nor should we throw off all sense of fear and solicitude for it.

[572] Ez 18:21
[573] Cf. Lk 15

"Wherefore he that thinketh himself to stand, let him take heed lest he fall."[574] "I am not conscious to myself of anything, yet I am not hereby justified; but he that judgeth me is the Lord."[575] "Justify not thyself before God, for he knoweth the heart."[576] "With fear and trembling work out your salvation."[577] "I chastise my body, and bring it into subjection; lest perhaps; when I have preached to others, I myself should become a castaway."[578]

450. **What sins are chiefly opposed to the love of God?**
In general, all mortal sins; but in particular, 1) indifference and aversion to God and divine things; and 2) hatred and repugnance to him and his paternal dispensations.

451. **How do we honor God also "exteriorly"?**
We honor God also exteriorly when we manifest our interior respectful sentiments toward him by exterior actions; as by our uniting with others in the public services of religion or in prayer, in common with others, by kneeling, and generally by our reverent demeanor during religious exercises.

452. **Why are we also commanded to honor God exteriorly?**
1) Because the body has been created by God as well as the soul, and, therefore, both should pay him honor and homage; 2) because it is quite natural to man to manifest his interior worship of God also exteriorly; 3) because the interior worship is intensified by exterior worship; and 4) because exterior worship is conducive and necessary for our mutual edification, for fortifying ourselves in our faith, and for preserving and propagating our religion.

Example. Daniel, who chose to be cast into the den of the lions rather than to give up the exterior adoration of God as prescribed by the law.[579]

[574] 1 Cor 10:12
[575] 1 Cor 4:4
[576] Ecclus 7:5
[577] Phil 2:12
[578] 1 Cor 9:27
[579] Cf. Dn 6

453. **How do we sin against the exterior worship of God?**

By neglecting to attend divine service, or by behaving irreverently when we are present.

Example. Punishment of the men at Bethsames because they approached the ark of the Lord in an irreverent manner.[580]

454. **May we sin in any other way against the reverence due to God?**

Yes, we sin also against it by idolatry, superstition, witchcraft, sacrilege, and simony.

455. **When does a person commit idolatry?**

He commits idolatry (worship of images) when he pays divine honor to any creature or thing, as the heathens did.

456. **When do we sin by superstition?**

1) When we honor God or the saints in a manner contrary to the doctrine or practice of the Church; 2) when we attribute to things a certain power which they cannot have, either by nature, or by the prayers of the Church, or by virtue of divine dispensation.

Examples. When we consult fortune-tellers and make them tell us our fortunes by cutting cards or by inspecting our hands; or when we have recourse to the interpretation of dreams, or to vain and foolish signs and practices, in order to know hidden things, or to obtain luck or health; still more, when for that purpose we abuse even holy names and blessed things.

457. **Is such superstition a grievous sin?**

It is generally a very grievous sin, because he who practices such things mostly expects the assistance of the evil spirit, if not openly, at least secretly; but, at all events, puts that confidence in idle or delusive things which he ought to place in God alone.

[580] Cf. 1 Kgs 6:19

458. **Is it also superstitious to wear on our persons images (medals) of the saints, or blessed things?**

On the contrary, it is praiseworthy, if it is done with a pious intention—that is to say, with confidence in God, in the intercession of the saints, or in the prayer and blessing of the Church.

459. **How do people become guilty of witchcraft?**

When they try, with the help of the evil spirits, to find hidden treasures, to injure others, or to work wonderful things.

Thus one day that wicked one, Antichrist, will do: "Whose coming is according to the working of Satan, in all [deluding] power, and signs, and lying wonders, and in all seduction of iniquity to them that perish."[581] This God will permit for the just punishment of those who rejected the Christian truth and the divine miracles.

460. **What is to be thought of consulting spiritistic mediums, engaging in spiritistic meetings, evoking the spirits of the dead, and other such practices?**

Such practices are forbidden by the first commandment, and are highly sinful and dangerous.[582]

461. **What is sacrilege?**

Sacrilege is a profanation of holy things, holy persons, or holy places; for instance, the unworthy receiving of a sacrament, the ill-treatment of an ecclesiastic, the desecration of a church or of sacred vessels, etc.

Examples: Punishment of King Baltassar,[583] of Heliodorus.[584] How Christ cast the sellers out of the Temple.[585]

[581] 2 Thes 2:9-10
[582] Cf. Dt 18
[583] Cf. Dn 5
[584] Cf. 2 Mc 3
[585] See Jn 2:15.

462. **When does a person commit simony?**
When he buys or sells spiritual things, preferments, and the like, for money or money's worth; as Simon the Magician intended to do.[586] This sin has been forbidden by the Church under the most severe penalties, even under pain of excommunication.

Application. Make every day acts of faith, hope, and charity, and never neglect to say your morning and evening prayers. At church, behave with reverence, and pray with attention, on your knees, and with your hands joined. Never use forbidden or suspicious means in order to cure diseases or to discover hidden things. Are you in doubt whether the use of certain things is permitted or not, ask the priest or your confessor.

The Veneration and Invocation of the Saints

463. **What does the Catholic Church teach respecting the veneration and invocation of the saints?**
She teaches that it is right and available to salvation to honor and invoke the saints.

464. **But is not the honor which we pay to the saints against the first commandment?**
By no means; for 1) we pay no divine honor to the saints; and 2) we honor and praise in the saints God himself, who has shown himself so powerful and merciful in them.

465. **What is the difference between the honor which we show to God and that which we show to the saints?**
1) We honor and adore God alone as our sovereign Lord and the author of all good things; but we honor the saints only as his faithful servants and friends. 2) We honor God for his own sake, or on account of the infinite perfections which he has of himself; but we honor the saints on account of the gifts and advantages which they have received from God.

[586] Cf. Acts 8

466. **But do we not kneel down when we honor the saints? Do we not build churches and altars, and offer the Sacrifice of the Mass to them, as to God himself?**

We kneel down, it is true; but we do not adore the saints any more than a courtier adores his king when, on his knees, he asks a favor of him. We consecrate churches and altars, and offer the Holy Sacrifice of the Mass to God alone, although, at the same time, we honor the memory of the saints, and implore their intercession.

From the most ancient times the Church has approved and cherished such veneration, has instituted festivals, built churches and altars in commemoration of the saints, and implored their intercession at the holy sacrifice; and God often confirmed such devotion by extraordinary graces. Churches are not consecrated to the saints whose names they bear, but to God, under the invocation of the saints.

467. **What should we have principally in view when we venerate the saints?**

We should imitate their virtues, and strive to become like them, that we may also one day share in their eternal happiness.

468. **In what does our praying to God differ from our praying to the saints?**

We pray to God that he may help us by his omnipotence; but we pray to the saints that they may help us by interceding with God for us.

469. **Is it, then, in the power of the saints in heaven to obtain anything from God in our behalf?**

It was in their power when they were living on earth; much more must it be so now that they are in heaven; for death does not dissolve the communion between them and us.[587]

"Pray one for another, that you may be saved; for the continual prayer of a just man availeth much."[588]—No one but a most obstinate infidel can

[587] See the ninth article of the Creed, above, p. 233ff.

[588] Jas 5:16

deny the miracles which were, and are still, wrought by the intercession of the saints.[589]

470. **Does the holy scripture also testify that the saints in heaven pray for us?**
Yes, the holy scripture says: 1) that the angels pray for man; 2) that the prophet Jeremias, long after his death, "prayeth much for the people, and for all the holy city";[590] and 3) that the four-and-twenty ancients incessantly offer up the prayers of the saints at the throne of the Most High.[591]

"And the angel of the Lord answered, and said: 'O Lord of hosts, how long wilt thou not have mercy on Jerusalem, and on the cities of Juda?'"[592] "When thou didst pray with tears,...I offered thy prayer to the Lord,"[593] said the angel Raphael to Tobias.

471. **Do, then, the saints in heaven know anything of us?**
If they did not know anything of us, the archangel Raphael could not have offered the prayer of Tobias to God, nor could there be joy before the angels of God upon one sinner doing penance, as the gospel testifies.[594]

472. **But is it not a mark of distrust in Jesus Christ when we address ourselves to the saints?**
No; for 1) we expect grace and salvation from God alone through the merits of Jesus Christ; and 2) if it were a mark of distrust, St. Paul would not have applied to the faithful, saying: "I beseech you, brethren, through our Lord Jesus Christ,...that you may help me in your prayers for me to God."[595]

[589] Proceedings of the Church at a beatification or canonization
[590] 2 Mc 15:14
[591] Cf. Apoc 5:8
[592] Zac 1:12
[593] Tb 12:12
[594] Cf. Lk 15:10
[595] Rom 15:30

473. **Why does God grant us many graces through the intercession of the saints?**
Because it is the will of God that we should acknowledge our own unworthiness and the merits of his faithful servants. Therefore, he himself, in former times, commanded the friends of Job, saying: "Go to my servant Job,...and my servant Job shall pray for you."[596]

474. **Whom should we in particular honor and invoke above all the angels and saints?**
Mary, the Blessed Virgin and Mother of God.

475. **Why should we particularly honor and invoke Mary?**
1) Because she is the Mother of God, and therefore far surpasses all the angels and saints in grace and glory; 2) because, for that very reason, her intercession with God is most powerful.

476. **Should we also honor the images of Jesus Christ and of the saints?**
Yes, certainly; for if even a child honors the likenesses of his parents, and a subject the image of his prince, so much the more must we honor the images of our Lord and of his saints.

How strictly the veneration of holy images was at all times observed in the Church was shown in the eighth century when the heretics, called "iconoclasts" (image-breakers), arose. They were supported by the Greek emperor, and they raged most obstinately and furiously against the images and those who revered them. But they were not able to abolish the pious practice. The faithful firmly suffered all imaginable ill-treatment, even torture and death; and in the year 787, the new heresy was solemnly condemned by the Seventh General Council.

[596] Jb 42:8

477. **But does not the scripture say: "You shall not make to yourselves any idol or graven thing"?**
True; but it is also immediately added: "To adore it,"[597] as the heathens did. But we Catholics detest the adoration of images.

God himself commanded Moses to "make two cherubim of beaten gold on the two sides of the oracle,"[598] and also to "make a brazen serpent, and set it up for a sign,"[599] which was a figure of our crucified Redeemer.

478. **But is it not superstitious to pray before images?**
Not at all; for when we pray before the images of Jesus Christ and his saints, we pray, not to the images, but to Jesus Christ and to the saints, whom they represent.

479. **Does it not prove that we put our trust in images when we go on pilgrimages to them?**
No; for we do not visit holy places because we trust in the images that are honored there, but because we know that God has been pleased to bestow many graces and benefits in such places, and therefore feel ourselves animated to pray there with greater fervor and confidence.

480. **What is the use of placing images of Christ and of the saints in our churches?**
They instruct and strengthen us in our faith, and incite us to live in conformity to it, whilst they represent before our eyes the mysteries of our religion, the history of our redemption, and the holy lives of the saints.

481. **Why do we honor the relics of the saints?**
Because their bodies were living members of Jesus Christ, and temples of the Holy Ghost, and will one day rise again from the dead to eternal glory.

At all times, relics have been kept in honor in the Church. As early as in the second century, the Christians in Antioch and Smyrna, as they

[597] Lv 26:1
[598] Ex 25:18
[599] Nm 21:8

testified themselves, honored the relics of their holy bishops, Ignatius and Polycarp, who had suffered death for Jesus Christ.

482. **Whence do we know for certain that the veneration of relics is pleasing to God?**

From this: that God has frequently been pleased to work great miracles through their means, as we read in the holy scripture and in the history of the Church.

"When the man [whom they were burying] had touched the bones of Eliseus, he came to life, and stood upon his feet."[600] "And God wrought by the hand of Paul more than common miracles; so that even there were brought from his body to the sick, handkerchiefs and aprons, and the diseases departed from them, and the wicked spirits went out of them."[601] St. Augustine, St. Ambrose, and others give us an account of the miracles which were wrought at the graves of St. Stephen, St. Felix of Nola, St. Gervasius, and of many other saints.

The authenticity of a relic which is exposed to the veneration of the faithful is not a matter of faith, but rests simply on human, but nevertheless credible, testimonies.

Application. Honor the blessed saints in heaven with great devotion, especially the most Blessed Virgin, St. Joseph, and your patron saint. Diligently read their lives, and faithfully imitate their examples. Keep in your dwellings no immodest pictures, but have, by all means, holy images, and, above all, an image of your crucified Redeemer. Do not help to circulate unauthorized prayers, or aid unauthorized persons to promote what are called chain prayers, as abuses may easily arise from these practices.[602]

[600] 4 Kgs 13:21
[601] Acts 19:11-12
[602] Feast of All Saints

THE SECOND COMMANDMENT OF GOD

"Thou shalt not take the name of the Lord thy God in vain."

483. **What does the second commandment forbid?**

The second commandment forbids all profanation of the holy name of God.

484. **How do we profane the name of God?**

We profane the name of God: 1) by irreverently pronouncing it; 2) by deriding religion; 3) by blasphemy; 4) by sinful swearing, and by cursing; and 5) by breaking vows.

485. **How do we sin by irreverently pronouncing God's holy name?**

By pronouncing the name of God in jest, or in anger, or in any other careless manner.

This applies also to other names and words worthy of reverence, as the name of the Blessed Virgin, the holy cross, the holy sacraments, etc., and to the words of the holy scripture, which are never to be abused in jest or by way of derision.

"The Lord will not hold him guiltless that shall take the name of the Lord his God in vain."[603]

486. **How do we sin by deriding religion?**

By scoffing at religion, at the rites or ceremonies of the Church, or by turning them into ridicule, in which cases we may also become guilty of blasphemy.

"Knowing this first, that in the last days there shall come deceitful scoffers, walking after their own lusts,... you, therefore, brethren, knowing these things before, take heed, lest being led aside by the error of the unwise, you fall from your own steadfastness."[604]

[603] Ex 20:7
[604] 2 Pt 3: 3, 17

487. **What is meant by *blasphemy*?**

By *blasphemy* is meant contemptuous and abusive language uttered against God, the saints, or holy things.

This sin is so great that, in the old law, those who were found guilty of it were put to death. "He that blasphemeth the name of the Lord, dying let him die; all the multitude shall stone him."[605] How Sennacherib, king of the Assyrians, was punished for blaspheming the Lord, see 4 Kings 19.

488. **May we also become guilty of blasphemy by thoughts?**

Yes, when we voluntarily think contemptuously of God or of the saints.

489. **What is swearing or taking an oath?**

Swearing or taking an oath is to call the all-knowing God to witness that we speak the truth, or that we will keep our promise.

We call God also to witness when we swear by heaven, by the holy cross, or by the gospel, etc. "Whosoever shall swear by the temple, sweareth by it, and by him that dwelleth in it; and he that sweareth by heaven, sweareth by the throne of God, and by him that sitteth thereon."[606]

490. **Is it ever lawful to take an oath?**

Yes; it is lawful and even obligatory when we are called upon to do so by competent authority in the interests of justice, as is the case of witnesses in a legal trial.

491. **Are we bound to keep a lawful oath?**

Yes; it is a grievous sin not to fulfill a lawful oath, if we are able to do so.

492. **How do we sin by swearing?**

We sin by swearing: 1) when we swear falsely or in doubt; 2) when we swear, or induce others to swear, without necessity; 3) when we swear to do what is evil, or to omit what is good.

[605] Lv 24:16
[606] Mt 23:21-22

"Thou shalt swear…in truth, and in judgment, and in justice."[607]

493. **What means "swearing falsely," or "in doubt"?**

It means: 1) to assert with an oath that something is true, though we know that it is untrue, or do not know whether it is true or not; 2) to promise with an oath something which we do not intend to perform.

494. **What are we to think of perjury or a false oath?**

Perjury, especially in a court of justice, is one of the greatest crimes; because he who commits it: 1) mocks God's omniscience, sanctity, and justice; 2) destroys the last means of preserving truth and faith among men; and 3) almost solemnly renounces God, and calls down his vengeance upon himself.

"And the Lord said to me: 'This flying volume which thou seest is the curse that goeth forth over the face of the earth; for every one that sweareth shall be judged by it. I will bring it forth, saith the Lord of hosts, and it shall come to the house of him that sweareth falsely by my name, and it shall remain in the midst of his house, and shall consume it, with the timber thereof, and the stones thereof.'"[608]

495. **When a person has sworn to do something evil, or to omit something that is good, is he bound to keep such an oath?**

No; for as it was a sin to take such an oath, so it would be another sin to keep it.—*Example*: Herod.[609]

496. **What do you mean by *cursing*?**

Cursing means to wish any evil either to ourselves or to our neighbor, or to any of God's creatures, whereby the name of God is frequently dishonored.

Cursing is something very hateful, which betrays a rude, angry temper. From the mouth of a Christian or child of God nothing but blessing ought

[607] Jer 4:2
[608] Cf. Zac 5:3-4; Cf. also Ez 17
[609] Cf. Mk 6:23-28

to come forth.[610] Cursing is at the same time an oath, when we call upon God to punish us if we speak an untruth.

497. **What is a vow?**

A vow is a voluntary promise made to God to do something that is agreeable to him, although there be no obligation to do it.

Accordingly, a vow is: 1) a real promise, by which we deliberately bind ourselves, and not a mere desire or resolution; 2) a promise made to God, because it is to God alone we make vows; and 3) a promise to do something that is agreeable to God; therefore it cannot be anything trifling, sinful, or injurious to others, nor anything good in itself, but by which something better is prevented or higher duties neglected.

498. **What does the Church teach with regard to vows?**

1. That they please God, because they are voluntary offerings made to him. Thus God kindly accepted the vows of the patriarch Jacob, and of the pious Anna, the mother of Samuel, and granted their petitions.

"And Jacob made a vow, saying: 'If God shall be with me,...and I shall return prosperously to my father's house,...of all things that thou shalt give to me, I will offer tithes to thee."[611] "Anna made a vow, saying: 'O Lord of hosts, if thou...wilt be mindful of me,...and wilt give to thy servant a man child, I will give him to the Lord all the days of his life."[612]

2. That it is a sacred duty to keep them, unless it be impossible to do so. People should therefore be very cautious about making vows, and should, in general, ask advice of their confessor, or some other prudent priest.

"If thou hast vowed anything to God, defer not to pay it...It is much better not to vow, than after a vow not to perform the things promised."[613]

[610] Cf. 1 Pt 3:9
[611] Gn 28:20-22
[612] 1 Kgs 1:11
[613] Eccles 5:3-4

499. **If it should become very difficult to keep a vow, in whole or in part, what is to be done?**

One's confessor ought to be consulted who may, if necessary, seek a dispensation from the bishop or the pope, according to the character of the vow.

500. **Is it sufficient not to dishonor the name of God?**

No; we must also honor and revere it—i.e., we must gratefully praise it, devoutly call upon it, steadily confess it, and exert ourselves to promote its honor.

Application. Carefully avoid the shameful habit of cursing and swearing. "A man that sweareth much shall be filled with iniquity, and a scourge shall not depart from his house."[614] On the contrary, often invoke with devotion the names of Jesus and Mary, especially in temptations against purity.

THE THIRD COMMANDMENT OF GOD

"Remember that thou keep holy the sabbath day."

501. **What are we commanded by the third commandment?**

By the third commandment, we are commanded to sanctify the Lord's day by performing works of piety and abstaining from servile works.

502. **Which is the Lord's day?**

In the old law, it was the seventh day of the week, or the sabbath day (day of rest), in memory of God's resting on that day, after he had finished the work of creation in six days. In the new law, it is the first day of the week, or the Sunday, in memory of the accomplishment of our redemption, which is a new spiritual creation.[615]

[614] Ecclus 23:12

[615] Cf. Gal 6:15

"In six days the Lord made heaven and earth, and the sea, and all things that are in them, and rested on the seventh day; therefore the Lord blessed the seventh day, and sanctified it."[616]

503. **How was our redemption accomplished on the Sunday?**
It was on a Sunday that our Savior rose from the dead, and it was also on a Sunday that he sent down the Holy Ghost upon his Church.

504. **What works of piety should we perform on the Sunday?**
1) We are bound to hear Mass, and, if possible, we should also attend the other divine service, especially the sermon and catechetical instruction; and 2) we should receive the holy sacraments, read books of devotion, or meditate on the great truths of our religion, and occupy ourselves in works of mercy, either corporal or spiritual.[617]

505. **Which works are servile and forbidden?**
All bodily works which are commonly performed by servants, day laborers, and tradesmen.

Works by which the mind only is exerted are not numbered amongst the servile works. But all those noisy and those merely worldly employments, which disturb quiet religious observance, such as lawsuits, buying and selling, etc., are also forbidden.

506. **Is it never lawful to do servile work on a Sunday?**
It is lawful: 1) when the pastors of the Church, for weighty reasons, give a dispensation; and 2) as often as a) the honor of God, b) the good of our neighbor, or c) urgent necessity require it.

It is lawful to engage in occupations which on account of public welfare cannot be interrupted on Sunday, as for example, those of railroad employees, watchmen, bakers, etc.

[616] Ex 20:11; Cf. Gn 2:2-3
[617] Cf. Jas 1:27

Persons compelled to work on Sunday should consult a confessor or pastor.

Examples: a) Officiating in the Temple.[618] b) Parable of the sheep that falls into a pit.[619] c) The disciples plucking ears of corn.[620]

507. **Are they only guilty who themselves do forbidden work?**

No; those also are guilty who without any necessity require their inferiors, as servants, day laborers, or tradesmen, to do such work, or allow them to do it; for God says: "That thy manservant and thy maidservant may rest, even as thyself."[621]

508. **Is the Sunday profaned only by servile work and staying away from divine service?**

No; it is likewise profaned by debauchery, intemperance, and extravagant games, sports, and amusements, which make of the Lord's day a day of revelry and public scandal.

509. **What should we particularly consider in order to be deterred from profaning the Sunday?**

We should consider:

1. The temporal and eternal punishment with which God threatens such as break the sabbath. "They grievously violated my sabbaths; I said, therefore, that I would pour out my indignation upon them in the desert, and would consume them."[622] "Keep you my sabbath; for it is holy unto you: he that shall profane it shall be put to death."[623]
2. That it is an unjustifiable heedlessness not to devote even so much as one day to the care of our immortal soul, after the body has been taken care of during six days.

[618] Cf. Mt 12:5
[619] Cf. Mt 12:11-12
[620] Cf. Mt 12:1-4
[621] Dt 5:14
[622] Ez 20:13
[623] Ex 31:14

3. That the observance of the Sunday is a public profession of our Christian faith, and, consequently, that by its profanation we bring disgrace on our religion, and give great scandal to our fellow Christians. *Example.* Zeal of the Jews in keeping holy the sabbath day.[624]

Application. Always observe the Lord's day conscientiously, and never be induced to violate it, either by thoughtlessness and excessive fondness for amusements, or by the example of wicked or infidel people. "God be merciful unto us; it is not profitable to us to forsake the law."[625]

THE FOURTH COMMANDMENT OF GOD

"Honor thy father and thy mother."

510. **What is commanded by the fourth commandment?**
By the fourth commandment, children are commanded to show reverence, love, and obedience to their parents, and inferiors to their superiors.

511. **Why must children reverence, love, and obey their parents?**
Because, next to God, their parents are their greatest benefactors, and supply his place in their regard.

512. **How should children reverence their parents?**
They should venerate their parents as the representatives of God, and should therefore always show them respect in word and deed.

"Honor thy father in work and word, and all patience."[626]

513. **How should children love their parents?**
They should: 1) be grateful to them, and wish them well from their heart; 2) they should make them happy by their good conduct; 3) they should assist them in their necessities, and take care of them in their old age; and 4) they should bear with their faults and weaknesses.

[624] Cf. 2 Mc 6:11
[625] 1 Mc 2:21
[626] Ecclus 3:9

"With thy whole heart, honor thy father, and forget not the groanings of thy mother. Remember that thou hadst not been born but through them, and make a return to them as they have done for thee."[627]—*Example* of Jesus, who, when dying on the cross, still provided for his Mother.

514. **How should children obey their parents?**
1) They should do what their parents command, and not do what they forbid, provided they order nothing bad or unjust; and 2) they should willingly receive, and readily follow, their advice and admonitions.

"Children, obey your parents in all things; for this is well pleasing to the Lord."[628]—*Example* of Jesus, who, though "God blessed for ever," yet was subject to Mary and Joseph.

515. **What have children to expect who faithfully observe the fourth commandment?**
In this life, they may be sure of God's protection and blessing, and in the other, of eternal happiness.

"Honor thy father and thy mother, which is the first commandment with a promise; that it may be well with thee, and thou mayest be long lived upon earth."[629] "Honor thy father,...that a blessing may come upon thee from him, and his blessing may remain in the latter end. The father's blessing establisheth the houses of the children, but the mother's curse rooteth up the foundation."[630]—*Examples*: Sem, Isaac, Ruth, Samuel, young Tobias.

516. **When do children sin against the reverence they owe to their parents?**
They sin against the reverence they owe to their parents: 1) when in their heart they despise or disregard them; 2) when they speak ill of them; 3) when they are ashamed of them; and 4) when they treat them harshly and insolently.

627 Ecclus 7:28-30
628 Col 3:20
629 Eph 6:2-3
630 Ecclus 3:9-11

"The eye that mocketh at his father, and that despiseth the labor of his mother in bearing him, let the ravens of the brooks pick it out, and the young eagles eat it."[631]

517. **When do children sin against the love they owe to their parents?**
They sin against the love they owe to their parents: 1) when they wish or do them evil; 2) when, by their bad behavior, they give them trouble, and bring disgrace upon them, or otherwise grieve them, or put them in a passion; 3) when they do not assist them in their need or old age; 4) when they do not bear with their failings; and 5) when they do not pray for their parents, whether living or dead.

"He that striketh his father or mother shall be put to death...He that curseth his father or mother shall die the death."[632] "Son, support the old age of thy father, and grieve him not in his life; and if his understanding fail, have patience with him, and despise him not when thou art in thy strength; for the relieving of the father shall not be forgotten."[633]

518. **When do children sin against the obedience due to their parents?**
They sin against the obedience due to their parents: 1) when they obey them badly, or not at all; 2) when they do not willingly listen to their admonitions; and 3) when they offer resistance to their corrections.

"If a man have a stubborn and unruly son, who will not hear the commandments of his father or mother, and being corrected, slighteth obedience, they shall take him, and bring him to the ancients of the city,...and shall say to them: 'This our son is rebellious and stubborn, he slighteth hearing our admonitions, he giveth himself to reveling, and to debauchery and banquetings': the people of the city shall stone him, and he shall die; that you may take away the evil out of the midst of you, and all Israel hearing it may be afraid."[634]

631 Prv 30:17
632 Ex 21:15, 17
633 Ecclus 3:14-15
634 Dt 21:18-21

519. **What have those children to expect who do not fulfill their duties toward their parents?**

In this life they have to expect the curse of God, disgrace, and ignominy; and in the life to come, eternal damnation.

"Cursed be he that honoreth not his father and mother, and all the people shall say: 'Amen.'"[635] "Remember thy father and thy mother,... lest God forget thee, and thou...wish that thou hadst not been born, and curse the day of thy nativity."[636]—*Examples*: Cham, Absalom, the sons of Heli the high priest.

520. **What superiors, besides our parents, must we honor, love, and obey?**

Our guardians, tutors, teachers, employers, masters and mistresses, and all our spiritual and civil superiors.

521. **What are our duties toward our guardians, tutors, teachers, and employers?**

We must consider them as the representatives and assistants of our parents; and, therefore, our duties towards them are in proportion to those which children owe to their parents.

522. **What are the particular obligations of servants to their masters and mistresses?**

They should, for the Lord's sake, show them respectful obedience, and honestly fulfill their contracts toward them.[637]

"Servants, obey in all things your masters according to the flesh, not serving to the eye, as pleasing men, but in simplicity of heart, fearing God. Whatsoever you do, do it from the heart, as to the Lord, and not to men; knowing that you shall receive of the Lord the reward of inheritance."[638] "Servants, be subject to your masters with all fear, not only to the good and gentle, but also to the froward."[639]

635 Dt 27:16
636 Ecclus 23:18-19
637 Cf. 1 Pt 2:9-10
638 Col 3:22-24
639 1 Pt 2:18

523. **How do servants sin against their masters and mistresses?**

1) By disobedience, obstinacy, moroseness, and ill will; 2) by laziness, by pilfering dainties, and by wasting and embezzling their goods; 3) by calumny, detraction, and tale-hearing; and, most of all, 4) by teaching evil to their children, by assisting them to do evil, or by conniving at it.

524. **What are our duties toward our spiritual superiors?**

We are bound: 1) to honor and love them as the representatives of God, and our spiritual fathers; 2) to submit to their ordinances; 3) to pray for them; and 4) to provide for their support in the manner established by law and custom.

"With all thy soul fear the Lord, and reverence his priests."[640] "Obey your prelates, and be subject to them; for they watch as being to render an account of your souls, that they may do this with joy, and not with grief; for this is not expedient for you."[641] "The Lord ordained that they who preach the gospel should live by the gospel."[642]—*Example* of the Christians, when Peter was in prison.[643]

525. **When do we sin against our spiritual superiors?**

1) When, by word or deed, we violate the reverence due to them, or when, by speaking ill of them, we lower their character; 2) when we oppose them, and thereby may be the cause of schism and scandal; and 3) when, contrary to our duty, we refuse to contribute toward their support, and to provide for the divine service.

"He that despiseth you, despiseth me."[644] "The Lord knoweth how to... reserve the unjust unto the day of judgment to be tormented; and especially them who...despise government, audacious, self-willed, they fear not to bring in sects, blaspheming. They allure by the desires of fleshly riotousness those who for a little while escape, such as converse in error: promising

640 Ecclus 7:31
641 Heb 13:17
642 1 Cor 9:14; Cf. Lk 10:7; 1 Tm 5:17-18
643 Cf. Acts 12; Cf. also Gal 4:14-15
644 Lk 10:16

them liberty, whereas they themselves are the slaves of corruption."[645] "Woe unto them, for they have gone in the way of Cain,...and have perished in the contradiction of Core."[646]—*Examples*: Core, Dathan, and Abiron, swallowed up by the earth;[647] forty-two boys torn by two bears.[648]

526. **What are our duties toward our civil, or temporal, rulers?**

We are bound: 1) to show to our civil rulers, ordained by God, respect, fidelity, and conscientious obedience, and to suffer anything rather than raise sedition against them; 2) to pay the taxes imposed by them; and 3) to assist them in their necessities and dangers; and even to sacrifice our property and life in defense of our country against its enemies.

"Let every soul be subject to higher powers; for there is no power but from God, and those that are, are ordained of God. Therefore, he that resisteth the power, resisteth the ordinance of God; and they that resist, purchase to themselves damnation...Wherefore be subject of necessity, not only for wrath, but also for conscience' sake...Render therefore to all men their dues: tribute to whom tribute is due; custom to whom custom; fear to whom fear; honor to whom honor."[649]—*Examples*: Jesus and the first Christians; David toward Saul.[650]

527. **How do we sin against our civil rulers?**

1) By hatred and contempt; 2) by reviling and blaspheming them; 3) by refusing to pay the taxes due to them; 4) by resistance and rebellion; and 5) by any sort of treason, violence, or conspiracy, against our government and country.

Of those "who despise dominion, and blaspheme majesty," the apostle St. Jude says: "These are murmurers, full of complaints, walking according

[645] 2 Pt 2:9-10, 18-19
[646] Jude 1:11
[647] Cf. Nm 16
[648] Cf. 4 Kgs 2:24
[649] Rom 13:1-2, 5, 7
[650] Cf. 1 Kgs 24:7

to their own desires, and their mouth speaketh proud things, admiring persons for gain's sake."[651]

528. **When are parents, superiors, and sovereigns not to be obeyed?**
When they command anything unlawful before God.

"We ought to obey God rather than men."[652]—*Examples*: Joseph in the house of Putiphar; Susanna; the three young men at Babylon; the seven Machabees; the apostles before the council.

529. **How should young people behave toward the aged?**
Young people should treat the aged respectfully, listen to their good advice, and, as far as possible, lighten the burden of their old age.

"Rise up before the hoary head, and honor the person of the aged man, and fear the Lord thy God."[653]

Application. Hearken now to your parents, teachers, pastors, etc., and follow them, lest "thou mourn at the last,...and say: 'Why have I hated instruction, and my heart consented not to reproof, and have not heard the voice of them that taught me, and have not inclined my ear to masters?'"[654]

530. **Does the fourth commandment regard children and inferiors only?**
It includes also the duties of parents and superiors.

531. **What are the duties of parents toward their children?**
The first and most sacred duty of parents is to bring up their children for God and for eternal life. Therefore they should: 1) teach them well themselves, and get them well instructed in the Catholic religion; 2) train them up, as early as possible, to a pious and virtuous life; 3) set them good example; 4) guard them against being led into sinful or dangerous courses; and 5) correct their faults with Christian charity.

[651] Jude 1:8, 16
[652] Acts 5:29
[653] Lv 19:32
[654] Prv 5:11-13

"And you, fathers,...bring your children up in the discipline and correction of the Lord."[655] "The child that is left to his own will bringeth his mother to shame."[656] "Withhold not correction from a child; for if thou strike him with the rod, he shall not die, and thou shalt...deliver his soul from hell."[657]

532. **How do parents sin when they neglect these their duties?**
They sin grievously, and, moreover, render themselves accessory to the sins of their children, and often are the cause of their eternal damnation (hell).

533. **Have parents charge only of the eternal salvation of their children?**
They have charge also of their temporal welfare and success; therefore, they sin: 1) when they inconsiderately squander their property; 2) when they do not take proper care of the food, clothing, or health of their children; or 3) when they neglect to accustom them early to labor, and to make them learn something useful.

Parents must not unreasonably interfere with their children's liberty in the choice of a state of life or a partner in marriage.

534. **What are the duties of masters and mistresses toward their servants?**
They should: 1) not treat them harshly, but kindly; 2) give them their just wages and sufficient nourishment; 3) urge them, by word and example, to fulfill their religious duties, and to do all that is right; and 4) keep them from evil and all occasions of sin.

"If thou have a faithful servant, let him be to thee as thy own soul: treat him as a brother."[658] "Masters, do to your servants that which is just and equal, knowing that you also have a master in heaven."[659] "But if any

[655] Eph 6:4
[656] Prv 29:15
[657] Prv 23:13-14
[658] Ecclus 33:31
[659] Col 4:1

man have not care of his own, and especially of those of his house, he hath denied the faith, and is worse than an infidel."[660]

535. **What are the obligations of civil rulers to their inferiors?**

Civil rulers are ordained by God for the good of the people; therefore they should: 1) promote public welfare as much as lies in their power; 2) perform the duties of their office with wisdom and incorruptible justice; 3) punish evil; and 4) be to all a pattern of a Christian life.

"The power is God's minister to thee for good."[661] "And charging the judges, [Josaphat] said: 'Take heed what you do; for you exercise not the judgment of man, but of the Lord; and whatsoever you judge, it shall redound to you...There is no iniquity with the Lord our God, nor respect of persons, nor desire of gifts.'"[662] Therefore, at elections for public offices, it is necessary, above all things, to consider piety, judgment, and an honest and energetic will in the person to be elected.

Application. Always honor your civil rulers as the ministers of God for your own good, and never listen to those enemies of all law and order, who "promise liberty, whereas they themselves are the slaves of corruption."[663] Besides observing the laws, all are bound to live together in harmony, as far as possible, and to endeavor, each according to his means and ability, to promote virtue, peace, good order, and the common welfare.

THE FIFTH COMMANDMENT OF GOD

"Thou shalt not kill."

536. **What sins does the fifth commandment forbid?**

The fifth commandment forbids all sins by which we may injure our neighbor or ourselves, whether as to the life of the body or of the soul.

[660] 1 Tm 5:8
[661] Rom 13:4
[662] 2 Par 19:6-7
[663] 2 Pt 2:19

537. **When do we injure our neighbor as to the life of his body?**
1) When we kill, strike, or wound him in an unjust manner; and 2) when, by vexation or harsh treatment, we embitter and shorten his life.

538. **What sin does he commit who deliberately kills his neighbor in an unjust manner?**
He commits the heinous sin of murder that cries to heaven for vengeance: for 1) he wantonly invades the rights of God; 2) he undermines the safety of human society; and 3) he plunges his neighbor into the greatest temporal, and often into eternal, ruin.

The deliberate destruction of infant life before birth, even in its earliest stages, as is sometimes done by surgeons, physicians, nurses, and others is nothing less than willful murder.

"Whosoever shall shed man's blood, his blood shall be shed; for man was made to the image of God."[664] How murder is punished, even in this life, by tormenting remorse, and often by an ignominious death, we learn from the examples of Cain,[665] of Ahab and Jezabel.[666]

539. **Is it ever lawful to destroy human life?**
Yes, it is lawful: 1) for the supreme authority to do so in the execution of criminals;[667] and 2) for others, in defense of their country, or, when necessary, in protecting life from unjust attack.

540. **Is it also lawful to send a man a challenge, or to accept his, to a duel in defense of our honor?**
No; for such a duel in any case, even if it be not for life and death, is a great crime, which is in direct opposition to all order established by God and man; therefore, all those who are accessory to it, even all voluntary witnesses, incur excommunication.

[664] Gn 9:6
[665] Cf. Gn 4:16
[666] Cf. 3 Kgs 21-22; 4 Kgs 9
[667] Cf. Rom 13:4

541. **Does the fifth commandment forbid only the actual crime of taking away the life of our neighbor?**
It also forbids everything that leads and induces to the crime; as anger, hatred, envy, quarreling, abusive words, and imprecations.

"Whosoever hateth his brother is a murderer."[668] "But I say to you, that whosoever is angry with his brother, shall be in danger of the judgment."[669]

542. **When do we injure ourselves as to the life of our body?**
1) When we take away our life; and 2) when we impair our health, or shorten our life, by intemperance in eating and drinking, by violent anger, by immoderate grief, etc.

543. **What sin does he commit who deliberately makes away with himself?**
He commits three horrible crimes: 1) a crime against the Divine Majesty, who alone has power over life and death; 2) a crime against his own soul, which he mercilessly plunges into eternal hell fire; and 3) a crime against human society, and especially against his relations, on whom he brings inexpressible grief and disgrace.

544. **How does the Church, therefore, punish suicide, or self-murder?**
She refuses Christian burial to the self-murderer, for his own punishment, as well as to deter others from doing the same.

545. **Are we never allowed to expose our life or our health to danger?**
Never without necessity; but, when a higher duty requires it, we may.[670]

546. **May we desire our own death?**
No, we may not when the desire proceeds from dejection or despair; but we may when we ardently desire to offend God no more, and to be united with him in heaven.

[668] 1 Jn 3:15
[669] Mt 5:22
[670] Cf. Mt 10:28

"I desire to be dissolved, and to be with Christ."[671]

547. **When do we injure our neighbor as to the life of his soul?**

When we scandalize him; that is, when we deliberately seduce him to sin, or voluntarily influence him, and give him occasion to commit it.

548. **Who render themselves guilty of this sin?**

In general, all those who in any way incite, advise, or help others to do evil, command them to do it, or approve of it; and in particular those: 1) who use impious or filthy language, or dress themselves immodestly; 2) who spread abroad bad books and pictures; 3) who open their houses to thieves, drunkards, gamblers, or other wicked men, for their unlawful meetings; and 4) those superiors who give bad example, or who do not hinder evil, as they are in duty bound to do.

549. **What should in particular deter us from giving scandal?**

1. The thought that he who gives scandal is a minister of Satan, destroying those souls which Jesus Christ has ransomed with his blood, by seducing them to sin. "He [the devil] was a murderer from the beginning."[672] "Destroy not him...for whom Christ died."[673]

2. The dreadful consequences of seduction, since those who have themselves been seduced generally seduce others, and thus the sin is continually propagated.—*Examples*: The whole human race corrupted through the descendants of Cain.[674] Jeroboam's sin and punishment.[675]

3. The awful sentence of Jesus Christ. "He that shall scandalize one of these little ones that believe in me, it were better for him that a millstone should be hanged about his neck, and that he should be drowned in the depth of the sea. Woe to the world because of scandals;...woe to that man

[671] Phil 1:23
[672] Jn 8:44
[673] Rom 14:15
[674] Cf. Gn 6
[675] Cf. 3 Kgs 12-14

by whom the scandal cometh."[676]—*Example* of Eleazar, who chose to die rather than scandalize young men;[677] and of St. Paul.[678]

550. **What must we do when we have injured our neighbor as to his body or soul?**
We must not only repent and confess the sin, but we must also, as far as it is in our power, repair the evil we have done.

551. **What are we commanded by the fifth commandment?**
We are commanded: 1) to live in peace and union with our neighbor; 2) to promote, according to our condition, his spiritual as well as his corporal welfare; and 3) to take also reasonable care of our own life and health.

Application. Never presume to curse, to abuse, or to strike anyone; but, as it is becoming to a child of God, be peaceable, kind, and meek. Shun a seducer as the devil; for he is about to kill your soul, let his words or promises be ever so charming and pleasing. Beware of murdering your neighbor's soul by any scandalous act or word.

THE SIXTH AND NINTH COMMANDMENTS OF GOD

"Thou shalt not commit adultery."

"Thou shalt not covet thy neighbor's wife."

552. **What does the sixth commandment forbid?**
The sixth commandment forbids: 1) adultery and all sins of impurity; as unchaste looks, words, jests, touches, and whatsoever else violates modesty; and 2) everything that leads to impurity.

"But fornication and all uncleanness,...let it not so much as be named among you, as becometh saints, or obscenity, or foolish talking, or scurrility."[679]

[676] Mt 18:6-7
[677] Cf. 2 Mc 6
[678] Cf. 1 Cor 8:13
[679] Eph 5:3-4

553. **What is it that generally leads to impurity?**

1) Curiosity of the eyes; 2) immodest dress; 3) flatterers or seducers; 4) obscene books and scandalous pictures; 5) nocturnal interviews, indecent plays and dances; 6) a too-free intercourse with the other sex; 7) drunkenness and revelry; and 8) idleness and effeminacy.

554. **What does the ninth commandment forbid?**

The ninth commandment especially forbids the desire to have another man's wife, and, in general, all impure thoughts and desires.

"Whosoever shall look on a woman to lust after her, hath already committed adultery with her in his heart."[680]

555. **Are impure thoughts and desires always sins?**

As long as they displease us, and we endeavor to banish them from our mind, they are not sins.

556. **When do we sin by impure thoughts?**

We sin by impure thoughts when we voluntarily represent immodest things or actions to our mind, and when we voluntarily take pleasure in them.

As it is a sin against purity designedly to look at immodest things, so it is also a sin to represent such things to our mind, or, when such representations are involuntary, willingly to take complacency or pleasure in them.

557. **When do we sin by impure desires?**

We sin by impure desires when we voluntarily wish to see, hear, or do something that is contrary to chastity or purity.

558. **What should we do when we are tempted by impure thoughts and desires?**

1) We should, in the very beginning, earnestly resist them, and implore the assistance of God; and 2) when the temptation continues, we should not be discouraged, but persevere in our resistance, and endeavor to occupy our minds with some good subject.

[680] Mt 5:28

"As I knew that I could not otherwise be continent, except God gave it,...I went to the Lord, and besought him...with my whole heart."[681] "Blessed is the man that endureth temptation; for when he hath been proved, he shall receive the crown of life."[682]

559. **Why must we most carefully guard against impurity?**

1) Because no sin is more shameful; and 2) because none is attended with such dreadful consequences.

560. **Why is this sin so shameful?**

Because man, who, as the image and temple of God, is called to a pure and holy life, is degraded by it to the level of an impure or unclean animal; whence it is styled, "sin of impurity" or "uncleanness."[683]

561. **What are the consequences of impurity?**

1) It robs man of his innocence, and infects his body and soul; 2) it leads him to many other sins and vices, and often to murder and despair; and 3) it plunges him into misery, ignominy, and shame, and finally into eternal damnation.

"He that joineth himself to harlots will be wicked: rottenness and worms shall inherit him."[684] "The whoremongers...shall have their portion in the pool burning with fire and brimstone."[685]

Examples. Impurity led David, Solomon, the two elders,[686] Herod, and Herodias into the greatest crimes. Chiefly on account of impurity, nearly the entire human race was destroyed by the deluge; Sodom and Gomorrha, by a rain of brimstone and fire; twenty-four thousand Israelites were put to death in the desert; and almost the whole tribe of Benjamin perished by the sword.

[681] Ws 8:21
[682] Jas 1:12
[683] Cf. 1 Cor 3:17
[684] Ecclus 19:3
[685] Apoc 21:8
[686] Cf. Dn 13

562. **Is every sin of impurity a grievous sin?**

Yes, every sin of impurity which one commits knowingly and willingly, either with himself or with others, is a mortal sin; for "know you this and understand," says St. Paul, "that no fornicator, or unclean person, hath inheritance in the kingdom of Christ and of God."[687]

563. **Are all sins of impurity equally grievous?**

No; some are more grievous than others, according to the persons with whom the sin is committed; or according as the sin is more heinous and unnatural, and its consequences are more pernicious.

564. **What are we to do when we doubt whether anything is a sin against purity?**

We must consult our director, and in the meantime carefully avoid what we are doubtful of.

565. **What are we commanded by the sixth and ninth commandments?**

We are commanded to be decent and modest in all our thoughts, looks, words, and actions, and to preserve most carefully the innocence of our soul as the greatest good and the most beautiful ornament of man.

566. **What means should we employ in order to preserve our innocence?**

We should: 1) shun all bad company and all occasions of sin;[688] 2) carefully guard our senses, especially our eyes;[689] 3) often receive the holy sacraments; 4) in temptation, recommend ourselves to God and to the Blessed Virgin; 5) remember that God sees everything, and that we may die at any moment;[690] and 6) we should earnestly exercise ourselves in humility, in the mortification of the flesh, and in self-denial.[691]

Application. Love the innocence of your soul; often meditate on these words of the holy scripture: "Oh! how beautiful is the chaste generation

[687] Eph 5:5
[688] Cf. Ecclus 3:27
[689] Cf. Ps 118:37
[690] Cf. Ecclus 7:40
[691] Cf. Gal 5:24

with glory; for the memory thereof is immortal, because it is known both with God and with men…It triumpheth crowned for ever, winning the reward of undefiled conflicts."[692] Therefore, whether you are by yourself or with others, never say or do anything that may not be said or done before people of propriety; and should any one attempt to lead you to what is wrong, repulse him or seek for the protection of others. "My son, if sinners shall entice thee, consent not to them. If they shall say: 'Come with us';…my son, walk not thou with them."[693] Avoid all immoral books, magazines, and newspapers.[694]

THE SEVENTH COMMANDMENT OF GOD

"Thou shalt not steal."

567. **What does the seventh commandment forbid?**

The seventh commandment forbids us to injure our neighbor in his property by robbery or theft, by cheating, usury, or in any other unjust way.

568. **Who are guilty of robbery or theft?**

Not only those who are properly called robbers and thieves, but also all those 1) who give them advice or assistance; 2) who buy, sell, hide, or keep stolen goods; 3) who do not return the things they have found or borrowed; 4) who do not pay their debts; and 5) all those who beg without need, and thus defraud the real poor of their alms.

569. **How is fraud committed?**

1) By injuring, openly or secretly, our neighbor's property or business; 2) by giving false weight or measure, or bad money, or practicing any other deceit in buying or selling; 3) by refusing to pay our lawful debts when we can do so.

[692] Ws 4:1-2

[693] Prv 1:10-11, 15

[694] See the second paragraph to q. 439, on p. 280, "The First Commandment."

570. **How, also, may servants and employees be guilty of fraud?**
1) By disposing of their employer's property without his consent; 2) by wasting time or material; and by disregarding just agreements or contracts which they have made with their employers.

Servants may not give alms of the property of their employers without their consent.

571. **In what other ways may we sin against the seventh commandment?**
1) By gambling and other extravagances injurious to one's family; 2) by evading our just share of public burdens, such as paying taxes; 3) by wasting or appropriating public money unjustly; 4) by usurious practices.

572. **Who are guilty of usurious practices?**
1) Those who exact unlawful interest for money loaned; 2) those who purchase in large quantities articles of food and other necessaries, in order to obtain more than a just price for them; 3) in general, those who in trade take unfair advantage of their neighbor's ignorance or necessity.

573. **May we also grievously sin against the seventh commandment by petty thefts or frauds?**
Yes: 1) when we so often repeat them that the owner suffers a considerable loss, and even when we have only the intention of thus repeating them; and 2) when the loss of a thing, trifling in itself, causes our neighbor a considerable injury.

574. **What must we do when we are in possession of illgotten goods or have unjustly injured our neighbor?**
We must restore the ill-gotten goods, and repair, as far as we are able, the injury done; without this we cannot obtain pardon from God.

575. **Who is bound to make restitution or reparation?**
1. He who is in possession of the things stolen, or of their value, or who has really done the injury.

2. If he does not do it, the obligation devolves on those who, by counsel or action, were accessory to the sin, or who did not hinder it, although they were able to do so, and were bound by the duties of their station or office to hinder the wrong.

576. **How much must be restored?**

1. If one has knowingly and unjustly taken or detained his neighbor's goods, he must fully compensate him.

2. If he did it unknowingly and unwillingly, he must, as soon as he comes to know that it is another man's property, restore all that is still left and as much more as his wealth has increased by it.

In the former case, full restitution must be made not only of the things stolen, or, if they are gone, of their value, but also of that which, in the meantime, they have produced; those expenses, however, being deducted which even the owner would not have been able to avoid. And, in general, the owner must be compensated for all the profits which he has been deprived of, and for all the losses he has suffered. In the latter case, we are bound to restore all that which, after deducting the expenses, is still remaining of the ill-gotten goods and of their produce, and, in general, as much as, by their possession and temporary use, we have become the richer.

577. **To whom must restitution of the ill-gotten goods be made?**

To the owner or to his heirs; but if this be not possible, they must be given to the poor or be appropriated to religious and charitable purposes.

578. **What must they do who cannot immediately make restitution?**

They must sincerely have the intention of doing so as soon as they can; and, in the meantime, they must employ all reasonable means to enable themselves to perform this duty.

579. **What should we bear in mind in order to guard against stealing, or against neglecting to make restitution?**

1) That death will at length wrest the ill-gotten goods from us, and perhaps sooner than we expect; 2) that the stolen property will bring us, not happiness

and blessing, but misfortune and malediction, uneasiness and a miserable end; and 3) that there is no greater foolishness than to forfeit heaven for the perishable things of this world, and to plunge our soul into unquenchable fire.

"He who soweth iniquity shall reap evils."[695] "What doth it profit a man if he gain the whole world, and suffer the loss of his own soul? Or what exchange shall a man give for his soul?"[696]

580. **What are we commanded by the seventh commandment?**

We are commanded to give to everyone his due, and to be charitable to our neighbor.

Application. Give to everyone his own, and be contented with what you have. "A little, justly gained, is better than much, gained unjustly."[697] Never steal anything, be it ever so little, and mind this true saying: "Small beginnings make great endings." Beware of daintiness, drunkenness, idleness, gambling, vain show, and finery; for all this leads people to robbery and theft, and brings them to ruin.

THE EIGHTH COMMANDMENT OF GOD

"Thou shalt not bear false witness against thy neighbor."

581. **What does the eighth commandment forbid?**

The eighth commandment forbids above all to give false evidence; that is, to say in a court of justice what is not true.

"And bringing two men, son of the devil, they made them sit against him [Naboth]; and they, like men of the devil, bore witness against him before the people."[698]

582. **How are we to give evidence in a court of justice?**

We must tell the exact truth, just as we know it, and neither more nor less.

695 Prv 22:8
696 Mt 16:26
697 Cf. Prv 16:8
698 3 Kgs 21:13

583. **What other sins are forbidden by the eighth commandment?**

1) Lies and hypocrisy; 2) detraction and calumny or slander; 3) false suspicion and rash judgment; and, in general, all sins by which the honor or character of our neighbor is injured.

584. **What is meant by a lie?**

To say knowingly and deliberately what is not true, with the intention of deceiving.

585. **Is it ever lawful to tell a lie?**

No; it is never lawful to tell a lie, neither for our own nor for another's benefit, not even in jest or need; for every lie is essentially opposed to God, who is truth itself.

"A lie is a foul blot in a man."[699] "Lying lips are an abomination to the Lord."[700]—*Example*: Punishment of Ananias and Saphira.[701] Although it is never lawful to tell an untruth, yet we are sometimes bound by charity or official duty to conceal the truth.

586. **How do we sin by hypocrisy?**

By pretending to be better or more pious than we really are, in order to deceive others.

"Woe to you, scribes and Pharisees, hypocrites! because you are like to whited sepulchres, which outwardly appear to men beautiful, but within are full of dead men's bones, and of all filthiness. So you also outwardly indeed appear to men just, but inwardly you are full of hypocrisy and iniquity."[702]

587. **How do we sin by detraction?**

By revealing the faults of others without any necessity.

[699] Ecclus 20:26
[700] Prv 12:22
[701] Cf. Acts 5
[702] Mt 23:27-28

588. **When is it allowed to reveal the faults of others?**
We are allowed, and even bound, to reveal them: 1) when it is for the good of the guilty person; or 2) when it is necessary for preventing a greater evil.

589. **What is to be observed in making such revelation?**
1) The revelation must proceed from a pure motive of charity, and be made to such only as are able to remedy the evil; 2) the fault is not to be exaggerated, nor is what is uncertain to be represented as certain.

590. **How do we sin by calumny or slander?**
By imputing faults to our neighbor which he has not at all, or by exaggerating his real faults.

"If a serpent bite in silence, he is nothing better that backbiteth secretly."[703]—*Example*: Aman.[704]

591. **Is every calumny or detraction equally sinful?**
No; the sin is the greater: 1) the more important the fault is, and the more considerable the person of whom it is mentioned; 2) the greater the loss and injury is which he suffers by it; 3) the more people there are who hear it; and 4) the worse our intention is in divulging it.

A most injurious and detestable sin is tale-bearing or whispering—i.e., when we relate to a person what another has said of him, and thus create hatred and dissension between them. "The whisperer and the double tongued is accursed; for he hath troubled many that were at peace."[705]

592. **Is it also a sin even to listen to detraction or calumny?**
Yes, it is a sin: 1) to listen with pleasure to detraction or calumny; 2) not to prevent it when it is in our power; and 3) to occasion and encourage it by asking questions or approving of it.

703 Eccles 10:11
704 Cf. Est 13
705 Ecclus 28:15

"Hedge in thy ears with thorns, hear not a wicked tongue."[706] "The north wind driveth away rain, as doth a sad countenance a backbiting tongue."[707]

593. **What is he obliged to do who, by slander or abusive language, has injured the character of his neighbor?**

He is obliged: 1) to retract the slander or to beg pardon; and 2) to repair all the injury he has done him.

"A good name is better than great riches."[708] Therefore, it is an obligation to restore the former as well as the latter.

594. **Must we also retract when we have divulged true but hidden faults?**

No; in such a case we should try to excuse our neighbor, and to repair his honor by some other lawful means.

595. **When do we sin by false suspicion and rash judgment?**

We sin: 1) by false suspicion, when, without sufficient reason, we deliberately surmise evil of our neighbor; and 2) by rash judgment, when, without sufficient reason, we believe the evil to be true and certain.

"Judge not, that you may not be judged...Why seest thou the mote that is in thy brother's eye, and seest not the beam that is in thine own eye?"[709]

596. **What are we commanded by the eighth commandment?**

We are commanded: 1) to speak the truth in all things; 2) to be solicitous for the honor and reputation of everyone; and 3) to bridle especially our tongue.

597. **How far should we also be solicitous for our own honor?**

As far as the honor of God, the edification of our neighbor, and the duties of our state of life require it.

[706] Ecclus 28:28
[707] Prv 25:23
[708] Prv 22:1
[709] Mt 7:1, 3

"We forecast what may be good not only before God, but also before men."[710] Yet we should always be ready to suffer also reproach and ignominy for our own and our neighbor's salvation, or for the sake of Jesus Christ. In this sense, it is said: "If one strike thee on thy right cheek, turn to him also the other";[711] and, "If you be reproached for the name of Christ, you shall be blessed."[712] "And they [the apostles] indeed went from the presence of the council, rejoicing that they were accounted worthy to suffer reproach for the name of Jesus."[713]

598. **How are we to be solicitous for our own reputation?**
Above all, 1) by continually leading a Christian life, and 2) by avoiding, to the best of our power, even the least appearance of evil. In defense of our reputation when attacked we can use none but lawful means.

"But with modesty and fear, having a good conscience: that whereas they speak evil of you, they may be ashamed who falsely accuse your good conversation in Christ."[714] "From all appearance of evil refrain yourselves."[715]

599. **How may we best guard against the sins of the tongue?**
1) By not talking inconsiderately, and by bearing in mind that we have to give an account of every idle word we speak;[716] and 2) by keeping our heart free from ambition, envy, hatred, vengeance, etc.

"He that keepeth his mouth, keepeth his soul; but he that hath no guard on his speech, shall meet with evils."[717] "O generation of vipers, how can you speak good things, whereas you are evil? for out of the abundance of the heart the mouth speaketh."[718]

[710] 2 Cor 8:21
[711] Mt 5:39
[712] 1 Pt 4:14
[713] Acts 5:41
[714] 1 Pt 3:16
[715] 1 Thes 5:22
[716] Cf. Mt 12:36
[717] Prv 13:3
[718] Mt 12:34

Application. Detest all lies and falsehoods. Never speak uncharitably of your neighbor, nor grieve him by reproachful words: "The stroke of a whip maketh a blue mark; but the stroke of the tongue will break the bones."[719] However, do not conceal faults from those who can correct them.

THE TENTH COMMANDMENT OF GOD

"Thou shalt not covet thy neighbor's goods."

600. **What does the tenth commandment forbid?**
The tenth commandment forbids all voluntary desire of our neighbor's goods.

"The desire of money is the root of all evils."[720]—*Example*: Achab.[721]

601. **What are we commanded by the tenth commandment?**
We are commanded to be contented with what is our own, and not to be envious of what belongs to others.

602. **How can a Christian, even in poverty, be easily contented with his own?**
By bearing in mind: 1) that a clean conscience is the greatest treasure; 2) that our true home is in the other world; 3) that Christ also has become poor for our sake, and that one day he will magnificently reward all those who patiently suffer poverty for his sake.

603. **Why does God forbid not only all evil actions, but also all evil thoughts and desires?**
Because evil thoughts and desires defile the heart, and finally lead also to evil actions.

719 Ecclus 28:21
720 1 Tm 6:10
721 Cf. 3 Kgs 21

"Man seeth those things that appear, but the Lord beholdeth the heart."[722] "From the heart come forth evil thoughts, murders, adulteries,"[723] etc.

Application. Turn your thoughts toward eternity, and you will have no difficulty to despise all that is temporal. "Walk in the spirit," i.e., love God, the supreme good, "and you shall not fulfill the lusts of the flesh."[724] Happy is he who can truly say: "My soul longeth and fainteth for the courts of the Lord; my heart and my flesh have rejoiced in the living God."[725]

The Six Commandments of the Church

604. **Are there, besides the commandments of God, any others which Christians are bound to keep?**
Yes, the commandments of the Church.

605. **Whence has the Church a right to give commandments?**
From Jesus Christ himself, who has commissioned his Church to guide and govern the faithful in his name.[726]

Therefore, to despise the commandments of the Church is to despise Christ himself. "He that heareth you, heareth me; and he that despiseth you, despiseth me."[727]

606. **Has the Church no further right than to give commandments?**
She has also a right to watch over the observance of these commandments, and to punish those who break them; for instance, to refuse them the holy

722 1 Kgs 16:7
723 Mt 15:19ff
724 Gal 5:16
725 Ps 83:3
726 See p. 245–246, q. 309-311.
727 Lk 10:16

sacraments,[728] and finally to exclude them from the Church, and to deprive them of Christian burial when they die.[729]

607. **Which are the general or chief commandments of the Church?**
These six:

1. To abstain from servile work and to hear Mass on all Sundays and holy days of obligation.
2. To fast and to abstain on the days appointed by the Church.
3. To confess our sins at least once a year.
4. To receive worthily the Blessed Eucharist at Easter or within the time appointed.
5. To contribute to the support of our pastors.
6. Not to marry persons within the forbidden degrees of kindred or otherwise prohibited by the Church; nor to solemnize marriage at the forbidden times.

608. **Why has the Church given us these commandments?**
1) To explain the commandments of God more precisely, and to determine more particularly how they are to be kept; and 2) to lead us to a religious and penitential life, and thereby to secure our eternal salvation.

609. **How do these commandments of the Church bind us?**
They bind us strictly—that is, under pain of grievous sin.

"If he will not hear the Church, let him be to thee as the heathen and publican."[730] Even in the old law, God had ordained: "He that will be proud and refuse to obey the commandment of the priest,...that man shall die, and thou shalt take away the evil from Israel; and all the people hearing it shall fear, that no one afterward swell with pride."[731]

Application. Be determined always humbly and conscientiously to observe the commandments and ordinances of the Church, that one day

[728] Cf. Mt 18:18
[729] Cf. 1 Cor 5:3-5. See p. 235, q. 277.
[730] Mt 18:17
[731] Dt 17:12-13

Jesus Christ may own you as a faithful sheep of his flock, which he has charged St. Peter and his successors to feed.

THE FIRST COMMANDMENT OF THE CHURCH

610. **What are we commanded by the first commandment of the Church?**

By the first commandment, we are commanded, in the first place, to keep holy the Sundays and the holy days which the Church has instituted in honor of our Lord and of his saints, by resting from servile work.

As in the old law, on certain occasions—for instance, after the victory gained by the Jews over Holofernes,[732] and over Aman[733]—festivals were instituted in memory of the blessings received from God; so also has the Christian Church, in different times, most justly commanded that several holy days or anniversaries should be celebrated in honor of Jesus Christ, of his glorious Mother, and of the saints, his glorified friends.

611. **For what purpose were the feasts of our Lord instituted?**

They were instituted that we should: 1) devoutly meditate on the mysteries of our redemption; 2) thank God for his graces; and 3) renew our zeal in serving him, and thus render ourselves worthy of the fruits of redemption.

In the course of each ecclesiastical year, the whole life of Jesus Christ is so represented to us in its principal parts as if the mysteries which we commemorate were renewed before our eyes. Therefore, it is the intention of the Church that we should every year contemplate with her the life of Christ from its beginning to its end. In Advent, we should, by repentance and longing expectation, prepare the way for the coming of our Redeemer into our hearts; in Lent, we should, by penance and mortification, participate in his sufferings, die to sin, and spiritually rise with him to a new life at Easter. At the approach of the feast of Pentecost, we should ardently long for the gifts of the Holy Ghost, and then continually endeavor to cooperate with the graces received.

[732] Cf. Jdt 16:31
[733] Cf. Est 9

612. **Why were the feasts of the saints instituted?**

That we may: 1) praise the Lord for the graces which he has bestowed upon them, and, through them, upon us also; 2) represent to our mind their exemplary virtues upon earth and their eternal bliss in heaven, and resolve to imitate them; and 3) implore their intercession with God.

613. **Can the Church also suppress holy days?**

As she has full power to institute holy days, so she has also a right to suppress them again, to transfer them, or to limit them to certain places, when time and circumstances require it.

The doctrine of the Church always is, and must be, one and the same, because it comes from God; but it is not so with her regulations and laws of discipline, which she makes after the lapse of ages, and must adapt to variety of times and places. Therefore, without detriment to the unity of her doctrine, there may be a difference in the celebration of her festivals.

Besides the Sundays, the following festivals are holy days of obligation in the United States: The Circumcision of Our Lord, January 1; Ascension of Our Lord; Assumption of the Blessed Virgin, August 15; All Saints, November 1; The Immaculate Conception of the Blessed Virgin, the patronal festival of the American Church, December 8; and Christmas, or The Nativity of Our Lord, December 25.

Application. Prepare yourself, in conformity with the spirit of the Church, as fervently for every chief festival of the year as if it were the last in your life. Beware of profaning the holy days of obligation by servile work, by excesses, or sinful amusements.

614. **What are we further commanded to do by the first commandment of the Church?**

By the first commandment, we are further commanded to assist on all Sundays and holy days of obligation at the Holy Sacrifice of the Mass with due attention, reverence, and devotion.

615. **Why are we commanded especially to hear Mass on Sundays and holy days of obligation?**
Because the Sacrifice of the Mass is the most holy and salutary of all divine services, and that in which the Most High is honored in the most worthy manner.

616. **Who are obliged to hear Mass on Sundays and holy days of obligation?**
All who are seven years of age and have attained the use of reason (which is generally the case at that age) are strictly bound to hear Mass, unless weighty reasons, as illness, nursing the sick, etc., excuse them from it.

617. **When do we sin against this command of the Church?**
1) When, through our own fault, we lose either the entire Mass or a great part of it; and 2) when, during Mass, we give way to voluntary distractions, look about through curiosity, talk, laugh, or otherwise behave so that we cannot follow the Mass.

618. **Where should the faithful hear Mass on Sundays and holy days?**
In the parish church, when it is possible; also in any church or public oratory.

619. **Why does the Church wish that the faithful should attend divine service especially in their parish church?**
Because in the parish church the pastor preaches and offers the Sacrifice of the Mass principally for his parishioners.

620. **Does this commandment of the Church also command us to hear the sermon?**
According to the letter it does not; but according to the spirit it certainly does; for the hearing of the word of God also belongs to the worthy celebration of the Sundays and holy days, and is, in general, an essential duty of a Christian.

In the primitive Church, the sermon was generally preached at Mass after the gospel; therefore the Church, which commands us to hear Mass, had no occasion for giving a particular and express commandment to hear the sermon.

621. **Why are all Christians bound to hear the word of God?**

1) Because the word of God is for all a most powerful means of sanctification, ordained by God himself; 2) because it is indispensable to all to be repeatedly reminded of the truths of religion, and to be admonished to live up to them; and 3) because all are obliged to mutual edification, by setting one another an example of Christian piety.

"He that is of God, heareth the words of God; therefore you hear them not, because you are not of God."[734] It is therefore a bad sign when people neglect to hear the word of God.

622. **How should we hear the word of God?**

We should 1) listen to it with earnest attention, and with an ardent desire of working out our salvation; and 2) we should reflect well upon it, apply it to ourselves, and faithfully follow it.

"Blessed are they who hear the word of God and keep it."[735]

Application. Make it a rule to assist with devotion on Sundays and holy days at the divine service in the morning and in the afternoon, and to prefer your parish church to any other.

Missions, retreats, and Lenten courses of instructions are seasons of special grace and mercy, particularly for those who have been leading irregular lives: to neglect these opportunities is to despise the mercy of God.

THE SECOND COMMANDMENT OF THE CHURCH

623. **What does the second commandment of the Church oblige us to do?**

The second commandment of the Church obliges us to observe the laws of abstinence and fasting laid down by the Church.

[734] Jn 8:47

[735] Lk 11:28; Cf. Lk 8:5-15

624. **What does the law of abstinence forbid?**
The law of abstinence forbids the eating of flesh meat and of broth or soup made of meat; but it permits the use of eggs, milk, cheese, and butter; also seasonings of food which are made from the fat of animals.

625. **What does the law of fasting prescribe?**
It prescribes that only one full meal a day may be taken. But it does not forbid a small quantity of food in the morning and evening, the quality and quantity to be regulated according to the approved custom of one's locality.

626. **Is it permitted to eat both flesh and fish at the same meal on days of fasting which are not also days of abstinence?**
Yes; we may eat flesh and fish at the same meal. Also, we may take the full meal in the evening and a collation in the middle of the day.

627. **What days does the law of abstinence, as apart from the law of fasting, oblige us to observe?**
The law of abstinence, apart from the law of fasting, obliges us to abstain on all the Fridays of the year.

628. **On what days are both the laws of abstinence and of fasting to be observed?**
The laws both of abstinence and of fasting are to be observed on: 1) Ash Wednesday, the Fridays and Saturdays of Lent; 2) the Wednesdays, Fridays, and Saturdays of the Ember days, 3) the Vigils of Pentecost, of the Assumption of the Blessed Virgin Mary, of the feast of All Saints, and of Christmas day.

The forty days of Lent are ordained in imitation of the forty days' fast of Jesus Christ, in remembrance of his bitter passion and death, and that we may worthily prepare ourselves for the celebration of Easter. The Ember days are ordained that the faithful may thank God for the blessings they have received in each quarter of the year; that in each season they may be reminded to do penance; and also, that they may obtain of God worthy priests, these being generally the days of their ordination. By the vigils, the faithful prepare themselves for the worthy celebration of great festivals.

The four weeks preceding the feast of Christmas are called the holy season of Advent. It is time of special prayer and devotion.

629. **On what days is the law of fasting, apart from the law of abstinence, to be observed?**
The law of fasting, apart from the law of abstinence, is to be observed on all week days in Lent that have not been already mentioned. (See preceding question.)

630. **Do the laws either of abstinence or fasting bind on Sundays or holy days of obligation?**
No; on Sundays and holy days of obligation, neither fast nor abstinence need be observed; also the Lenten obligations of abstinence and fast end at noon on Holy Saturday, because the Lenten season closes at the end of Mass on that day.

631. **Who are bound by the laws of abstinence and of fasting?**
The law of abstinence binds all who have completed their seventh year; the law of fasting binds those who have completed their twenty-first year and have not yet entered upon their sixtieth year.

632. **May any persons within these ages be excused from fasting or abstinence?**
Yes; the sick, convalescent, those in feeble health, and those who would be unable properly to discharge their duties of life if they were obliged to observe fast and abstinence may be excused from either or both, according to circumstances.

633. **What are they to do who believe they have a good reason to be excused from fulfilling the obligations of abstinence and fasting?**
They ought to apply to their confessors or pastors for counsel.

A bishop may, for special grave local reason, in his diocese sometimes dispense from the general laws of abstinence and fasting on particular occasions; or order a fast or abstinence to be observed which is not imposed by the general laws.

While the faith of the Church remains the same in all ages, from time to time she introduces changes in her discipline. By "her discipline" is meant the laws and regulations which she prescribes for her own government and for the direction of Christian life. Her disciplinary laws and precepts comprise, among other matters, divine worship, the administering and receiving of the sacraments, the duties of fasting and abstinence. The collection of these disciplinary regulations is called the Canon Law. Owing to the changes which time brings about in the ways of life, habits, customs, and conditions of the faithful, the Church, for the welfare of her children, introduces changes in her discipline to adapt it the better to the changed conditions. The Holy See has recently issued a complete Code of Canon Law in which is laid down some modifications of former discipline, especially with regard to the laws of fasting and abstinence.

634. **Is it not superstitious to abstain from certain kinds of food?**

1) It is superstitious, if we abstain from certain food as if it were evil and unclean in itself, as some heretics asserted; but 2) it is not so by any means if we do it in the spirit of obedience and penance, as the Catholic Church prescribes.

1) St. Paul combated this heresy;[736] and also the Catholic Church has at all times combated and condemned it. 2) God himself forbade certain meats to the Jews,[737] and the apostles to the first Christians.[738] St. John the Baptist ate nothing but locusts and wild honey.[739] Eleazar and the seven Machabean brothers, with their mother, chose to suffer the most painful death, rather than transgress the law of God by eating swine's flesh.[740]

[736] Cf. 1 Tm 4:1-4
[737] Cf. Lv 11:2ff
[738] Cf. Acts 15:29
[739] Cf. Mk 1:6
[740] Cf. 2 Mc 6-7

635. **But does not our Savior clearly say: "Not that which goeth into the mouth defileth a man"?**

Yes; but the disobedience which proceeds from the heart defiles him,[741] as it is proved by the fall of our first parents.

Let, however, no one believe that the breaking of the fast is only then a grievous sin when it proceeds from a contempt of the commandment or from a deliberate resistance to the Church. This opinion is erroneous, and has been expressly condemned by the Church.[742] Nay, there is a culpable disobedience when one knowingly and deliberately does what the Church has forbidden, even though it be neither attended with obstinacy nor contempt of the commandment, but is done either through gluttony or through a weak complaisance to others.

636. **Should we, on fasting days, content ourselves with abstaining from food?**

No; we should, according to the intention of the Church, spend these days in the spirit of penance, and sanctify them by prayer and good works.[743]

Application. Respect the commandment of fasting and abstinence as a commandment which God himself has given you through his Church, and consider it an honor to observe it strictly.

THE THIRD, FOURTH, AND FIFTH COMMANDMENTS OF THE CHURCH

637. **What are we commanded by the third and fourth commandments of the Church?**

By the third and fourth commandments, we are commanded: 1) to confess our sins faithfully at least once a year; and 2) to receive the Holy Communion worthily at Easter or during the Easter time; that is, from the First Sunday in Lent till Trinity Sunday, inclusive.

741 Cf. Mt 15:11, 18

742 Cf. Alexander VII, Proposition 23

743 Cf. Is 58:6-7

638. **To whom must the confession be made?**

To any priest authorized by the bishop to hear confessions.

In former times, the faithful were commanded by the Church to confess their sins once a year to their own parish priest, or to ask leave of him if they wished to confess to another priest. Hence comes this form of the commandment, which is still in use in some dioceses: "Thou shalt confess thy sins once a year to thy parish priest, or, with his permission, to another."

639. **Where are we to receive Easter Communion?**

Conformably to a precept of the Church, we are to receive it in the parish church, or at least notify our pastor if we receive it elsewhere.

640. **At what age are we obliged to go to confession and Communion?**

Decrees of popes and laws of the Church make it clear that at the age of reason, which is about seven years, all are bound by the precept of Easter Communion. The parents, as well as the confessor and pastor, are obliged to see that children make their first Communion in time to fulfill this duty.

In a decree dated August, 1910, the Sacred Congregation of the Sacraments declares that the obligation of satisfying the precepts of both Communion and confession begins when the child commences to reason, which, the decree says, is at the age of seven or thereabouts.

641. **Why has the Church commanded that the Blessed Sacrament should be received during Easter time?**

1) Because Jesus Christ instituted the Holy Eucharist within this time; and 2) because, within this time, he died, and rose again from the dead, and, therefore, we also should die to sin and lead a new life.

642. **Ought we to think it sufficient to receive Holy Communion once in the year?**

No; it is the intention and most earnest desire of holy mother Church that we should frequently, and even daily, partake of this august sacrament.

The Church does not bind us under pain of sin to go oftener than once a year at Easter time, but her laws manifest her fervent wishes for daily Communion among all the faithful, irrespective of age or sex.

643. **Why, then, does the Church not command us to communicate oftener?**
1) Because the love of God and the care for our souls should alone be sufficient motives to induce us to do so; and 2) because the Church wishes to prescribe, under pain of mortal sin, only what she deems absolutely necessary.

Application. Make it a rule to go to confession and Communion at least once a month.

644. **What are we commanded to do by the fifth commandment of the Church?**
We are commanded to contribute cheerfully, according to our means, to the support of our pastors and of our churches, schools, and religious institutions, and of religion generally.

645. **Are we bound in conscience and in justice to contribute to the support of our pastors?**
Yes; and by a divine precept also. St. Paul says: "So the Lord ordained, that they who preach the gospel should live by the gospel."[744]

Under the old law, God commanded the people of Israel to give tithes and offerings for the support of the priesthood and the maintenance of worship. In the Church, from the beginning, this was a sacred duty. "For as many as were owners of lands or houses sold them and brought the price of the things they sold, and laid it down before the feet of the apostles, and distribution was made to every one, according as he had need."[745]

646. **Does this commandment of the Church apply only to heads of families?**
No; it applies also to all who earn or enjoy an income of their own.[746]

[744] 1 Cor 9:14

[745] Acts 4:34-35

[746] On the sixth commandment of the Church, "Not to marry within certain degrees of kindred, or privately without witnesses, nor to solemnize marriage at the forbidden times," see the sacrament of matrimony, below, p. 423ff.

The Violation of the Commandments

On Sin in General

647. **What is actual sin?**

Actual sin is a willful violation of the law of God.

648. **In how many ways may we sin?**

We may sin: 1) by bad thoughts, desires, words, and actions; and 2) also by the omission of the good which we are bound to do.

649. **Are all sins equally grievous?**

No; there are grievous sins which are called mortal; and there are lesser ones, which are called venial.

Some sins in the holy scripture are compared to motes, and others to beams;[747] and it is also written of the just man that "he shall fall seven times."[748]

650. **When do we commit mortal sin?**

We commit mortal sin when we willfully violate the law of God in a matter which we know or believe to be important.

651. **Why are grievous sins called "mortal" sins?**

Because grievous sin deprives the soul of supernatural life—that is, sanctifying grace—and renders us guilty of eternal death, or everlasting damnation.

"Sin, when it is completed, begetteth death."[749] "I know thy works, that thou hast the name of being alive, and thou art dead."[750]

747 Cf. Mt 7:3
748 Prv 24:16
749 Jas 1:15
750 Apoc 3:1

652. **When do we commit venial sin?**
We commit venial sin when we transgress the law of God in a matter not of grave importance, or when our transgression is not quite voluntary.

653. **When is the transgression not quite voluntary?**
When, with our understanding, we do not sufficiently perceive the evil, or, with our will, we do not fully consent to it.

654. **Why are lesser sins called "venial" sins?**
Because they can be forgiven more easily, and even without confession.

655. **Should we dread only mortal sins?**
No; we should dread and carefully avoid any sin, whether it be grievous or venial, as the greatest evil on earth.

"How can I do this wicked thing, and sin against my God?"[751]

656. **What should deter us from committing sin?**
The consideration of its malice and evil consequences.

657. **In what does the malice of mortal sin principally consist?**
In this, that mortal sin is: 1) a grievous offense against God, our supreme Lord, and the most criminal disobedience to his holy will; 2) the most shameful ingratitude to God, our greatest benefactor and best Father; 3) detestable infidelity to our most amiable Redeemer, and contempt of his graces and merits.

1) "Thou hast broken my yoke,...and thou saidst: 'I will not serve.'"[752] 2) "Hear, O ye heavens, and give ear, O earth, for the Lord hath spoken: 'I have brought up children and exalted them; but they

[751] Gn 39:9
[752] Jer 2:20

have despised me.'"[753] 3) Of those "who were once illuminated, have tasted also the heavenly gift, and were made partakers of the Holy Ghost,...and are fallen away [from God by mortal sin]," St. Paul says that they "crucify again to themselves the Son of God, and make him a mockery."[754] "If any man love not our Lord Jesus Christ, let him be anathema."[755]

658. **Can we comprehend the full malice of an offense against God?**
We cannot, because we do not comprehend the infinite greatness and goodness of the Lord our God, who is offended by sin.

659. **What most of all shows us the malice of an offense against God?**
1) The grievous punishment of the wicked angels and of our first parents; 2) the everlasting punishment in hell which every mortal sin deserves; and 3) the most bitter passion and death which the only Son of God suffered for our sins.

660. **What are the consequences of mortal sin?**
Mortal sin 1) separates us from God, and deprives us of his love and friendship; 2) it disfigures in us the image of God, and disturbs the peace of our conscience; 3) it robs us of all merits, and of our heirship to heaven; and 4) it draws upon us the judgments of God, and, lastly, eternal damnation.

"They that commit sin and iniquity are enemies of their own soul."[756]—*Examples*: Cain, Antiochus, Judas; parable of the rich man.

661. **Why should we also carefully avoid venial sin?**
1) Because venial sin also is an offense against God, and is, therefore, after mortal sin, the greatest of all evils; 2) because it weakens the life of the soul, and hinders many graces which God intends to give us; and 3) because it

[753] Is 1:2
[754] Heb 6:4-6
[755] 1 Cor 16:22
[756] Tb 12:10

also brings many punishments of God upon us, and leads us by degrees to grievous sins.

"He that is unjust in that which is little, is unjust also in that which is greater."[757] "Behold how small a fire, what a great wood it kindleth."[758]

Application. "[My son,] all the days of thy life have God in thy mind, and take heed thou never consent to sin…We lead indeed a poor life; but we shall have many good things, if we fear God, and depart from all sin, and do that which is good."[759]

On the Different Kinds of Sin

662. **What particular kinds of sin are there?**

1) The seven capital or deadly sins; 2) the six sins against the Holy Ghost; 3) the four sins crying to heaven for vengeance; and 4) the nine ways of being accessory to another person's sins.

663. **Which are the seven capital sins?**

1) Pride; 2) covetousness; 3) lust; 4) anger; 5) gluttony; 6) envy; and 7) sloth.

664. **Are these sins always grievous?**

They are grievous sins as often as a weighty duty either to God, our neighbor, or ourselves is violated by them.

665. **Why are they called capital sins?**

Because they are also vices; that is, main sources from which all other sins take their rise.

666. **When do we sin by pride?**

When we think too much of ourselves, do not give God the honor due to him, and despise our neighbor.

[757] Lk 16:10
[758] Cf. Jas 3:5
[759] Tb 4:6, 23

From pride spring especially: vanity, ambition, hypocrisy, disobedience, and resistance to superiors; coldness and hard-heartedness toward inferiors; an inordinate desire of ruling; quarrel and strife; ingratitude, envy, cruelty, infidelity and heresy, hatred of God.—*Examples*: Lucifer, Nabuchodonosor, Holofernes, Aman, Herod, the Pharisee, etc. "Pride is hateful before God and men...[It] is the beginning of all sin; he that holdeth it shall be filled with maledictions, and it shall ruin him in the end."[760]

667. **When do we sin by covetousness?**

When we inordinately seek and love money or other worldly goods, and are hard-hearted toward those who are in distress.

Covetousness, or avarice, leads people to an excessive care for earthly things, to hardness of heart, lying, perjury, theft, fraud, usury, simony, treachery, superstitious seeking after hidden treasures, to manslaughter and murder.—*Examples*: Achan, Ahab, Giezi, Judas, Ananias, and Saphira. "There is not a more wicked thing than to love money; for such a one setteth even his own soul to sale."[761] "They that will become rich fall into temptation, and into the snare of the devil, and into many unprofitable and hurtful desires which drown men into destruction and perdition."[762]

668. **How do we sin by lust?**

By indulging in immodest or impure thoughts, desires, words, or actions.

The ordinary effects of lust, or impurity, are: aversion to prayer and to all that is good; excessive fondness for amusement and dissipation; neglect of the duties of our state of life; great desire of attracting notice; insensibility and cruelty; all sorts of shameless excesses and of unnatural crimes; seduction of innocence; false promises and oaths; theft, ruin of health and of domestic happiness; enmity, duels, suicide or self-murder; and likewise atheism, sacrilege, worship of the devil, madness, and despair.[763]

[760] Ecclus 10:7, 15
[761] Ecclus 10:10
[762] 1 Tm 6:9
[763] See the sixth commandment of God, above, p. 310ff.

669. **When do we sin by anger?**

When we are exasperated at that which displeases us, fly into a passion, and suffer ourselves to be carried away by a violent desire of revenge.

Anger leads to hatred, enmity, quarreling, cursing, blaspheming, reviling, and to all the sins and crimes against the fifth commandment of God.—*Examples*: Esau, whilst in anger, designs to kill his brother Jacob; Absalom kills his brother Amnon. "Let all bitterness, and anger, and indignation, and clamor, and blasphemy, be put away from you, with all malice."[764]

670. **When do we sin by gluttony?**

When we eat and drink too much, or when, out of time and in an inordinate manner, we long for eating and drinking.

From this vice proceed: daintiness, profusion, idleness, drunkenness, destruction of domestic peace and comfort, indecent jests and buffooneries, lewdness, adultery, debauchery, impenitence; and likewise cursing, railing, striking, and murdering.—*Examples*: The rich man;[765] King Baltassar. "Take heed to yourselves, lest perhaps your hearts be overcharged with surfeiting and drunkenness,...and that day [of judgment] come upon you suddenly."[766] "Their [the intemperate] God is their belly."[767]

671. **When do we sin by envy?**

When we repine at our neighbor's good, and are sad when he is in possession of temporal or spiritual blessings, and rejoice when he is deprived of them.

Envy produces: ingratitude and murmuring against God, blasphemy, blindness, whispering and calumny; hatred, desire of revenge, deceit and knavery, persecution and murder.—*Examples*: Satan, Cain, the brothers

[764] Eph 4:31
[765] Cf. Lk 16:19ff
[766] Lk 21:34
[767] Phil 3:19

of Joseph, Saul, the Pharisees. "By the envy of the devil, death came into the world; and they follow him that are of his side."[768]

672. **When do we sin by sloth?**
When we give way to our natural repugnance to labor and exertion, and thus neglect our duties.

673. **What sort of sloth is particularly hateful to God?**
Lukewarmness, or laziness in whatsoever concerns the service of God or the salvation of our soul. Therefore, God says: "I would thou wert cold or hot. But because thou art lukewarm, and neither cold nor hot, I will begin to vomit thee out of my mouth."[769]

The effects of sloth in general are: neglect of the duties of our calling, ruin of property, lying, deceit, effeminacy, and a great many sins against the sixth and seventh commandments. "Idleness hath taught much evil."[770] "Go to the ant, O sluggard, and consider her ways, and learn wisdom."[771] The effects of spiritual sloth, or lukewarmness, are: aversion to all religious exercises, contempt of the word of God and of all means of grace, irritation at salutary admonitions, love of the world, pusillanimity, impenitence, infidelity.—*Examples*: The slothful servant; the foolish virgins.[772]

674. **What benefit should we reap from the doctrine of the capital sins?**
We should carefully avoid them as the sources of all evil, and most earnestly endeavor to acquire the opposite virtues.

Application. Every morning, when you get up, resolve to guard most carefully during the day against your chief fault. At night, examine your conscience on it; and if you have failed, repent, and purpose to confess it as soon as possible.

768 Ws 2:24-25
769 Apoc 3:15-16
770 Ecclus 33:29
771 Prv 6:6
772 Cf. Mt 25

The Different Kinds of Sin (Continued)

675. **Which are the six sins against the Holy Ghost?**

1) Presumption of God's mercy; 2) despair; 3) resisting the known Christian truth; 4) envy at another's spiritual good; 5) obstinacy in sin; and 6) final impenitence.

Examples. Cain, Pharao, the Pharisees, Elymas the Magician.[773]

676. **Why are they called "sins against the Holy Ghost"?**

Because by them we resist, in an especial manner, the Holy Ghost, since we knowingly and willingly despise, reject, or abuse his grace.

"You stiff-necked and uncircumcised in heart and ears, you always resist the Holy Ghost: as your fathers did, so do you also."[774]

677. **Why should we particularly avoid these sins?**

Because they obstruct the entrance of God's grace into the heart, and therefore hinder our conversion, or render it very difficult.

Speaking of these sins, Jesus Christ says that they "shall not be forgiven, neither in this world, nor in the world to come";[775] that is to say, that they are hardly ever forgiven, because it is very, very seldom that people truly repent of them.

678. **Which are the four sins crying to heaven for vengeance?**

1) Willful murder; 2) sodomy; 3) oppression of the poor, of widows and orphans; 4) defrauding laborers of their wages.

"The voice of thy brother's blood crieth to me from the earth."[776] "The cry of Sodom and Gomorrha is multiplied, and their sin is become exceedingly grievous...We will destroy this place, because their cry is grown loud before the Lord."[777] "Do not the widow's tears run down the cheek, and

[773] Cf. Acts 13
[774] Acts 7:51
[775] Mt 12:32
[776] Gn 4:10
[777] Gn 18:20; 19:13

her cry against him that causeth them to fall? From the cheek they go up even to heaven."[778] "Behold the hire of the laborers,...which by fraud has been kept back by you, crieth, and the cry of them hath entered into the ears of the Lord of Sabaoth."[779]

679. **Why are they called "sins crying to heaven for vengeance"?**
Because, on account of their heinous malice, they cry, as it were, for vengeance, and call on divine justice to punish them signally.

680. **In how many ways may we become accessory to another person's sin, and be answerable for it?**
In these nine ways: 1) by counsel; 2) by command; 3) by consent; 4) by provocation; 5) by praise or flattery; 6) by silence; 7) by connivance; 8) by partaking; 9) by defense of the ill done.

[We are accessory by silence] when we could and should prevent another's sin either by kindly admonishing him or by giving information to his parents, his pastor, etc. "If thou declare it not to the wicked, that he may be converted from his wicked way, and live, the same wicked man shall die in his iniquity, but I will require his blood at thy hand."[780]

[We are accessory by connivance] when we could and should punish the sinner. Thus Heli sinned, "because he knew that his sons did wickedly, and did not chastise them."[781]

681. **Why are we answerable for the sin which another commits?**
Because, in any of the above ways, we are either the cause of his sin or cooperate with him in it, and thus are as guilty before God as if we had committed it ourselves; or, it may be, even more so.

"Not only they that do such things are worthy of death, but they also that consent to them that do them."[782]

[778] Ecclus 35:18-19
[779] Jas 5:4
[780] Cf. Ez 3:18
[781] 1 Kgs 3:13
[782] Cf. Rom 1:32

Application. Always receive wholesome admonitions willingly and gratefully. Never participate in the sins of others; on the contrary, endeavor, to the utmost of your power, to hinder them; and when, for that reason, you are to reveal them, do not say: "I do not like to denounce others, because I should not like them to denounce me." Ought you, then, to be sorry, if someone were to snatch from your hands the knife with which you were about to kill yourself?

Virtue and Christian Perfection

682. **Should we be contented with avoiding grievous sins and crimes?**
No; we should also diligently endeavor to become more and more virtuous, and to attain the perfection suitable to our condition.

"He that is just, let him be justified still; and he that is holy, let him be sanctified still."[783] "Be not afraid to be justified even to death."[784]—*Example* of St. Paul: "Not as though I had already attained, or were already perfect; but I follow after...One thing I do: forgetting the things that are behind, and stretching forth myself to those that are before."[785]

Virtue

683. **Why should we endeavor to become more and more virtuous?**
Because man is only good, and pleasing to God, inasmuch as he is virtuous.

684. **In what does Christian virtue consist?**
Christian virtue, in general, consists in the perseverance of the will, and in its constant exertions to do what is acceptable to God.

[783] Apoc 22:11
[784] Ecclus 18:22
[785] Phil 3:12-13

685. **How is Christian virtue divided with regard to its origin?**
Into infused and acquired virtue.

686. **What is infused virtue?**
Virtue is called "infused," inasmuch as it is a gift of God, which together with sanctifying grace is imparted to the soul, in order to qualify and dispose us for the practice of supernatural virtues—i.e., for the performance of such pious actions as are worthy of life everlasting.[786]

687. **Which virtues are chiefly infused into the soul?**
The three theological virtues: faith, hope, and charity.

688. **Why are they called "theological virtues"?**
Because they come directly from, and directly relate to, God.

689. **When should we make acts of faith, hope, and charity?**
We should make them frequently, but especially: 1) in great temptations against these virtues; 2) when we receive the holy sacraments; and 3) when we are in danger of losing our life, or on our deathbed.

690. **How may we make acts of faith, hope, and charity?**
We may make them in this manner:

An act of faith. O my God! I firmly believe that thou art one God in three divine Persons, Father, Son, and Holy Ghost. I believe that the divine Son became man, and died for our sins, and that he will come to judge the living and the dead. I believe these and all the truths which the holy Catholic Church teaches, because thou hast revealed them, who canst neither deceive nor be deceived.

An act of hope. O my God! relying on thy infinite goodness and promises, I hope to obtain pardon of my sins, the help of thy grace, and life everlasting, through the merits of Jesus Christ, my Lord and Redeemer.

[786] Cf. Rom 5:5

An act of charity.[787] O my God! I love thee above all things, with my whole heart and soul, because thou are all-good and worthy of all love. I love my neighbor as myself for the love of thee. I forgive all who have injured me, and ask pardon of all whom I have injured.

691. **What is acquired virtue?**
Virtue is called "acquired," inasmuch as it is a faculty which, with the assistance of God, we acquire by constant practice.

692. **What do we generally call those virtues which can be acquired by practice?**
We call them "moral virtues," because they regulate our moral conduct according to the will of God.

693. **Which among them are the four cardinal or principal virtues in which all the others are included?**
1) Prudence; 2) justice; 3) fortitude; and 4) temperance.[788]

They are called "cardinal" virtues, because they are, as it were, the hinges (*cardines*) by which the whole moral life of a Christian is supported, and on which it must constantly move.

694. **What is prudence?**
Prudence is a virtue which makes us discern what is truly good and agreeable to God from what only appears to be so, and thus prevents our being seduced to evil.

"Be not conformed to this world, but be reformed in the newness of your mind, that you may prove what is the good, and the acceptable, and the perfect will of God."[789] "Beware of false prophets."[790]—*Examples*: The imprudent Josaphat;[791] the wise virgins.[792]

[787] *Charity* here means "love."
[788] Cf. Ws 8:7
[789] Rom 12:2
[790] Mt 7:15
[791] Cf. 2 Par 19:2
[792] Cf. Mt 25

695. **What is justice?**

Justice is a virtue by which we are always determined to do what is right, and, therefore, always disposed to give everyone his due.

"Render to Caesar the things that are Caesar's; and to God, the things that are God's."[793]—*Example*: Tobias.[794]

696. **What is fortitude?**

Fortitude is a virtue which enables us to endure any hardship or persecution, rather than abandon our duty.

Examples. The seven Machabees and their mother, who esteemed the torments as nothing.[795]

697. **What is temperance?**

Temperance is a virtue which restrains our sensual inclinations and desires, that they may not allure us from virtue.

"Refrain yourselves from carnal desires, which war against the soul."[796]—*Example*: Esther.[797]

698. **What virtues are especially opposite to the seven capital sins?**

1) Humility; 2) liberality; 3) chastity; 4) meekness; 5) temperance in eating and drinking; 6) brotherly love; and 7) diligence.

699. **What is humility?**

Humility is a virtue which teaches us to acknowledge our own unworthiness, weakness, and sinfulness, and to look upon all good as coming from God.

793 Mt 22:21
794 Cf. Tb 2:21
795 Cf. 2 Mc 7:12
796 1 Pt 2:11
797 Cf. Est 14:14-18

Examples. Abraham;[798] the publican;[799] St. Paul.[800] "Unless you…become as little children, you shall not enter into the kingdom of heaven."[801]

700. **What is liberality?**

Liberality is a virtue which inclines us to use our property for the relief of the needy, or for other laudable purposes.

Examples. Tobias;[802] Solomon;[803] the first Christians.[804] "Give, and it shall be given to you."[805]

701. **What is chastity?**

Chastity is a virtue which subdues all impure inclinations and desires by which modesty is violated.

Examples. Joseph, Susanna, and, above all, the Blessed Virgin Mary. "They that are Christ's have crucified their flesh with the vices and concupiscences."[806]

702. **What is meekness?**

Meekness is a virtue which suppresses all desire of revenge, and any motion of unjust anger and displeasure.

Examples. David;[807] St. Stephen.[808] "Learn of me, because I am meek and humble of heart."[809]

[798] Cf. Gn 18:27
[799] Cf. Lk 18:13
[800] Cf. 1 Cor 15:8-9
[801] Mt 18:3
[802] Cf. Tb 1:19-20
[803] Cf. 3 Kgs 5-8
[804] Cf. Acts 2:45
[805] Lk 6:38
[806] Gal 5:24
[807] Cf. 1 Kgs 24, 26
[808] Cf. Acts 7:58
[809] Mt 11:29

703. **What is temperance in eating and drinking?**

Temperance in eating and drinking is a virtue by which we control ourselves, especially our appetite for eating and drinking.

Examples. Daniel, Ananias, Misael, and Azarias;[810] John the Baptist.[811] "Let us walk honestly,...not in rioting and drunkenness."[812]

704. **What is brotherly love?**

Brotherly love is a virtue by which we wish everyone well, and sincerely rejoice and condole with our neighbor.

Examples. The history of Ruth and of Tobias. "Love one another with the charity of brotherhood...Rejoice with them that rejoice; weep with them that weep."[813]

705. **What is diligence?**

Diligence is a virtue which enables us to serve God readily and cheerfully, to promote his honor as much as lies in our power, and faithfully to perform all our duties.

Examples. Mathathias;[814] St. Paul.[815] "In carefulness [be] not slothful; in spirit fervent; serving the Lord."[816]

Application. Unless you perseveringly struggle with your wicked inclinations, you will never acquire the Christian virtues; therefore, fight faithfully until death, and God will give you the crown of life.[817]

[810] Cf. Dn 1
[811] Cf. Mt 3:4
[812] Rom 13:13
[813] Rom 12:10, 15
[814] Cf. 1 Mc 2
[815] Cf. Phil 3:13-14
[816] Rom 12:11
[817] Cf. Apoc 2:10

On Christian Perfection

706. **Why should we all endeavor to attain the perfection suitable to our condition?**

1) Because our Lord and Savior says to all: "Be you perfect, as also your heavenly Father is perfect";[818] 2) because we are commanded to love God with our whole heart, and with our whole soul, and with our whole mind, and with our whole strength;[819] 3) because the more holy our life is upon earth, the greater will be our happiness in heaven; and 4) because we easily fall into grievous sin, and finally run into eternal perdition, if we do not continually endeavor to increase in virtue.[820]

707. **In what does Christian perfection consist?**

Christian perfection consists in this: that, free from all inordinate love of the world and of ourselves, we love God above all, and all in God.

"What have I in heaven? and besides thee what do I desire upon earth?...Thou art the God of my heart, and the God that is my portion for ever."[821]

708. **Which is in general the way to perfection?**

The imitation of Jesus Christ.

"If thou wilt be perfect,...and come, follow me."[822]

709. **What particular means of attaining perfection have been recommended by Jesus Christ?**

Chiefly those which are called "evangelical counsels."

[818] Mt 5:48
[819] Cf. Mk 12:30
[820] Cf. Mt 25:29
[821] Ps 72:25-26
[822] Mt 19:21

710. **Which are the evangelical counsels?**

1) Voluntary poverty; 2) perpetual chastity; and 3) entire obedience to a spiritual superior.

711. **What is voluntary poverty?**

It is a free renunciation of all temporal things, in order to be less distracted in striving for those that are eternal.

"If thou wilt be perfect, go sell what thou hast, and give to the poor, and thou shalt have treasure in heaven; and come, follow me."[823]

712. **What is perpetual chastity?**

It is a free and perpetual renunciation, not only of all impure pleasure, but even of marriage, in order that we may render undivided service to God.[824]

"Now concerning virgins, I have no commandment of the Lord, but I give counsel:...he that giveth his virgin in marriage, doth well; and he that giveth her not, doth better."[825] "If any one shall say that the marriage state is to be preferred to the state of virginity, or of celibacy, and that it is not better and more blessed to remain in virginity, or in celibacy, than to be united in matrimony, let him be anathema."[826]

713. **What is entire obedience?**

It is a renunciation of one's own will, in order to do the divine will more surely under a superior who represents God.[827]

714. **Why are the evangelical counsels special means of perfection?**

1) Because by them the chief obstacles to Christian perfection are removed—namely, the inordinate love and desire of earthly goods, sensual pleasures, and the pride of independence; and 2) because by them man sacrifices to the Lord his God all that he has and is: his exterior goods, by

[823] Ibid.
[824] See Mt 19:10-12.
[825] 1 Cor 7:25, 38
[826] Council of Trent, Session 24, Can. 10
[827] Cf. Mt 16:24

the vow of poverty; his body, by the vow of chastity; and his mind or will, by the vow of obedience.

Of these evangelical counsels our divine Redeemer meant to speak when he said: "All men take not this word, but they to whom it is given."[828]

715. **Who are obliged to observe the evangelical counsels?**

All religious, and all those who have bound themselves by vow to keep them.

The secular clergy also, when they receive the greater orders, bind themselves to perpetual chastity, in order to be able to devote themselves entirely, and with an undivided heart, to the service of God and of their neighbor. "He that is without a wife is solicitous for the things that belong to the Lord, how he may please God. But he that is with a wife is solicitous for the things of the world, how he may please his wife; and he is divided."[829]

716. **Can people in the world also lead a perfect life?**

Yes, if they do not live according to the spirit of the world, but according to the spirit of Jesus Christ.

"If any man love the world, the charity of the Father is not in him; for all that is in the world is the concupiscence of the flesh, and the concupiscence of the eyes, and the pride of life."[830] "Whosoever will be a friend of this world becometh an enemy of God."[831] "If any man have not the Spirit of Christ, he is none of his."[832]

717. **Is, then, the spirit of the world at variance with the Spirit of Christ?**

Most certainly it is, as we distinctly see from those sentences of our Savior which are called the "eight beatitudes."

[828] Mt 19:11
[829] 1 Cor 7:32-33
[830] 1 Jn 2:15-16
[831] Jas 4:4
[832] Rom 8:9

718. **Which are the eight beatitudes?**

1. Blessed are the poor in spirit; for theirs is the kingdom of heaven.
2. Blessed are the meek; for they shall possess the land.
3. Blessed are they that mourn; for they shall be comforted.
4. Blessed are they that hunger and thirst after justice; for they shall have their fill.
5. Blessed are the merciful; for they shall obtain mercy.
6. Blessed are the clean of heart; for they shall see God.
7. Blessed are the peacemakers; for they shall be called the children of God.
8. Blessed are they that suffer persecution for justice' sake; for theirs is the kingdom of heaven.[833]

719. **How do we know from the eight beatitudes that the spirit of the world is at variance with the Spirit of Christ?**

We know it from this: that the world esteems those very persons miserable and foolish whom Christ our Lord calls "blessed."

The world is accustomed to set forth riches, reputation, honors, and sensual pleasures as the sources of happiness; Jesus Christ, on the contrary, teaches us in the eight beatitudes to seek our happiness in God and in his holy service, and, therefore, willingly and cheerfully to endure poverty, persecution, and any hardships that may fall to our lot.

720. **What means must a Christian use, let his condition be what it may, in order to attain to perfection?**

He must 1) delight in prayer, diligently hear the word of God, and often receive the holy sacraments; 2) he must steadily subdue and deny himself; and 3) he must perform his daily actions in the state of grace, and in a manner acceptable to God.

"They were persevering in the doctrine of the apostles, and in the communication of the breaking of bread, and in prayers."[834] "If any man will

[833] Mt 5:3-10
[834] Acts 2:42

come after me, let him deny himself, and take up his cross, and follow me."[835] "Whether you eat or drink, or whatsoever else you do, do all to the glory of God."[836]

721. **How should we deny ourselves?**
We should refuse ourselves many things that are dear and agreeable to us, and should deprive ourselves of lawful things, that we may the more easily abstain from unlawful ones.

722. **How may we most easily perform our daily actions in a manner acceptable to God?**
By representing to ourselves how Jesus Christ performed them, and by striving to imitate him for his sake.

723. **How should we do our daily work after the example of Christ?**
We should do it diligently, patiently, and with a view to please God. Therefore, we should form a good intention at the beginning, and renew it sometimes when the work is of long continuance.

724. **What should we do when we take our meals?**
We should before and after meals say grace, reverently and devoutly, and be temperate and modest at table.

725. **May we also be allowed to take recreation?**
Yes; for nothing forbids our taking proper recreation in due time. We should, however, sanctify it by a good intention and by the remembrance of God, and keep within the bounds of modesty.

726. **What should our intercourse with our neighbor be?**
It should be: 1) kind, that we may not offend anyone; and 2) prudent, that we may not in any manner be seduced to evil.

[835] Mt 16:24
[836] 1 Cor 10:31

727. **How should we act in our afflictions?**

We should remember and feel that they come from God, and we should offer them up to him, and beg of him the grace necessary to make a good use of them.

Application. Think that these words, which God spoke to Abraham, are also addressed to you: "Walk before me, and be perfect."[837] Strive earnestly to become daily more pious and virtuous. Let this be every morning your resolution, and every night examine your conscience upon it. "My son,... serve [God] with a perfect heart and a willing mind; for the Lord searcheth all hearts, and understandeth all the thoughts of minds. If thou seek him, thou shalt find him; but if thou forsake him, he will cast thee off for ever."[838]

[837] Gn 17:1
[838] 1 Par 28:9

SECTION III

On the Means of Grace

Grace in General

728. **Can we, by our own natural strength, keep the commandments and be saved?**

No; we cannot, without the grace of God.

"Without me you can do nothing,"[839] says Christ. "I will put my spirit in the midst of you, and I will cause you to walk in my commandments."[840]

729. **What do we understand by "the grace of God"?**

By "the grace of God," we understand here an internal supernatural help or gift which God communicates to us, through the merits of Jesus Christ, for our eternal salvation.

730. **How many kinds of this supernatural help and gift, or of "grace" properly so called, are there?**

There are two kinds: 1) the grace of assistance, called also "actual" or "transient grace"; and 2) the grace of sanctification or justification, called also "sanctifying" or "habitual grace."

The grace of assistance is called "actual" and "transient," because it acts transiently upon the soul, whereas the grace of sanctification or justification remains habitually in the soul, beautifies it, and makes it holy and just in the eyes of God.

[839] Jn 15:5
[840] Ez 36:27

The Grace of Assistance

731. **In what does actual grace, or the grace of assistance, consist?**
Actual grace consists in this: that God enlightens our understanding, and inclines our will to avoid evil, and both to will and to do what is good.

"Give me understanding, and I will search thy law, and I will keep it with my whole heart...Incline my heart unto thy testimonies,"[841] etc.

732. **How far is the assistance of grace necessary to us?**
It is so necessary to us that, without the grace of God, we can neither begin, continue, nor accomplish the least thing toward our salvation.

"For it is God who worketh in you, both to will and to accomplish."[842]

733. **Why is grace so indispensable to everything that relates to salvation?**
1) Because eternal salvation is a good of a supernatural order, and, consequently, can be obtained only by a supernatural power and help—that is, by grace; 2) because by grace alone we enter into connection with Christ, and partake of his infinite merits, which are the source of everything that leads to salvation.

1) "Not that we are sufficient to think anything [conducive to salvation] of ourselves, as of ourselves; but our sufficiency is from God."[843] 2) "I cast not away the grace of God; for if justice be by the law, then Christ died in vain"[844]—i.e., if the observance of the law alone, without being united by grace with Christ, did justify us, or lead us to eternal salvation, it would not have been necessary for Christ to die in order to merit salvation for us.

By this, however, it is not meant that man is naturally quite incapable of performing any action that is morally good, but only that by such morally good actions as proceed from his naturally good will he can neither merit, nor in any way obtain, grace or salvation; by them he can only prepare himself for grace, insofar as he does not, by bad actions, still increase

[841] Ps 118:34, 36
[842] Phil 2:13
[843] 2 Cor 3:5
[844] Gal 2:21

the obstacles of it. "No man can come to me," says Christ, "unless it be given him by my Father."[845]

734. **Does God give his grace to all men?**

Yes; God gives to all men sufficient grace to enable them to keep, as they are in duty bound, the commandments, and to work out their salvation.

"The Son of man is come to save that which was lost."[846] "[God] will have all men to be saved, and to come to the knowledge of the truth."[847] "God is faithful, who will not suffer you to be tempted above that which you are able, but will make also with temptation issue, that you may be able to bear it."[848] "God does not command impossibilities; but, when commanding, he admonishes us to do what we are able, and to pray for what we are not able to do, and aids us, that we may be able."[849]

735. **But what must we do on our part, in order that the grace of God may conduce to our salvation?**

We must not resist it, but faithfully cooperate with it.

"We exhort you, that you receive not the grace of God in vain."[850] God stretches forth his hand to save us; if we really wish to be saved, we must take hold of it, and not reject it.—*Example* of St. Paul: "I have labored more abundantly than all they; yet not I, but the grace of God with me."[851]

736. **Is it, then, also in our power to resist the grace of God?**

Most certainly; for God's grace does not force the human will, but leaves it perfectly free.

"Jerusalem, Jerusalem,...how often would I have gathered together thy children, as the hen doth gather her chickens under her wings, and

[845] Jn 6:66
[846] Mt 18:11
[847] 1 Tm 2:4
[848] 1 Cor 10:13
[849] Council of Trent, Session 6, "Decree on Justification," Ch. 11
[850] 2 Cor 6:1
[851] 1 Cor 15:10

thou wouldst not!"[852] "Today, if you shall hear his voice, harden not your hearts."[853]

Application. Pray daily to God to give you his grace, and take particular care not to close your heart against it. "Behold, I stand at the gate, and knock. If any man shall hear my voice, and open to me the door, I will come in to him, and will sup with him, and he with me."[854] In order to make his grace operate the more easily in the human heart, God often connects it with exterior events; as sudden death, diseases, good and bad fortune. Do not heedlessly disregard such divine warnings; for nothing is more dangerous than not to know the time of the visitation of God.—*Example*: Jerusalem.[855]

On the Grace of Sanctification or Justification

737. **What is sanctifying grace?**

Sanctifying grace is a gratuitous supernatural gift, which the Holy Ghost communicates to our souls, and by which from sinners we are made just, children of God, and heirs of heaven.

Together with sanctifying grace, "the charity of God is poured forth in our hearts by the Holy Ghost, who is given to us."[856] With it God enters into our hearts, according to the words of Jesus: "If any one love me,...my Father will love him, and we will come to him, and will make our abode with him."[857] Through it we are born again children of God, and our soul receives supernatural life: "Behold what manner of charity the Father hath bestowed upon us, that we should be called, and should be the sons of God."[858]

852 Mt 23:37
853 Ps 94:8
854 Apoc 3:20
855 Cf. Lk 19:44
856 Rom 5:5
857 Jn 14:23
858 1 Jn 3:1

738. **Why is sanctifying grace called "a gratuitous gift"?**
Because it is an entirely free gift, flowing from the compassionate love of God.

"For all have sinned, and do need the glory of God; being justified freely [i.e., without their desert] by his grace, through the redemption that is in Christ Jesus."[859]

739. **Why is sanctifying grace also called "grace of justification"?**
Because by sanctifying grace man is justified—that is, passes from the state of sin to the state of righteousness and holiness.

740. **What, then, does the justification of the sinner include?**
Justification includes: 1) cleanness from all grievous sins at least, together with the remission of eternal punishment; and 2) the sanctification and renewal of the interior man.

"You are washed, you are sanctified, you are justified in the name of our Lord Jesus Christ and the Spirit of our God."[860]

741. **What first gives rise to the justification of the sinner?**
God by grace enlightens the sinner, and excites him to turn to him.

742. **What must the sinner do on his part, in order to attain to justification?**
He must, with the assistance of grace, voluntarily turn to God, and believe all that God has revealed, especially that we are justified by Jesus Christ.

743. **What effect has this belief on the sinner?**
1) The sinner is struck with a wholesome fear of the justice of God, but hopes to obtain pardon from his mercy; 2) then he begins to love God, is sorry for his sins, resolves to lead a new life, agreeable to God, and receives the sacrament of baptism, or, if he is baptized, the sacrament of penance.

[859] Rom 3:23-24
[860] 1 Cor 6:11

744. **What does the sinner receive in the sacrament of baptism or penance?**
He receives sanctifying grace, and together with it the remission of his sins and interior sanctification, by which he is really made just, acceptable to God, a child of God, and heir of heaven.[861]

745. **How long does sanctifying grace remain in the soul of the justified man?**
As long as he does not commit mortal sin.

746. **What fruits does the justified man produce by the help of grace?**
He produces good—i.e., meritorious—works; for "every good tree bringeth forth good fruit."[862]

747. **Cannot a man who is in mortal sin do good?**
He can do good, but without any merit for heaven.[863]

748. **Is, then, the good done in mortal sin useless?**
No; it is, on the contrary, 1) very useful to obtain from the divine mercy the grace of conversion, 2) sometimes also the averting of temporal punishment.

1) "Redeem thou thy sins with alms, and thy iniquities with works of mercy to the poor: perhaps he will forgive thy offenses."[864]—*Example*: Manasses.[865] 2) Achab;[866] the Ninivites.

749. **What do we merit by the good works which we perform in the state of grace?**
We merit: 1) an increase of sanctifying grace; and 2) eternal salvation.[867]
"If any one shall say that the justified man by the good works which he performs through the grace of God and the merit of Jesus Christ, whose

[861] Cf. Council of Trent, Session 6
[862] Mt 7:17
[863] Cf. Jn 15:4-5
[864] Dn 4:24
[865] Cf. 2 Par 33:12
[866] Cf. 3 Kgs 21:29
[867] Cf. 2 Tm 4:8

living member he is, does not truly merit increase of grace and eternal life, let him be anathema."[868]

750. **Whence do such good works derive their intrinsic value or meritoriousness?**
From the infinite merits of Jesus Christ, whose living members we are through sanctifying grace.

"I am the vine, you are the branches: he that abideth in me, and I in him, the same beareth much fruit; for without me you can do nothing."[869]

751. **Is every Christian bound to do good works?**
Yes; for "every tree that doth not yield good fruit, shall be cut down, and cast into the fire."[870]

752. **What good works should we perform before all others?**
1) Those the performance of which is commanded to all Christians by the commandments of God and of the Church; and 2) those which are necessary or useful to fulfill the duties of our state of life.

753. **What other good works are especially recommended to us in holy scripture?**
Prayer, fasting, and alms; by which, in general, are understood the works of devotion, mortification, and charity.

"Prayer is good with fasting and alms, more than to lay up treasures of gold."[871]

754. **What does God especially regard in our good works?**
Our good intention, by which we may obtain from God great reward even for small works.

[868] Council of Trent, Session 6, Can. 32
[869] Jn 15:5; Cf. Council of Trent, Session 6, "Decree on Justification," Ch. 16
[870] Mt 3:10
[871] Tb 12:8

"Whosoever shall give to drink to one of these little ones a cup of cold water only in the name of a disciple, amen I say to you, he shall not lose his reward."[872]—*Example* of the poor widow.[873]

755. **What is a good intention?**
The purpose or positive act of the will to serve God, and to honor him.

756. **How may we make a good intention?**
We may say, for instance, thus: "O my God, I offer up to thee all my thoughts, words, and deeds, for thy honor and glory"; or: "My Lord and my God, all for thy honor."

757. **When should we make a good intention?**
It is very useful to make it several times a day, and especially every morning.

758. **What means must we particularly use in order to obtain grace?**
The holy sacraments and prayer.

759. **Do both these means give us grace in the same manner and in the same measure?**
No; for 1) the sacraments produce grace in us; prayer obtains it for us; 2) through the sacraments, we obtain those special graces for which they were instituted; but through prayer, we receive all sorts of graces, except those which can be obtained only by the sacraments.

Application. Strive most carefully to preserve sanctifying grace continually in your heart by avoiding sin and performing good works. "A man making void the law of Moses dieth without any mercy under two or three witnesses: how much more, do you think, he deserveth worse punishments, who hath trodden underfoot the Son of God, and hath esteemed the blood of the testament unclean by which he was sanctified, and hath offered an affront to the Spirit of grace?"[874]

[872] Mt 10:42
[873] Cf. Mk 12:41-44
[874] Heb 10:28-29

The Sacraments

760. **What is a sacrament?**

A sacrament is a visible, or sensible, sign, instituted by Jesus Christ, by which invisible grace and inward sanctification are communicated to our souls.

By *sensible* is meant something that can be perceived by some of the senses.

761. **How many things are necessary to constitute a sacrament?**

These three: 1) a visible sign; 2) an invisible grace; and 3) the institution by Jesus Christ.

762. **Why has Christ instituted visible signs for imparting his grace to us?**

1) That we may have a visible pledge of the inward invisible grace; and 2) that by sharing in these visible means of grace, we may manifest our communion with the one Church of Christ.

Thus Christ himself sometimes made use of certain signs when he conferred spiritual and corporal blessings on people; for instance, when he breathed on his disciples, and said: "Receive ye the Holy Ghost";[875] when "he spat on the ground and made clay of the spittle, and spread the clay upon the eyes" of the man born blind;[876] when "he put his fingers into the ears [of the man deaf and dumb] and spitting, he touched his tongue, and looking up to heaven, he groaned, and said to him: 'Ephpheta,' which is, 'Be thou opened.'"[877]

[875] Jn 20:22
[876] Jn 9:6
[877] Mk 7:33-34

763. **Do these signs only signify grace?**
No; they also effect or produce the grace which they signify, unless we, on our part, put an obstacle in the way; therefore, they are also called "efficacious signs."

764. **What grace do the sacraments effect?**
1) They communicate, or increase, sanctifying grace; 2) each sacrament communicates other special graces according to the end for which it has been instituted.

765. **How must we receive the sacraments, in order that they may produce these graces in us?**
We must prepare ourselves well for them, and then receive them worthily.

766. **What sin does he commit who receives a sacrament unworthily?**
He commits a very grievous sin—a sacrilege.

767. **Does not the efficacy of the sacraments also depend on the worthiness or unworthiness of those who administer them?**
No; for the sacraments have their efficacy, not from him who administers them, but from the merits of Jesus Christ, by whom they were instituted.

The sacraments are, as it were, channels through which flow to us the graces which Jesus has merited for us by his bitter passion and death.

768. **Were all the sacraments instituted by Christ?**
Yes; for God alone can give to outward signs the power of producing grace and sanctification.

769. **How many sacraments has Christ instituted?**
These seven: 1) baptism; 2) confirmation; 3) Holy Eucharist; 4) penance; 5) extreme unction; 6) holy orders; and 7) matrimony.

Our Lord Jesus Christ has instituted just as many sacraments as are necessary and conducive to the supernatural life of man. For as he is first born into this natural life, then grows up and acquires strength, is frequently supplied with nourishing food in order to preserve life and to increase his strength, etc.; so also he is 1) born in baptism to the supernatural life; gains, then, 2) in confirmation, strength and growth; 3) receives in the Holy Eucharist a divine nourishment; 4) finds in penance a remedy to heal all the diseases of his soul, and to restore him to the state of grace; and 5) gets in extreme unction assistance and strength against despair and the last assaults of the devil; 6) in holy orders, the powers of administrating the means of grace necessary to the supernatural life are propagated; and 7) in matrimony, the union between husband and wife is blessed, that, being sanctified themselves, they may also bring up their children to a holy, and consequently to eternal, life.

770. **How do we know that there are seven sacraments?**

We know it because such has been at all times the teaching and practice of the Church, which is "the pillar and ground of the truth."[878]

Not only have the Catholics of all ages held them, but the modern Greeks, the Russians, and all those sects who in the first centuries separated themselves from the Catholic Church, have ever retained and still hold these seven sacraments; which evidently proves that the doctrine of seven sacraments is as old as the Church itself.

771. **How are the sacraments divided?**

They are divided: 1) into sacraments of the living and sacraments of the dead; and 2) into such as can be received only once, and such as can be received more than once.

772. **Which are the sacraments of the living?**

The sacraments of the living are: 1) confirmation; 2) Holy Eucharist; 3) extreme unction; 4) holy orders; and 5) matrimony.

773. **Why are they called sacraments of the "living"?**

Because, in order to receive them, we ought to have supernatural life—that is, sanctifying grace.

[878] 1 Tm 3:15

774. **Which are the sacraments of the dead?**
The sacraments of the dead are these two: baptism and penance.

775. **Why are they called sacraments of the "dead"?**
Because, when we receive them, we either have not, or at least are not obliged to have, the life of grace.

776. **Which sacraments can be received only once?**
Baptism, confirmation, and holy orders.

777. **Why can they be received but once?**
Because they imprint upon the soul an indelible character, or spiritual mark, which consecrates and dedicates him who receives it in a special manner to the service of God, remains forever, and will add either to his glory in heaven or to his misery in hell.

778. **Whence have we received those ceremonies which, in the administration of the sacraments, are used together with the signs instituted by Christ?**
From the Church, which, under the assistance of the Holy Ghost, has ordained them for the increase of our devotion and reverence.

Application. Esteem the holy sacraments as most precious means of grace instituted by Christ; give fervent thanks to God for them, and beware of profaning them by imprecations or by unworthily receiving them.

BAPTISM

779. **Which is the first and most necessary sacrament?**
The first and most necessary sacrament is baptism.

780. **Why is baptism the first sacrament?**
Because before baptism no other sacrament can be validly received.

781. **Why is baptism the most necessary sacrament?**
Because without baptism no one can be saved.

"Unless a man be born again of water and the Holy Ghost, he cannot enter into the kingdom of God."[879]

God has not revealed to us what becomes of those children who die without baptism. All we know is that they are not admitted to enjoy the sight or beatific vision of God, nor are they punished like those who have sinned of their own free will. However, it is to be supposed that their life hereafter is also to them a benefit of God.

782. **What is baptism?**

Baptism is a sacrament in which, by water and the word of God, we are cleansed from all sin, and reborn and sanctified in Christ to life everlasting.

783. **Why do you say that we are baptized "by water and the word of God"?**

Because baptism is administered by pouring water over the head or over the body of him who is baptized, and, at the same time, pronouncing these words: "I baptize thee in the name of the Father, and of the Son, and of the Holy Ghost."

784. **Why do you say that "in baptism we are cleansed from all sin"?**

Because, in baptism, original sin and all the sins committed before baptism are forgiven.

785. **Is also the punishment due to sin remitted?**

Yes; the temporal as well as the eternal punishment is remitted in baptism.

786. **Why are we, even after baptism, still subject to some defects of original sin, as death, concupiscence, and many tribulations and infirmities?**

1) That we ourselves may experience how punishable and pernicious sin is, and hate it so much the more; and 2) that we may increase our merits for heaven by our combats and sufferings.

[879] Jn 3:5

787. **Why do you further say that we are "reborn and sanctified to life everlasting"?**
Because, in baptism, we are not only cleansed from all sin, but are also transformed in a spiritual manner, made holy, children of God, and heirs of heaven.

"He saved us by the laver of regeneration, and renovation of the Holy Ghost, whom he hath poured forth upon us abundantly through Jesus Christ our Savior; that, being justified by his grace, we may be his heirs, according to hope, of life everlasting."[880]

788. **By what is this spiritual rebirth and sanctification effected?**
It is effected by the grace of sanctification, which, together with the theological virtues of faith, hope, and charity, the Holy Ghost infuses into the soul in baptism.

"The charity of God is poured forth in our hearts by the Holy Ghost, who is given to us."[881]

789. **And why do you say that we are reborn and sanctified "in Christ"?**
To signify that all these graces are given to us, because by baptism we are united with Christ and incorporated into his Church.

"There is now, therefore, no condemnation to them that are in Christ Jesus."[882]

790. **When did Christ give the commandment to baptize?**
Before his ascension, when he said to his apostles: "Going therefore, teach ye all nations; baptizing them in the name of the Father, and of the Son, and of the Holy Ghost."[883]

[880] Ti 3:5-7
[881] Rom 5:5
[882] Rom 8:1
[883] Mt 28:19

791. **Who can validly baptize?**

Any person; but, except in cases of necessity, only priests, who have care of souls, are allowed to baptize.

792. **Is the baptism given by non-Catholics also valid?**

Yes; it is valid, if they strictly observe in it all that is necessary for baptism.

When heretics are converted, if it is found, after diligent examination, either that baptism had not been conferred at all, or else conferred improperly, they must be baptized. If, upon investigation, there remains a reasonable doubt of the validity of their former baptism, they must be baptized conditionally. If the former baptism was valid, they are not to be baptized again. There are three ways, therefore, of receiving converts into the Church.

I. If baptism is conferred absolutely, neither abjuration nor absolution follows, since all the past is wiped out by baptism.

II. If baptism is repeated conditionally, the following order is to be observed: 1) the abjuration, or profession of faith; 2) conditional baptism; 3) sacramental confession.

III. If the former baptism is held to be valid, the abjuration or profession of faith alone is to be made, followed by absolution from censures.

793. **What sort of water should be used in baptism?**

Any natural water will do for the validity of baptism. However, when possible, baptismal water, or water blessed for that purpose, should be used.

794. **What intention must he have who baptizes?**

He must have the intention to baptize indeed—that is, to do what the Church does, or what Christ has ordained.

795. **What name should be given to the child in baptism?**

The name of some saint, in whom the child may have an intercessor with God, and an example for imitation.

796. **Why must the person to be baptized renounce Satan, all his works, and all his pomps, before baptism?**
Because no one can belong to Christ, unless he renounce not only Satan, but also his works—i.e., sin and his pomps—i.e., the spirit and the vanities of the world, by which Satan blinds men and entices them to sin.[884]

In baptism, we promise to believe, to avoid sin, and to lead a new life pleasing to God. On the other hand, God promises us his grace and eternal salvation. These mutual promises are called the covenant of baptism.

797. **Why does the priest place a white linen cloth upon our head in baptism?**
To remind us that we should preserve the innocence we have received pure and spotless until death; therefore, when he puts it on us, he says: "Receive this white garment, and see thou carry it without stain before the judgment seat of our Lord Jesus Christ, that thou mayest have eternal life."

798. **What does the lighted candle, which is put into the child's hand after he is baptized, signify?**
That a Christian ought to shine by his faith and virtuous life before the whole world.

"So let your light shine before men, that they may see your good works, and glorify your Father who is in heaven."[885]

The other ceremonies of baptism are also very ancient, and have all a deep meaning. 1) The person to be baptized remains at first without the church, because only baptism gives him entrance into it. 2) The priest breathes three times in his face, to signify the new and spiritual life he receives by the grace of the Holy Ghost.[886] 3) The sign of the cross made upon his forehead and upon his breast denotes that he is becoming the property of his crucified Redeemer, whose doctrine he is to carry in his heart, and to profess openly. 4) The blessed salt, which is put into his mouth, is an emblem of Christian wisdom, and of preservation from the corruption of sin. 5) By the exorcisms, which are repeated several times, the power of

[884] Cf. Mt 4:8-9
[885] Mt 5:16
[886] Cf. Gn 2:7; Jn 20:22

the devil, "who has the empire of death,"[887] is broken in the name of the Blessed Trinity. 6) The laying of the priest's hand upon the person to be baptized signifies the protection of God; and the stole laid upon him, and his being led by it into the church, is a sign of the ecclesiastical power, in virtue of which the priest admits him into the Church. 7) The touching of the child's ears and nostrils with spittle, in imitation of our Savior,[888] signifies that, by the grace of this sacrament, his spiritual senses are opened to the doctrine of Christ. 8) After having renounced the devil and all his works, and all his pomps, he is anointed with holy oil on the breast and between the shoulders, because, as a champion of Christ, he has now manfully to fight against the devil and the world. 9) After the baptism, the crown of the head is anointed with chrism, to intimate that he is now a Christian—i.e., an anointed of God, etc.

799. **What should sponsors, or godfathers and godmothers, be particularly mindful of?**
Sponsors should bear in mind that they become, as it were, the spiritual parents of the infant that is baptized, and make in his name the profession of faith and the baptismal vows; that therefore: 1) they should be good Catholics themselves; 2) they should take care that the child be instructed in the Catholic religion, and well educated, if his natural parents should neglect their duty in this respect, or be prevented from performing it; and 3) that they cannot marry their godchild; but they are not forbidden to marry each other.

800. **How many godfathers and godmothers does the Church admit?**
The Church generally admits but one godfather for a boy, and one godmother for a girl; or, at most, one godfather and one godmother for one person to be baptized. The others who may be admitted besides are only to be considered as witnesses of his baptism, and, consequently, contract no spiritual relationship.

[887] Heb 2:14
[888] Cf. Mk 7:33

801. **Can the baptism of water never be supplied?**
When it is impossible to have it, it may be supplied by the baptism of desire or by the baptism of blood.

802. **What is the "baptism of desire"?**
An earnest wish and a determined will to receive baptism, or to do all that God has ordained for our salvation, accompanied with a perfect contrition, or a pure love of God.

"Every one that loveth is born of God, and knoweth God."[889]

803. **What is the "baptism of blood"?**
Martyrdom for the sake of Christ.

"He that shall lose his life for me shall find it."[890]

Application. Never forget what you owe to God for the inestimable grace of baptism; and often, if possible every Sunday, renew your baptismal vows.

CONFIRMATION

804. **What is confirmation?**
Confirmation is a sacrament in which, through the bishop's laying on of hands, unction, and prayer, those already baptized are strengthened by the Holy Ghost, in order that they may steadfastly profess their faith, and faithfully live up to it.

805. **Who teaches us that the sacrament of confirmation was instituted by Christ?**
The infallible Catholic Church, 1) in accordance with the holy scripture, 2) with the doctrine of the holy fathers, and 3) with the practice of the most ancient times.

[889] 1 Jn 4:7
[890] Mt 10:39

1) The holy scripture reckons the doctrine of confirmation, as well as that of baptism and penance, amongst the fundamental truths of Christianity.[891] It testifies that Christ promised the Holy Ghost to the faithful, and that the apostles imparted him by prayer and imposition of hands. "When the apostles, who were in Jerusalem, had heard that Samaria had received the word of God, they sent unto them Peter and John; who, when they were come, prayed for them, that they might receive the Holy Ghost; for he was not as yet come upon any of them, but they were only baptized in the name of the Lord Jesus; then they laid their hands upon them, and they received the Holy Ghost."[892] "They [the disciples of Ephesus] were baptized in the name of the Lord Jesus; and when Paul had imposed his hands on them, the Holy Ghost came upon them, and they spoke with tongues and prophesied."[893]

2) The holy fathers designate this sacrament by various names; as "confirmation" (i.e., "strengthening"), "imposition of hands," "sealing," "unction," "chrism," "mystery of the Holy Ghost." "The sacrament of chrism," says St. Augustine, "is just as holy as baptism."

3) History attests that even in the earliest days of the Church, the bishops traveled about to lay their hands on those that were baptized, and to call down the Holy Ghost upon them.

806. **What are the effects of confirmation?**

1) Confirmation increases sanctifying grace in us; 2) it gives us the Holy Ghost, to enable us to fight against evil and to grow in virtue; and 3) it imprints on us, as soldiers of Christ, a spiritual mark which can never be effaced.

"He that confirmeth us with you in Christ, and that hath anointed us is God: who also hath sealed us, and given the pledge of the Spirit in our hearts."[894]

[891] Cf. Heb 6:1-2
[892] Acts 8:14-17
[893] Acts 19:5-6
[894] 2 Cor 1:21-22

807. **Who has power to confirm?**
The bishops, as successors of the apostles, have power to confirm; in urgent cases, however, the pope can delegate this power also to a priest who is not a bishop.

808. **How does the bishop give confirmation?**
He extends his hands over all those who are to be confirmed, and prays for them all in general, that the Holy Ghost may come down upon them; then he lays his hand upon each one in particular, and anoints him with holy chrism; and he concludes by giving to all in common the episcopal benediction.

809. **How does the bishop anoint those to be confirmed?**
He makes the sign of the cross with holy chrism upon the forehead of each one, saying at the same time: "*N.*, I sign thee with the sign of the cross, and I confirm thee with the chrism of salvation, in the name of the Father, and of the Son, and of the Holy Ghost."

810. **Of what does the chrism, blessed by the bishop, consist?**
Of oil of olives and balsam.

811. **What does the oil signify?**
The oil signifies the inward strength which we receive for the combat against the enemies of our salvation.

812. **Why is fragrant balsam mixed with the oil?**
To signify that he who is confirmed receives the grace to preserve himself from the corruption of the world, and to send forth by a pious life the sweet odor of virtue.

813. **Why does the bishop make the sign of the cross on the forehead of him whom he confirms?**
To intimate that a Christian never must be ashamed of the cross, but boldly profess his faith in Jesus crucified.

"I am not ashamed of the gospel; for it is the power of God unto salvation to every one that believeth."[895]

814. **Why does the bishop, after he has anointed him, give him a slight blow on the cheek?**

To remind him that, being now strengthened, he ought to be prepared to suffer patiently any kind of humiliation for the name of Jesus.

815. **Is confirmation necessary to salvation?**

Confirmation is not absolutely necessary to salvation; yet it would be a sin not to receive it through neglect or indifference.

Whatever has been instituted by God for the sanctification of all must also ardently be desired, and thankfully accepted, by all.

816. **Who is capable of receiving confirmation?**

Everyone who is baptized.

817. **How is a person to prepare himself for receiving the sacrament of confirmation?**

1) He must cleanse his conscience at least from all grievous sins; 2) he must get himself well instructed in the fundamental truths of our faith, particularly in those which regard this sacrament; and 3) he must heartily desire the grace of the Holy Ghost, and, for that purpose, he must fervently pray, and perform good works.

818. **How are we to receive confirmation?**

We must: 1) earnestly ask for the gifts of the Holy Ghost; 2) promise God that we will live, and die, as good Christians; and 3) not leave the church before the bishop has given his benediction.

[895] Rom 1:16

819. **What should we do after confirmation?**
We should: 1) give humble thanks to God; 2) spend that day especially in devotion; and 3) preserve and increase the grace of the Holy Ghost by perseverance in our struggle against the enemies of salvation, and by an ardent zeal in all that is good.

820. **Why are sponsors, or godfathers and godmothers, required also in confirmation?**
That they may present to the bishop those who are to be confirmed, and afterward advise and help them in their spiritual combat for which they are consecrated in this sacrament.

The sponsor enters into this engagement by laying his hand on the right shoulder of the person to be confirmed. Thus he becomes his spiritual parent and guardian, and has to preserve him from losing the grace of confirmation; and there arises from it the same spiritual relationship, but not the same impediment of marriage, as in baptism.

821. **What qualities does the Church require in the godfathers and godmothers of those who are confirmed?**
They must be Catholics, must have been confirmed, be blameless in their conduct, and of such age that they are able to fulfill their duties as sponsors. Parents cannot be the sponsors of their children; and the sponsor in confirmation is to be different from the sponsor in baptism.

Application. Pray frequently and earnestly that the gifts of the Holy Ghost may be strengthened in you. Perform without fear all the duties of a Catholic Christian. Should you have to suffer ignominy and persecution on account of your faith, consider it an honor, and rejoice in it after the example of the apostles.[896]

[896] Cf. Acts 5:41

THE HOLY EUCHARIST

The Real Presence of Christ in the Blessed Sacrament

822. **What is the Holy Eucharist?**

It is the true body and the true blood of our Lord Jesus Christ, who is really and substantially present under the appearances of bread and wine for the nourishment of our souls.

It is called "Eucharist" from the Greek word *eucharistia*, which means "good grace," because it contains Christ our Lord, the true grace, and the source of all heavenly gifts; or "thanksgiving," because, when we offer this most spotless victim, we render to God a homage of infinite value, in return for all the benefits which we have received from his bounty, particularly for the inestimable treasure of grace bestowed on us in this sacrament. It is also called the "Blessed" or "Most Holy Sacrament," because it contains Jesus Christ himself, the author of all the sacraments, and of all sanctity. The "Sacrament of the Altar," because it is on the altar it is offered and reserved. The "holy host," because it contains Jesus Christ, the true host or victim, immolated for us. The "viaticum" (i.e., "provision for a journey"), as well because it is the spiritual food by which we are supported during our mortal pilgrimage, as also, because it prepares for us a passage to eternal happiness and everlasting glory.[897]

823. **Is there in the Holy Eucharist all that is requisite for constituting a sacrament?**

Yes; there are: 1) the visible sign, i.e., the appearances of bread and wine; 2) the invisible grace, i.e., Jesus Christ himself, the author and dispenser of all graces; and 3) the institution by our Lord Jesus Christ.

824. **When did Jesus Christ institute this sacrament?**

He instituted it at the last supper, the evening before his bitter passion.

[897] Cf. *Catechism of the Council of Trent*. Editor's note: See p. 241-243 of Volume VII of this series.

825. **How did he institute it?**
Jesus took bread, blessed it, and broke and gave it to his disciples, saying, "Take ye, and eat: this is my body." After that, in like manner, he took the chalice with wine in it, blessed and gave it to his disciples, saying, "Drink ye all of this: this is my blood. Do this for a commemoration of me."[898]

826. **What became of the bread and wine, when Jesus pronounced these words over them: "This is my body, this is my blood"?**
The bread was, in an invisible manner, changed into the true body, and the wine into the true blood, of Jesus Christ.

827. **After these words of Christ, what did still remain of bread and wine?**
Nothing but their species or appearances.

828. **What is understood by the "appearances" of bread and wine?**
All that which the senses perceive of bread and wine; as form, color, taste, smell, etc.

829. **How do we know that with these words, "This is my body, this is my blood," Christ gave his true body and his true blood to the apostles?**
We know it: 1) because Christ had long before promised to his disciples that he would give them his real flesh to eat and his real blood to drink; and 2) because, at the last supper, he expressly declared that that which he then gave them as food and drink was really his body and his blood; and 3) because the apostles and the Catholic Church have at all times believed and taught so.

1) "'The bread that I will give is my flesh for the life of the world.' The Jews therefore strove among themselves, saying: 'How can this man give us his flesh to eat?' Then Jesus said to them: 'Amen, amen, I say unto you: Except you eat the flesh of the Son of man, and drink his blood, you shall

[898] See "Short History of Revealed Religion," p. 112, above.

not have life in you. For my flesh is meat indeed, and my blood is drink indeed.'"[899]

2) Christ foresaw that the Church would understand his most clear and distinct words in their proper and literal meaning. Had he wished to be understood in a different manner, he would also have spoken differently, that he might not in such most important matter give occasion to misunderstanding and error.

3) The teaching of the apostles, especially of St. Paul, is evident from 1 Corinthians 10:16 and 11:23-29; the teaching of the whole Church, from her prayers and rites relating to the divine service; from the decrees of her councils; from the numerous testimonies of the holy fathers and ecclesiastical writers. For instance, St. Justin Martyr says: "As Jesus Christ took flesh and blood, so also is the food consecrated by his words flesh and blood of the incarnate Jesus."[900] St. Cyril, bishop of Jerusalem, gives this evidence: "As Christ himself declared and said, 'This is my body,' who would dare to doubt it? As he openly protested, saying, 'This is my blood,' who would hesitate, and think that it is not his blood? Once he changed water into wine; and should we question whether he could change wine into blood?"[901] No less plain and precise are the testimonies of St. John Chrysostom, St. Ambrose, St. Augustine, and of many other fathers, even of the first centuries. We have also a strong proof of the antiquity of the Catholic doctrine in this, that the schismatic Greek Church, and the other older Oriental Churches, believe and teach precisely the same.

830. **Did Christ give also to his apostles power to change bread and wine into his sacred flesh and blood?**

Yes; he gave them that power with these words: "Do this for a commemoration of me."[902]

[899] Jn 6:52ff
[900] Justin Martyr, *First Apology*, Ch. 66
[901] Cyril of Jerusalem, *Catechetical Lecture 22*, n. 1-2
[902] Lk 22:19

831. **To whom did this power pass from the apostles?**
It passed from the apostles to the bishops and priests.

832. **When do the bishops and priests exercise this power?**
At Mass, when they pronounce over the bread and wine these words: "This is my body, this is my blood."

833. **Is there, then, after the consecration any longer bread and wine on the altar?**
No; there is then on the altar the true body and the true blood of Jesus Christ under the appearances of bread and wine.

This change is properly called "transubstantiation," which means a real conversion of the whole substance of the bread into the substance of the body of Christ our Lord, and of the substance of the wine into the substance of his blood.[903]

834. **How long does Christ remain present with his sacred flesh and blood?**
As long as the appearances of bread and of wine continue to exist.

835. **Is the body of Christ alone present under the appearance of bread, and the blood of Christ alone present under the appearance of wine?**
No; under each appearance, Christ is present entire and undivided, as he is entire and undivided in heaven.

836. **When the priest breaks or divides the sacred host, does he also break the body of Christ?**
No; he breaks or divides the appearances only: the body of Christ itself is present in each part entire and living, in a real though mysterious manner.

[903] Cf. Council of Trent, Session 13, "Decree concerning the Most Holy Sacrament of the Eucharist," Ch. 4; Can. 2

837. **What does the real presence of Jesus Christ in the Holy Eucharist require us to do?**

To visit him frequently, and to adore him with the most profound humility and awe, and with the most ardent love and gratitude.

"Let all the angels of God adore him."[904] In order to show due honor to the Blessed Sacrament, the Church exposes it for public adoration, gives benediction with it, carries it reverently about in solemn procession, has established feasts and confraternities (of the Most Holy Sacrament, of the Sacred Heart of Jesus, and others). As an emblem of adoration and love, a lamp is kept burning day and night before the altar where the Blessed Sacrament is reserved in the tabernacle.

838. **Is Christ present in the Holy Eucharist only that he may be also as man with us?**

He is also present for two other reasons: 1) that he may offer himself for us in the Holy Sacrifice of the Mass; and 2) that in Holy Communion he may give himself to us for the nourishment of our souls.

Application. Rejoice that our Lord and Savior is pleased to remain in the Blessed Sacrament amongst us to the end of the world. Thank him for this exceedingly great favor; love him, and visit him often and with devotion. Pour out all your sufferings before this amiable comforter, and have full confidence in his help; for he himself invites you, saying: "Come to me, all you that labor, and are burdened, and I will refresh you."[905]

On the Holy Sacrifice of the Mass

839. **What is a sacrifice?**

A sacrifice is that first and highest act of religion in which a duly authorized person offers to God some sensible thing which is visibly immolated either physically or mystically, in token and acknowledgment of God's supreme dominion over all things and of our total dependence on him.

[904] Heb 1:6
[905] Mt 11:28

He who sacrifices is styled a "priest"; the sensible thing which is sacrificed is called the "victim"; the place where it is sacrificed is the "altar." These four—priest, victim, altar, and sacrifice—are inseparable. Each one of them calls for the others.

840. **Have there been sacrifices at all times?**

Yes, there have been sacrifices from the beginning of the world, and under the old law they were strictly commanded by God himself.

841. **Why were the sacrifices of the old law abolished?**

Because they were only figures of the unspotted sacrifice of the new law, and were, therefore, not to last longer than the old law itself.

"For the law having a shadow of the good things to come, not the very image of the things, by the self-same sacrifices, which they offer continually every year, can never make the comers thereunto perfect;...for it is impossible that with the blood of oxen and goats sin should be taken away. Wherefore when he [Christ] cometh into the world he saith: 'Sacrifice and oblation thou [O God] wouldst not; but a body thou hast fitted to me... Then said I: Behold, I come: in the head of the book it is written of me, that I should do thy will, O God...' He taketh away the first, that he may establish that which followeth."[906]

842. **What is the sacrifice of the new law?**

The sacrifice of the new law is the Son of God himself, Jesus Christ, who, by his death on the cross, offered himself to his heavenly Father for us.[907]

843. **Was all sacrifice to cease with the death of Christ?**

No; there was to be in the new law of grace a perpetual sacrifice, in order to represent continually that which was once accomplished on the cross, and to apply the fruits of it to our souls.

[906] Heb 10:1, 4-5, 7, 9
[907] Cf. Heb 9:14

844. **Was such a sacrifice promised to us by God?**

Yes, 1) even in the old law it was prefigured by the sacrifice of Melchisedech, and 2) was foretold by the prophet Malachias.

1) As Melchisedech offered bread and wine,[908] so also Christ offers himself under the species of bread and wine unto the end of the world. Therefore, it is said in Psalm 109: "The Lord hath sworn, and he will not repent: 'Thou art a priest for ever according to the order of Melchisedech.'" 2) "I have no pleasure in you [Jews], saith the Lord of hosts, and I will not receive a gift of your hand; for from the rising of the sun even to the going down, my name is great among the Gentiles, and in every place there is sacrifice, and there is offered to my name a clean oblation."

845. **Which is this perpetual sacrifice, foretold by Malachias?**

It is the Sacrifice of the Mass.

846. **By whom was the Sacrifice of the Mass instituted?**

It was instituted by Jesus Christ, when, at the last supper, he offered himself up under the appearances of bread and wine to his heavenly Father, and commanded his apostles thenceforth to celebrate this his sacrifice.

847. **What, then, is the Mass?**

The Mass is the perpetual sacrifice of the new law, in which Christ our Lord offers himself, by the hands of the priest, in an unbloody manner, under the appearances of bread and wine, to his heavenly Father, as he once offered himself on the cross in a bloody manner.

848. **What is the difference between the Sacrifice of the Mass and the sacrifice of the cross?**

The Sacrifice of the Mass is essentially the same sacrifice as that of the cross; the only difference is in the manner of offering.

[908] Cf. Gn 14:18

849. **Why is the Sacrifice of the Mass the same sacrifice as that of the cross?**
Because in both it is the same high priest who offers, and the same victim who is offered—namely, Jesus Christ our Lord; and because, in the Sacrifice of the Mass, the oblation which Christ made of himself on the cross for us to the Father is commemorated and continued.

The priest is only the minister and visible representative of Christ; therefore, he does not speak in his own name, but in the name of Christ: "This is my body; this is my blood."

850. **How is the manner of offering different in both?**
On the cross, Christ offered himself in a bloody manner; but in the Mass, he offers himself in an unbloody manner, whilst he renews the sacrifice accomplished on the cross, without suffering or dying anymore.

851. **If Christ dies no more, how, then, can the sacrifice which he consummated on the cross be renewed in the Mass?**
It is renewed, because in the Mass Christ offers himself really and truly under the emblems of the bloody death which he suffered on the cross—that is, under the separated appearances of bread and wine.

By virtue of the words which the priest pronounces, the body of Christ becomes present under the appearance of bread, and his blood under the appearance of wine; and both these appearances being visibly separated from each other, the separation of the blood from the body, consequently the bloody death on the cross is represented in an unbloody, mystical manner. This unbloody renewal is, however, not made in order that we may be redeemed anew, for the sacrifice of the cross was sufficient for the redemption of the whole world; but that we may have a standing memorial, and a lively, though unbloody, representation of the bloody sacrifice of the cross, by which God is perfectly honored, and the abundant fruits of the redemption are applied to our souls.

852. **How do we prove that, from the time of the apostles, the Mass has always been celebrated?**

We prove this: 1) by the words of St. Paul, which clearly show that, as early as in the times of the apostles, the Christians had an altar of their own; for where an altar is, there must also be a sacrifice; and 2) by the undeniable testimonies of the holy fathers, the decrees of the councils, the most ancient prayers of the Mass, and by many other memorials of the Eastern and Western Churches.

"We [Christians] have an altar, whereof they have no power to eat who serve the tabernacle,"—i.e., the Jews.[909]

853. **To whom do we offer the Sacrifice of the Mass?**

We offer it to God alone; however, we also celebrate the memory of the saints in it.

854. **How do we celebrate the memory of the saints in the Mass?**

1) By rendering thanks to God for all the graces bestowed upon them in this life, and for the glory they now enjoy in heaven; and 2) by imploring their intercession for us.

855. **What are the ends for which we offer the Mass to God?**

We offer it to God: 1) as a sacrifice of praise for his honor and glory; 2) as a sacrifice of thanksgiving for all the graces and benefits received from him; 3) as a sacrifice of propitiation for the many offenses given to him; and 4) as a sacrifice of petition, in order to obtain his assistance in all our necessities of soul and body.

856. **What effects has the Mass as a sacrifice of propitiation?**

By it we obtain from the divine mercy: 1) graces of contrition and repentance for the forgiveness of sins; and 2) remission of temporal punishment deserved for sins.

[909] Heb 13:10; Cf. 1 Cor 10:18-21

857. **To whom are the fruits of the Mass applied?**
The general fruits are applied to the whole Church, both the living and the dead; the special fruits are applied: 1) chiefly to the priest who celebrates the Mass; 2) next, to those for whom in particular he offers it up; and 3) to all those who assist at it with devotion.

858. **Which are the principal parts of the Mass?**
The principal parts of the Mass are: 1) the offertory; 2) the consecration; and 3) the communion.

859. **What do you think of the ceremonies which the Church has added to the Sacrifice of the Mass?**
The ceremonies of the Mass have all been handed down to us from the most ancient times, many from the times of the apostles themselves, and their sublime and mysterious signification is intended to fill our hearts with devotion and reverence.

1) The priest first prays with heartfelt sorrow, and profoundly bowing, at the foot of the altar; then having ascended the steps, he kisses it reverently, reads the introit, and prays again in the spirit of humility to God, by reciting alternately with the server the *Kyrie eleison* ("Lord, have mercy on us"). 2) He intones joyfully the hymn of the angels (*Gloria*), and turns then toward the people, to wish them the divine blessing. 3) He prays at the side of the altar, in the name of all who are present, to God for the necessities of all. After that, he reads two portions of the holy scripture, the epistle and the gospel, the latter, however, at the other side of the altar, to intimate that the evangelical doctrine, rejected by the Jews, passed over to the heathens. 4) The gospel is followed, on certain days, by the Nicene Creed. This is the preparation for the sacrifice. It was anciently called the "Mass of the Catechumens"—i.e., of those who were still in the first rudiments of Christianity, because they were permitted to assist at it thus far before they were baptized.

Next begins 5) the sacrifice itself by the offertory: the priest, united with the people, offers bread and wine, and then washes his hands, to show the purity of heart with which we should assist at the holy sacrifice. 6) He invites all to fervent prayer, and, praising God, he joins with the choirs of angels, saying: "Holy, holy, holy," etc. 7) Next follow prayers, said in a low voice, for the Church, her rulers, and all the faithful, under the invocation of the Blessed Virgin and all the saints.

8) Then he pronounces the mysterious words of consecration, adores, making a genuflection, and elevates the sacred body and the sacred blood above his head. At the ringing of the bell, the people adore on their knees, and strike their breasts in token of repentance for their sins. 9) The priest begs of God graciously to accept the sacrifice, to have mercy on all mankind, also on the souls in purgatory, and concludes with the Lord's Prayer, which contains the substance of all petitions.

10) After a preparatory prayer, during which, at Solemn Masses, the kiss of peace is given, follows the Holy Communion, of which all those who are present should partake, at least spiritually. 11) The Communion being over, the whole concludes with a prayer of thanksgiving, the blessing of the people, and the reading of the gospel of St. John.

860. **Why is the Mass said in Latin?**

1) Because this language comes from Rome, whence we received our faith; 2) because, being a dead language, it does not change in the course of time like living languages; and 3) because thereby the unity and uniformity of the Church, even in her public service, is represented and preserved.

Out of respect for very ancient usage, the Holy See permits the Greeks and some other bodies of Eastern Christians to retain their own languages in the celebration of Mass and other rites.

861. **Why has the Church assigned particular vestments for the priest whilst officiating at the altar?**

That we may remember that the priest does no act at the altar in his own person, but as the representative of Jesus, and that he celebrates a most holy divine mystery.

In the old testament, God himself minutely appointed the vestments for the priests, and said: "Aaron and his sons shall use them…when they approach to the altar to minister in the sanctuary, lest being guilty of iniquity they die."[910]

The different colors of the priest's vestments have also their meaning. The white signifies innocence and spiritual joy; the red, the love of God; the green, the hope of eternal life; the violet or purple, humility and penance; the black, deep mourning.

Application. Endeavor to assist daily at the Holy Sacrifice of the Mass with sincere devotion and profound reverence; for there is no other act so holy and divine, so rich in graces and heavenly blessings. At the offertory, offer yourself with Jesus Christ to your heavenly Father; at the consecration, humbly adore your Savior, and beg his pardon; at the communion, communicate, at least spiritually—that is to say, desire most earnestly to be united with your dearest Lord in this sacrament of love.

On Holy Communion

862. **What is Holy Communion?**

Holy Communion is truly the receiving of the real body and blood of Jesus Christ for the nourishment of our souls.

Communion means "union of the faithful with Christ and with one another"; or, "common participation of the body and blood of Jesus Christ." The Communion is also called the "Lord's supper," "the receiving of the Blessed Sacrament," "of the Holy Eucharist," etc.

863. **Was it God, or is it the Church only, that has commanded us to receive Holy Communion?**

God has commanded it, and the Church also; for Christ our Lord says expressly: "Amen, amen I say unto you: Except you eat the flesh of the Son of man, and drink his blood, you shall not have life in you."[911]

[910] Ex 28:43
[911] Jn 6:54

864. **Must we also drink the chalice in order to receive the blood of Christ?**
No; for under the appearance of bread we receive also his blood, since we receive him whole and entire, his humanity and his divinity.

Therefore, Christ promises eternal life to those also who receive him under the appearance of bread alone: "If any man eat of this bread, he shall live for ever; and the bread that I will give is my flesh, for the life of the world."[912] "This is the bread that came down from heaven. Not as your fathers did eat manna, and are dead. He that eateth this bread shall live for ever."[913]

865. **But why, then, did Christ institute the Holy Eucharist in both kinds?**
Because he instituted it not only as a sacrament, but also as a sacrifice, for which both kinds are required.

Accordingly, the words of Christ, "Drink ye all of this,"[914] are by no means a command to all the people, but only to the apostles, and their successors the bishops and priests, when they celebrate the Holy Sacrifice of the Mass. Therefore, priests also, when they do not actually celebrate Mass, communicate under one kind only.

866. **Why does the Catholic Church give Holy Communion to the faithful in one kind only—namely, under the form of bread?**
1) To prevent the sacred blood from being profaned, since, under the appearance of wine, it might easily be spilled, and could not well be reserved; 2) to make it easy for all to receive the Blessed Sacrament, as many feel a disgust at drinking out of a common chalice; and 3) to declare thereby against the heretics that Christ is present whole and entire under each kind.

In the very first times of the primitive Church, the sick, prisoners, and all those who communicated at home, received the Blessed Sacrament only under the form of bread. Thus, only the breaking of bread is mentioned by St. Luke: "Whilst he was at table with them, he took bread, and blessed and

[912] Jn 6:52
[913] Jn 6:59
[914] Mt 26:27

brake, and gave to them";[915] and in the Acts: "And they were persevering in the doctrine of the apostles, and in the communication of the breaking of bread, and in prayers."[916] Subsequently, it is true, Pope Leo and Pope Gelasius commanded the chalice to be received by the faithful in the public Communion, but only in order to combat the erroneous doctrine of the Manicheans, who detested wine as something diabolical, and to prevent these heretics from approaching with the Catholics to Communion. But this was only for a time and to meet an emergency. When that heresy disappeared, the faithful could return to the ancient and general usage.

867. **Why does our Lord communicate himself to all the faithful as food?**
1) To give us a proof of his tender, superabundant love, and to unite himself most intimately with us: "He that eateth my flesh, and drinketh my blood, abideth in me, and I in him";[917] and 2) to unite us also most closely together with one another by a bond of love and concord: "For we, being many, are one bread, one body, all that partake of one bread."[918]

868. **What graces does Holy Communion impart to our souls?**
By uniting us in the most intimate manner with Jesus Christ, the source of all divine graces, it imparts to us innumerable graces, especially these: 1) it preserves and increases sanctifying grace; 2) it weakens our evil inclinations, and gives us a desire and strength to be virtuous; 3) it cleanses us from venial and preserves us from mortal sin; and 4) it is to us a pledge of our future resurrection and everlasting happiness.[919]

869. **Does everyone receive in Holy Communion the graces it is intended to give?**
No; he who receives Holy Communion unworthily—that is, in the state of mortal sin—brings damnation upon himself.

[915] Lk 24:30
[916] Acts 2:42; Cf. Acts 2:46
[917] Jn 6:57
[918] 1 Cor 10:17
[919] Cf. Jn 6:55

"Whosoever shall eat this bread or drink the chalice of the Lord unworthily, shall be guilty of the body and of the blood of the Lord. But let a man prove himself, and so let him eat of that bread, and drink of the chalice; for he that eateth and drinketh unworthily, eateth and drinketh judgment to himself, not discerning the body of the Lord."[920]—Comparison with the ark of the covenant, which brought happiness and blessing upon the pious Israelites, but misfortune and a curse upon the impious Philistines.

870. **What sin does he commit who dares to communicate unworthily?**
1) He commits, like Judas; a horrible sacrilege, because he is "guilty of the body and of the blood of the Lord";[921] and 2) he renders himself guilty of the blackest ingratitude, because he treats his divine Redeemer with the foulest indignity in the very same instant in which he is favored by him with the greatest proof of his immense love.[922]

871. **What are frequently the consequences of an unworthy Communion, even in this life?**
Blindness and hardness of heart, and sometimes also sudden death, and other temporal punishment.

Example. Miserable end of Judas, of whom our Savior said: "It were better for him, if that man had not been born."[923] And of such St. Paul says: "Therefore [on account of unworthily receiving], are there many infirm and weak among you, and many sleep [the sleep of death]."[924]

872. **What, then, must we do when we have committed a grievous sin?**
We must make a good confession before we receive.

"Let a man prove himself, and so let him eat of that bread, and drink of the chalice."[925]

[920] 1 Cor 11:27-29
[921] 1 Cor 11:27
[922] Cf. Ps 54:13ff
[923] Mt 26:24
[924] 1 Cor 11:30
[925] 1 Cor 11:28

873. **How must we further prepare ourselves, as to the soul?**
We must endeavor: 1) to cleanse our souls also from venial sin; and 2) to excite in our hearts sentiments of fervor and devotion.

874. **Does venial sin also render our Communions unworthy?**
Venial sin does not render them unworthy or sacrilegious, but it diminishes the graces which they otherwise would produce.

875. **How can we excite sentiments of fervor and devotion in our heart?**
By pious meditations and devout exercises.

876. **Which are the best exercises before Holy Communion?**
The acts: 1) of faith and adoration; 2) of humility and contrition; and 3) of hope, love, and an ardent desire.

877. **How do you make an act of faith?**
O my Jesus, I firmly believe all that thou hast revealed, but especially that thou art really present in this most Holy Sacrament, because thou, the eternal and infallible truth, hast declared it.

878. **How do you make an act of adoration?**
O my Jesus, in union with all the angels and saints, I adore thee in this most Holy Sacrament, in which thou art concealed for the love of me; I adore thee as my Lord and my God, my Creator and my Redeemer.

879. **How do you make an act of contrition?**
O my Jesus, I am most heartily sorry for all my sins, because by them I have provoked and offended thee, my most bountiful God, whom I love above all things.

880. **How do you make an act of humility?**
My Lord and my Savior, how dare I approach thee after having so often offended thee! Indeed, I am not worthy to receive thee into my heart; but only say the word, and my soul shall be healed.

881. **How do you make an act of hope?**

Yes, my most amiable Jesus, thy mercy is unbounded! Thou vouchsafest to come to me, and to dwell in my heart; so thou wilt also, I confidently hope, sanctify me, and replenish me with thy grace.

882. **How do you make an act of love?**

O my Jesus, thou hast loved me unto the death of the cross, and, for the love of me, thou wilt now become also the food of my soul. Oh! what return can I make for thy love? In life and in death, I will love thee, and none but thee.

883. **How do you make an act of desire?**

Come, O Jesus, come and take possession of my heart; make it entirely thine own. Come, my Jesus, come and visit me, and strengthen me with thy grace.

884. **How must we prepare ourselves as to the body?**

1) We must be fasting; that is, from twelve o'clock the night before we must not have taken even the least thing by way of eating or drinking.—The Church commands this under pain of a grievous sin, in order to prevent great abuses that would follow from the disregard of this law.—2) We must be decently dressed.

885. **Who are dispensed from this command to receive fasting?**

Those who are dangerously ill, and receive the Blessed Sacrament by way of viaticum—i.e., as a preparation for their passage into eternity.

The Holy See grants to invalids, even though not dangerously ill, permission to take some liquid food after midnight before going to Communion, with the approval of their confessor, provided that they have been laid up at least a month, and that they have no definite hope of a speedy recovery. They may thus receive once or twice a week as long as their illness lasts.

886. **How should we approach the altar rail, in order to receive Holy Communion?**

With the greatest reverence, with hands joined and raised, and eyes cast down.

887. **What should we do at the time of our receiving the sacred host?**

We should spread the Communion cloth over our hands and under our chin, hold the head erect and firm, extend the tongue a little upon the under lip, and then most reverently receive the sacred host.

Do not keep the sacred host in your mouth until it is quite dissolved; but let it moisten a little upon your tongue, and then swallow it. Should it stick to the roof of your mouth, remove it with your tongue, and not with your finger. Gloves should not be worn.

888. **What must we do after receiving Holy Communion?**

We must retire with the greatest modesty to our place, and spend some time in devout prayer.

No time is more precious and more favorable for obtaining graces than that which immediately follows Holy Communion; therefore, we should avail ourselves of it in the best manner we can. It is, indeed, a bad sign if we cannot, in meditation and prayer, entertain ourselves for half an hour, or at least for fifteen minutes, with our dear Redeemer.

889. **What sort of prayers ought we especially to say after Holy Communion?**

Those in which we humble ourselves before the Lord, thank him, offer ourselves up to him, express our love, and implore his graces.

890. **In what manner may we say these prayers?**

We may say them in the following manner:

An act of humility. O my Jesus, whence is this to me that thou, my God, shouldst have vouchsafed to come to me, a poor sinner!

An act of thanksgiving and oblation. Most amiable Jesus, what return can I make to thee for all that thou hast done for me? I offer to thee my body, and my soul, and all that I possess. All my thoughts, my desires, my words, and all that I do, shall be thine, shall be for thee.

An act of love. O Jesus, inflame my cold heart with the fire of thy love, in order that I may love thee more than all things, more than myself.

An act of petition. O my Lord and my God, grant me, a poor creature, all the graces I stand in need of; for thou art, indeed, infinitely rich and infinitely good.

O most bountiful Jesus, remain within me with thy grace; strengthen and bless me by the virtue of this Holy Sacrament, now and at the hour of my death. Amen.

891. **How should we spend the day of Communion?**

We should spend it, as much as possible, in pious exercises, and avoid worldly recreations and amusements.

Application. Consider how the Lord pours forth, in the most Holy Sacrament of the Altar, the treasures of his divine love for mankind; and resolve, therefore, to approach to the holy table as often as you can with permission, and to receive the bread of angels with as much devotion and purity of heart as you can possibly attain to.

PENANCE

892. **What is understood by *penance*?**

By *penance* is understood: 1) the virtue or disposition of heart by which man repents of his sins and is converted to God; 2) the punishment by which he atones for the sins committed; and 3) the sacrament of penance.

893. **What is the sacrament of penance?**

It is a sacrament in which the priest, in the place of God, forgives sins, when the sinner is heartily sorry for them, sincerely confesses them, and is willing to perform the penance imposed upon him.

894. **Does the priest truly forgive the sins, or does he only declare that they are remitted?**
The priest does really and truly forgive the sins in virtue of the power given to him by Christ.

895. **When did Christ give the power to forgive sins?**
When after his resurrection he breathed on the apostles, and said to them: "Receive ye the Holy Ghost. Whose sins you shall forgive, they are forgiven them; and whose sins you shall retain, they are retained."[926]

896. **Did not Christ impart this power to the apostles alone?**
No; he imparted it also to all those who were to succeed the apostles in the priesthood, as the Church has always believed and taught.

897. **Why was the power of forgiving sins to pass from the apostles to their successors also?**
Because Christ instituted his means of salvation for all times, and for all men, who stand in need of them.

898. **Can all sins be forgiven by the sacrament of penance?**
Yes, all the sins we have committed after baptism can be forgiven, if we confess them with the necessary disposition of repentance.

"If we confess our sins, he is faithful and just, to forgive us our sins, and to cleanse us from all iniquity."[927]

Yet not all sins can be forgiven by every priest. For, 1) in order that a priest may be able to absolve validly from sins, it is not only required that he should have received this power in holy order, but also that he should have been especially authorized by the bishop to administer the sacrament of penance in his diocese. 2) According to an ancient, lawful, and salutary practice, the pope and the bishops are accustomed to reserve to themselves the absolution from certain very grievous sins, from which,

[926] Jn 20:22-23
[927] 1 Jn 1:9

therefore, other priests can absolve only in virtue of a particular authorization. When, however, there is immediate danger of death, and no priest especially authorized to hear confessions is present, any other priest can absolve from all sins.

899. **But why must we confess our sins in order to have them forgiven?**
Because Christ ordained it so when he instituted the sacrament of penance.

900. **How do we prove that Christ has ordained confession?**
We prove it: 1) by his own words: "Whose sins you shall forgive," etc., for unless we declare our sins, and the whole state of our soul, to the priest, he cannot know whether, in virtue of the judicial power which God has conferred on him, he is to forgive or to retain them.

2) By the testimony of the holy fathers of the Church, who unanimously teach that we have not to expect from God forgiveness of our sins, if we are ashamed to confess them to the priest: "Whosoever is ashamed to declare his sins to man, and will not confess them, he shall be confounded in the day of judgment in the face of the whole world." "If the sick man is ashamed to discover the wounds of his soul to the physician, he cannot be cured." Thus, likewise, Origen, St. Cyprian, St. Basil, St. Pacian, St. John Climacus, St. Gregory the Great, and others.

3) By the existence of confession in the Church at all times and among all nations; for if confession had been instituted by human laws, and not by Christ himself, people would certainly never have generally complied with it; that confession was practiced as early as in the times of the apostles, is proved by tradition; and even the holy scripture testifies that, when the apostle St. Paul was at Ephesus, "many of them that believed came confessing and declaring their deeds."[928]

[928] Acts 19:18

901. **But to receive forgiveness of our sins is it not sufficient to confess them to God alone?**

By no means; or else the full power which Christ gave to the priests, of retaining or remitting them according to their judgment, would, indeed, be vain and useless.

"Confess your sins one to another [not, then, to God alone],...that you may be saved."[929] "Let no one say: 'I do penance privately before God; God, who knows me, sees what is going on in my heart.' Was it, then, said in vain: 'Whatsoever ye shall loose on earth, it shall be loosed also in heaven?' Were, then, the keys given in vain to the Church of God?"[930]

902. **Is, then, the sacrament of penance necessary for salvation to all those who have sinned?**

It is necessary for salvation to all those who have committed a grievous sin after baptism.

903. **Can the sacrament of penance never be supplied?**

When the sacrament of penance cannot be received, it can be supplied by a perfect contrition, and a firm resolution to confess our sins as soon as an opportunity offers.

904. **What are the effects of the sacrament of penance?**

1) It remits the guilt of sins committed after baptism; 2) it remits the eternal, and at least a part of the temporal, punishment due to our sins; 3) it restores, or, if it is not lost, it increases, sanctifying grace; and 4) it also confers other particular graces to enable us to lead a holy life.

905. **How many things are required on our part, in order to receive the sacrament of penance worthily?**

These five: 1) examination of conscience; 2) contrition; 3) resolution of amendment; 4) confession; and 5) satisfaction.

[929] Jas 5:16
[930] Augustine

The Examination of Conscience

906. **What is meant by "examining our conscience"?**
To examine our conscience means to meditate seriously upon our sins, in order that we may know them well.

907. **How must we begin the examination of conscience?**
By imploring the assistance of the Holy Ghost, that he may give us the grace rightly to know, to repent, and to confess our sins.

908. **How do we implore the assistance of the Holy Ghost?**
Come, O Holy Ghost, enlighten my understanding, that I may rightly know my sins; and move my heart, that I may properly repent of them, sincerely confess them, and truly amend my life.

909. **In what manner should we examine our conscience?**
1) We should examine when it was that we last made a good confession, and whether we performed the penance then laid upon us; and 2) we should go through the commandments of God and of the Church, and through the obligations of our state of life, and also through the different kinds of sin, carefully examining in what way and how often we have offended God by thoughts, words, actions, and omissions.

910. **Must we also examine ourselves on the number and the circumstances of our sins?**
Yes; at least, when they are mortal.

911. **Against what faults are we to guard in the examination of conscience?**
1) We must not examine ourselves too hastily and superficially; 2) we must not conceal our favorite sins from ourselves; 3) we must not take all that to be trifling which the world considers as such; but we should place ourselves in spirit before the tribunal of God; 4) on the other hand, we must avoid becoming too scrupulous.

912. **How much time ought we to employ in the examination of conscience?**
The more carelessly we have lived, and the longer we have stayed from confession, the more time and diligence ought we to employ in examining ourselves.

913. **How can we facilitate this examination?**
By examining our conscience every day, and by going frequently to confession.

On Contrition

914. **What is contrition?**
Contrition is a hearty sorrow for our sins, and a detestation of them.

915. **What qualities must contrition have that our sins may be forgiven?**
These three: it must be 1) interior; 2) universal; and 3) supernatural.

916. **How must contrition be interior?**
We must not grieve merely in words for our sins, but we must also detest them in our hearts as the greatest evil, and sincerely wish we had not committed them.

"Rend your hearts, and not your garments."[931] "A sacrifice to God is an afflicted spirit; a contrite and humbled heart, O God, thou wilt not despise."[932]

917. **How must contrition be universal?**
We must be sorry for all the sins we have committed, or, at least, for all mortal sins.

[931] Jl 2:13
[932] Ps 50:19

918. **If a penitent has no sorrow for his venial sins, would his confession nevertheless be valid?**

If he has to confess venial sins only, and is not truly sorry for any one of them, his confession is null.

If since our last confession we have to accuse ourselves of venial sins only, and, because they do not seem to be grievous, we doubt whether we have sufficient contrition for them, it is advisable to repent again of some grievous sin of our former life, which we have already confessed, and to include it in our confession, saying at the end of it: "For these, and all my other sins which I cannot at present call to my remembrance, and also for the sins of my past life, especially for...I am heartily sorry," etc. This should also be done when we are not quite certain whether we have committed any sin since the last confession.

919. **How must contrition be supernatural?**

The sorrow for our sins must arise not from the consideration of their natural evil consequences, but from supernatural motives; namely, because we have offended God, lost his grace, deserved hell, etc.

920. **Would it not, then, be sufficient to be sorry for our sins on account of the temporal loss incurred by them?**

To be sorry for our sins only because we have lost by them our health, property, reputation, etc., is nothing but a natural sorrow, which is of no avail for everlasting life.

Thus the sorrow of King Saul, Antiochus, and others was a merely natural sorrow; on the contrary, that of King David, Mary Magdalen, Zacheus, the apostles Peter and Paul, and other scripture penitents, was supernatural.

921. **What should we do in order to obtain supernatural contrition?**

We should 1) earnestly ask God for his grace; and 2) we should seriously call to our mind what faith teaches us concerning the malice of sin, and its fatal consequences;[933] for supernatural contrition must proceed from grace and motives of faith.

922. **Why must contrition proceed from motives of faith?**
1) Because faith is the foundation and root of all justification; and 2) because, otherwise, contrition does not prompt us to renounce evil entirely and forever, but only inasmuch as we have to dread temporal losses.

923. **How many kinds of supernatural contrition are there?**
Two: perfect contrition and imperfect contrition, commonly called "attrition."

924. **When is contrition perfect?**
When it arises from perfect love; i.e., when we detest sin more than all other evils, for the reason that it offends God, the supreme good.

Since perfect contrition proceeds from perfect love, in order to excite ourselves to perfect contrition it is very profitable, previously, or at the same time, to excite ourselves to perfect love of God.

925. **When is contrition imperfect?**
When our love is not perfect, and when, therefore, our fear of hell and of the loss of heaven, or our sense of the heinousness of sin itself, must unite with it in causing us to detest sin above all other evils, and to resolve to offend God no more.

Perfect contrition is, therefore, a sorrow for sin arising from the perfect love of God; imperfect contrition is, on the contrary, a sorrow for sin arising from any other motive which, though good and supernatural, is not perfect. In order to excite ourselves to perfect contrition, let us consider how much God deserves to be loved by us, on account of his infinite goodness—i.e., on account of that perfection which he, as the sovereign good, possesses; and how, nevertheless, we have despised and insulted him, our most loveable Father; how we have expelled him from our heart, and

[933] See p. 336–338, q. 657-661, and p. 232, q. 266.

renounced his love and friendship forever. In order to excite ourselves to imperfect contrition, let us consider how terrible are the pains of hell or of purgatory, which we have deserved; how beautiful heaven, which we have lost; how detestable sin, which nailed the Son of God to the cross, has deprived our soul of grace, disfigured it, rendered it foul and execrable before God and his angels, etc.; and let us, therefore, repent of the offense given to God, and detest it more than any other evil in the world.

926. **Must contrition necessarily be perfect?**
It is not necessary for the remission of sins that we should have perfect contrition; we should, however, strive to obtain it.

927. **Why should we strive to obtain perfect contrition?**
Because the more perfect our contrition is, the more is our repentance meritorious and acceptable to God, and the more certainly it obtains our pardon.

928. **When should we make an act of perfect contrition, even without the sacrament of penance?**
1) In danger of death; and 2) as often as we have the misfortune to commit a mortal sin and cannot immediately go to confession.

929. **When must we make the act of contrition in the sacrament of penance?**
We must make it before our confession, or, at least, when the priest gives us absolution.

930. **Can contrition ever be supplied in case of necessity?**
No; contrition is so necessary that it cannot be supplied by anything or in any case.

The Resolution of Amendment

931. **What must contrition necessarily include?**
Contrition must necessarily include: 1) hope of pardon; and 2) resolution of amendment.

932. **What is a "resolution of amendment"?**
A "resolution of amendment" is a sincere determination to amend our life and to sin no more.

933. **What must be the qualities of our resolution of amendment?**
Our resolution of amendment must be, like our contrition: 1) interior or sincere; 2) universal; and 3) supernatural.

934. **What must he be determined to do who forms a firm and sincere resolution of amendment?**
He must be determined: 1) to avoid, at least, all grievous sins, so that he will suffer anything rather than commit even one; 2) to shun the danger, and especially the proximate occasion, of sin; 3) to use the necessary means of amendment; 4) to make due satisfaction for his sins; and 5) to repair whatever injury he may have done to his neighbor.

935. **What is meant by "the proximate occasion of sin"?**
By "the proximate occasion of sin" is meant a person, a company, an amusement, and such like, by which people usually have been, or, if they do not avoid them, probably will be, led into sin.

936. **Is it a strict duty to shun the proximate occasions of sin?**
Yes, whenever it is possible; for he who will not avoid the occasion of sin has not a sincere purpose to avoid sin itself.

937. **What ought they to consider who will not avoid the proximate occasion, or will not desist from their habitual sins?**
That the priest's absolution is of no avail to them, but only aggravates their guilt.

938. **How can we make an act of imperfect and perfect contrition together with a resolution of amendment?**
In this manner: O my God! I am heartily sorry for having offended thee, and I detest all my sins, because I dread the loss of heaven and the pains of hell, but most of all because they offend thee, my God, who art all-good and deserving of all my love. I firmly resolve, with the help of thy grace, to confess my sins, to do penance, and to amend my life. Amen.

Confession

939. **What is confession?**
Confession is a sorrowful declaration of our sins to a priest, in order to obtain absolution from him.

940. **What are the necessary qualities of confession?**
Confession must be: 1) entire; 2) sincere; and 3) clear.

941. **When is confession "entire"?**
When we confess, at least, all grievous sins which we remember, together with their number and necessary circumstances.

942. **But what must we do if we do not recollect the number rightly?**
We must declare it as well as we are able, and say, for instance: "I have committed this sin about…times a day, week, or month.

943. **What sort of circumstances must we confess?**
We must: 1) especially confess such circumstances as change the nature, or aggravate the guilt, of our sins; and 2) mention in general everything

by which the confessor may be enabled to judge rightly of the state of our conscience, and to put us on our guard against relapsing into sin.

1) Should a person have stolen Church property, wished his parents dead, coveted his neighbor's wife, injured someone by telling a lie, etc., it would not be sufficient for him to confess merely that he has stolen, wished some persons dead, had an evil desire, told a lie. 2) Therefore, we must also declare whether we have injured our neighbors much or little, knowingly or unknowingly; whether the occasion of sin still continues; whether we have often before confessed the evil habit, and never corrected it.

944. **What is to be observed in the declaration of the circumstances?**
We must avoid making known any person who may be concerned in our sins; we must refrain from all superfluous narrations, and must express ourselves in as modest and decent a manner as the nature of the sin allows.

945. **Must we also confess venial sins?**
We are not, indeed, obliged to confess venial sins; yet it is good and wholesome to do so.

946. **But if we do not know whether something is a mortal or a venial sin, what are we to do?**
We are to confess it, because many people mistake mortal sins for venial ones.

947. **When is confession sincere?**
When we accuse ourselves just as we sincerely believe ourselves guilty before God, without concealing or disguising anything, or excusing it by vain pretenses.

948. **What should the penitent consider if he is ashamed to make a sincere confession?**
He should consider: 1) that a confession which is not sincere procures him neither remission of sins nor peace of conscience; but that the confession, as well as the Communion which follows it, is another grievous sin—a

sacrilege—and deserves eternal damnation; and 2) that it is much better for him to confess his sins to one priest, bound by secrecy, than to live always uneasy in sin, to die unhappy forever, and to be put to shame at the last day before the whole world.

As the confessor is bound to suffer even martyrdom rather than reveal anything heard in confession, so is everyone else, who may have accidentally overheard any part of a confession, bound to the strictest secrecy.

949. **What must we do if we have omitted something in confession which we were obliged to declare?**

1) If we have omitted it without our fault, it is only required to mention it in the next confession; but 2) if we have omitted it, either because we were ashamed to confess it or because we did not sufficiently examine our conscience, we must also say in how many confessions we have omitted it through our fault, and repeat them all.

950. **When is confession clear?**

When we so express ourselves that the confessor can understand everything well, and clearly see the state of our conscience.

951. **Would our confession be clear if we accused ourselves in general only?—for example, that we have not loved God, that we have thought or spoken evil?**

By no means; we must distinctly name and specify the different sins.

952. **What is a general confession?**

A general confession is that in which we repeat all or some of our former confessions.

953. **When is a general confession necessary?**

As often as our former confessions were sacrilegious, either through want of sincerity, or of sorrow and resolution, or through a culpable negligence in the examination of our conscience.

954. **When principally is a general confession useful and advisable?**
1) As a preparation for first Communion; 2) on entering on a state of life; 3) in dangerous illness; 4) at the time of a jubilee, a mission, etc.

955. **How do you begin your confession?**
Having made the sign of the cross, I say: "I, a poor and miserable sinner, accuse myself to God, the Almighty, and to you, my Father, in his stead, that since my last confession, which was..., I have committed the following sins." (Here I confess my sins.)

Or in the following manner:

Having arrived at the confessional, I kneel down, make the sign of the cross, and ask the priest's blessing by saying: "Bless me, Father, for I have sinned." After receiving his blessing, I say the first part of the *confiteor* as far as "through my most grievous fault." Then I say how long it is since my last confession, whether I then received absolution and performed my penance. After this, I confess all the sins I can recollect, beginning with those which I may have forgotten in my last confession.

956. **How do you finish your confession?**
In conclusion, I say: "For these, and all the sins of my whole life, I am most heartily sorry, because by them I have offended God, the supreme and most amiable good. I detest all my sins, and am firmly resolved to amend my life, and to sin no more. I humbly ask penance and absolution of you, my ghostly Father."

Or, I conclude by saying: "For these, and all my other sins which I cannot at present call to my remembrance, and also for the sins of my past life, especially for...,[934] I am heartily sorry, purpose amendment for the future, and most humbly ask pardon of God, and penance and absolution of you, my ghostly Father." Here I finish the *confiteor*: "Therefore I beseech the Blessed Mary ever Virgin," etc.

[934] See p. 402, q. 918.

957. **What should we do after this?**

We should listen with attention to the instruction which the confessor may think proper to give, and to the penance he enjoins; and when he asks us questions, we should answer them with sincerity and humility.

Take care not to leave the confessional before the priest has given you notice, by saying, for instance: "Go in peace"; or, "May God Almighty bless you!" or something similar.

958. **What are we to do if we should not receive absolution?**

We should humbly submit to the decision of the confessor, and, by true amendment, render ourselves worthy of it.

Satisfaction

959. **What is satisfaction in the sacrament of penance?**

It is the performance of the penance enjoined by the confessor.

960. **For what purpose does the confessor impose a penance on us?**

1) For the expiation of the temporal punishment of sin; and 2) for the amendment of our life.

961. **When God remits the sin, does he also remit all punishment due on account of it?**

With the sin, God always remits the eternal punishment, but he does not always remit the temporal punishment due for it: therefore the prophet Nathan said to David: "The Lord hath taken away thy sin;...nevertheless,...the child that is born to thee shall surely die."[935]

962. **What is the temporal punishment due to our sins?**

It is that punishment which we have to suffer either here on earth, or in purgatory.

[935] 2 Kgs 12:13-14

963. **Why does God not always remit the temporal punishment together with the eternal?**
1) Because his justice demands that, by the enduring of the punishment, we should make some reparation for the injury done to him; and 2) because in his mercy he will, by the fear of such punishment, render us more cautious, and guard us against relapsing into sin.

964. **Has not Christ, then, made full satisfaction for our sins?**
Yes, Christ has abundantly satisfied for our sins; nevertheless, he requires that we also, in union with him, should make satisfaction; just as he has prayed for us, and nevertheless requires that we also should pray in order to be saved.

"[I] fill up those things that are wanting of the sufferings of Christ."[936] "If we suffer with him, we shall be also glorified with him."[937]

965. **From whom has the priest the power to impose works of penance?**
From Jesus Christ, who gave to his Church the power not only to loose, but also to bind.[938]

966. **Is the confession invalid if the penitent does not perform the penance enjoined?**
If after confession, through his own fault, he does not perform the penance which in confession he was willing and sincerely intended to perform, the confession is not rendered invalid; but he commits a new sin, and deprives himself of many graces.

967. **When should we comply with the penance enjoined?**
If the confessor has fixed no time for it, the best way is to comply with it directly, and before we have fallen again into any grievous sin.

[936] Col 1:24
[937] Rom 8:17
[938] Cf. Mt 18:18

968. **What should we do if the penance seems to be too severe?**
We should consider how light the present penances are in comparison with the ancient canonical penances, and with the eternal punishment we have deserved; but if we should really be unable to do the penance, we should respectfully mention it to the confessor.

969. **Should we perform that penance only which the confessor lays upon us?**
We should also endeavor to satisfy the divine justice by other voluntary penitential works, and by patience in our sufferings.

970. **What shall we have to expect if we neglect to make due satisfaction to the divine justice?**
We shall have so much the more to suffer in purgatory, and that without any merit for heaven.

971. **Are we, after confession, under no other obligation than to satisfy the divine justice?**
We are also obliged: 1) to repair, to the utmost of our power, the scandal we have given and the injury we have unjustly done to our neighbor; and 2) to employ the means necessary not to relapse into sin, and to amend our life.

1) *Example* of Zacheus: "Behold, Lord, the half of my goods I give to the poor; and if I have wronged any man of anything, I restore him fourfold."[939] 2) "Behold, thou art made whole: sin no more, lest some worse thing happen to thee."[940]

972. **What should they think who always relapse into their former grievous sins?**
That their confessions are much to be suspected, and that their state is extremely dangerous.

"When the unclean spirit is gone out of a man…he goeth and taketh with him seven other spirits more wicked than himself, and entering in

[939] Lk 19:8
[940] Jn 5:14

they dwell there; and the last state of that man becomes worse than the first."[941]

973. **What means should we especially use in order that we may not relapse into sin?**

We should: 1) strictly follow the instructions and directions of our confessor; 2) carefully avoid the occasions of sin; 3) daily examine our conscience; 4) be assiduous in praying, in hearing the word of God, and receiving the sacraments of penance and of the Holy Eucharist; and 5) we should often meditate on the four last things of man.

Application. When you have sinned, go to confession without delay, but never without a diligent examination of conscience, a true contrition, a firm resolution of amendment, and a sincere declaration of your sins; that the sacrament of penance, so replete with grace, may not become for you a source of eternal perdition.

Indulgences

974. **By what means does the Church assist us in the discharge of the temporal punishment due to our sins?**

By the grant of indulgences.

975. **What is an indulgence?**

An indulgence is a remission, granted out of the sacrament of penance, of that temporal punishment which, even after the sin is forgiven, we have yet to undergo, either here or in purgatory.

976. **How does the Church remit the punishment due to our sins?**

By making to the divine justice compensation for us from the inexhaustible treasure of the merits of Christ and his saints.

Indulgences, therefore, derive their value and efficacy from the spiritual treasure of the Church, which consists of the superabundant merits and

[941] Lk 11:24, 26

satisfactions of Christ and the saints. This treasure is to be considered as the common property of the faithful, committed to the administration of the Church; since, by virtue of the communion of saints, by which we are united as members of one body, the abundance of some supplies the want of others.

"In this present time, let your abundance supply their want, that their abundance also may supply your want, that there may be an equality."[942]

977. **What is generally required to gain an indulgence?**
It is required: 1) that we should be in the state of grace, and have already obtained, by true repentance, forgiveness of those sins the temporal punishment of which is to be remitted by the indulgence; and 2) that we should exactly perform the good works prescribed for the gaining of the indulgence.

978. **What must we believe with regard to indulgences?**
We must believe: 1) that the Catholic Church has power to grant indulgences; and 2) that the use of them is very salutary to us.[943]

979. **From whom has the Catholic Church the power of granting indulgences?**
From Jesus Christ, who made no exception when he said: "Whatsoever thou shalt loose on earth, it shall be loosed also in heaven."[944]

That the Catholic Church has from the earliest times exercised this full power is evident even from 2 Corinthians 2:10.

980. **Who has a right to grant indulgences?**
This right belongs especially to our most holy father the pope, who, being the successor of St. Peter, has received from Christ the keys of the kingdom of heaven; the bishops, however, have also the power of granting some partial indulgences.

[942] 2 Cor 8:14
[943] Cf. Council of Trent, Session 25
[944] Mt 16:19; 18:18

981. **For what reasons are indulgences very salutary to us?**
For these: 1) they discharge our debt of temporal punishment; 2) they encourage us to make our peace with God, by substituting easier exercises of piety for the very severe canonical penances of the ancient Church; 3) they incite us to true repentance and amendment, since without these requisites they cannot be gained at all; 4) they urge us to receive frequently the sacraments of penance and of the Holy Eucharist, and to perform good works; 5) they console fervent penitents in their fear of the judgments of God.

To assert that, by an indulgence, the Church forgives sins, past or future, or that she grants indulgences for money, is a gross calumny. It is true that, when granting an indulgence, she has sometimes, besides the conditions of a sincere repentance, prescribed almsdeeds for charitable purposes; for instance, for the building of a church or of a hospital; but as this, laudable as it was in the beginning, gave nevertheless, in the course of time, occasion to abuses, the Council of Trent abolished the abuses, declaring, however, that "the use of indulgences is very salutary to Christian people, and approved of by the authority of the sacred councils."[945]

982. **Is it, then, not true that the Church, by indulgences, frees us from the obligation of doing penance?**
No; she does not free us from the obligation of doing penance according to our capacity, since, the greater is our penitential zeal and love to God, the more do we participate in the indulgence; she will only assist us in our inability to expiate all temporal punishment in this life, and thus, by a generous indulgence, effect what, in ancient times, she endeavored to attain by the rigorous penitential canons.

983. **How many kinds of indulgences are there?**
There are two kinds: a plenary indulgence, which is the remission of the whole debt of temporal punishment due to sin; and a partial indulgence, which is the remission of a part of it only.

[945] Council of Trent, Session 25, "Decree concerning Indulgences"

984. **What is meant by an indulgence of "forty days" or "seven years"?**
A remission of such a debt of temporal punishment as a person would discharge if he did penance for forty days or seven years, according to the ancient canons of the Church.

985. **What is meant by a jubilee?**
A jubilee is a plenary indulgence which the holy father grants every twenty-fifth year, or upon extraordinary occasions; during which time, in order to increase the fervor of repentance in the faithful, confessors have a special power to commute private vows into other works of piety, and to absolve in reserved cases.

986. **Can indulgences also be gained for the benefit of the souls in purgatory?**
Yes, all those which the pope has expressly declared to be applicable to them.

Application. Value and esteem indulgences, and avail yourself of every opportunity of gaining them worthily for yourself, as well as for the souls of the faithful departed.

EXTREME UNCTION

987. **What is extreme unction?**
Extreme unction is a sacrament in which the sick, by the anointing with holy oil, and by the prayer of the priest, receive the grace of God for the good of their souls, and often also of their bodies.

This sacrament is called "extreme unction," because it is usually the last of the holy unctions which are administered by the Church.

988. **Whence do we know that the sacrament of extreme unction was instituted by Christ?**
We know this: 1) from the holy scripture; and 2) from the constant doctrine of the Church.

989. **What does holy scripture say of the sacrament of extreme unction?**
The apostle St. James says in his epistle: "Is any man sick among you, let him bring in the priests of the Church, and let them pray over him, anointing him with oil in the name of the Lord; and the prayer of faith shall save the sick man, and the Lord shall raise him up, and if he be in sins, they shall be forgiven him."[946]

990. **Why do we infer from these words that Christ has instituted extreme unction?**
Because the anointing with oil could have no sacramental power of forgiving sins if Christ had not so ordained it.

991. **How is extreme unction administered?**
The priest anoints the different senses of the sick person with holy oil, and uses, at each anointing, this form of prayer: "Through this holy unction, and his most tender mercy, may the Lord forgive thee whatever sins thou hast committed by thy sight" ("by thy hearing," etc.).

992. **What effects does extreme unction produce in the soul?**
Extreme unction 1) increases sanctifying grace; 2) it remits venial sins, and also those mortal sins which the sick person can no more confess; 3) it removes the remains of sins already forgiven; and 4) it strengthens the soul in her sufferings and temptations, especially in her agony.

By "remains of sins" we understand the temporal punishment, the evil inclinations of the heart, and the weakness of the will, which are the consequences of sins committed, and remain even after the sins have been forgiven.

993. **What effects does extreme unction produce in the body?**
It often relieves the pains of the sick person, and sometimes restores him even to health, if it be expedient for the salvation of his soul.

[946] Jas 5:14-15

994. **Who can and ought to receive extreme unction?**
Every Catholic who has come to the use of reason, and is so ill as to be in danger of death; but not persons in health, even though they are in danger of death.

995. **How are we to receive extreme unction?**
We are to receive it: 1) in the state of grace; wherefore we must previously, if possible, confess our sins, or, at least, make an act of perfect contrition; and 2) with faith, hope, and charity, and resignation to the will of God.

Acts of these and similar virtues should often be made by the sick person during illness, especially when his end approaches, and all present ought to help him to do so. It may be briefly done in the following words:

I believe, my God, in thee,
I most firmly hope in thee,
And I love most truly thee,
And all men are dear to me.
All my sins are grieving me,
Which, I beg thee, pardon me.
I resign myself to thee,
Thank for good and evil thee;
Nay, I'll live and die for thee. Amen.

996. **When should we receive extreme unction?**
We should receive it, if possible, whilst we are still in our senses, and after having received the viaticum.

997. **How often can extreme unction be received?**
In each dangerous illness it can be received once; it can, however, be repeated on relapse into danger that had passed.

998. **Is it not unreasonable for a person, from fear of death, to defer, or even neglect, the receiving of extreme unction until he is at the point of death?**
Certainly; for 1) extreme unction has been instituted even for the health of the body; 2) the sick person will recover more probably if he employs

in time the remedy ordained by God, than if he waits until he cannot recover except by a miracle; and 3) if his sickness be mortal, what should he wish for more earnestly than to die happy, which this holy sacrament gives him grace to do?

Relatives also, or attendants, of the sick person, sin grievously, if through their fault the last sacraments are not administered to him in due time. "His sisters, therefore, sent to him, saying: 'Lord, behold, he whom thou lovest is sick.'"[947] The person who goes to call the priest should be able to explain the condition of the patient, in order that the priest may be able to decide whether or not he is to bring the holy viaticum with him.

Application. When God in his mercy visits you with a dangerous illness, be sure not to put off the receiving of the holy sacraments to the last moment; otherwise, death may surprise you when it is no longer possible to have the attendance of a priest.

HOLY ORDERS

999. **On whom did Christ himself confer the priesthood?**
On his apostles.

1000. **Was the priesthood to end with the death of the apostles?**
No; no more than the Church was to end at their death.

1001. **How was the priesthood continued?**
By the sacrament of holy orders.

1002. **What is holy orders?**
Holy orders is that sacrament which communicates to those who receive it the full power of priesthood, together with a special grace to discharge their sacred duties well.

[947] Jn 11:3

1003. **What are the principal powers of the priesthood?**

1) The power to change bread and wine into the body and blood of our Lord; and 2) the power to forgive sins.

The power of consecrating bread and wine Christ gave to his Church at the last chapter;[948] and the power of forgiving sins he gave after his resurrection.[949]

1004. **Is there in holy orders also a visible sign which indicates the communicating of the invisible power and grace?**

Yes, there are several: the imposition of hands and the prayer of the bishop, and the delivery of the chalice with wine, and of the paten with bread.

The imposition of hands and prayer are also mentioned in holy scripture: "I admonish thee, that thou stir up the grace of God which is in thee by the imposition of my hands."[950] Thus wrote St. Paul to Bishop Timothy; and in a similar manner, 1 Timothy 4:14. By prayer and imposition of hands Paul and Barnabas were also ordained: "Then they, fasting and praying, and imposing their hands upon them, sent them away."[951]

1005. **But are not all Christians true priests by their baptism?**

No; as the true priesthood of the old law was propagated by natural descent from Aaron, so it is also in the new law propagated by a spiritual descent from the apostles—that is, by ordination.

1006. **Why, then, does St. Peter say that all Christians are "a kingly priesthood"?**[952]

Because all, by their baptism, are obliged to offer up to God internal or spiritual sacrifices[953] of faith, hope, and charity, of prayer and mortification. From this passage it can no more be inferred that all Christians are true priests than that all are true kings. In the old law, also, God said to the

[948] Compare p. 380, q. 830, above.

[949] Compare p. 397, q. 895, above.

[950] 2 Tm 1:6

[951] Acts 13:3

[952] 1 Pt 2:9

[953] Cf. 1 Pt 2:5

Israelites: "You shall be to me a priestly kingdom";[954] nevertheless, there was a particular priesthood, which alone was authorized to offer sacrifices.—*Example*: Punishment of King Ozias.[955]

1007. **Who can validly administer the sacrament of holy orders?**
Bishops only, who have received this power by a particular consecration.

As no one can be made a priest except by the sacrament of holy orders, which can validly be administered only by a bishop, who again has received the power of administering it from another bishop lawfully consecrated, it is evident that, by an uninterrupted succession of bishops lawfully ordained and consecrated, the priesthood ascends to the apostles, on whom Christ himself conferred the priestly and episcopal powers, both for themselves and for their successors.

1008. **Cannot also civil authorities, or Christian communities, confer spiritual powers?**
No; they cannot confer spiritual powers on others, because they have none themselves.

Hence the Council of Trent decrees "that all those who, being only called and instituted by the people, or by the civil power and magistrate, ascend to the exercise of these ministrations, and those who of their own rashness assume them to themselves, are not to be looked upon as ministers of the Church, but as thieves and robbers, who have not entered by the door."[956]

1009. **Can a priest be deprived of his ordination?**
No; he can as little be deprived of ordination as of baptism, because it imprints an indelible character upon the soul.

A priest, therefore, or a bishop, cannot be deprived of the powers which he has received in his ordination or consecration to change bread

[954] Ex 19:6
[955] 2 Par 26
[956] Council of Trent, Session 23, "The True and Catholic Doctrine, touching the Sacrament of Order," Ch. 4; Cf. Jn 10:1, 8

and wine into the body and blood of Jesus Christ, and to offer up the Holy Sacrifice of the Mass, to administer confirmation, extreme unction, and holy orders; but the power of remitting sins by sacramental absolution can be taken from him, because the valid administration of the sacrament of penance is also dependent on jurisdiction—that is to say, on his mission or authorization by a lawful spiritual superior.[957] For this very reason, the priest and bishops of the schismatical Greek Church, and all those who ever have fallen away from the Catholic Church, retain the powers of their ordination and consecration which originally they received from the Catholic Church; but all other spiritual power which depends on the apostolical mission, and comes from the head of the Catholic Church, expires with their separation from the Church.

1010. **Are there any other orders besides those of priest and bishop?**
Yes; there are others which are preparatory degrees to the priesthood.

1011. **Which are these other orders?**
1) The four minor orders, by which those who receive them are qualified for various offices connected with the divine service; namely, those of porter, lector, exorcist, and acolyte; 2) the order of subdeacon, who has to assist the deacon when serving at the altar; and 3) the order of deacon, who immediately assists the priest at the altar, and helps him also in baptizing, preaching, and giving Holy Communion.

1012. **Who can and ought to embrace the ecclesiastical state?**
He only who is called to it by God.

Parents who, actuated by temporal interests, force their children to take holy orders, sin most grievously, and are responsible for all the evil consequences resulting from it.

[957] Compare p. 397–398, q. 898, above.

1013. **What should the faithful do in order to obtain worthy priests and pastors?**
They should often and fervently pray to God for that grace, and render themselves worthy of it by their love of the Church and respect for the priesthood.

"Pray ye, therefore, the Lord of the harvest, that he send forth laborers into his harvest."[958]

Application. Always show due respect and submission to priests, as the representatives of God and the dispensers of his holy mysteries: and should you happen to perceive in any of them human failings and infirmities, do not be scandalized, but "whatsoever they shall say to you, observe and do; but according to their works, do ye not."[959]

MATRIMONY

1014. **By whom was matrimony instituted?**
Matrimony was instituted by God himself, when he gave to Adam in paradise Eve for his wife, that they both might lead a godly life, and live together in faithful and indissoluble love.

1015. **Was the sanctity of matrimony always respected according to its original institution?**
No. When by sin the entire human race had fallen away from God, the contract of marriage was no longer kept so holy, until our Savior came, and not only restored matrimony as God had originally instituted it, but also elevated it to the dignity of a sacrament.

1016. **How did Christ restore matrimony to its original institution?**
He ordained that marriage should again, as it was from the beginning, subsist between one man and one woman only, and that unto the death of either of them; and he proposed, therefore, his spiritual union with the Church as an example to married people.[960]

958 Mt 9:38
959 Mt 23:3
960 Cf. Eph 5

"Moses, by reason of the hardness of your heart, permitted you to put away your wives; but from the beginning it was not so. And I say to you, that whosoever shall put away his wife,...and shall marry another, committeth adultery; and he that shall marry her that is put away committeth adultery."[961]

1017. **Can, then, the bond of marriage never be dissolved?**

Spiritual superiors can, indeed, for important reasons, allow a husband and wife to live separated from each other; but, nevertheless, they continue married people, and neither of them can validly contract a second marriage whilst the other party is living.

"To them that are married, not I, but the Lord commandeth that the wife depart not from her husband. And if she depart, that she remain unmarried, or be reconciled to her husband. And let not the husband put away his wife."[962] The bond of Christian marriage cannot be dissolved by the civil law, because the civil authority cannot interfere with the sacrament, and cannot put asunder what God has joined.

1018. **How do we know that matrimony is a sacrament?**

1) St. Paul teaches so, who calls matrimony in the Church "a great sacrament";[963] 2) the Church has at all times believed and taught so, as is evident not only from the holy fathers, but also from the fact that those sects who in the first ages separated themselves from us agree in holding this doctrine.

St. Paul teaches that husbands and wives should be united with each other, as Christ and his Church are united. Now, the union that subsists between Christ and his Church is supernatural and replete with graces; consequently, matrimony is a sign to which invisible grace is attached, and, therefore, a sacrament.

[961] Mt 19:8-9; Cf. Lk 16:18; Mk 10:11-12
[962] 1 Cor 7:10-11
[963] Eph 5:32

1019. **What, then, is matrimony in the Church of Christ?**
Matrimony is a sacrament by which two single persons, man and woman, are married to each other, and receive grace from God to discharge the duties of their state faithfully until death.

1020. **How is this sacrament received?**
The bridegroom and the bride declare before a duly authorized priest and two witnesses that they take each other for wife and husband, whereupon the priest blesses their union.

1021. **What are the duties of married persons?**
1) They should take the mutual love of Christ and his Church for their model and live with each other in peace and conjugal fidelity, until death separates them; 2) they should edify each other by leading a holy life; 3) they should concur together in bringing up their children in the fear of God, and suffer no servants to be in their house who might endanger their innocence; 4) the husband should treat his wife with kindness, support and cherish her; the wife should obey her husband in all that is just and honorable, and conscientiously manage the domestic concerns.

"Marriage honorable in all, and the bed undefiled; for fornicators and adulterers God will judge."[964] "As the Church is subject to Christ, so also let the wives be to their husbands in all things"—i.e., that are just and honorable. "Husbands, love your wives, as Christ also loved the Church, and delivered himself up for it...For no man ever hated his own flesh, but nourisheth and cherisheth it, as also Christ doth the Church."[965]

1022. **What should married people consider when they are tempted to break their conjugal fidelity?**
1) That by adultery they break the solemn contract they have made in the presence of God and of the Church; 2) that they break the most sacred bond by which, according to God's disposal, human society is united and

[964] Heb 13:4
[965] Eph 5:24-29

kept together; 3) that they disturb domestic peace, hinder the good education of their children, and destroy the happiness of the whole family; and 4) that they expose themselves to the danger of falling into disgrace and misery, and all sorts of sins and vices, and even of being severely chastised, and ultimately entirely rejected by God himself.

"He that is an adulterer...shall destroy his own soul; he gathereth to himself shame and dishonor, and his reproach shall not be blotted out."[966]

In the old law, adultery was, by God's command, punished with death, and, in the primitive Church, with public penance of many years, like manslaughter.

1023. **What should these people bear in mind who intend to enter the married state?**

1) They should not thoughtlessly, and without due reflection, enter into an engagement to marry; 2) they should be properly instructed, confirmed, and be free from impediments; 3) they should live innocently whilst they are engaged, and should not think that, during that time, they are allowed sinful liberties on that account; 4) they should enter the marriage state with a pure and holy intention; and 5) before they marry, they should make a good confession and worthily receive Holy Communion.

"We are the children of saints, and we must not be joined together like heathens, that know not God."[967]

1024. **Who may be said to espouse each other thoughtlessly?**

1) All who neglect to have previous recourse to God, and disregard his will, the advice of their parents, and the salvation of their own soul in the affair;[968] 2) those who, in their choice, care less for religion and virtue than for temporal advantages, etc.; and 3) those who do not first consider whether they will be able to fulfill the weighty duties of the married state.

The husband should be able to maintain his wife and children; he should not be a freethinker, or addicted to gambling, drinking, quarreling,

[966] Prv 6:32-33
[967] Tb 8:5
[968] Cf. Prv 19:14

cursing, etc. The wife should be free from vanity, love of finery, and capriciousness; she should be chaste, pious, modest, industrious, and economical. Both should possess the virtue, intelligence, and knowledge in religious matters requisite to give their children a Christian education.

1025. **How is a binding engagement to marry entered into?**
The engagement must be in writing and signed by the two parties, in presence of the pastor of one of them, or the bishop, or two other witnesses.

1026. **What sin do they commit who receive the sacrament of matrimony with an unholy intention, or in the state of moral sin?**
They render themselves guilty of sacrilege, and, therefore, unworthy of all the divine graces and blessings attached to the sacrament.

1027. **What is meant by an "invalid marriage"?**
It is one that is entirely destitute of effect in the eyes of God and of the Church.

1028. **What should they do who are married invalidly?**
They should go at once to the priest and be properly married, or else separate.

1029. **What things make a marriage invalid?**
Three things: 1) imperfect consent; 2) want of proper form; or 3) existence of an impediment.

1030. **What is meant by "imperfect consent"?**
It is consent that is given out of ignorance or fear.

1031. **What is meant by "the proper form of marriage"?**
It is that formality without which the Church will not recognize the marriage, and consists in the presence of a duly qualified priest and at least two witnesses.

1032. **What are impediments?**

Impediments are circumstances which, from the nature of the case or the law of God or of the Church, prevent the marriage.

1033. **How many kinds of impediments are there?**

There are two kinds: 1) such as render the marriage illegal, as for instance, certain vows, and difference of religion between the parties where both are baptized; 2) such as render it not only illegal, but null if attempted. These are: lack of proper age, physical incapacity, bond of previous marriage still existing, difference of religion between a Catholic and an unbaptized person, sacred orders, solemn religious profession, relationship by blood or marriage, spiritual relationship, public propriety, abduction and crime.

1034. **What is understood by the "forbidden times"?**

1) The time which begins with the First Sunday of Advent and ends with the Epiphany of our Lord; and 2) that which begins with Ash Wednesday and ends with Low Sunday, within which times the Church forbids the solemnizing of marriage because they have been particularly set apart for penance and prayer.

This commandment of the Church does not forbid marriages during Lent and Advent; it forbids them to be solemnized—that is, the priest is not allowed to say the Mass appointed in the missal for the bridegroom and bride, nor to give the solemn nuptial benediction.

1035. **Can the impediments of marriage never be dispensed with?**

The Church can dispense with some when there are sufficient reasons, but not with all; on this subject, the parties must confer with their pastor.

That the reasons must be weighty is evident from the decree of the Council of Trent, which says that impediments of marriage are either never, or but rarely, to be dispensed with.[969]

[969] Cf. Council of Trent, Session 24, "Decree on the Reformation of Marriage," Ch. 5

1036. **What should we think of mixed marriages—i.e., of marriages which are contracted between Catholics and non-Catholics, especially protestants?**
That the Church has, at all times, disapproved of such marriages, and never permits them, except on certain conditions.

1037. **Why does the Church disapprove of such marriages?**
1) Because the Catholic party is exposed to great danger of either losing the faith or of becoming indifferent; 2) because the Catholic education of the children is generally deficient, and not seldom impossible; 3) because the non-Catholic party usually does not acknowledge matrimony either as a sacrament or as indissoluble, and can, therefore, according to his or her principles, separate and marry again, which the Catholic consort is not permitted to do; and 4) because, for that very reason, such a marriage never is a true emblem of the most intimate, indissoluble union of Christ with his Church, which every Christian marriage ought to be; 5) because the happiness of married life depends, above all, on unity of faith.

1038. **On what conditions does the Church consent to a mixed marriage?**
On these: 1) that the Catholic party be allowed the free exercise of religion; 2) that all the children be brought up in the Catholic religion;[970] and 3) that the Catholic party earnestly endeavor to gain by persuasion the non-Catholic consort to the true Church.

1039. **Is the Church obliged to require such conditions?**
Yes; otherwise, she would either be indifferent to the eternal welfare of her children, or deny that she alone is the true saving Church.

1040. **Can, then, a person never be permitted to contract a mixed marriage, unless the Catholic education of the children be previously secured?**
No; for such a marriage would be a grievous sin against the Catholic Church and the spiritual welfare of the children that may be born; wherefore the Church can in no case give her consent to it.

[970] Cf. Briefs of Pius VIII and Gregory XVI

Parents who freely consent to such a marriage of their child render themselves guilty of the same sin as the child, and incur a severe responsibility before God.

Application. In the choice of a state of life, consult above all things God and the salvation of your soul. Should you, after a mature deliberation, think yourself to be called to the married state, prepare yourself for it by prayer, good works, and especially by a good, general confession, and be careful not to follow those who, by sin and vice, draw the curse of God upon their heads.

Prayer

Prayer in General

1041. **What is prayer?**

Prayer is the raising up of our minds and hearts to God, either to praise him, or to thank him, or to beg his grace; and therefore, it is divided into prayer of praise, prayer of thanksgiving, and prayer of petition.

1042. **What does "to praise God" mean?**

"To praise God" means to rejoice at his infinite perfections, and to glorify and adore him on that account.[971]

Examples. David in his psalms; the three children in the fiery furnace;[972] the Blessed Virgin.[973]

[971] Cf. Ps 9:3
[972] Cf. Dn 3
[973] Cf. Lk 1:46; etc.

1043. **Are we bound to praise God?**

Yes, we are; for this we were created, and this will one day be our eternal occupation in heaven.[974]

"My mouth shall speak the praise of the Lord, and let all flesh bless his holy name for ever, yea, for ever and ever."[975] "Be ye filled with the Holy Spirit, speaking to yourselves in psalms, and hymns, and spiritual canticles, singing and making melody in your hearts to the Lord."[976]

1044. **Must we also thank God for his gifts?**

Yes; for ingratitude is a detestable vice, whereas gratitude is the best means to obtain new benefits.

"In all things give thanks; for this is the will of God in Christ Jesus."[977]

1045. **Must we also beg graces of God?**

"Ask," says Jesus Christ himself, "and it shall be given you; seek, and you shall find; knock, and it shall be opened to you."[978]

1046. **Is prayer necessary to all?**

Prayer is necessary for salvation to all who have sufficiently the use of reason.

1047. **Why is prayer necessary to all?**

Because God has commanded it, and because, without it, we do not receive the graces necessary to persevere to the end.

1048. **But does not God already know what we stand in need of?**

Most certainly; but we do not pray to tell God what we stand in need of, but to acknowledge him as the giver of all good gifts, to testify our dependence on him, and thereby to render ourselves more worthy of his gifts.

[974] Cf. Apoc 4
[975] Ps 144:21
[976] Eph 5:18-19
[977] 1 Thes 5:18
[978] Lk 11:9

1049. **What are the principal fruits of prayer?**

Prayer: 1) unites us to God; 2) makes us heavenly-minded; 3) strengthens us against evil; 4) gives us zeal and energy for good; 5) comforts us in adversity; and 6) obtains help for us in time of need, and the grace of perseverance unto death.

Examples. Moses;[979] Samuel;[980] Judith;[981] Esther;[982] the Machabees;[983] the first Christians whilst Peter was in prison.[984]

1050. **How must we pray that we may obtain these fruits?**

We must pray: 1) with devotion; 2) with humility; 3) with confidence; 4) with resignation to the will of God; and 5) with perseverance.

1051. **When do we pray with devotion?**

When our prayer comes from the heart, and we avoid all distracting thoughts as much as possible.

"This people honoreth me with their lips; but their heart is far from me."[985]

1052. **Are all the distractions in prayer sinful?**

They are sinful when we ourselves are the cause of them, or willfully admit or entertain them; but when we struggle against them, they increase our merit.

1053. **What should we do in order that we may be less distracted in our prayers?**

Before our prayers, we should, as far as possible, banish all worldly thoughts, and represent the omnipresent God in a lively manner to our mind.

979 Cf. Ex 17:11
980 Cf. 1 Kgs 12:18
981 Cf. Jdt 9; etc.
982 Cf. Est 14; etc.
983 Cf. 2 Mc 15:27
984 Cf. Acts 12:5; etc.
985 Mt 15:8

"Before prayer, prepare thy soul, and be not as a man that tempteth God."[986]

1054. **When do we pray with humility?**

When we address our prayers to God with a sincere acknowledgment of our weakness and unworthiness.

"The prayer of him that humbleth himself shall pierce the clouds."[987]—*Example*: The Pharisee and the publican.[988]

1055. **When do we pray with confidence?**

When we firmly hope that God will hear our prayer, inasmuch as it is conducive to his honor and to our salvation.

"Let him ask in faith, nothing wavering; for he that wavereth is like a wave of the sea, which is moved and carried about by the wind. Therefore, let not that man think that he shall receive anything of the Lord."[989]

1056. **Why may and ought we to have this firm hope?**

Because God can give us all good things, and, for the sake of Jesus, will also really do so, as our Savior himself solemnly assures us, saying: "Amen, amen I say to you, if you ask the Father anything in my name, he will give it to you."[990]

1057. **But why do we not always receive what we ask for?**

1) Either because we do not pray as we ought; or 2) because that which we ask for is prejudicial to our salvation; or 3) because we do not persevere in praying; therefore we must also pray with resignation to the will of God, and perseverance.

[986] Ecclus 18:23
[987] Ecclus 35:21
[988] Cf. Lk 18
[989] Jas 1:6-7
[990] Jn 16:23; Cf. Mk 11:23-24

1058. **When do we pray with resignation to the will of God?**
When we leave it entirely to him to hear us when and how he thinks proper.

"Father,...not my will, but thine be done."[991]

1059. **When do we pray with perseverance?**
When we do not desist, although we are not aware of being heard, but continue to pray the more fervently.

Example of the woman of Chanaan;[992] parable of the friend who asks for three loaves.[993]

Meditation

1060. **Must we always use a set form of words in our prayers?**
No; this may be done in vocal prayer; but there is also an interior or mental prayer, called "meditation."

1061. **In what does meditation consist?**
It consists in reflecting upon the life and sufferings of Jesus, upon the divine perfections, or other truths of our religion, in order to excite in our hearts pious sentiments, and especially good and efficacious resolutions.

1062. **When ought we to pray?**
Christ says that "we ought always to pray, and not to faint."[994]

1063. **How is it possible to pray always?**
We pray always when we frequently raise up our minds and hearts to God, and offer up to him all our labors, sufferings, and pleasures. Yet at certain times we are to pray in an especial manner.

[991] Lk 22:42
[992] Cf. Mt 15
[993] Cf. Lk 11:5-10
[994] Lk 18:1

1064. **When are we thus especially to pray?**
1) In time of temptation and other pressing need, and during private and public calamities; 2) in the morning and at night; before and after meals; when the *Angelus* bell rings; and when we are in the Church.

1065. **Why should we pray in the Church especially?**
Because the Church is especially the house of God and of prayer, where all that we see and hear is intended to raise our minds and hearts to the meditation on divine things.

1066. **For whom must we pray?**
We must pray for all men: for the living and the dead; for friends and enemies; especially for our parents, brothers and sisters, benefactors, spiritual and temporal superiors, and also for heretics and infidels.

"I desire therefore, first of all, that supplications, prayers, intercessions, and thanksgivings be made for all men, for kings, and for all that are in high station, that we may lead a quiet and a peaceable life in all piety and chastity."[995]

Application. Consider how happy you are that you, a miserable worm of the earth, are allowed to speak to God, the Most High, as a child speaks to his father. Pray, therefore, often and willingly, and always with as much devotion as you possibly can, both at home and in the Church.

The Lord's Prayer

1067. **Which is the most excellent of all prayers?**
The most excellent of all prayers is the Our Father, or the Lord's Prayer.

1068. **Why is the Our Father called the "Lord's Prayer"?**
Because Christ our Lord has taught it to us, and commanded us to say it.[996]

[995] 1 Tm 2:1-2
[996] Cf. Mt 6:9-13

1069. **What does the Lord's Prayer contain?**
It contains a short preface and seven petitions.

1070. **What do you call its preface?**
These words: "Our Father who art in heaven."

1071. **What does the Father remind us of?**
That God is our Father, so good and so worthy of veneration that there is no earthly father like him; and that we, therefore, ought to pray to him with a childlike reverence, love, and confidence.

1072. **Why do we say "Our Father," and not "My Father"?**
Because, God being the Father of all men, we are all his children, and should therefore love one another as brothers, and pray for one another.[997]

1073. **Why do we add these words: "Who art in heaven"?**
To call to our mind: 1) that God, though he is everywhere, dwells especially in heaven, where we shall one day see him face-to-face;[998] 2) that we are but pilgrims upon earth, and that our true country is in heaven; and 3) that when we pray, we must detach our hearts from all earthly things, and raise them up to heaven.

1074. **What do we ask for in the first petition: "Hallowed be thy name"?**
That the name of God may never be profaned or blasphemed, but that God may be rightly known, loved, and honored by us and by all men.

1075. **Why is this the first petition?**
Because we are to esteem the honor and glory of God more than all things else.

[997] Cf. Mal 2:10
[998] Cf. 1 Cor 13:12

1076. **What do we ask for in the second petition: "Thy kingdom come"?**
1) That the kingdom of God, the Church, may be more and more extended upon earth; 2) that the kingdom of divine grace and love may now be established in our hearts, in order that, 3) after this life, we may all be admitted into the kingdom of heaven.

1077. **What is the meaning of the third petition: "Thy will be done on earth as it is in heaven"?**
1) We ask that we and all men may do the will of God on earth as faithfully and cheerfully as the angels and saints do it in heaven; and 2) we profess that, in all things, we submit ourselves to the holy will of God.

1078. **What do we ask for in the fourth petition: "Give us this day our daily bread"?**
We ask that God would give us all that is daily necessary for our soul and body.

1079. **Why does Christ bid us ask for our daily bread only?**
To teach us that we should wish only for necessaries, not for riches and abundance.

"Having food, and wherewith to be covered, with these we are content."[999]

1080. **What do we ask for in the fifth petition: "Forgive us our trespasses, as we forgive them that trespass against us"?**
That God would so forgive us all our sins as we forgive others who have offended us.

1081. **May those who do not forgive expect forgiveness themselves?**
No; on the contrary, they pass judgment upon themselves as often as they say the Our Father.

"Forgive thy neighbor if he hath hurt thee; and then shall thy sins be forgiven to thee when thou prayest."[1000]

[999] 1 Tm 6:8
[1000] Ecclus 28:2

1082. **What do we ask for in the sixth petition: "Lead us not into temptation"?**

We ask that God would remove from us all temptations and all the dangers of sin, or, at least, give us grace sufficient to resist them.

1083. **By whom are we tempted to sin?**

1) By our own flesh or concupiscence; "for the flesh lusteth against the spirit";[1001] 2) by the world—i.e., by its vain pomps, bad examples, and wicked maxims; and 3) by the devil, who, "as a roaring lion, goeth about seeking whom he may devour."[1002]

1084. **Why does God permit us to be tempted?**

1) To keep us humble; 2) to try our faithfulness or to punish our unfaithfulness; and 3) to increase our zeal for virtue, and our merits.

"Lest the greatness of the revelations should exalt me, there was given me a sting of my flesh, an angel of Satan, to buffet me."[1003] "The Lord your God trieth you, that it may appear whether you love him with all your heart and with all your soul, or no."[1004] "Blessed is the man that endureth temptation; for when he hath been proved he shall receive the crown of life, which God hath promised to them that love him."[1005]

1085. **Is temptation in itself a sin?**

Temptation in itself is not a sin; but to expose ourselves heedlessly to temptation, or to yield to it, is a sin.

For our consolation and instruction, Christ himself allowed the devil to tempt him.[1006]

[1001] Gal 5:17
[1002] 1 Pt 5:8
[1003] 2 Cor 12:7
[1004] Dt 13:3
[1005] Jas 1:12
[1006] Cf. Mt 4

1086. **What must we do in order that we may not yield?**

We must especially watch and pray, as Christ our Lord says: "Watch ye and pray that ye enter not into temptation."[1007]

1087. **What do we ask for in the seventh petition: "But deliver us from evil"?**

That God would preserve us from all evil of soul and body, especially from sin and eternal damnation.

1088. **Why do we add the word *Amen*, or "So be it"?**

To express by it our ardent desire, and also our confidence, of being heard.

Application. Always say the Lord's Prayer with reverential attention, remembering that we have received it from our divine Redeemer himself.

The Angelical Salutation

1089. **What prayer do Catholics usually say after the Our Father?**

The prayer which is said in honor of the Mother of God, and is called the "Angelical Salutation," or "Hail Mary."

1090. **Why do we add the Angelical Salutation to the Lord's Prayer?**

That the most Blessed Mother of God may second our weak prayer by her powerful intercession with her divine Son.

1091. **How many parts has the Hail Mary?**

Two parts: a prayer of praise and a prayer of petition.

1092. **Of what is the prayer of praise composed?**

1) Of the words of the archangel Gabriel: "Hail [Mary], full of grace, the Lord is with thee; blessed art thou among women," and 2) of the words of St. Elizabeth: "And blessed is the fruit of thy womb," to which we add the name of *Jesus*.

[1007] Mt 26:41

Hail is a term of salutation, equivalent to *Ave* or *Salve*, and means, "Be well," or, "I salute thee."

1093. **When did the archangel Gabriel speak those words?**
When he announced to the Blessed Virgin Mary that she should become the Mother of God.[1008]

1094. **When were the above words spoken by St. Elizabeth?**
When Mary went into the hill country, and visited her cousin Elizabeth.[1009]

1095. **Why do we address Mary by these words: "Full of grace"?**
1) Because Mary received great grace, even before her birth; 2) because she always increased in grace; and 3) because she brought forth the author of all grace.

1096. **Why do we say: "The Lord is with thee"?**
Because God is, in a most particular manner, with the Blessed Virgin, wherefore she is justly called the chosen daughter of the heavenly Father, the true Mother of the divine Son, and the immaculate spouse of the Holy Ghost.

1097. **What is the meaning of these words of praise: "Blessed art thou among women"?**
That Mary is the happiest of all the daughters of Eve: 1) because she was chosen before all to be the Mother of God; 2) because she alone is a Mother and, at the same time, a Virgin; and 3) because the first woman brought a curse on the world; Mary, on the other hand, brought us salvation.

1098. **Why do we add these words: "Blessed is the fruit of thy womb, Jesus"?**
To show that the veneration of Mary is inseparable from the veneration of Christ, and that we praise the Mother for the sake of the Son.

[1008] Cf. Lk 1:28
[1009] Cf. Lk 1:42

1099. **Of what is the prayer of petition composed?**
Of the words which were added by the Church: "Holy Mary, Mother of God, pray for us sinners, now, and at the hour of our death. Amen."

1100. **Why were these words added by the Church?**
1) That we may profess by them before the whole world that Mary is truly Mother of God, because her child is truly God; and 2) that we may often implore the assistance of her prayers in all our necessities, and especially for obtaining the grace of a happy death.

1101. **Why should we often pray for a happy death?**
1) Because our eternal salvation depends on the last moments of our life; 2) because, at that critical time, the temptations are commonly more violent and more dangerous; and 3) because perseverance to the end of life is a special grace, for which we ought continually to pray.[1010]

1102. **Is the Blessed Virgin powerful with God?**
Certainly; for it has never been heard yet that anyone who had recourse to Mary, and with true devotion implored her intercession, has ever been abandoned by God.[1011]

1103. **What prayer do we say when, morning, noon, and night the bell is rung for the *Angelus*?**
We say the following:

"The angel of the Lord declared unto Mary. And she conceived of the Holy Ghost. Hail, Mary, etc.

"Behold the handmaid of the Lord. Be it done unto me according to thy word. Hail, Mary, etc.

"And the Word was made flesh. And dwelt among us. Hail, Mary, etc.

"Pray for us, O Holy Mother of God!

"That we may be made worthy of the promises of Christ.

[1010] Cf. Council of Trent, Session 6, Can. 16, 22
[1011] Cf. Bernard

"Let us pray:

"Pour forth, we beseech thee, O Lord, thy grace into our hearts, that we, to whom the incarnation of Christ thy Son was made known by the message of an angel, may, by his passion and cross, be brought to the glory of his resurrection, through the same Christ our Lord. Amen."

Even if we live in countries or in places where such public signal is not given, nevertheless, as this pious exercise is strongly recommended by the Church, and several popes have granted many spiritual favors and indulgences to those who daily and devoutly practice it, let us be careful to say this prayer with great devotion every day in the morning, at noon, and in the evening.

1104. **Why do we say this prayer?**

1) To give thanks to God for the incarnation of Christ; and 2) to honor the Blessed Virgin, and to recommend ourselves to her protection.

1105. **What is the rosary?**

It is a very useful and easy form of prayer, mental as well as vocal, which was spread by St. Dominic in the thirteenth century, was approved by the Church, and has, since then, always been practiced and recommended by her.

This form of prayer is called "rosary" because it is, as it were, a chaplet of the most beautiful prayers and meditations, wherein the principal mysteries of our religion are wreathed like fragrant roses. Hence the name. It is divided into three parts, each part consisting of five mysteries. The first five, called "the joyful mysteries," are: the annunciation, the visitation, the birth of our Lord, the presentation of our Lord in the Temple, the finding of our Lord in the Temple. The second five, called "the sorrowful mysteries," are: the prayer and bloody sweat of our Lord in the garden, the scourging of our Lord at the pillar, the crowning of our Lord with thorns, our Lord carrying his cross, the crucifixion of our Lord. The third five, called "the glorious mysteries," are: the resurrection of our Lord, the ascension of our Lord into heaven, the descent of the Holy Ghost on the apostles, the assumption of the Blessed Virgin Mary into heaven, the crowning of the Blessed Virgin Mary in heaven. It is true that in the rosary the same salutation is often repeated; but this ought not to surprise us more than that, in Psalm 135, the words, "his mercy endureth for ever," are repeated twenty-seven times; or that the angels in heaven incessantly sing, "Holy, holy, holy." Nor ought this practice to appear tedious to us, since the mind is, in the meantime, to be occupied with the contemplation of the holy mysteries.

The titles of honor, which are given to our Blessed Lady in the Litany of Loretto, as "Mystical Rose," "Tower of David," "Morning Star," etc., are figurative expressions taken from the holy scripture, and are applied to her on account of the eminent privileges and graces conferred on her.

Application. Honor the Blessed Virgin in a most particular and childlike manner. Implore her assistance in all your necessities and concerns, and strive eagerly to imitate her charity, patience, purity, and other virtues.

Sacramentals

1106. **What do we usually understand by *sacramentals*?**

By *sacramentals*, we understand: 1) all those things which the Church blesses or consecrates for the divine service, or for our own pious use: as holy water, oil, salt, bread, wine, palms, altars, chalices, etc.; 2) also the exorcisms, blessings, and consecrations used by the Church.

1107. **Why are such things called "sacramentals"?**

They are called "sacramentals," because they resemble the sacraments, though they are essentially different from them.

1108. **What is the difference between the sacramentals and the sacraments?**

1) The sacraments were instituted by God, and operate by the power which God gave them; the sacramentals, on the contrary, were instituted by the Church, and produce their effects by the prayers and blessings of the Church;

2) the sacraments have an infallible effect, unless we put an obstacle in their way; but the effect of the sacramentals depends principally on the pious intention of the person who makes use of them; 3) the sacraments effect immediately inward sanctification, whereas the sacramentals, by imparting minor graces, only contribute toward it, and protect us also from temporal evils; 4) the sacraments are in general necessary, and commanded by God; but the sacramentals are only recommended by the Church as useful and wholesome.

1109. **Why does the Church consecrate or bless the things belonging to the divine service?**

The Church consecrates or blesses all those things that belong to the divine service, as churches, altars, bells, vestments, etc., 1) in order to sanctify them, and dedicate them peculiarly to the divine service; and 2) to render them more venerable and salutary to us.[1012]

"Every creature...is sanctified by the word of God and prayer."[1013] Thus, even in the old law, the altar and all the vessels thereof were sprinkled and anointed, as the Lord had commanded.[1014]

1110. **Why does the Church bless also bread, wine, the fruits of the field, and such like things?**

The Church blesses these things: 1) after the example of Jesus Christ, who also blessed loaves and fishes;[1015] 2) that "to them that love God, all things [may] work together unto good";[1016] and 3) that as by the sin of Adam the curse of God extended to all the creatures of the earth,[1017] so also his blessings may be poured out over all.

From our birth to our death the Church incessantly shows her love and solicitude for us: she prays for us, consoles us, helps us, blesses us; even over our last place of rest—the cemetery and grave—she pronounces her blessing.

1012 Anniversary of the dedication of a church
1013 1 Tm 4:4-5
1014 Cf. Lv 8:11
1015 Cf. Lk 9:16
1016 Rom 8:28
1017 Cf. Gn 3:17; Rom 8:20-22

1111. **Why should we especially make a devout use of the sacramentals?**
Because we share through them in the prayer and blessing of the whole Church, in the name of which the priest consecrates and blesses.

If in the old law the blessing of the patriarchs was so highly esteemed, how much more should we esteem the blessing of the Church, which Christ has entrusted with the inexhaustible treasure of his means of grace and salvation!

1112. **Has, then, the prayer of the Church a particular efficacy?**
Yes, the prayer of the Church has a particular efficacy: 1) because she is the body of Christ, animated and guided by his Spirit; and 2) because her prayer is always united with the prayer of Jesus and his saints.

1113. **What does the Church usually pray for when she consecrates or blesses?**
She prays for the averting of the judgments of God, for protection against the devil, for peace, blessing, well-being of the soul and body, etc.

That the Church should use symbolical signs, especially the sign of the cross, and blessed things, as holy water, holy oils, *agnus dei's*, palms, etc., in imparting her blessing and the fruits of her prayer, ought not to surprise us more than that God, both in the old and new testament, was pleased to distribute his graces and blessings to the people by means of various signs and things.[1018]

1114. **How should we use holy water?**
A pious Christian sprinkles himself with holy water not only when he enters or leaves the church, but also in his house, when rising and going to bed, when going out and returning, and on many other occasions; and, at the same time, he begs of God that, through the blood of Jesus Christ, he may be more and more purified, and be protected in all dangers of soul and body.

[1018] See Nm 21:9; Tb 6:8, 11; 4 Kgs 5, 13; Mk 6:13; etc.

1115. **Why are the people sprinkled with holy water before High Mass?**

Because we should be pure and holy when we appear in the presence of God, and pray to him.

Application. Beware of being indifferent to the prayers and blessings of the Church, but respect and esteem them, and use all things blessed by the Church, especially holy water, with due reverence and devotion.

Religious Practices and Ceremonies in General, and on Some in Particular

1116. **What do we understand by "religious ceremonies"?**

By "religious ceremonies," we understand certain significant signs or actions, which the Church has established for the celebration of the divine service.

1117. **Why is the instruction on prayer and the sacramentals followed here by the explanation of religious practices and ceremonies?**

1) Because religious ceremonies have been instituted to give praise and glory to God, no less than prayer itself; and 2) because they help us to raise our souls to God and to the contemplation of divine things, and consequently to pray with attention and devotion.

1118. **How do ceremonies help us to raise our souls to God and divine things?**

They help us: 1) because they render the divine service more solemn, and thereby hold our attention, and draw it from earthly objects to God; and 2) because they represent in a visible manner before our eyes mysteries invisible in themselves, and thereby render it easier for us to meditate on them.

1119. **Are not ceremonies idle observances?**

Not at all; for 1) God himself prescribed, under severe penalties, several kinds of ceremonies to the Jews; 2) Christ our Lord also used various ceremonies; and 3) he himself instituted sacramental signs or ceremonies.

Examples. 1) See the book of Leviticus. 2) For instance, when he healed the man that was deaf and dumb;[1019] when he gave sight to the man born blind;[1020] when he breathed on his disciples, and imparted to them the Holy Ghost.[1021] 3) When he instituted the Holy Eucharist, baptism, etc.

1120. **But must we not adore God in spirit and in truth?**[1022]

By all means; and therefore, the Church wishes that we should not merely assist at the ceremonies, but also understand their meaning, and accompany them with prayer and pious sentiments.

1121. **Has, then, every religious ceremony a meaning?**

Yes; all things which the Church makes use of for celebrating the divine service have a mystical signification, and are intended to excite our souls to lively sentiments of devotion.[1023]

1122. **But are there not also religious ceremonies and practices which are useless and superfluous?**

No; that which the holy infallible Church ordains, approves, or practices, cannot but be useful and profitable to us, because she is always guided by the Holy Ghost.

1123. **What is, then, the use of incense?**

Incense is an emblem of reverence and of prayer which should ascend to heaven as a sweet odor before God.[1024]

[1019] Cf. Mk 7

[1020] Cf. Jn 9

[1021] Cf. Jn 20

[1022] Cf. Jn 4:24

[1023] For the ceremonies of baptism, see p. 370–372; of confirmation, p. 373–376; of the Mass, p. 384–389; of the blessing of water, salt, oil, etc., see p. 443ff.

[1024] Cf. Ps 140:2

1124. **What do the lighted candles signify?**

They signify faith which enlightens, hope which soars above this world, and charity which inflames; and they recall also to our mind those times of persecution when the Christians celebrated the divine service in catacombs or subterranean caverns.

1125. **What do the candles blessed on the feast of the Purification of the Blessed Virgin Mary especially call to our mind?**

The words of Simeon, that Jesus is "a light to the revelation of the Gentiles,"[1025]—that is to say, a light to be revealed to the Gentiles, or to lighten the Gentiles—and that we also are to walk as "children of the light."[1026]

1126. **What does the paschal candle remind us of?**

It reminds us of Jesus Christ, risen from the dead, who rescued us from the slavery of Satan, as formerly the pillar of fire led the children of Israel out of the bondage of the Egyptians.[1027]

1127. **What do the ashes blessed on Ash Wednesday call to our remembrance?**

That we should humble ourselves, and sincerely repent; therefore the priest, whilst he puts ashes on our heads, says: "Remember, man, that thou art dust, and into dust thou shalt return."[1028]

Ashes were even in the old testament an emblem of penance and humility.—*Examples*: The Ninivites, Judith, Esther, etc.

1128. **What do the palms on Palm Sunday call to our mind?**

The triumphal entrance of our Lord into Jerusalem, and his victory over hell; and that we also should strive to gain the palm of eternal life.

[1025] Lk 2:32
[1026] Eph 5:8
[1027] Cf. Ex 14:20
[1028] Cf. Gn 3:19

1129. **For what end are public supplications and processions made?**

1) To praise God also publicly, to thank him, to draw down, by our prayers, his protection and blessing upon town and country, and to avert his chastisements; 2) to proclaim the victory and triumph of the Catholic religion, for which purpose the cross and banner precede; and 3) to remind us that we are but pilgrims in this world, and that we should constantly walk before God.

We meet with examples of such public supplications and processions as early as the most ancient times of Christianity.

1130. **What should we think of pilgrimages?**

When they are made according to the intentions of the Church, they are certainly much to be commended; nay, they are even confirmed by the example of the saints, and by the indulgences of the Church.

It is true that God is, and hears us, everywhere; nevertheless, he may be more disposed to hear us in certain places, as well as at certain times. Moreover, in places of pilgrimage, there are many things calculated to excite us to pray with greater fervor and confidence, and, therefore, with more chances of being heard. Should abuses intervene, not the pilgrimages, but the abuses should be condemned.

1131. **How does the Church wish pilgrimages to be made?**

The Church wishes: 1) that we should not neglect for them the urgent duties of our state or profession; 2) that we should have a good intention; 3) that we should well employ the time engaged in them, and patiently endure the hardships which attend them; and 4) that we should pray fervently at the holy place, and, if possible, go there to confession and Communion.

1132. **Have pilgrimages long been in use?**

They were in use even under the old law, where we see that, by an express command of God, the Israelites went on a pilgrimage to the Temple of Jerusalem, as did also Jesus and Mary. And the first Christians went frequently to the place where Christ lived and suffered, and to the tombs of the apostles and holy martyrs.

1133. **What are confraternities?**

They are pious associations, generally approved of by the popes, and established for the purposes of mutual prayer, encouragement, and assistance in the performance of good works and the frequentation of the sacraments.

Since confraternities conduce much to holiness of life, when the rules—which, however, as such, do not bind under pain of any sin—are well kept, the Church has granted them ample indulgences; yet all are free to apply or not for admittance into them.

Application. Take part with great devotion in the religious practices and ceremonies of the Church, and never suffer yourself to be diverted from them either by the mockery or example of impious or thoughtless people.

Recapitulation

"Our religion is divine."

This is proved by her history from the creation of the world to the present time; viz., by her age, her founder, her propagation, her duration, her blessings, and fruits, etc.[1029]

"This our divine religion teaches."

That we are in this world in order that we may serve God in this life, and be eternally happy with him hereafter in heaven.[1030] For this end we must: 1) believe all that God has revealed (Section I); 2) keep all the commandments which God has given us either himself or through his Church; consequently, also avoid sin, by which the divine command is broken, and strive to lead a virtuous life (Section II); 3) but this we cannot do without the grace of God. Therefore we must also make use of the means of grace which God has ordained; namely, the sacraments and prayer (Section III).

[1029] See "Short History of Revealed Religion."

[1030] See "Introduction," p. 163–164, above.

ABOUT THIS SERIES

Tradivox was first conceived as an international research endeavor to recover lost and otherwise little-known Catholic catechetical texts. As the research progressed over several years, the vision began to grow, along with the number of project contributors and a general desire to share these works with a broader audience.

Legally incorporated in 2019, Tradivox has begun the work of carefully remastering and republishing dozens of these catechisms which were once in common and official use in the Church around the world. That effort is embodied in this *Tradivox Catholic Catechism Index*, a multi-volume series restoring artifacts of traditional faith and praxis for a contemporary readership. More about this series and the work of Tradivox can be learned at www.Tradivox.com.

SOPHIA INSTITUTE

Sophia Institute is a nonprofit institution that seeks to nurture the spiritual, moral, and cultural life of souls and to spread the Gospel of Christ in conformity with the authentic teachings of the Roman Catholic Church.

Sophia Institute Press fulfills this mission by offering translations, reprints, and new publications that afford readers a rich source of the enduring wisdom of mankind.

Sophia Institute also operates the popular online resource Catholic Exchange.com. *Catholic Exchange* provides world news from a Catholic perspective as well as daily devotionals and articles that will help readers to grow in holiness and live a life consistent with the teachings of the Church.

In 2013, Sophia Institute launched Sophia Institute for Teachers to renew and rebuild Catholic culture through service to Catholic education. With the goal of nurturing the spiritual, moral, and cultural life of souls, and an abiding respect for the role and work of teachers, we strive to provide materials and programs that are at once enlightening to the mind and ennobling to the heart; faithful and complete, as well as useful and practical.

Sophia Institute gratefully recognizes the Solidarity Association for preserving and encouraging the growth of our apostolate over the course of many years. Without their generous and timely support, this book would not be in your hands.

www.SophiaInstitute.com
www.CatholicExchange.com
www.SophiaInstituteforTeachers.org

Sophia Institute Press® is a registered trademark of Sophia Institute.
Sophia Institute is a tax-exempt institution as defined by the
Internal Revenue Code, Section 501(c)(3). Tax ID 22-2548708.